"Although the use of apostles and prophets as ecclesiastical titles and offices has become fashionable within contemporary Christianity, not many Christians understand their actual meanings and functions. This book provides great insights into the ministry of apostles and prophets from biblical, church-history, and contemporary perspectives. I strongly recommend it to all Christians who are seeking to have a fresh understanding of the ministry of apostles and prophets."

—ALFRED KODUAH,
former General Secretary, The Church of Pentecost

"Opoku Onyinah has provided us with a very thoughtful treatment of a fascinating topic. Whether or not you agree that apostles and prophets exist today in a continuing line from biblical times, you will be challenged to rethink the question. Onyinah's . . . theological definitions and conclusions based upon the biblical text are rich, clear, and easily understood. I believe that church leaders of all kinds, as well as seminary students and informed laypeople, will benefit from this work as they think about Christian leadership."

—CECIL M. ROBECK JR.,
Fuller Theological Seminary

"With the ongoing debates on apostles and prophets today, this book takes us back to where they all began: the Bible. As an apostle of his church in Africa, Onyinah presents a thorough study of the biblical, historical, and theological evidence to help the world church establish a healthy understanding of the function and office of apostles and prophets today."

—WONSUK MA,
Oral Roberts University

"Opoku Onyinah is filling a great need by his book *Apostles and Prophets*. Many Pentecostals have been hesitating to use these titles, which has caused limitation of God-given ministries and gifts. On the other hand, there is also too much misuse of those terms. Opoku offers us sound biblical tools to reflect the leadership and serving aspects of these ministries."
—ARTO HÄMÄLÄINEN,
Chairman, the Africa Pentecostal Mission (APM)

"Onyinah distills a life lived at the intersection of scholarship and pastoral ministry to present a delightful cornucopia of literature spanning biblical, extra-biblical, church fathers, church history, and contemporary realties on the subject of apostles and prophets. . . . With the phenomenal growth of global Pentecostalism, this is doubtless a legacy book, recommended for Christians everywhere—as much for Pentecostals as for non-Pentecostals."
—CASELY BAIDEN ESSAMUAH,
Secretary, Global Christian Forum

Apostles and Prophets

Apostles and Prophets

The Ministry of Apostles and Prophets
throughout the Generations

OPOKU ONYINAH

Foreword by
Paul Yaw Frimpong Manso

WIPF & STOCK · Eugene, Oregon

APOSTLES AND PROPHETS
The Ministry of Apostles and Prophets throughout the Generations

Copyright © 2022 Opoku Onyinah. All rights reserved. Except for brief quotations in critical publications or reviews, no part of this book may be reproduced in any manner without prior written permission from the publisher. Write: Permissions, Wipf and Stock Publishers, 199 W. 8th Ave., Suite 3, Eugene, OR 97401.

Wipf and Stock
An Imprint of Wipf and Stock Publishers
199 W. 8th Ave., Suite 3
Eugene, OR 97401

www.wipfandstock.com

PAPERBACK ISBN: 978-1-6667-3333-4
HARDCOVER ISBN: 978-1-6667-2788-3
EBOOK ISBN: 978-1-6667-2789-0

JANUARY 24, 2022

Scripture quotations marked KJV are taken from The Authorized (King James) Version. Rights in the Authorized Version in the United Kingdom are vested in the Crown. Reproduced by permission of the Crown's patentee, Cambridge University Press.

Scriptures quotations marked NIV are taken from the Holy *Bible*, New International Version®, *NIV*®. Copyright © 1973, 1978, 1984, 2011 by Biblica, Inc.™ Used by permission of Zondervan.

Scripture quotations marked NKJV are taken from the New King James Version®. Copyright © 1982 by Thomas Nelson. Used by permission. All rights reserved.

Scripture quotations marked ESV are taken from the Holy Bible, English Standard Version® copyright © 2001 by Crossway Bibles, a publishing ministry of Good News Publishers. ESV Text Edition: 2016. The ESV® text has been reproduced in cooperation with and by permission of Good News Publishers. All rights reserved.

Scripture quotations marked NASU are taken from the (NASB®) New American Standard Bible Updated Edition®, Copyright © 1960, 1971, 1977, 1995, 2020 by The Lockman Foundation. Used by permission. All rights reserved.

Scripture quotations marked NLT are taken from the Holy Bible, New Living Translation, copyright © 1996, 2004, 2015 by Tyndale House Foundation. Used by permission of Tyndale House Publishers, Carol Stream, Illinois 60188. All rights reserved.

Dedicated to
Pastors Peter Ernest Nsiah and Emmanuel David Aninkorah
and Thomas Nyarko
Apostles Daniel Kwabena Arnan and Fred Stephen Safo
and Prophet Martinson Kwado Yeboah

Contents

Foreword by Paul Yaw Frimpong Manso | vii

Acknowledgments | xi

INTRODUCTION | 1

Part 1: The Prophet | 13

Chapter 1　The Messengers of God | 14
Chapter 2　The Prophet as God's Messenger in the Old Testament | 22
Chapter 3　The Making of a Prophet | 31

Part 2: The Constitution of a Prophet | 49

Chapter 4　The Gifts of Speaking under Inspiration | 51
Chapter 5　The Gifts of Revelation | 60
Chapter 6　Gifts of the Word | 75

Part 3: The Functions of the Prophet in the Old Testament | 93

Chapter 7　The Man of God's Word | 95
Chapter 8　Access to the Council of God | 102
Chapter 9　The Man with the Presence of God | 109

Part 4 : The New Testament Prophet | 117

Chapter 10　The Spirit to Fall on All Flesh | 119
Chapter 11　Every Believer Has the Potential to Prophesy | 125

Part 5: The Apostle | 132

Chapter 12　Identifying an Apostle | 134

Chapter 13	The Making of Apostles	144
Chapter 14	The Constitution of an Apostle	162
Chapter 15	Who Then Is an Apostle?	174

Part 6: The Functions of an Apostle | 179

Chapter 16	Foundation Layers	181
Chapter 17	Government of the Church	190
Chapter 18	Spiritual Authority	202
Chapter 19	Broader Perspective of God's Kingdom	208
Chapter 20	The Apostle Works in Teams	215
Chapter 21	The Difference between Apostles and Prophets	221

Part 7: From Apostles to Bishops | 227

Chapter 22	The New Testament Church Was Led by Apostles	229
Chapter 23	After the Death of the Apostles	235
Chapter 24	From the Church Fathers	243
Chapter 25	Deductions on Apostleship from Ancient Literature	252
Chapter 26	The Need for Apostles and Prophets	259

Part 8: Receiving Revelations | 269

| Chapter 27 | How to Receive Revelation | 271 |
| Chapter 28 | Hindrances to Hearing from the Lord | 291 |

Part 9: Limitations of Apostles and Prophets | 301

Chapter 29	Identifying a True Prophet	303
Chapter 30	Prophetic Flaws	312
Chapter 31	How to Test Prophetic Utterance	324

CONCLUSION | 330

Bibliography | 337

Subject Index | 343

Scripture Index | 373

Foreword

SOME FORTY YEARS AGO (1981), when I was in my first year at Bible college, I heard of a young pastor who was being used by the Lord mightily in the Church of Pentecost, Kumasi, Ghana. Kumasi is the second-largest city as well as the center of culture in Ghana. Some of my friends who were members of the Church of Pentecost kept on telling me about the developments in the church. During the period, the Church of Pentecost was known for being a prayerful church, but not so much in the area of teaching. However, I heard of this young man whose teaching ministry attracted many people in Kumasi and caused great excitement in the city. People defied rains and ran to listen to his teachings. He was not only a teacher but also a great worshipper and a prayerful person. He was training many young people and releasing them for ministry, planting new churches within the city and its vicinities. Soon the Church of Pentecost in Kumasi grew astronomically. No doubt within three years, his ministry attracted the attention of the leadership of the Church of Pentecost and he was appointed a regional head, supervising the work of pastors and ministers. Two years after this appointment, he was confirmed by his church as an apostle. I realized that wherever he went, the church under his supervision grew. As a young man myself, who had by then completed Bible college and was pastoring a church in the city, I was attracted to his ministry and followed him wherever he went. I did not know that thirty-six years later, I would take over from him as the president of the Ghana Pentecostal and Charismatic Council, and as the chairman of the Ghana Evangelism Committee.

From a very humble beginning, he grew in the ministry and was given the opportunity by his church to study up to a PhD level. With the special graces endowed him by the Lord, he initiated what is called Pentecost International Worship Centre, a ministry of the church that caters for expatriates and people whose cultures have changed within their cultures. He became the first international missions director, the first rector of the Pentecost University College, and the fifth chairman of the Church of Pentecost. He served and continues to serve on many national and international boards, councils, and commissions. It was his work as the president of the Ghana Pentecostal and Charismatic Council that brought us even more closely together. I consider him an excellent team player, a man of God with great wisdom, and an embodiment of many gifts: a teacher, pastor, worshipper/psalmist, theologian, ecumenist, of prophetic and apostolic grace. If I were consulted to recommend one person to write on the subject of apostles and prophets, he would be the first person I would recommend, since I know that he would not only write as an academician (check) but also as an experienced practitioner. Thus, he qualifies to write this book. I am pleased that he has come out with such a balanced book on the subject.

In this book, Professor Opoku Onyinah brings new insight about apostles and prophets by diligently dividing the "Word of Truth," interacting with early church history, and applying practical illustrations. He shows that apostles and prophets have been in existence since God started communicating with his people. Yet, the focus of the Old Testament minister of God was the prophet, while the focus of the New Testament is the apostle. The call, the making of, the functions, and the spiritual gifts, which constitute an apostle or a prophet, are dealt with thoroughly. He contends that God used apostles such as Joseph, Moses, Nehemiah, Peter, Paul, Martin Luther, and John Wesley in their generations, and he will continue to use apostles in generations unborn. A significant contribution of the study is the discussion on why the government of the church dropped from apostles to bishops. Similarly, the part that you need spiritual illumination to comprehend is the chapters on how to receive revelations; you need to digest this part to take you to another spiritual realm. The limitations of the apostolic and prophetic is analyzed against the need to test all manifestations of the Spirit. Onyinah's desire is that God will raise more apostles and prophets in our generations to deal with the modern challenges that we face. I highly recommend that you read the book to get abreast of the new face of the apostolic and prophetic ministry that my friend Opoku brings to us.

Reverend Professor Paul Yaw Frimpong Manso
    General Superintendent of the Assemblies of God, Ghana
    President, Ghana Pentecostal and Charismatic Council
    Chairman, Ghana Evangelism Committee

Acknowledgments

THIS BOOK HAS COME about because the Lord found me, called and shaped me to work as his servant. I give him glory. I also give thanks to the Church of Pentecost, which gave me the opportunity in active service for forty-two years (1976–2018) to serve the Lord in many capacities, as a district pastor, a regional apostle, the first international missions director (IMD), the first rector of Pentecost University College, and the chairman of the church for ten years. All of these gave me the opportunity to exercise the gifts in me that have helped me write this book. Thus, I write not just from a theoretical perspective but also from practical experience.

In view of this, I want to honor my mentors who discovered the grace of God in my life as a young man of twenty-two years, then, recommended and trained me in the ministry. A few among them are Pastor P. E. Nsiah, the then-Apostle E. D. Aninkorah, Apostle B. K. Arthur, Prophet Thomas Nyarko, Apostles D. K. Arnan, F. S. Safo, and Prophet M. K. Yeboah.

In the Church of Pentecost, I extend special thanks to all the chairmen, general secretaries, international missions directors, Executive Council members present and past, directors of ministries, committees and board chairpersons, national heads, area heads, and colleague apostles and prophets, active and retired, that I worked with. In fact, I am grateful to General Council members, and Pentecost University College Council members I worked with. I am also indebted to the Staff Representative Council (SRC), and the entire headquarters staff for their unflinching support for me during my forty-two years in full-time pastoral ministry, out of which twenty-one were spent at the headquarters.

The general secretaries are Apostles Rigwell Ato Addison (when I was the IMD), Albert Amoah, Dr. Alfred Koduah, and Alexander Nana Yaw Kumi-Larbi. The international missions directors are Apostles Dr. S. K. Baidoo and Emmanuel Gyesi-Addo.

The Executive Council members I worked with are: Apostles Ekow Badu Wood, Ousmane Zabre, Francis Ofori-Yeboah, James Smith Gyimah, Emmanuel Owusu Bediakoh, Emmanuel Owusu, David Tekper, Joseph Asabil, M. O. Andoh, Samuel Osei Asante, Nii Kotei Dzani, Yaw Agyei Kwarteng, Eric Kwabena Nyamekye, Prophets J. E. Ameyaw, and James Osei Amaniampong.

The staff I worked with were very helpful and supportive, and they greatly contributed to sharpening my life and ministry. These include Elders Stephen Ahedor, D. K. Siaw, Joseph Tekpetey, E. K. Yeboah, Arthur Kaye, Akwasi Akowuah, Peter Nimakoh, Emmanuel Eshun, Samuel Agyei Wilson, Kwasi Boakye Yiadom, Erasmus Okpoti, Patrick Opoku Onyinah; Mrs. Rianon Seesi, Mrs. Trish Waller, Mrs. Akotsen Faustina Enninful, Mrs. Henrietta Awuah, Mrs. Selina Osei Owusu; Ms. Joyce Hammond; Pastor Johnny Peprah, Apostle Samuel Otu and Mrs. Gifty Appiah, Apostles Emmanuel Gyesi-Addo and Komi Edna Agbavitor. Others include Elder Dr. Gibson Annor-Antwi, Rev. Dr. Emmanuel and Emily Anim, Elder Professor K. B. and Mrs. Victoria Omane-Antwi, and Elder J. M. K. Nyadie.

I am greatly appreciative to Apostle Dr. Michael K. Ntumy, my predecessor as chairman of the Church of Pentecost, for his friendship and support over the years and for reading through the book and offering very useful suggestions. Similarly, I am grateful to Apostle Eric Kwabena Nyamekye who is my successor as the chairman of the church for exhibiting apostolicity in the discharge of his duties as a sign of apostolic succession within the Church of Pentecost system.

My special friends have been key contributors in my ministry. Together with others behind the scenes, their prayer support, encouragement and availability in good and bad times have helped me. These include Apostle E. K. and Mrs. Esi Barabu, Mrs. Dorcas Barabu of blessed memory, Prophet and Mrs. Georgina James Osei Amaniampong (and his twin brother, John, and wife, Mary), Apostle Emmanuel and Patience Owusu, Apostle Dr. Emmanuel and Mrs. Faustina Owusu Bediakoh, Elder Stephen and Grace Agyei, Elder Dr. Gibson and Mrs. Joyce Annor-Antwi.

Other friends and pastors who have assisted in various parts of my ministry include Mrs. Faustina France, Mrs. Grace Dwomoh, Deaconess Lynda Kuffour, Elder Boniface and Mrs. Comfort Oppong, Deaconess Theresa Owusu and husband, Michael Owusu, Rev. Professor Peter Ohene and Dr. Abigail Kyei, Rev. Johnson and Mrs. Margaret Agyemang Badu, Apostle Daniel Kwame and Mrs. Fedelia Noble-Atsu, Apostle Samuel and Mary Antwi, Apostle Abraham Lincoln and Theresa Angoh, Apostle Patrick and Mrs. Roberta Aseyoro, Apostle Nicholas Yaw and Mrs. Love Siaw, Apostle Michael and Mrs. Sheila Agyemang Amoako (USA), and Apostle Samuel and Mary Arthur (USA).

I express gratitude to my wife, Grace, my children and their spouses (Nicholas, Mark, Daniel, Caleb, Grace, and Stephen) and my siblings led by Apostles Dr. Stephen Waye Onyinah, Onyinah Gyamfi, Dr. Onyina Agyei, my mother, Rebeca Akosua Afriyie, the entire extended family, my in-laws, especially my mother-in-law, Madam Akosua Acheampomaah, and those in our household, both past and present. Other siblings Mrs. Mary Waye and Elder Ameyaw Gyamfi; Mrs. Gladys and Elder Eric Yamoah, Mrs. Veronica Acheampong, Ms. Mary Onyinah, Ms. Annah Onyinah Yeboah, Mr. Onyinah Gyau, Mrs. Grace Temah and Apostle Kojo Yeboah, Mr. Kwame Arhin, Mrs. Achiah Onyinah, Honorable Elder Maxwell Adu Agyei. They have been supportive and helped to shape me.

On the national front, I have enjoyed the fellowship, encouragement, and support of fellow heads of churches, leaders of parachurch organizations, other eminent personalities, and ministers. The Ghana Pentecostal and Charismatic Council and the Ghana Evangelism Committee both offered me leadership positions to serve. A few of the personalities I worked with here include Apostle Adottey, Rt. Rev. Sam Korankye-Ankrah; Aps. Dr. Stephen K. Amoani; Bishop Dr. Charles Agyinasare, Aps. Samuel Y. Antwi; Rev. Clement Anchebah; Rt. Rev. Dr. S. K. Ofori; Rev. Dr. Seth Ablorh; Bishop Dr. Prince Baah, Rev. Christopher Marfo-Ahenkora; Bishop S. N. Mensah; Bishop Dr. Gordon Kisseih; Aps. Peter O. Mankralo, Aps. Dr. Nana Anyani Boadum.

Other parachurch organizations I related to are the Christian Council, Catholic Secretariat, National Peace Council, National Coalition of Proper Sexual Behaviour and Family Values. Some personalities I would also like to acknowledge are Most Rev. Aboagye Mensah, Very Rev. Yaw Frimpong Manso, Most Rev. Emmanuel Asante, Most Rev. Dr. Asante Antwi, Rev. Dr. Joyce Aryee, Archbishop Charles Palmer-Buckle; Very Rev. Professor Emmanuel Martey, Most Rev. Justice Ofei Akrofi, Most

Rev. Awotwi Pratt, Very Rev. Professor Cephas Omenyo, Prophet Robert Dentu, Rev. Dr. Kwame Bansah, Dr. Paul Opoku-Mensah, Archbishop Duncan Williams, Prophet Victor Kusi Boateng, Nana S. K. B. Asante, George Amo, Shaibu Abubakar, Imam Awal Shueib, Maulvi Mohammed Bin Salih, Skeikh M. M. Gedel, Rev. Dr. Nii Amoo Darku, Osofo Kofi Atabuatsi, Nana Agyakoma Difie II, and Lawyer Moses Fo-Amoani. I am also grateful to the Ghana National Chief Imam, Dr. Osamanu Nuhu Sharubutu, for the cordial relationship that exists between us.

The various governments and the presidents I have worked with have all been very helpful and favorable to us in many ways. They attended our programs such as General Council meetings, conferences, and offered us the opportunity to serve on the National Peace Council, the Board of Trustees of the National Cathedral and they assisted us whenever necessary. I am deeply grateful to all of them including Presidents Atta Mills, John Dramani Mahama, and Nana Addo Danquah Akuffo-Addo and his vice, Dr. Mahamudu Bawumia.

Thanks also to our friends at the international level who continue to pray for, encourage, and offer me opportunities to serve in various capacities, including cochair of Scholars Consultation, Empowered21, cochair of Empowered21, Africa; Commissioner of World Mission and Evangelism of the World Council of Churches; member of Pentecostal theologians in dialogue with the Catholic Church; member of the Steering Committee of Africa Pentecostal Missions Fellowship, member of the Commission of Religious Liberty of the World Pentecostal Fellowship, and member of the Commission of Christian Unity of the World Pentecostal Fellowship.

The Lord raised some business men and women who in various ways supported our ministry. These include Elders Dr. Joseph and Mrs. Cynthia Araba Siaw Agyepong (CEO of Zoomlion and Jospong Group of Companies), Nana K. and Mrs. Josephine Gyasi, Nana Dr. Michael Agyekum and Mrs. Ernestina Serwah Addo (KAMA), Mr. Daniel Ofori, CEO of White Chapel, and Nana Samuel and Mrs. Mercy Amo Tobbin (CEO of Tobinco Pharmacy). Others include Elder Nana Samuel and Mrs. Gladys Fredua Agyeman, Hon. Deaconess Eunice Buah Asoma Hinneh, Elder Patrick Kwame and Mrs. Gifty Danso and Elder Prince and Mrs. Margaret Amoah and Deaconess Mrs. Faustina France. I am very grateful to all of them.

I register my sincerest appreciation to Stephanie Selawe Adenyo of Comms Havilah for editing and proofreading the project. My special gratitude also goes to Mrs. Florence Simpson and Faustina Enninful for proofreading the script, and Ms. Alberta Joyce Hammond and Felix Ekow Nkrumah for effecting some corrections for me.

Finally, I am grateful to all ministers of the Church of Pentecost for their support and encouragement. I salute the officers (elders, deacons, and deaconesses) and members of the church for their trust and support accorded us as I carried out my duties. May your labor of love in the Lord's vineyard never go unrewarded!

Opoku Onyinah

Introduction

THE LORD CALLED ME to the full-time pastoral ministry of the Church of Pentecost at age twenty-two, at a time when it was uncommon for people of my age to be called into the ministry of the church. The regional superintendent of the Northern and Upper Regions, Rev. Emmanuel David Aninkorah, who recommended me, said he had hitherto decided to stop making such recommendations. He had a reason for this. The three people he recommended earlier had all failed. However, according to him, when he recognized the grace of God in my life, he could not resist the temptation of recommending me to the ministry.

Truly, to his observation, after I had been called to the ministry and transferred to my second station, Kumasi, which happened to be the second-largest city of Ghana, that same grace was at work. During my teaching sessions, people would come in much earlier than the service was scheduled, in order to secure a seat. This tendency followed me wherever I went and many times people defied rains to attend meetings; a phenomenon which was not common in our side of the world. Some of the church elders and senior pastors began to say that "this young man is an apostle." After eight years in the ministry, at age thirty, the executive council of the church appointed me a regional superintendent, supervising the work of sixteen pastors. Within a year, thirteen new churches were planted and 1,409 new converts were baptized and added to the church.[1] I was then confirmed as an apostle in the structure of the Church of Pentecost. In the same year, 1986, the executive council of the church sponsored two pastors, Pastor Daniel Kwame Noble-Atsu and myself, to study at the Elim Bible College (now Regents Theological College) in the UK. One of the issues of discussion during the period was "apostles." The

1. Church of Pentecost, "Annual Report on Volta Region."

question was, "Are there apostles today?" Since then, I became interested in discovering all that the Bible has to say about apostles.

As I began to research into it, I realized that not only were there problems with the concept of apostleship but there were also challenges with the term "apostle" itself. However, this is not our concern now.[2] The question "Are there apostles today?" continues to prevail after the death of the original apostles. The common view of the period was cessationism; the belief that spiritual gifts, such as speaking in tongues, healing, miracles, and prophecy, died with the apostolic age. The claim is that the Lord appointed apostles for the early days of the church, to establish standard doctrines hence the church is built on the foundation of the apostles and prophets (Eph 2:20), and that everything we need to know has been taught by the apostles and canonized in Scripture. The understanding here is that the early church did not have the complete Scripture. Thus, they needed reliable apostles and prophets to lay down the foundation of the church. Now that we have the complete canon of Scripture, there is no longer a need for apostles and prophets. Hence, if someone claims to be an apostle or prophet, there should be concern since it is perceived that he opens up for false teachings to be developed.[3]

Notwithstanding, throughout the history of the church, some people have always sought for something more than "dead traditions." In the third century, Mani of Persia (216–274) claimed to be the last apostle— "the Apostle of Light" and "supreme illuminator." He established what came to be known as Manichaeism, which taught the dualistic concept of good and evil. He was considered a heretic by the church and subsequently excommunicated.[4]

Prophet Mohammed also arose at the time when religious images had saturated the church. He considered himself the last apostle (messenger) and prophet of all times. His passion was to deliver humanity from the idolatrous worship he believed the church had placed on people. He had to destroy 360 idols in Mecca.[5]

---

2. For discussion on this, see Agnew, "On the Origin of the Term *apostolos*"; Agnew, "Origin of the NT Apostles Concept"; Barrett, "Shaliah and Apostle"; Schnackenburg, "Apostles before and during Paul's Time"; Taylor, "Apostolic Identity and the Conflicts in Corinth and Galatia"; Taylor, "Conflict as Context for Defining Identity."

3. For reading on cessation, see Ruthven, *On the Cessation of the Charismata*; Grudem, *Are Miraculous Gifts for Today*.

4. Shelton, *History of the Christian Church*, vol. 1; Synan, *Eye Witness*.

5. Hamon, *Eternal Church*; Synan, *Eye Witness*, 174.

One other person who brought the church's mind to the supernatural was Edward Irving (1792–1834) of Scotland. Irving was not settled with the cessationist view because he believed in the continuation of the spiritual gifts after the death of the apostles. As an ordained Presbyterian minister, pastoring Caledonian Chapel, in Hatton Garden, London, he encouraged his congregation to pray for the gifts. It is said that in the 1830s, speaking in tongues, prophecy, and healings were manifested in his congregation, although he himself did not speak in tongues.[6] Eventually, the Church of Scotland excommunicated him in 1832, and he then became a wandering preacher. His followers started the Holy Catholic Apostolic Church and ordained him as a deacon of the church, but he died in 1834. His movement could not survive the first generation in Britain.[7]

Still, in the nineteenth century, arose Joseph Smith (1805–1844), who established the Mormon Church or the Church of Jesus Christ of Latter-day Saints in the United States. Mormons believe that God has placed in the church presidents, apostles, high priests, seventies, and elders.[8] They also believe in the operations of the Holy Spirit, especially the "Spirit of prophecy" and speaking in tongues.[9] In the services of the church, it is said that Smith could lay hands on people to receive the Holy Spirit and that he himself often spoke in tongues.[10] Mormons however have been considered a sect as a result of their strange teaching which originates from the book of Mormon.

During the outpouring of the Holy Spirit in the early part of the twentieth century, which was climaxed at Azusa Street in the United States, there was the manifestation of some of the spiritual gifts, including speaking in tongues, healing, and prophecy. However, most of the denominations which came out of the move of the Spirit, including the largest Pentecostal denomination in the world, the Assemblies of God, did not recognize the offices of the apostles and prophets. They believed that there is apostolic function or ministry today but not the office of apostle;

---

6. Synan, *Eye Witness*, 175.
7. Body, "Irvin, Edward"; Strachan, *Pentecostal Theology of Ewald Irving*.
8. Martin, *Kingdom of the Cults*, 228.
9. Thomas, *Pentecostal Reads the Book of Mormon*, 210–13.
10. Synan, *Eye Witness*, 177.

simply stated, the missionaries are doing the work of the apostles. This is a view similar to cessationism.[11]

Some Pentecostals, however, acknowledged the offices of apostles and prophets. One of such persons is William Oliver Hutchinson. Having been influenced by both the Welsh revival in 1904 and that of Azusa Street in 1906, Hutchinson established the Apostolic Faith Church, and was the first to recognize the offices of the apostles and prophets in 1912.[12]

Two of the members who were called to these offices were Daniel Powel Williams who was ordained an apostle and his brother, William Jones Williams who was also called to the office of prophet. According to the *Dictionary of Welsh Biography*, both were called on the same day, March 5, 1911.[13] Their callings occurred through a "directive prophecy."[14] In 1916, Daniel Williams (and his brother William Jones) seceded from Hutchinson and his Apostolic Faith Church to form the Apostolic Church as a result of disagreements. One common factor of these apostolic churches was the formation of the college of the apostles and prophets that became the governing body of the church. Initially, within the Apostolic Church, prophecy was almost considered infallible as they equated it with Scriptures. However, later, the church acknowledged the possibility of error depending on the state of the person who prophesied. By 1939, the leaders of the Apostolic Church in the UK had agreed to discontinue the practice of prophets singling out people in public meetings and pronouncing them to certain church positions.[15]

Meanwhile, the Apostolic Church established missions in all the continents, including New Zealand, Australia, Canada, the United States, and Africa. Some of the churches that came out of the Apostolic Church or were influenced by it include: the Church of Pentecost with its headquarters in Ghana, Christ Apostolic Church of Ghana, and Christ Apostolic Church of Nigeria, and the ACTS churches of New Zealand which were formerly the Apostolic Church of New Zealand.

---

11. Schmithals, *Office of Apostle*; Johnson, *Apostolic Functions*, 52–62.

12. Worsfold, *Origins of the Apostolic Church in Great Britain*, 91. For further reading, see Hathaway, "Role of William Oliver Hutchinson," 40–56.

13. Although Evan David Jones is aware T.N. Turnbull says that it was at a conference in London in 1913 that Daniel Powell was called to the apostleship, he thinks otherwise. Jones "Williams, Daniel Powell ('Pastor Dan')."

14. Directive prophecy is the situation where someone speaks with the first person singular on behalf of God instructing people to do specific things.

15. Koduah, "Role of Directive Prophecy," 297–325.

Equippers Churches and Activate Churches were part of the network of the ACTS churches. The mission churches of ACTS also adopted the process of calling people into the offices of apostles and prophets. Contrary to what Vinson Synan said, "In these churches, apostles 'usually twelve' were duly elected and ordained,"[16] a statement which somewhat implied a mystification of the number twelve, there is nothing said about the number twelve in regards to calling and ordination in these churches.[17] Of course, Synan did not substantiate his claim. The call to the apostolic ministry was strengthened by the Latter Rain movement in mid-twentieth century.[18] The Latter Rain movement believed in the restoration of the fivefold ministry of apostles, prophets, evangelists, pastors, and teachers (Eph 4:11–12). They also believed that the laying-on of hands by apostles and prophets is followed by the baptism of the Spirit, manifestation of spiritual gifts, and other supernatural occurrences.[19] The Latter Rain movement also laid emphasis on deliverance and was opposed to the establishment of "human organizations."

Consequently, the churches influenced by the Latter Rain movement were independent local churches with little or no central organization. Other features of the Latter Rain movement were the "praise dance," fasting, and prayers. Still, others included the "New thing" in Isa 43:19 (and Acts 17:19–21) which, to them, centered on revelation, and the Feast of Tabernacles.[20] The Latter Rain ministers did not only hold on to these beliefs, but, as it has been shown by Riss and Bill Hamon, the crusades of some of the key leaders of the movement, such as William Branham, Gordon Lindsay, T. L. Osborn, and Oral Roberts were characterized by reports of healing and other miraculous phenomena.[21] The ministers of Latter Rain, especially those just mentioned, greatly contributed to the ministry of the Full Gospel Business Men's Fellowship, which also

16. Synan, *Eye Witness*, 180.

17. Having associated myself with these churches for several years, I have never suspected any mystification of the number twelve in connection with the ordination of apostles, and neither do we find it in their constitution, principles and practices. For example, see the Apostolic Church, *Apostolic Church: Its Principles and Practices*.

18. Riss, "Latter Rain Movement," 830–33; Riss, "Latter Rain Movement of 1948," 32–45.

19. Hamon, *Eternal Church*, 263; Riss, "Latter Rain Movement," 533; Hocken, *Streams of Renewal*, 26; Worsfold, *Origins of the Apostolic Church in Great Britain*, 292.

20. Worsfold, *Origins of the Apostolic Church in Great Britain*, 292; Hocken, *Streams of Renewal*, 26.

21. Hamon, *Eternal Church*, 246; Riss, *20th Century Revival Movements*, 105–12.

influenced the Charismatic renewal within the mainline churches.[22] The Latter Rain movement, however, was opposed by the classical Pentecostal churches including the Assemblies of God, the Church of God, the Pentecostal Holiness Church, and the Apostolic Church.[23]

Even though most of the classical Pentecostals rejected the Latter Rain movement, their teaching on apostles and prophets was strengthened by the network that has been known as the New Apostolic Reformation (NAR). By the close of the twentieth century, C. Peter Wagner, having been influenced by David Cannistraci's book *The Gift of Apostles*, coined the term New Apostolic Reformation (NAR), to describe what he observed was a new trend within Christianity.[24]

Initially, the trend he referred to was largely a congregational life, with what he observed as "minimal adjustments in theology."[25] Thus, what he observed was not an association with membership, but independent churches who believed in the restoration of the apostolic and prophetic offices. Through his initiative, some of these churches formed a network, which was headed by himself (Peter Wagner).[26] Some critics of this network, however, associate whatever trend differs from the classical Pentecostal and Charismatic renewal mainstream churches and groups, with the NAR. The NAR, nevertheless, is a global network of ministers who believe in the restoration of the fivefold ministry in Eph 4:12, which are apostles, prophets, evangelists, pastors, and teachers. This network believes that God's intent for the government of the church is that apostles and prophets lead it. They believe that the role of apostles and prophets does continue, since this role did not end with the original apostles. They believe that the church lost this truth but has now been restored.[27] The

---

22. Peter Hocken has pointed out the renewal within the mainline churches was greatly influenced by the ministry of David Johannes Du Plessis. Hocken, "Charismatic Movement," 477–520.

23. Assemblies of God, "Twenty Third General Council," 26; Synan, *Eye Witness*, 180. Thomas, *God of Our Fathers*, 144–45.

24. Cannistraci, *Gifts of Apostle*, 12.

25. Wagner, *Apostle and Prophets*, 22. For further reading, see Wagner, *New Apostolic*; Wagner, *Church Quake*; Wagner, *Apostle Today*.

26. Wagner, *Apostle Today*, back page.

27. Some literature published by contemporary apostles and prophets: Joyner, *Apostolic Ministry*; Evans, *Apostolic Ministry*; Price, *ABC'S of Apostleship*; Jacobs, *Voice of God*; Bickle with Sullivant, *Growing in the Prophetic*; Deere, *Surprised by the Voice of God*; Goll, *Coming of Prophetic Revolution*; Chironna, *Prophetic Perspective*; Price, *Prophetic Handbook*.

NAR is still a movement that is not an association with membership and constitution yet it has come under strong criticism.

At its early stage, Wagner indicated how he felt Synan represented the opposing view. He cited Synan's thoughts that "it is axiomatic to say that anyone who claims to be an apostle probably is not one. An apostle is not self-appointed or elected by any ecclesiastical body, but is chosen by the Lord Himself."[28] Synan was comfortable with the term ministry rather than office. Writing in 2010, however, Synan mellowed down his reservations. He believes that if the move is not abused, the NAR will bring the gospel to many unreached people of the world.[29]

The Assemblies of God is resolute on the NAR. In its General Council held on August 11, 2000, it adapted a paper which implies that the offices of contemporary apostles and prophets is a departure from Scripture. Although the paper accepts that the ministry still functions, it denies that there is indication in Scripture that the offices of apostles and prophets continue.[30]

Notwithstanding the Assemblies of God official stance on apostles and prophets, David Petts, who served for twenty-seven years (1977–2004), as the principal of Mattersey Hall, a Bible College owned by the Assemblies of God, UK, wrote a textbook which indicates that there are apostles today. Petts was not concerned about the difference between the terms "office" and "ministry," he simply assumed that "despite the views of the cessationists who argue that some of these gifts are not for today, that all the gifts mentioned in the New Testament are important for the church of the 21st Century."[31] He believes that there are apostles today.[32] Similarly, the renowned Pentecostal New Testament scholar Gordon Fee, accepts that "part of the problem with the term is that it has a sense of function as well as office or position." And that "in Paul the functional and positional usages nearly coalesce."[33] This could mean that Fee sees the apostleship as both functional and positional; his view is similar to Petts's position. Petts's position has not been accepted by many Evangelicals and Pentecostals; still, many attack the concept of apostles and prophets

---

28. Synan, *Eye Witness*, 185–86.

29. Synan, *Eye Witness*, 185–86.

30. General Council of the Assemblies of God, "End time Revival–Spirit-Led and Spirit-Controlled." However, see Cartledge, *Apostolic Revolution*.

31. Petts, *Body Builders*, 6, 38.

32. Petts, *Body Builders*, 29–31, 38.

33. Fee, *First Epistle to the Corinthians*, 30.

today. Paramount among the opposing views is the advocacy against the New Apostolic Reformation led by R. Douglas Geivett and Holly Pivec, which is presented in their book, *God's Super-Apostles: Encountering the Worldwide Prophets and Movements*.[34] Geivett and Pivec argue among other reasons that the Bible does not teach that "apostles today must govern the church in the way the apostles of Christ governed" and that passages such as Eph 4:11–12; 2:20 and 1 Cor 12:28 do not speak "about governing offices."[35] Furthermore, they contend that the governing office of apostles was temporary."[36] They assigned three reasons for these: first, that the twelve apostles of Christ had a unique role to play; second, that Paul reasoned that he was the final apostle; and third, that Scripture gives no indication that apostles would be recognized after the death of the apostles of Christ.[37]

In addition to these, Geivett and Pivec accuse NAR ministers of using authority more than those of the Roman Catholic bishops.[38] They conclude that "screening their claims by multiple biblical criteria, NAR teachings about apostles fall short."[39] They, however, claim that there is a place for people "who function in some way as certain types of first-century apostles—as missionaries and church planters."[40] These arguments are not directly from the cessationists' perspective, however, when pressed hard, they reflect the same stance since the core of cessationism is that the miraculous gifts of the Holy Spirit ceased after the apostolic age. One of the accusations levelled against the NAR is the excessive use of power, nevertheless, the desire to come under authority or to be one man's keeper is one of the reasons for the formation of the network of the NAR. One thing, however, that comes out from the criticisms is that none of them has completely branded the NAR a sect. Michael Brown, a renowned North American theologian, offers this counsel:

> My suggestion, then, for those who want to be constructive is this. First, get rid of the extreme rhetoric ("not Christian"; "aberrant movement"; etc.). You're slandering your brothers and

---

34. Geitvett and Pivec, *God's Super-Apostles*.
35. Geitvett and Pivec, *God's Super-Apostles*, 29–30.
36. Geitvett and Pivec, *God's Super-Apostles*, 31.
37. Geitvett and Pivec, *God's Super-Apostles*, 31.
38. Geitvett and Pivec, *God's Super-Apostles*, 10.
39. Geitvett and Pivec, *God's Super-Apostles*, 41.
40. Geitvett and Pivec, *God's Super-Apostles*, 32–33, 41.

sisters. . . . Fourth, identify the beliefs or practices you question, be sure you rightly understand them from an insider perspective, then respond to them based on Scripture and fruit. Fifth, recognize the wonderful things the Spirit is doing around the world today. This way, rather than scaring people with false accusations of a conspiratorial, worldwide, demonic movement, you can engage in constructive, fruitful interaction. That way, you can build up more than tear down. Isn't that the goal we all share?[41]

This book is not defending the NAR concept of apostles and prophets, neither is it a book to warn people about the NAR nor an academic treaty to argue about the existence or the cessation of apostles and prophets today. The book is an attempt from a pastor/theologian whose interest is to trace and find out the role of apostles and prophets in the Bible, and then share these findings in a practical way to help the church of today. In a way, it is a follow up of what Petts assumed by saying there are apostles and prophets today and Fee's analysis that the term "has a sense of function as well as office or position."[42]

However, while Petts's focus was on all the spiritual gifts, my focus is on apostles and prophets with the other spiritual gifts in the background. Accordingly, the terms office, and ministry of the apostle are used interchangeably unless otherwise stated. While I dwell on the Bible to make relevant points, I also make good use of ancient literature to find out the practices which were going on in the early church period, to make some assumptions. I make good use of secondary materials as well as personal illustrations to buttress some statements. While I write as a Pentecostal from the apostolic background, I hope Evangelicals and Pentecostals from the other side who read this book will find my presentation as an objective and fair assessment of the issues discussed.

In 1948, a man of God whom I identify as a Chinese "apostle," Watchman Nee, during his ministry to Christian workers, came out with three types of ministers in the Bible. These are: the prophet as the minister of the word of God in the Old Testament; the Lord Jesus as minister of the word of God in the gospels; and the apostle as the minister of the word of

---

41. Brown, "Dispelling the Myths about NAR (the New Apostolic Reformation)." https://www.christianpost.com/voice/dispelling-myths-new-apostolic-reformation-michael-brown.html. Assessed 28/01/2020

42. Fee, *First Epistle to the Corinthians*, 30.

God in the New Testament.[43] Watchman Nee was not a Pentecostal and he did not speak in tongues;[44] nonetheless, he was a man of the Spirit of God. I consider his ministry as that of an apostle and himself as one of the greatest apostles the Lord has raised for his church. I build upon his concept of the ministers of God's word.

My premise is that there have been apostles and prophets from the Old Testament period to date. However, the focus of the Old Testament minister of God was the prophet. The focus of the New Testament minister of God today is the apostle; in other words, apostles have never been put out of the system. Bishops and elders were raised to assist the work of the apostles in the New Testament. God has always raised apostles to champion his course. The prayer of the church today should, therefore, be that the Lord of the Harvest would raise up more apostles and prophets in our generation.

To advance my proposition, the book has been divided into nine parts. Part 1 begins with how God communicates with human beings from creation to today, with the prophet as the focus in the Old Testament. It indicates that there were few apostolic figures in the Old Testament. It continues with how the prophetic office was developed and the prophet made. Here, using the life of Samuel as a case study, the call of the prophet is discussed in detail since it forms a very important aspect of the prophetic ministry in general.

Part 2 deals with the constitution of the prophet. It looks at the gifts that come together to make up "the gift of a prophet." There is no direct way of getting these gifts. Thus, here, I dig from the Bible to identify the gifts which come together to constitute the prophetic office and discuss them in turns.

Part 3 discusses the functions of the prophet. It shows how the prophet becomes the interpreter of the covenant of God and continues with the prophet as the person who understands the times and speaks into it. The functions end by discussing the prophet as the person with spiritual authority over God's household.

Part 4 deals with the New Testament prophets. It has been argued throughout the book that the minister of the Old Testament is the prophet, and that of the New Testament is the apostle. This part attempts to find out if there are prophets in the New Testament. It begins with how the

---

43. Nee, *Ministry of God's Word*, 9–20.
44. Kinnear, *Against the Tide*, 104.

New Testament is linked with the Old Testament in connection with the fulfillment of its prophecies, and then shows how in the New Testament, there is the potential for each person to prophesy. It however shows that some could still specially possess the gift of prophecy and others could be called into the office of the prophet.

Part 5 presents the apostle as the messenger of God in the New Testament. It begins with the identification of the original apostles in the Bible, continues with the training that goes into the making of an apostle and then discovers other apostles besides the known and labeled ones. Part 5 also explores the gifts that come together to constitute an apostle and ends with how to recognize an apostle.

Part 6 discusses the functions of the apostles. My research shows that the functions of apostles are remarkably different from the functions of prophets in the Old Testament. However, there are some similarities. Thus, this section ends with similarities as well as dissimilarities between apostles and prophets.

Part 7 finds out why the leadership of the church dropped from apostles to bishops. It makes a brief survey from church history to find out how the apostles dropped to give way to bishops as the managers of the church. I dig out from some available first- and second-century books to find out the roles of church officers during those periods. I select a few church fathers and analyze the type of gifts they had, and how the community recognized them. I end by appealing to the Lord to raise up more apostles in our generation.

Part 8 gives a highlight of how to receive revelations. It shows that both prophets and apostles can receive revelations. It continues by showing the developments of receiving revelations and ends with the hindrances to hearing from God.

Part 9 deals with the limitations of apostles and prophets, with special focus on the challenges that go along with prophecy. It discusses how to identify both good and false manifestations. This is the part that deals with how to identify good prophets, the prophetic flaws and how to test prophecy.

In the book, unless otherwise stated or implied, the use of the male pronouns signifies both male and female genders.

PART 1

The Prophet

Part 1 begins with how God communicates with human beings. It shows that God has always spoken with his creation. God started to deal with some persons who were called prophets, nevertheless, there were also some apostles. God continued with the prophets until the coming of the Lord Jesus Christ, and now, after his death and resurrection, God deals with the apostles. This part has been divided into three chapters. Chapter 1 serves as introduction, chapter 2 deals with how the prophetic office developed, and chapter 3 shows how prophets are made.

Chapter 1

The Messengers of God

GOD ALWAYS SPEAKS TO people in every generation. The way God speaks to people in each generation may change but there is a clear indication that he always speaks. For example, the account of Gen 1:26—3 shows that God was constantly communicating with human beings. Immediately God created human beings, he spoke to them, "And God blessed them. And God said to them, 'Be fruitful and multiply and fill the earth and subdue it and have dominion over the fish of the sea and over the birds of the heavens and over every living thing that moves on the earth'" (Gen 1:28 ESV). From Gen 3:8, "And they heard the sound of the Lord God walking in the garden in the cool of the day, and Adam and his wife hid themselves from the presence of the Lord God among the trees of the garden" (NKJV), we get the indication that, before the fall, God was constantly sharing fellowship with Adam and Eve.

GOD CONTINUES TO SPEAK AFTER THE FALL

God was still speaking to people after the fall and this is evident in the presentation of offerings by Cain and Abel:

> In the course of time Cain brought some of the fruits of the soil as an offering to the Lord. But Abel brought fat portions from some of the firstborn of his flock. The Lord looked with favor on Abel and his offering, but on Cain and his offering he did not look with favor. So Cain was very angry, and his face was

> downcast. Then the Lord said to Cain, "Why are you angry? Why is your face downcast? If you do what is right, will you not be accepted? But if you do not do what is right, sin is crouching at your door; it desires to have, but you must master it." Now Cain said to his brother Abel, "Let's go out to the field." And while they were in the field, Cain attacked his brother Abel and killed him. Then the Lord said to Cain, "Where is your brother Abel?" "I don't know," he replied. "Am I my brother's keeper?" The Lord said, "What have you done? Listen! Your brother's blood cries out to me from the ground. Now you are under a curse and driven from the ground, which opened its mouth to receive your brother's blood from your hand. When you work the ground, it will no longer yield its crops for you. You will be a restless wanderer on the earth." Cain said to the Lord, "My punishment is more than I can bear. Today you are driving me from the land, and I will be hidden from your presence; I will be a restless wanderer on the earth, and whoever finds me will kill me." But the Lord said to him, "Not so; if anyone kills Cain, he will suffer vengeance seven times over." Then the Lord put a mark on Cain so that no one who found him would kill him. So Cain went out from the Lord's presence and lived in the land of Nod, east of Eden. (Gen 4:3–16 NIV)

How did Abel know that his offering had been accepted? How did Cain know that his offering had not been accepted? God might have communicated with them. When Cain conceived the idea of killing his brother, the Lord spoke to him and warned him. Again, when he eventually killed his brother, the Lord spoke to him (Gen 4:2–9). Cain also responded by telling the Lord that his punishment was too much. There was a dialogue between the Lord and Cain, which means that God does not only speak to righteous people; he also speaks to sinners. The great lesson here is that God continues to speak to people.

GOD SPOKE TO NOAH

God spoke to Noah, "I have determined to make an end of all flesh, for the earth is filled with violence through them. Behold, I will destroy them with the earth. Make yourself an ark of gopher wood. Make rooms in the ark, and cover it inside and out with pitch" (Gen 6:13–14 ESV). We do not know how God spoke to him. But it was very clear that Noah knew

God had spoken to him. He followed the directive of the Lord and it proved faithful by the falling of the rains and the subsequent flood.

However, it is also known from the story of Noah that God was not speaking to him on everything. He allowed him to use his own wisdom to decide on other factors. After the flood, God did not tell Noah that the water had dried and so he should settle down but Noah used his common sense to decide. Let us ponder over Gen 8:6–12:

> At the end of forty days Noah opened the window of the ark that he had made and sent forth a raven. It went to and fro until the waters were dried up from the earth. Then he sent forth a dove from him, to see if the waters had subsided from the face of the ground. But the dove found no place to set her foot, and she returned to him to the ark, for the waters were still on the face of the whole earth. So he put out his hand and took her and brought her into the ark with him. He waited another seven days, and again he sent forth the dove out of the ark. And the dove came back to him in the evening, and behold, in her mouth was a freshly plucked olive leaf. So Noah knew that the waters had subsided from the earth. Then he waited another seven days and sent forth the dove, and she did not return to him anymore. (ESV)

The Lord did not ask Noah to send a raven, neither did he tell him to send a dove, yet Noah used his common sense and it was workable and good. This is an indication that, for God, using one's wisdom and knowledge is not of itself a sin because these faculties are God-given; only they must be used in the right way. It must be noted that although God was speaking to people in this era, the people concerned were not being called prophets or apostles. Thus, the fact that God speaks to a person does not make that person a prophet because God speaks to his creation—the people he has created.

INTRODUCTION TO THE PROPHET

In Gen 12, God spoke to Abraham and his immediate descendants—Isaac and Jacob. They are often referred to as the Patriarchs. For example, Gen 12:1 reads, "Now the LORD said to Abram . . . " (cf. Gen 13:14; 15:1). It is not clear how God spoke to Abraham, but in other instances, he revealed himself to him, and to Jacob in dreams. For example, in Gen

15:12–14 and Gen 28:12–17, the Lord spoke to Abraham and Jacob in dreams, respectively:

> As the sun was going down, a deep sleep fell on Abram. And behold, dreadful and great darkness fell upon him. Then the Lord said to Abram, "Know for certain that your offspring will be sojourners in a land that is not theirs and will be servants there, and they will be afflicted for four hundred years. But I will bring judgment on the nation that they serve, and afterward they shall come out with great possessions." (Gen 15:12–14 ESV)

> And he dreamed, and behold, there was a ladder set up on the earth, and the top of it reached to heaven. And behold, the angels of God were ascending and descending on it! And behold, the Lord stood above it and said, "I am the Lord, the God of Abraham your father and the God of Isaac. The land on which you lie I will give to you and to your offspring." . . . And he was afraid and said, "How awesome is this place! This is none other than the house of God, and this is the gate of heaven." (Gen 28:12–17 ESV)

In these two instances, the Lord spoke to Abraham and Jacob through dreams. These examples are clear, but, in other places, it is not clear how the Lord spoke to them. However, what is certain during this period is that the Lord spoke to these people and they were sure that they heard the voice of God. They were the messengers of God at the time.

Abraham was the first person who was described as a prophet, by the Lord in a dream to King Abimelech, "Now then, return the man's wife, for he is a prophet, so that he will pray for you, and you shall live. But if you do not return her, know that you shall surely die, you, and all who are yours" (Gen 20:7 ESV). We shall pick up this later in our study. The emergence of Moses brings in another picture. God manifested himself and called him through the burning bush experience, he then commissioned him to go and deliver his people. Moses' experience with the Lord is described as "speaking to God face to face":

> Then He said,
>
> "Hear now My words: If there is a prophet among you,
>
> I, the Lord, make Myself known to him in a vision;
>
> I speak to him in a dream. Not so with My servant Moses;
>
> He is faithful in all My house.

> I speak with him face to face,
>
> Even plainly, and not in dark sayings; And he sees the form of the Lord.
>
> Why then were you not afraid
>
> To speak against My servant Moses?"
>
> (Num 12:6–8 NKJV)

The Lord makes it known here that he could reveal himself to prophets through visions and dreams but Moses was set apart as someone whose knowledge of God was higher than the prophet, because the Lord revealed himself to him by speaking with him face to face. Through this special dealing with Moses, God gave him the law, which became the standard way of knowing the will and ways of God, since God's purpose was well established in his law.

On the one hand, those who heard and obeyed the law were blessed. On the other hand, failure to obey the law resulted in curses and punishments. Nevertheless, new trends emerged, having no direct reference to the law of God as written down for his people. Along the line too, people lost the underlying principles of the law. Therefore, God continued to speak through individuals who were identified as "prophets." These prophets became the messengers of God, his mouthpiece, explaining the contents of God's law to the people. Seventeen books have been assigned to the prophets who were able to write down their revelations in the Bible. The law and the words of the prophets continued until the coming of the Lord Jesus.

THE PERIOD OF JESUS

The coming of Jesus began a new era. The person of Jesus was the embodiment of the word of God, he was the voice of God on earth, throwing light on God's word which had been misunderstood, and showing people the right path to God because he was the word himself. Jesus did not throw away the written law of God, rather, he made it clearer. For example, in Matt 5:17–18, he declared, "Do not think that I came to destroy the Law or the Prophets. I did not come to destroy but to fulfill. For assuredly, I say to you, till heaven and earth pass away, one jot or one title will by no means pass from the law till all is fulfilled" (NKJV). What did he mean by this? He wanted the people to know that the law of God was from God and it was perfect, but people had misunderstood it and applied it differently. His presence was to demonstrate to people the meaning of God's word and to make it relevant to generations.

Jesus did not need to receive revelations—seeing visions, dreams, and experiencing trances; he was the revelation. He did not need to say, "Thus saith the Lord"; he was the Lord speaking. He did not need the word of wisdom nor the word of knowledge; he was the word of wisdom and the word of knowledge. His very person on earth demonstrated the presence of God; he showed that God could live in the human body without pollution.

Ponder over this song which I received through an inspiration of the Holy Spirit in time of written:[1]

> Speak to me, Lord, speak, to me in Christ
>
> I am looking unto Christ
>
> Fullness of Godhead in bodily form
>
> Perfection manifests in Christ
>
> If I lift Christ up on high
>
> And I am obedient to you
>
> I shall be like a true servant
>
> who draws all people to his Master.

Our Lord Jesus Christ on earth was the manifestation of the word of God at the highest level; his very person and everything he did was the word of God. However, the people of Jesus' generation could not "hear" him, thus several times he told them, "He who has ears, let him hear" (Matt 11:15; 13:9 NIV; cf. Luke 8:8; 14:35; John 14:23–24).

Jesus appointed twelve men whom he called "apostles." He trained them and impacted their lives in such a way that they would continue the work which he began after his death. Often in his presence, he delegated his power for them to do his work (Luke 9:1–6; Matt 10:42). They could

---

1. Some Pentecostal members claim we receive songs instead of writing. Receiving a song comes through the inspiration of the Holy Spirit as one prays, meditate upon the word of God or appears before the presence of God. The song drops or flows easily to the spirit of the person. This can be sung and recorded or written down and taught later.

cast out demons and heal the sick in his name. They were, however, to wait for the Holy Spirit's empowerment before embarking on active ministry after his death. The Holy Spirit was to guide, teach and inform them of things which were to come (John 16:12–13). This means the Holy Spirit was going to communicate with them. However, the Holy Spirit would not come until after his death.

THE PERIOD OF THE APOSTLES

The death and resurrection of Jesus began an era, which continues up to our time—the period of the apostles. In this era, the apostles become the mouthpiece of God, the messengers of God. The coming of Jesus shows us that God could still speak through a person without saying, "Thus says the Lord." It shows us that the body of a human being can demonstrate the voice, power and glory of God. The apostolic era was the continuation of the era of our Lord Jesus but Jesus was different from the apostles; he was first the word of God, before he was clothed with the human body:

> In the beginning was the Word, and the Word was with God, and the Word was God. He was with God in the beginning. Through him all things were made; without him nothing was made that has been made. . . . The Word became flesh and made his dwelling among us. We have seen his glory, the glory of the One and Only, who came from the Father, full of grace and truth. (John 1:1–3, 14 NIV)

That is, in Jesus, the word comes first before the flesh. There was no pollution of the word, but with the apostles, the flesh comes before the word. The apostles had to believe before they would be born of God. John explains, "Yet to all who received him, to those who believed in his name, he gave the right to become children of God—children born not of natural descent, nor of human decision or a husband's will, but born of God" (John 1:12–13 NIV). Children born of God is the work of the Spirit, which comes about through a revelation of knowing and acknowledging Jesus as the Son of God—the Christ. When Peter was able to know and declare this, Jesus told him, "Flesh and blood has not revealed this to you, but My Father who is in heaven" (Matt 16:17 NKJV).

This means that considering the apostles as the mouthpiece of God is not the same as knowing Jesus as the word of God. With the apostles, the flesh comes before the word, which comes through the revelation of

Jesus as the Son of God—Christ. Nevertheless, what this means is that the ministry of the apostles was to come about through receiving the revelation of Jesus (the word), through the flesh (that is, the human body). In other words, the apostolic era has a combination of the ministry that was common in the Old Testament—revelation, and that of the Lord Jesus Christ—personality. In this era, the revelation of God settles in the body of a person for them to become a mouthpiece of God, a messenger of God.

Now, what we have identified so far is that God always speaks. He speaks to people of all caliber, sinners as well as righteous ones. There were no labels placed on those that God spoke to from the garden of Eden until it came to Abraham, who was called a prophet. The prophet was the messenger of God, who received revelation of God and carried his message and presence. Although Moses was a prophet, he was considered "above" the prophet as a result of his knowledge of the Lord. The Lord Jesus Christ also was God's word himself who did not need to say, "Thus says the Lord," since he was the word. The third messenger of God's word we have seen is the apostle. The apostle as the messenger of God was the combination of the Old Testament approach and that of our Lord Jesus Christ. Here, the person becomes the embodiment of God's word (a messenger) through the revelation of Jesus Christ as the Son of God.

Now we shall find in detail who the prophet was in the Old Testament.

Chapter 2

The Prophet as God's Messenger in the Old Testament

As we have already established, God always speaks. Nevertheless, people do not often hear him or even know it is the Lord who is speaking. Therefore, in the Old Testament, God chose some people to be his spokespersons by designating them as prophets. This means the prophets became the mouthpiece of God. If God spoke directly to all people, there would have been no concerns about prophets. However, because God chose to speak through these individuals, then, the persons he has chosen become a matter of concern, since human beings are flesh and blood, having their own preferences and challenges. We will therefore attempt to understand the term "prophet," discuss some of the people the Lord chose as prophets, and explore how he trained them to be his spokespersons.

ABRAHAM

The first person God addressed as a prophet was Abraham; the Lord told Abimelech, "Now return the man's wife, for he is a prophet, and he will pray for you and you will live. But if you do not return her, you may be sure that you and all yours will die" (Gen 20:7 NIV). The Hebrew word used here is *nabi* (the plural form is *nebi'im*)[1] which connotes an inspired spokesman; an ecstatic type of person.[2]

From the context in which the Lord used the term in connection with Abraham, the prophet is a person who is known by God, is God's friend, and someone God speaks for. He is also God's spokesperson, one who may instruct others on divine things, and a person God listens to. What the Lord told Abraham also implies that he was using Abraham to communicate his word to human beings, and Abraham was representing him. The call, life, and ministry of Abraham show partly how God uses prophets to speak to people.

MOSES

The next person that was addressed as a prophet was Moses. Deuteronomy 34:10 squarely declares, "There has not arisen a prophet since in Israel like Moses, whom the Lord knew face to face" (ESV). Moses himself confirms that he was a prophet: "The Lord your God will raise up for you a prophet like me from among your own brothers. You must listen to him" (Deut 18:15 NIV). It must however be shown that the functions of Moses went above the prophet. He was the apostolic type of figure. In Exod 7:1–3, "the Lord said to Moses, 'See, I have made you like God to Pharaoh, and your brother Aaron will be your prophet. You are to say everything I command you, and your brother Aaron is to tell Pharaoh to let the Israelites go out of his country'" (NIV). Moses was instructed to put words in the mouth of Aaron and then Aaron would speak those words that Moses would tell him.

Here, the Lord made Moses a god to Pharaoh, although not a god by nature or forever. This means that Moses was commissioned to have authority from God to act according to all things that the Lord would direct him to tell Pharaoh, because he was God's ambassador or representative to Pharaoh. He was authorized to command Pharaoh, and even

---

1. Some biblical scholars explain that the Hebrew term *nabi or navi* is related to the Arabian and Akkadian word *nabû* which means to call or announce. This word is found in the Hebrew text 115 times. Its usage has a wide range in the Old Testament and can reflect different meanings. But often it describes the prophet and his functions as the messenger of God under the influence of the Holy Spirit (cf. Ezek 22:8; Jer 29:27; Ezek 37:10). Vine, "Prophecy, Prophesy, Prophesying, Prophets," 221–22.

2. Hill, *Prophecy Past and Present*, 11. For reading on prophecy in early Christianity see, Aune, *Prophecy in Early Christianity and the Ancient Mediterranean World*.

punish him for his wrong doings. He could also exercise the power of life and death over him but notice that this authority was over Pharaoh only: "See, I have made you like God to Pharaoh" (Exod 7:1).

Aaron was going to speak on behalf of Moses; he was the mouth of Moses. A prophet speaks on behalf of God; he is the mouth of God. Moses hesitated to accept the call of the Lord in his life and his excuse was that he did not know how to speak, but the Lord said he was going to make Aaron his mouthpiece. The Lord declares:

> What about your brother, Aaron the Levite? I know he can speak well. He is already on his way to meet you, and his heart will be glad when he sees you. You shall speak to him and put words in his mouth; I will help both of you speak and will teach you what to do. He will speak to the people for you, and it will be as if he were your mouth and as if you were God to him. (Exod 4:14–16 NIV)

In a way, Aaron was the mouthpiece of Moses, or his interpreter, who was to present to Pharaoh whatever Moses would say. Aaron was also required to know the mind of God since Moses would declare the will of God revealed to him so as to inspire him to declare the words as they were. God was their helper: "I will help both of you speak and will teach you what to do" (Exod 4:15 NIV). Thus, Aaron was a prophet for Moses just as Moses was a prophet to God; Aaron as a prophet was the mouthpiece of Moses; and Moses as a prophet was the mouthpiece of God. The Hebrew term used by the author of Genesis to present Aaron as a prophet is *nabi*. This is the same term the Lord used to describe Abraham to King Abimelech.

MIRIAM AND DEBORAH

The next person addressed as a prophetess was Miriam, the sister of Aaron. She was also the first woman to be addressed as a prophetess:[3]

> Then Miriam the prophetess, the sister of Aaron, took a tambourine in her hand, and all the women went out after her with tambourines and dancing. And Miriam sang to them: "Sing to

---

3. She is addressed as the sister of Aaron not Moses, though she was likewise the sister of Moses. The reason could be that Miriam was older than Moses; that is, she was Aaron's sister before Moses. Again, she lived most of her life with Aaron, as Moses was in the king's palace, and in the desert with Jethro.

the Lord, for he has triumphed gloriously; the horse and his rider he has thrown into the sea." (Exod 15:20–21 ESV)

The Hebrew term used, *nebiyah*, is the feminine form of the Hebrew *nabi*. In Num 12:2, as the Lord was dealing with Miriam and Aaron, something came out that is relevant for our study. It reads, "'Has the Lord spoken only through Moses?' they asked. 'Hasn't he also spoken through us?' And the Lord heard this" (NIV). This statement by Aaron and Miriam showed discontentment. Instead of being grateful for what God was using them for, they challenged the special mission and exclusive authority he had granted Moses. The Lord punished her, thereby teaching us to be content with what he gives to us, and respect authorities that he has assigned. However, the context shows that Miriam, just like Aaron, could be a "prophet." The Lord even added, saying, "Hear my words: If there is a prophet among you, I the Lord make myself known to him in a vision; I speak with him in a dream" (Num 12:6–7 ESV). Miriam was endowed with the gift of prophecy and prophetic songs. She led the women to sing when they crossed the Red Sea.

Following Miriam was Deborah, who was also referred to as a prophetess, *nebiyah*, in Judg 4:4:

> Now Deborah, a prophetess, the wife of Lappidoth, was judging Israel at that time. She used to sit under the palm of Deborah between Ramah and Bethel in the hill country of Ephraim, and the people of Israel came up to her for judgment. She sent and summoned Barak the son of Abinoam from Kedesh-naphtali and said to him, "Has not the Lord, the God of Israel, commanded you, 'Go, gather your men at Mount Tabor, taking 10,000 from the people of Naphtali and the people of Zebulun. And I will draw out Sisera, the general of Jabin's army, to meet you by the river Kishon with his chariots and his troops, and I will give him into your hand'?" Barak said to her, "If you will go with me, I will go, but if you will not go with me, I will not go." And she said, "I will surely go with you. Nevertheless, the road on which you are going will not lead to your glory, for the Lord will sell Sisera into the hand of a woman." Then Deborah arose and went with Barak to Kedesh. And Barak called out Zebulun and Naphtali to Kedesh. And 10,000 men went up at his heels, and Deborah went up with him. (Judg 4:4–10 ESV)

She was both a judge (a ruler) and a prophetess. As a prophetess, the Lord used her to tell things to come; she told Barak that the Lord was prepared to defeat the huge army of a Canaanite king called Jabin under his army commander Sisera. She named the place where the army would camp, the victory to be gained over the commander, and how he would be delivered into the hands of a woman (Judg 4:4–10, 17–22). Like Miriam, she also had the prophetic gift of songs (Judg 5:1–31).

SAMUEL

Samuel was another person whose prophetic office came to the limelight early in Scriptures. First Samuel 3:20–21 reads, "And all Israel from Dan to Beersheba knew that Samuel was established as a prophet of the Lord. And the Lord appeared again at Shiloh, for the Lord revealed Himself to Samuel at Shiloh by the word of the Lord" (ESV). The same word *nabi* is used here. The people knew that Samuel was established as a prophet because every word that came from him did not fall to the ground, and then again, the Lord revealed himself to Samuel. This means that not only does the Lord speak through the prophet, but he also honors every word that a prophet speaks. Furthermore, it implies that God reveals himself to the prophet.

TERMS USED TO DESCRIBE THE PROPHETS

Nabi (Ecstatic Spokesman) and *Ro'eh* (Seer)

Now, I will like us to pay attention to the words used to describe the prophet. The common Hebrew root word used to describe most of the prophets in the Old Testament was *nabi*. However, there was another word also used; the word is seer, from the Hebrew root word *ro'eh* (1 Sam 9:9, 11). The term was first used to describe Samuel, when Saul wanted to consult him; Samuel also saw himself as a seer (1 Sam 9:18–19). The term "seer" comes from the English verb "see"; a seer is the one who sees, or has visions and tells.

The two terms were used interchangeably and many of the prophets were described as both seers (*ro'eh*) and ecstatic spokesmen (*nebi'im*). For example: Samuel was spoken of as a prophet and seer (1 Sam 3:20; 9:11, 18–19); Gad was addressed as David's seer (2 Sam 24:11; 1 Chr 21:9) and a prophet of God (1 Sam 22:5; 2 Sam 24:11). Iddo was referred to as a seer (2 Chr 9:29; 2 Chr 12:15) and then as the prophet of God (2 Chr 13:22);

Jehu son of Hanani was addressed as a seer (2 Chr 19:2) and then as a prophet (1 Kgs 16:7).

Summary of the Two Terms

From the above discussion, it is clear that the Old Testament prophet was both a seer and an inspired spokesman, the mouthpiece and the messenger of God on earth. He could hear from God, receive revelations from God and was required to speak what God had revealed to him—God's mind, word, or will to his people, and the nations. The prophet was therefore to stand in the council of the Lord and reveal his confidential matters to people on earth saying all he could see and hear. This means that the prophet's task did not depend on factors, such as age, experience, gender, or education since God could speak to whoever he wished; it was a matter of getting into his council. Let us consider the following Scriptures:

> For who among them has stood in the council of the Lord to see and to hear his word, or who has paid attention to his word and listened? (Jer 23:18 ESV)

> For the Lord God does nothing without revealing his secret to his servants the prophets. (Amos 3:7 ESV)

> Now Elijah the Tishbite, of Tishbe in Gilead, said to Ahab, "As the Lord the God of Israel lives, before whom I stand, there shall be neither dew nor rain these years, except by my word." (1 Kgs 17:1 ESV)

Notably, as Elijah was standing before the king, he claimed he was still standing in the presence of God; he was in God's council.

A prophet often received a specific message for his time, on a situation, or for his generation, or generations. Whatever the message is, whether foretelling (predictive) or "forth telling" (inspired spontaneous encouragement, instruction or rebuke), it served the benefit of those who initially received the message and those in the future who would put their faith in the promises of God. Such fulfilled promises cause the immediate recipients and those who hear of it later to place their faith in the Lord, knowing that he never changes and that he is a covenant fulfilling God.

TYPES OF PROPHETS

There were two types of prophets in the Old Testament. These include those who wrote their revelations and those who did not write theirs. The non-writing prophets in the Old Testament included persons such as Nathan (2 Sam 7:1–2), Gad (2 Sam 24:11), Ahijah (2 Chr 9:29; 10:15), Elijah (1 Kgs 17–18), Elisha (2 Kgs 1:15–25), Iddo (2 Chr 9:29; 2 Chr 12:15), Shemaiah (2 Chr 12:15), Jehu son of Hanani (2 Chr 19:2; 1 Kgs 16:7); and the five women who were addressed as prophetesses in the Bible. These are Miriam (Exod 15:20), Deborah (Judg 4:4), Huldah (2 Kgs 22:14), Isaiah's wife (Isa 8:3), and Noadiah, who was a false prophetess (Neh 6:14).[4]

The writing prophets are those whose books are found in the Bible among whom are those whose writings are many. They are Isaiah, Jeremiah, Ezekiel, and Daniel who are also labeled as major prophets. Those whose writings are few, such as Amos, Jonah, and Micah, seventeen in all, are called minor prophets. Of course, Samuel was also one of the prophets and two books of the Bible have been assigned to him. Other major prophets who did not write include Elijah and Elisha.

NOT ALL PEOPLE WHO PROPHESIED WERE PROPHETS

It is obvious that not all people who prophesied were prophets. A significant one is Jahaziel, the son of Zechariah. The Lord used him to strengthen King Jehoshaphat and Judah when Moab and Ammon came against them. The presentation makes it appear that he was not a prophet:

> Then the Spirit of the Lord came upon Jahaziel son of Zechariah, the son of Benaiah, the son of Jeiel, the son of Mattaniah, a Levite and descendant of Asaph, as he stood in the assembly. He said: "Listen, King Jehoshaphat and all who live in Judah and Jerusalem! This is what the Lord says to you: 'Do not be afraid or discouraged because of this vast army. For the battle is not yours, but God's.'" (2 Chr 20:14–15 NIV)

He appears to be someone who spoke once and never prophesied again. Others include Uriah, who is mentioned in Jer 26:20;[5] and a man of God who spoke to Eli (1 Sam 2:27).

---

4. Some of the texts cited indicate that some of these prophets wrote down their messages, but we do not have them.

5. It can be argued that Micah's name is mentioned in the same chapter (18). He

THE SCHOOL OF PROPHETS

It is assumed that Samuel established a school of prophets. Samuel directed Saul to Gibeah, where there was a procession of prophets, "After that you will go to Gibeah of God, where there is a Philistine outpost. As you approach the town, you will meet a procession of prophets coming down from the high place with lyres, tambourines, flutes and harps being played before them, and they will be prophesying" (1 Sam 10:5 NIV). Based upon this and another example cited below, some people think Samuel established the so-called school of the prophets, or what is referred to as the sons of the prophets, or the company of prophets. This assumption becomes a possibility if it is taken into consideration that in 1 Sam 19:20, Samuel was the head of some prophets who were prophesying. Perhaps, Samuel's experience with Eli caused him to establish such a school. He realized that ignorance can be a hindrance to hearing from God. The school was still very strong in the time of Elijah and Elisha (2 Kgs 2:3, 5; 4:1, 38; 6:1; 9:1; 1 Kgs 20:35). It appears that during this time, there were two schools, one at Bethel and the other at Jericho (2 Kgs 2:3, 5):

> *The company of the prophets at Bethel* came out to Elisha and asked, "Do you know that the Lord is going to take your master from you today?" "Yes, I know," Elisha replied, "but do not speak of it." Then Elijah said to him, "Stay here, Elisha; the Lord has sent me to Jericho." And he replied, "As surely as the Lord lives and as you live, I will not leave you." So they went to Jericho. *The company of the prophets at Jericho went up to Elisha and asked him*, "Do you know that the Lord is going to take your master from you today?" (2 Kgs 2:3–5 NIV, italics mine)

As Elijah (and Elisha) was passing by, the company of prophets at Bethel came to speak to Elisha. Again, when they reached Jericho, another company of prophets came to speak to Elisha. This signifies that there were two companies or schools of prophets.

It was thought that in the school of the prophets, the subjects which were taught included knowledge of the law and psalmody, with instrumental music, which is associated with "prophesying." That there was training alongside the school of the prophets is clear in 1 Chronicles:

---

was not addressed as a prophet but the book of Micah testifies that he was a prophet. Thus, not addressing the person as a prophet is not enough evidence to say that he is not a prophet.

> David, together with the commanders of the army, set apart some of the sons of Asaph, Heman and Jeduthun for the ministry of prophesying, accompanied by harps, lyres and cymbals. Here is the list of the men who performed this service. (1 Chr 25:1 NIV)

> Along with their relatives—all of them *trained and skilled in music* for the Lord-they numbered 288. Young and old alike, *teacher as well as student*, cast lots for their duties. (1 Chr 25:7-8 NIV, italics mine)

Thus, training and music went along with the training of the sons of the prophets. Elisha, for example, requested a musician to play for him, and then as he played, the hand of the Lord came upon him and he prophesied (2 Kgs 3:15).

Through this group of prophets, the prophetic office continued for a very long time in the Old Testament. In the books of Samuel, there were two other prophets who became prominent. They were Gad (1 Sam 22:5; 2 Sam 24:11) and Nathan (2 Sam 7:2ff.; 12:1ff.). Both became helpful to King David in his life and kingship. Elisha often interacted with some of the sons of the prophets. It was one of the wives of the sons of the prophets who appealed to Elisha that the husband had died and left her debts to deal with. Accordingly, the Lord used Elisha to perform the miracle of multiplication to settle her debts (2 Kgs 4:1-7). Furthermore, it was one of the sons of the prophets whose borrowed axe got into a river, of which the Lord used Elisha to perform the miracle of the floating iron to bring it back (2 Kgs 6:1-7).

Taken into consideration, the writing prophets, the non-writing prophets, and the school of the prophets, it may appear that there were a number of prophets during the period, however, reading the Old Testament, it appears that only few of them were from God. Perhaps, the school of the prophets despite its advantages also bred some false prophets. The role of the prophet was however very important. Since all who prophesied were not prophets, and the role of the prophet was important, who then is a prophet? Our attention will be drawn to this now.

Chapter 3

The Making of a Prophet

The discussion on the Old Testament prophets gives us a clue of who a prophet is. However, I have contended that while the prophet was the messenger of God in the Old Testament, the apostle is the messenger of God in the New Testament. This means that while there are similarities between the prophets of the Old and New Testaments, there will be some remarkable differences too. While we have discussed the meaning of the term "prophet," we have not discussed what constitutes the office of the prophet. This is what I want us to pick up in this chapter. I will select some of the major prophets and find out how they were called and trained. This will throw light on how prophets are made.

It is the Lord who raises up a person and calls him a prophet. What the Lord told Jeremiah is very significant for our study: "Now the word of the Lord came to me, saying 'Before I formed you in the womb I knew you, and before you were born I consecrated you; I appointed you a prophet to the nations'" (Jer 1:4–5 ESV). This implies that God works on a prophet even before he is formed in the womb of his mother. Thus, if we want to know how God prepares a prophet, we have to find out the life story of the prophets and know how God raised them up. We do not have many of the life stories of the prophets, but the story of Samuel is one of great prominence. Hence, while we will touch on the stories of some prophets, the life story of Samuel will be our main case study.

DEDICATION OF PARENTS

Samuel's parents were very dedicated to the Lord; his mother conceived him as a result of prayer. Though the Lord listens to the prayers of people who cry to him, that does not guarantee that the child born to a praying parent will instinctively become God-fearing or a Christian. The parent will need to train and continue to pray for him. The parents of Alfred Kinsey, the man who is credited as having started the sexual reformation in the twentieth century, were said to be very devout Christians in the Methodist Church.[1]

Madonna Louise Ciccone, often referred to, by the media, as the "Queen of Pop"[2] was born to Catholic parents Silvio Anthony Ciccone and Madonna Louise Fortin. Yet, instead of yielding to the Christian principles, she decided to rebel against everything Christianity stands for.[3] Her parents are not to be blamed for her actions. It takes the hand of the parents to bring up such a child in the Lord and the Lord also blesses the efforts of such parents. In spite of this, some children still go wayward.

Hannah prayed that if the Lord gave her a child, she would dedicate him to the Lord and no razor would touch his hair. "And she vowed a vow and said, 'O Lord of hosts, if you will indeed look on the affliction of your servant and remember me and not forget your servant, but will give to your servant a son, then I will give him to the Lord all the days of his life, and no razor shall touch his head'" (1 Sam 1:11 ESV). This means he was going to be a Nazirite to God (1 Sam 1:11; cf. Judg 13:5). A Nazirite is a person who does not shave his head, just like Rastafarians who wear dreadlocks. When the Lord responded to Hannah's prayer, and gave her Samuel, she presented him to the Lord when he was weaned, at about three years old, the age at which the Jews were said to wean their children. Perhaps, that was the reason why Hannah had to slaughter a three-year old bull. The bull represented the boy Samuel who was being dedicated to God. I wonder why the high priest accepted him at that age, considering that he was quite young (1 Sam 2:24–28). Training him at that tender age would require that the high priest does some additional

---

1. Onyinah, *Spiritual Warfare*, 55.

2. See Riley Baker, "Madonna's Career," https://www.guinnessworldrecords.com/news/2018/8/madonnas-career-in-10-records-as-queen-of-pop-turns-60-536857.

3. Onyinah, *Spiritual Warfare*, 56–57.

work on him. Sometimes, it is very rewarding to help children of such age, especially those who are orphans or needy.

The point here, however, is that the Lord used the dedication of Samuel's parents to prepare him as a prophet. This does not mean that if your parents are not Christians, the Lord cannot use you as a prophet. The Lord can use the experience that you will go through to prepare you for his mission but ultimately, parents are always encouraged to train their children in the Lord. Proverbs advises parents, "Train up a child in the way he should go; even when he is old he will not depart from it" (Prov 22:6 ESV).

A SERVING HEART

Samuel served at the house of the high priest Eli, who was old. His sons were serving as priests but they did not know the Lord (1 Sam 2:12). They were treating the priesthood with disrespect—fattening themselves with the offering of the Lord and sleeping with the women who served in the house of the Lord (1 Sam 2:12–17). It is sad and very dangerous to be a priest without knowing the Lord. Similarly, it is very bad to claim to be a Christian without knowing the Lord. Currently, there are many people serving as pastors who do not know the Lord. Who is a pastor who does not know the Lord? Any pastor who keeps on sinning without repentance does not know the Lord. This includes:

- Pastors who are immoral, defiling young girls and chasing other men's wives,
- Pastors who misuse church funds,
- Pastors who manipulate church systems for their own benefits,
- Pastors who are worldly: extremely focused on fashion, including those changing and acquiring clothes, vehicles, and houses at the expense of the kingdom work.

The priesthood is supposed to be a sacrificial service, not by mouth but by practice. When you see a pastor saying, "Had it not been the ministry, I would have been like this or that," as a means to stir people to give money, watch out for the tendency to get back into slavery in "Egypt" or the tendency to be "fleshy" is creeping in. He needs to review his life and pray. The true minister sees those "fleshy" things as vain. In life, we do not boast of the things which are garbage because garbage is filthy so we throw them away. True ministers of God have thrown these things away. Ministers who still run after them are like children who need to be taught the basic things of Christ again. The challenge with such ministers is that they are still leading the flock. They can cause havoc in churches and society. Eli's sons were still offering the sacrifice of the Lord and performing the duties of the priest in the house of God, having the right to carry or touch the ark of the Lord. What a responsibility the Lord has placed on ministers! How I wish all pastors would truly recognize the great responsibility the Lord has placed on us. "We have an altar from which those who minister at the tabernacle have no right to eat" (Heb 13:10 NIV).

When we consider the book of Hebrews which says that we have no right to eat on the altar on which we serve, the writer challenges his audience to shun sexual immorality; love of money; strange teaching (teaching which satisfies people's appetites); and ceremonial food (Heb 13:4–10). Pastors and all who claim to be the Lord's servants must be representatives of Christ on earth.

Eli's sons were eating from the "altar" of the Lord, yet it was they who were to teach Samuel the art of priesthood. How was Samuel going to make it through the unexemplary lives of Eli's sons? It is great that Samuel got closer to the old man instead. The moment the boy was left with the high priest, he started serving the Lord, by assisting him (1 Sam 2:11; 3:1). The New Living Translation puts 1 Sam 2:12 this way: "Then Elkanah returned home to Ramah without Samuel. And the boy served the Lord by assisting Eli the priest." By serving Eli the priest, he was serving the Lord. The Lord does not call people unexpectedly, he calls those who have servants' hearts.

Samuel got very close to Eli. Eli chose to bring Samuel to sleep closer to him than his children, and he was serving Eli in ways that Eli's sons did not. This is apparent in the sense that when the LORD called Samuel, his room was very close to Eli's to the point that Samuel thought the high priest was calling him to run errands, as he usually did for him. He was alert and ready to serve Eli even at night and did not pretend to be asleep. Sometimes people who stay with pastors in their homes serve more than the children of the pastors. They take with them all the blessings from pastors' homes. They learn how to cook, serve visitors, maintain a house, and serve the Lord; they leave the house with such blessings. Unlike human beings, God is no respecter of persons (Acts 10:34); he blesses all who call upon him.

You must serve if you want to be served. Those who will like to follow the footsteps of leaders must walk with them and assist them. Once you follow a leader, you are learning things that are taught, and catching things that cannot be taught. With things that are taught, all who come to hear of it learn of it. But with things that are caught, only those who follow and get closer catch them unknowingly. As leaders get along with others (both young and adults), they share their life stories and stories of their heroes—they share both good and bad moments; they share issues which they will not talk about officially or normally. These things come out during times of eating or conversations. It is during these unguarded moments that mentees catch the spirit and principles of their mentors. Mentors' aims and visions in life come out clearly during such moments. For example, it was during such private times with his disciples that Jesus asked his disciples about who they and other people thought he was. Right after, he revealed his purpose for coming on earth to them (Matt 16:13–21).

The little Samuel was constantly "drinking" from Eli, the high priest. He was benefitting in ways Eli's own children could not, because he was "drinking" from the old man. Notably, it was during this period that the Lord called him.

A CALL OF GOD

One of the most important aspects of being a prophet is the call of God. You cannot be a prophet without being called by the Lord. The prophetic office, unlike kingship and the priesthood, is not hereditary. Often God calls individuals from every walk of life to the ministry. It is this call that makes a prophet confident, bold, and so sure that the Lord is with him. The call of God humbles the person to know that he is nobody but a servant under the divine mission of the Almighty One. We shall examine the call of some prophets and end with the call of Samuel.

The Prophet Isaiah

Isaiah was prophesying to his own people about righteousness and God's judgment. He rebuked them of their evil deeds and brought them to repentance. Isaiah prophesied mainly to the people of Judah, although his prophecy cut across the whole of Israel, yet he had not been clearly called by God to the prophetic office. Isaiah was called to the prophetic office when King Uzziah died by receiving a revelation of the Lord at the temple.[4]

The book of Isaiah describes the experience:

> In the year that King Uzziah died, I saw the Lord sitting on a throne, high and lifted up, and the train of His *robe* filled the temple. Above it stood seraphim; each one had six wings: with two he covered his face, with two he covered his feet, and with two he flew. And one cried to another and said "Holy, holy, holy *is* the Lord of hosts; The whole earth *is* full of His glory!" And the posts of the door were shaken by the voice of him who cried out, and the house was filled with smoke. . . ."
>
> Also I heard the voice of the Lord, saying: "Whom shall I send, And who will go for Us?" Then I said, "Here am I! Send me." (Isa 6:1–4, 8 NKJV)

Isaiah's response was, "Woe *is* me, for I am undone! Because I *am* a man of unclean lips, And I dwell in the midst of a people of unclean lips; For my eyes have seen the King, The Lord of hosts" (v. 5). Isaiah was afraid, he thought he would die for seeing the King. Although he was prophesying, he saw his sins and sinful nature and felt he did not qualify to see the king, but the king had made a provision for him. The provision was that the Lord caused one of the creatures to fly down to him, carrying a burning coal that had been taken from the altar with a pair of tongs. He touched his lips with the burning coal and said, "This has touched your lips, and now your guilt is gone, and your sins are forgiven" (Isa 6:7).

The fire on the altar was first set by the Lord and it was to be kept burning without going off. Every fire needed at the temple worship was to be taken from the altar not from outside the altar. A censor full of coals of burning fire from the altar was taken into the holy of holiest in the Day of Atonement when sacrifice was made to atone for sin (Lev 16:12–13). The burning coal here was a token of forgiveness, since fire symbolized cleansing and purification. The altar was the place where atonement was made. One of the creatures or seraphim was merely the messenger whom God used to minister to him. God is the One who forgives, and his forgiveness is based upon the atonement of Jesus Christ. Isaiah received unconditional forgiveness. He heard the call of God, "Whom shall I send

---

4. For the call of Isaiah, Jeremiah and Ezekiel summarized here, see Onyinah, *No One will See God and Live.*

and who will go for Us" (Isa 6:8)? Accordingly, he responded affirmatively, "Here I am! Send me" (Isa 6:8), without hesitation to the divine call.

The sight of the glimpse of glory of God, as certified by his forgiveness and sanctification, certainly caused him to die to self. How do we know this? It was only after this that the Lord revealed the challenge of his unique call to him (Isa 6:9). Isaiah was to preach to the religious and arrogant people who would keep on hearing, but were destined to have their ears heavy (Isa 6:9–10; cf. 42:18–20). Isaiah wondered how long the people would continue to be unresponsive to his words of truth from God. The answer was, "Until the cities are laid waste and without inhabitant," but a remnant was to be saved and purified (Isa 6:11, 13 NKJV). The people had gone beyond hope. Isaiah was called to discipleship but not to stay at the temple and worship. Christians are to go and make others disciples of Christ. This is the work of all God's people now—making others the disciples of Christ.

The more Isaiah proclaimed the word of God, the less response he received from the people. This was a call to a very discouraging ministry. We must understand that the call of God is a call of faithfulness to him, to his word, and to the call itself, but not necessarily having "a successful ministry" from human point of view. Isaiah's ministry was not meant to produce a humanly acceptable result. How could a person respond to this, if it was not the Lord who called him? The revelation of the glory of God in the temple caused the prophet to die to self.

Do you want to respond to the call of God? Then, remember that you can no longer live for yourself. The ministry is not a matter of making money or acquiring wealth, it is a matter of being faithful to the Lord who has called you. You must be prepared to suffer, lose home, lose family members and be poor—you must be prepared to die. It is there and then that you may become a vessel of honor for the Lord.

God's call to Isaiah was a commission to speak to national and international issues or to the politics of the day. Before this time, Isaiah was concerned about the inner morals of his people, but after the special call, he was to engage himself with the effects of the sins and unrepentant hearts on the destiny of the people of Judah, Israel, the surrounding nations, and world events, which culminated in the birth of Christ. We must be prepared to be used by God "beyond the borders of Israel"; that is, beyond your local church or even national situations.[5]

---

5. Onyinah, *No One will See God and Live*, 42.

The Prophet Ezekiel

Ezekiel was the prophet to the exiles in Babylon. He was a priest (Ezek 1:3) from a priestly family of Zadokite priesthood (Ezek 44:15; 1 Kgs 1:32). He was preparing for service in the temple at Jerusalem, though he never had the privilege of serving there. Temple priests were consecrated at the age of thirty, but Ezekiel was taken captive along with King Jehoiachin at the age of twenty-five in 597 BC. His prophetic ministry began five years later in 593 BC (Ezek 1:2) and continued for at least twenty-two years (Ezek 29:17). Interestingly, the time he was called to the prophetic office would have been the year during which he would have been initiated into the temple priesthood. The desire to minister to the Lord warranted him the grace to be called into the prophetic ministry. His call was dramatic—an experience that could not be forgotten. He describes it:

> Now it came to pass in the thirtieth year, in the fourth *month*, on the fifth *day* of the month, as I *was* among the captives by the River Chebar, *that* the heavens were opened and I saw visions of God. . . . Like the appearance of a rainbow in a cloud on a rainy day, so *was* the appearance of the brightness all around it. This *was* the appearance of the likeness of the glory of the Lord. So when I saw *it*, I fell on my face, and I heard a voice of One speaking. (Ezek 1:1, 28 NKJV)

When Ezekiel saw this, he fell on his face, and there was no strength in the man who was called "strength." It was here that he died. The Lord had to speak to him and cause the Spirit to enter him, and set him on his feet (Ezek 2:1–2). Thereafter, he commissioned him.

Ezekiel was called to speak God's message to the children of Israel. But the people were rebellious against God and more specifically impudent and stubborn. They had broken the covenant relationship. If the rebellious people refused to listen to Ezekiel's message, Ezekiel would still prove himself a true prophet of God by continuing to proclaim God's messages (Ezek 2:7). Ezekiel's unique ministry to Israel was to be a divinely appointed "watchman," one who would not only warn the nation, but also issue warnings to individuals (Ezek 3:17–21). The warning was not only of physical death, but also of spiritual doom (see Ezek 33:1–9).

To equip Ezekiel, God commanded him to eat the scroll, that is, the word of God or God's message (Ezek 3:1–3). This assimilation of the message made the word of God part of the life of the prophet. The lesson here is that no one is ready or qualified to speak for God until he has consumed his word. This was a sign that whatever Ezekiel would say would be the word that he had swallowed. Ezekiel did not receive his prophetic call on a silver platter. There is always a price to pay in God's call. If God has not called you, do not bother to get into the prophetic ministry.[6]

The Prophet Jeremiah

Jeremiah was a priest who was called to the office of a prophet. He was shocked by the call and hesitated to accept it. He was a young man who perhaps had been prepared to be ordained as a full-fledged priest by then. He read the law and knew the suffering that some of the people of God had gone through. Let us listen to him:

> Now the word of the Lord came to me, saying, "Before I formed you in the womb I knew you, and before you were born I consecrated you; I appointed you a prophet to the nations." Then I said, "Ah, Lord God! Behold, I do not know how to speak, for I am only a youth." But the Lord said to me, "Do not say, 'I am only a youth'; for to all to whom I send you, you shall go, and whatever I command you, you shall speak. Do not be afraid of them, for I am with you to deliver you, declares the Lord." Then the Lord put out his hand and touched my mouth. And the Lord said to me, "Behold, I have put my words in your mouth. See, I have set you this day over nations and over kingdoms, to pluck up and to break down, to destroy and to overthrow, to build and to plant." (Jer 1:4–10 ESV)

The Lord made him aware that he called him before he was formed in his mother's womb, that is, even before the foundation of the world. It is God who calls people and when he does, he provides their needs. However, Jeremiah had problems. He did not know how to speak; he was not an orator, he was young and inexperienced. His specific age was not known, but it is suggested that he was in his twenties, since priests were ordained at age thirty. It is said that Isaiah, Hosea, and Zechariah were all young when they were called. The Lord knew he was afraid and, therefore, encouraged him to accept the call. For the Lord, inexperience is not an obstacle; what he demands is obedience.

What is seen here is that those who are truly called see the challenge of the ministry. They feel they are weak, not capable, unfit and unable

---

6. Onyinah, *No One will See God and Live*, 44.

to do it. They recognize the responsibility of the work, which has been placed on their shoulders. They come to the realization that nothing except the authority from God can help them accomplish it. They accept the call with fear and trembling. These people do not run for money, unlike the false prophets whose aim is to feed on people.

The Lord called Jeremiah as a prophet for the nations, not only to Judah, Israel, but also to the Babylonians and the surrounding nations (Jer 1:10). His ministry was difficult—"to pluck up and to break down, to destroy and to overthrow, to build and to plant" (Jer 1:10 ESV). He was not only to say "God bless you," but whatever the Lord tells him concerning the nations, whether good or bad. He was to foretell when a kingdom is to be uprooted as a tree or as a plant that is plucked up by the roots. He was to show a kingdom (the people of the kingdom) when it would be pulled, and thrown down, and destroyed, as a building is destroyed. The assignment was very difficult.

The glorious side was that he should also let a nation or kingdom know when it would be restored like a destroyed building that is being put up again, or an uprooted tree that is being planted again.

After the first encounter, the Lord showed him a vision again and assured him that his message would not be accepted but he would be with him and fortify him:

> The word of the Lord came to me a second time, saying, "What do you see?" And I said, "I see a boiling pot, facing away from the north." . . . But you, dress yourself for work; arise, and say to them everything that I command you. Do not be dismayed by them, lest I dismay you before them. And I, behold, I make you this day a fortified city, an iron pillar, and bronze walls, against the whole land, against the kings of Judah, its officials, its priests, and the people of the land. They will fight against you, but they shall not prevail against you, for I am with you, declares the Lord, to deliver you." (Jer 1:13, 17–19 ESV)

Such a call leaves an indelible mark on the person in such a way that he could not forget it, and it makes him aware that the Lord is with him.

This is how the Lord makes a prophet. The prophetic call is not a call to boast of the property that one has or live a flamboyant life, but it is a call to live the life that the Lord wants you to live—a call to declare the true words of God. Are you called by God? Examine your life.

EXAMPLES FROM THE PROPHET SAMUEL

Available to the Lord

When the Lord called Samuel, supernatural encounters such as seeing visions of God, hearing his audible voice, and experiencing the ministration of angels were rare. God was desiring to raise up a prophet or prophets for the people—a person or people who could hear from and see the Lord. God always desires to bless his people with all spiritual blessings, but people who are truly available and prepared to pay the price are lacking. Often the price is not just living a holy life, but living for the Lord.

Living for the Lord includes sometimes standing alone against populist ideas, loneliness (friends and family may shun you), saying the right thing at the right time, and rejecting worldly pleasures. Living for the Lord also includes allowing yourself "to be ashamed" for him in ways such as not following fashionable things and modern trends. For example, a young woman who is living for the Lord will not dress up to expose her cleavage, something others may consider as having self-confidence. A young man who is living for the Lord will not have sex with a woman he is not married to. An employer who is in need of money will have to reject taking bribe. A pastor who is living for the Lord will not take certain fringe benefits, which some pastors consider as their rights. Paul who was living for the Lord had this to say:

> Do we not have the right to eat and drink? Do we not have the right to take along a believing wife, as do the other apostles and the brothers of the Lord and Cephas? Or is it only Barnabas and I who have no right to refrain from working for a living? Who serves as a soldier at his own expense? Who plants a vineyard without eating any of its fruit? Or who tends a flock without getting some of the milk? (1 Cor 9:4–7 ESV)

> But I have made no use of any of these rights, nor am I writing these things to secure any such provision. For I would rather die than have anyone deprive me of my ground for boasting. For if I preach the gospel, that gives me no ground for boasting. For necessity is laid upon me. Woe to me if I do not preach the gospel! For if I do this of my own will, I have a reward, but not of my own will, I am still entrusted with a stewardship. (1 Cor 9:15–17 ESV)

This shows that there is a difference between living a holy life and living for the Lord. The prophet must be prepared to not only shun sin but live for the Lord. The little Samuel had chosen to live for the Lord. He chose not to follow the ways of Eli's sons, perhaps he heard Eli saying with his soft tone:

> "I have been hearing reports from all the people about the wicked things you are doing. Why do you keep sinning? You must stop, my sons! The reports I hear among the Lord's people are not good. If someone sins against another person, God can mediate for the guilty party. But if someone sins against the Lord, who can intercede?" But Eli's sons wouldn't listen to their father, for the Lord was already planning to put them to death. (1 Sam 2:23–25 NLT)

Samuel decided to listen to Eli, the high priest, rather than follow the evil examples of his sons. The Bible says, "But Samuel, though he was only a boy, served the Lord. He wore a linen garment like that of a priest" (1 Sam 2:18 NLT). He was serving the Lord and living as a priest, putting on the garment of priests.

God Reveals Himself to Samuel

Samuel was sleeping in one of the rooms in the temple, where the ark of the covenant was, closer to Eli when suddenly he heard a voice like Eli's calling him.[7] The voice sounded like Eli's so much that although God called three times, Samuel thought, in all three instances, that Eli was calling him. It is amazing how God's love overlooks our mistakes. Genuinely, Samuel thought it was Eli calling. It shows how the Lord will not bypass us when we make genuine mistakes. He will repeat the call until our ears are opened to him. You can never run away from the call of God, because it is clear and repeated several times that it becomes the passion of your life.

---

7. 1 Sam 3:3 shows that the lamp of God had not gone out. What lamp was he referring to? Was it the lamp in the tabernacle or generally referring to the light of God in Israel. The lamp of God in the tabernacle was never to be extinguished or put out (Exod 27:21; Lev 24:1–4). If the tabernacle was meant here, it means they had changed the prescribed instruction to keep the lamp burning. It was never to go off. However, the phrase "lamp of God" is also used to refer to hope (2 Sam 21:17; 1 Kgs 11:36; 2 Kgs 8:19). Yet, since the sacrificial offering had changed, and doors had been made for the tabernacle, it could be that the lamp here was referring to the lamp in the tabernacle.

What needs to be taken into consideration here, also, is why the boy Samuel heard the voice of the LORD as the voice of Eli. Eli had imparted his life; Eli was his mentor. Therefore, he was hearing the voice of God as the voice of Eli. If God calls you, what sort of voice will you hear? Who is your mentor? Who do you dream of?

In Ghana, because Christianity came first through the Roman Catholic priests, the visions of God or Jesus that people often see is that of the Roman Catholic priest wearing a white robe. God often appears to people in dreams and visions in forms that reflect the images of the mentors who trained them. In times of crises, sometimes, I see the vision of some of the founding leaders of the Church of Pentecost encouraging me in the Lord. Knowing your mentors is good, the Lord may use them in dreams and visions to speak to you or encourage you in your life challenges. However, God wants you to hear his voice within the voice of your mentors. This was what Samuel lacked—hearing the voice of God within the supposed voice of Eli.

In presenting Samuel's call, the author of 1 Samuel adds that Samuel did not know the Lord (3:7). He had said a similar thing concerning the sons of Eli but, for them, he said that because they were living in sin. It reads, "Now the sons of Eli were corrupt; they did not know the Lord" (1 Sam 2:12 NKJV). However, when the author of 1 Samuel said the boy Samuel did not know the Lord, he was trying to say that Samuel did not know that it was the Lord who was speaking, since the Lord had never spoken to him before (1 Sam 3:7). Tradition says that Samuel was about twelve years old when this happened.

The Need for Mentors

I have been wondering why God failed to speak to Samuel directly by saying, "Samuel, I am the Lord your God. It is not Eli who is calling you. Listen to me now." Many things could explain why the Lord did not take this approach. For example: first, Samuel could have been afraid, since he was a young boy who might still not have understood what was happening.

Second, the Lord wants parents and adults to pass on their knowledge of him to the young generation. When he created Adam and Eve, he told them to multiply. The Lord did not want to do the multiplication himself, rather, he wanted Adam and Eve to do it. With Abraham, the reason the Lord called him as stipulated here is illuminating, "For, I have chosen him, so that he will direct his children and his household after him to keep the way of the Lord by doing what is right and just, so that the Lord will bring about for Abraham what he has promised him" (Gen 18:19 NIV). God always wants human beings to cooperate with him to work, requiring adults to pass on what they know to others. Paul instructed Timothy, "And the things you have heard me say in the presence of many witnesses, entrust to reliable men who will also be qualified to teach others" (2 Tim 2:2–3 NIV). It is the responsibility of adults to mentor children in the way of the Lord.

Third, the Lord wanted Samuel to know that his obedience to Eli yielded fruits. Eli was the high priest who was teaching Samuel the ways of the Lord. He knew the ways of the Lord but his children did not. Since God shows no partiality, whoever obeyed the high priest would be blessed. He pronounced blessing on Hannah and she gave birth to Samuel. Again, he pronounced blessing on Hannah and she gave birth to other children: "Before they returned home, Eli would bless Elkanah and his wife and say, 'May the Lord give you other children to take the place of this one she gave to the Lord.' And the Lord gave Hannah three sons and two daughters. Meanwhile, Samuel grew up in the presence of the Lord"(1 Sam 2:20–21 NLT).

Fourth, the Lord wanted Samuel to know that hearing his voice did not mean that he did not need the training of Eli. He still needed his mentoring. Often, when people are granted some "graces" of God they think that they do not need their leaders again. This is a great mistake. The Lord still wanted Samuel to know the importance of submitting to the training of Eli. He needed not to follow the ways of Eli's sons who were disobedient to their father.

Eli taught Samuel the right way to respond to the Lord, "Speak, LORD, for your servant hears" (1 Sam 3:9 ESV). The term "LORD" here is Jehovah. Thus, he taught Samuel that it was the God of their fathers, Jehovah, who was speaking to him. To say that "your servant hears" is to say that your servant is listening to put into practice what you will communicate to him. Often, the Lord Jesus would tell his hearers, "He who has ears, let him hear" (Matt 13:9, 43 ESV; cf. Rev 2:7, 11, 17, 29; 3:6; 11:15; 13:9, 43). Everybody has ears, but why "he who has ears"? The implication is that anyone who is willing to hear what he, the Lord, is saying should listen, obey and put his words into practice. This is an indication that paying attention to what your master says is very important. Eli taught Samuel the right way to respond to the LORD.

Mentees, disciples, and church members should always be ready to hear from their leaders. Prophets must go through the mill before they can be refined for the use of the Master. It is one thing to say, "Yes Sir," and another to truly submit to your Master. Jesus says something about the scribes and Pharisees that is very deep:

> Then Jesus said to the crowds and to his disciples, "The teachers of religious law and the Pharisees are the official interpreters of the law of Moses. So practice and obey whatever they tell you, but don't follow their example. For they don't practice what they teach." (Matt 23:1–3 NLT)

> Jesus said to the crowds and to his disciples: "The teachers of the law and the Pharisees sit in Moses' seat. So you must obey them and do everything they tell you. But do not do what they do, for they do not practice what they preach." (Matt 23:1–3 NIV)

The Lord gave the law to the Jews through Moses. The authority of interpreting the law among the Jews had been delegated to the scribes and Pharisees. During the time of Jesus, the explanation of the law was often done in the synagogues and in the temple. The scribes and Pharisees sat while expounding the law, and rose when they read it. "Sitting in the seat of Moses" meant that they had been given the authority to teach the law. But they were not practicing what they were preaching.

I would have thought that Jesus would ask the people not to listen to the scribes and Pharisees at all, because he often condemned them for their external religiosity. Rather, he asked the people to obey whatever they are taught from the word of God. Jesus is teaching us that we must listen to whatever is truly taught from the word of God, even by evil teachers or leaders, but we must not follow their evil behavior. The reason is that God has set the order and respects it. He would therefore expect people to listen to his word even from the mouth of leaders and teachers who are hypocrites. Prophets will have to learn submission in their churches and to local leaders before the Lord will usher them to higher ministry, else they will blow it out when they get there.

You must take note that Jesus might be saying that the people must obey whatever the scribes and Pharisees say which is based upon the word of God, but they must not obey the traditions and the man-made rules of the Pharisees. This is plausible if you consider the fact that Jesus himself disobeyed the man-made rules of the Pharisees several times in the gospels (Matt 15:1–6; Mark 7:1–8; cf. Eph 6:1). In teaching children to obey their parents, Paul used the same principle, "Children, obey your parents *in the Lord*, for this is right" (Eph 6:1 NIV, italics mine). The principle of obeying "in the Lord" cuts across whenever the Christian is dealing with those in authority. If people in authority do not know the Lord, they will throw people out of gear. "Submission in the Lord" is the key.

Samuel was listening to Eli, who had been sitting on the seat of Moses, now he needed to listen to the one, in whose seat Eli was seated—the LORD.

Samuel was now placed in the right mood to receive from the Lord. Accordingly, "the LORD came and stood there, calling just as the other times, 'Samuel! Samuel!'" (1 Sam 3:10 NIV). What does the statement "the LORD came and stood there" mean? Was God really standing there?

It seems Samuel might have seen a form before his eyes like some visible human shape or a glorious splendorous light, which appears to him like God. On the other hand, and more appropriately, he might have heard the voice as if it was approaching nearer and nearer, then at last, he could imagine that it stopped approaching and he felt the LORD was standing with him. It appears that this was a way of presenting the story as a real experience. Later, the book refers to the whole incident as a vision: "Samuel lay down until morning and then opened the doors of the house of the Lord. He was afraid to tell Eli the vision" (1 Samuel 3:15 NIV). Furthermore, presenting the story this way shows that the revelation of God was an objectively real affair, and not a mere dream of Samuel.

On the one hand, the Lord is always calling people, but it is only those who are available who hear him. On the other hand, the Lord sometimes calls people for a specific assignment and commissions them. Samuel's call was specific.

Samuel's Response

In Samuel's response to the Lord, he left out one of the words that Eli taught him and, of course, a very important word—that is, "LORD." He rather said, "Speak, for Your servant hears," instead of, "Speak, LORD, for your servant hears." Why did he leave it out? Some suggestions are made here.

Perhaps, he was afraid to mention the name "LORD" (JEHOVAH), or he was thinking that it could be the voice of another human being. Maybe, he was thinking that it was the voice of any other spirit or he was probably being careful. In any way, I think receiving such an experience is quite frightening. People who receive such encounters often begin to shiver and speak quickly. It could be that in such a solemn moment, Samuel was shivering, frightened, and forgot to say LORD.

What Eli taught Samuel is how we must hear the LORD'S voice. We must pay attention to the Lord and allow him to speak. Once we pay attention to him, we will always hear his still small voice.

The Lord spoke and it was clear (1 Sam 3:10–15). The message was the same message of doom concerning Eli's family that a man of God had presented to Eli already. The message was too weighty to be given to a boy, but this was the LORD; he knew what he was doing. Sometimes when adults fail, the Lord may use children. However, here, it could not be that God did not have any adult since he had already carried the message to Eli. I think the Lord wanted to confirm to Eli and the people that he was raising a prophet for the nation—Samuel. Since there are many voices in the world, when God speaks sometimes his voice must be confirmed by others who also have the Spirit of God. Taking any word that comes from people without weighing them is unhealthy and quite dangerous. The Lord must confirm it in your spirit or through others.

Samuel got up the following morning and did his usual job of opening doors (1 Sam 3:15). Having a revelation from the Lord does not make you a prophet at once. Samuel was wise and humble to keep on doing what he used to do until the Lord would bring to pass what he had destined for him. People must not stop their schooling and jobs to do the work of God because they claim to have heard the voice of God. You need to continue to do what you do until the right time comes. Other things should be considered; the next part discusses these things.

PART 2

The Constitution of a Prophet

We have seen that it is the Lord who raises and calls someone a prophet. The call comes in such a dramatic way that it leaves an indelible mark on the person. The prophet no longer lives for himself. Several gifts may come together for a person to function in the call of the Lord. What are these gifts?

Since the Lord told Miriam and Aaron that "if there is any prophet among you, I speak to him in visions and dreams," it means that the prophet may have visions and dreams. Prophets including Samuel, Iddo, Gad, and Jehu were addressed as "seer." That means seeing visions is one of the gifts of the prophet. Daniel was one of the sharpest prophets in the Bible. He and his friends prayed that the Lord should reveal the dreams of King Nebuchadnezzar to him and give him the meaning (Dan 2). He thanked the Lord who made the secret known to him and gave him wisdom to understand it (Dan 2:23). Accordingly, the word of knowledge (ability to see or know) was one of the gifts that he possessed and so was the word of wisdom (ability to understand). Most of the prophets, including Micah, Elijah, Jeremiah, and Ezekiel, were able to discern the difference between good and bad prophets. The gift of the discerning of spirits was one of the gifts that these prophets had. Furthermore, most of the prophets were teaching the word of God, explaining the true meaning of God's word to the people and calling them to repentance. The gift of teaching and the gift of exhortation were some of the gifts that most of the prophets possessed. Miriam, Deborah, and Moses were prophets who possessed the gift of music. Music may be one of the gifts that a prophet possesses.

Against this backdrop, the following gifts and "graces" may constitute the gift of the prophet: the gift of prophecy, the word of knowledge (including visions and dreams), the word of wisdom, the discerning of spirits, the gift of teaching, the gift of exhortation and the gift of music. Since the gift of speaking in tongues and the gift of interpretation amount to prophecy, it can be one of the gifts that a prophet may exhibit.

This section, part 2, comprises three chapters that look at the gifts that come together to make up "the gift of the prophet." There is no direct way of getting these gifts. As such, I dig out the Bible and attempt to identify these gifts which come together to constitute the prophetic office. Three chapters have been assigned to this. The first chapter addresses three gifts which deal with speaking under inspiration: the gift of prophecy; the gift of speaking in diverse kinds of tongues; and the gift of interpretation. The second chapter deals with gifts of revelation, which are three: the gift of the word of knowledge; the gift of the word of wisdom; and the gift of discerning of spirit. The third handles the gifts of the word, which are three: the gift of teaching; the gift of exhortation; and the gift of music. The gifts will be explained in turns.

Chapter 4

The Gifts of Speaking under Inspiration

THE CHAPTER EXPLORES MANIFESTATIONS of the Spirit such as speaking under the inspiration of the Holy Spirit. There are three gifts which fall under this group. These are the gift of prophecy, the gift of speaking in diverse kinds of tongues, and the gift of interpretation, which will all be discussed in turns.

THE GIFT OF PROPHECY

The gift of prophecy is mentioned wherever spiritual gifts are mentioned (e.g., 1 Cor 12:10; Rom 12:6;[1] cf. 1 Pet 4:10; Eph 4:11). Obviously, it is the most popular gift among all the spiritual gifts.

Prophecy is the ability to receive a message from God and deliver it under the control of the Holy Spirit. Prophecy is not the same as preaching; it is often spontaneous and this is clear from the Scriptures. Biblical scholars show us that the Greek term *propheteia*, which is the root word for prophecy means "to speak the mind of God" or "foretelling." However, the Greek term *euangelizo*, which is translated as "preach," is meant to announce the good news to people. This shows that the two carry completely different meanings.[2]

---

1. Some believers consider the gifts mentioned in Rom 12:4–6 as natural talents. Hill, *Prophets, Past and Present*, 203. See also Turner, *Holy Spirit and Spiritual Gifts*; Lim, *Spiritual Gifts*.

2. See also Grudem, *Gift of Prophecy in the New Testament and Today*, 142–43.

The purpose of prophecy is very clear in Scripture. Paul explains, "But he who prophesies speaks edification and exhortation and comfort to men"(1 Cor 14:3 NKJV). Edification is very important to Paul who desires that everything done in the church should achieve the goal of edification. For example, church discipline and self-denial must be done toward this goal (2 Cor 10:8; 13:9; Rom 14:19). When people come to worship, and someone has a hymn, a revelation, a teaching, a tongue and an interpretation, it must all be done for the purpose of edifying the church. Prophecy is one of the ways through which the Lord edifies the church. The gift operates in the community of believers by building the individual members and promoting the spiritual growth of the body through the giving of the inspired spoken word.

The gift of prophecy also exhorts believers. It comes alongside to help a believer through the inspired message, just like counselling, which lifts up a believer in times of need.

The gift also operates to comfort people. Comfort has a greater degree of tenderness than exhortation. It requires speaking to a person in a very close and personal way, showing concern for their needs and offering help where possible. Thus, prophecy comes to address a person in such a way that discloses their personal needs.

At the same time, prophecy may operate to convince and convict a person. First Corinthians 14:24–25 clearly spells this out, "But if all prophesy, and an unbeliever or outsider enters, he is convicted by all, he is called to account by all, the secrets of his heart are disclosed, and so, falling on his face, he will worship God and declare that God is really among you" (ESV). Thus, a prophetic message may be released in such a way that the secret of someone's heart will be exposed. This will convince the person of the reality of God and convict him to honor God or even to believe in him and worship, if he did not believe him.

The prophet needs the gift of prophecy to function. It is the basic gift of the prophet to declare the words that the Lord has put in his mouth. The gift of prophecy usually operates in various ways; it may drop through hearing an audible voice or receiving a deep insight into issues. It may also drop in pictorial forms for the prophet to describe it or through inspiration as the person speaks spontaneously.[3]

---

3. See chap. 27, "How to Receive Revelation."

THE GIFT OF SPEAKING IN DIVERSE KINDS OF TONGUES

One of the gifts that a prophet may possess is the gift of speaking in diverse kinds of tongues. First Corinthians 12:10 reads, "To another the working of miracles; to another prophecy; to another discerning of spirits; to another diverse kinds of tongues; to another the interpretation of tongues" (1 Cor 12:10 KJV). There are types of tongues. The one which, the Pentecostals believe, is the evidence that one is baptized in the Holy Spirit. This belief is based on the following scriptures: first is Acts 2:1–4:

> When the Day of Pentecost had fully come, they were all with one accord in one place. And suddenly there came a sound from heaven, as of a rushing mighty wind, and it filled the whole house where they were sitting. Then there appeared to them divided tongues, as of fire, and one sat upon each of them. And they were all filled with the Holy Spirit and began to speak with other tongues, as the Spirit gave them utterance." (Acts 2:1–4 NKJV)

It was realized here that when the day of Pentecost had come, there was a rushing mighty wind, there appeared divided tongues of fire that sat upon the disciples, and then they spoke in tongues. The people who had gathered there also heard them speaking their own languages and praising God, "'We hear them speaking in our own tongues the wonderful works of God.' So they were all amazed and perplexed, saying to one another, 'Whatever could this mean?'" (Acts 2:10–12 NKJV). This is similar to interpretation of tongues or prophecy. This was very special on that day of Pentecost. Together, the signs were four—the mighty wind, tongues of fire, speaking in tongues, and speaking in people's languages, which were considered wonderful works of God. The four signs did not continue in subsequent experiences. This brings us to the next experience in Acts 8:14–19:

> Now when the apostles who were at Jerusalem heard that Samaria had received the word of God, they sent Peter and John to them, who, when they had come down, prayed for them that they might receive the Holy Spirit. For as yet He had fallen upon none of them. They had only been baptized in the name of the Lord Jesus. Then they laid hands on them, and they received the Holy Spirit. And when Simon saw that through the laying on of the apostles' hands the Holy Spirit was given, he offered them

money, saying, "Give me this power also, that anyone on whom I lay hands may receive the Holy Spirit." (NKJV)

When the people of Samaria received the word of God and accepted it, they needed the baptism in the Holy Spirit. This means receiving the word of God does not mean the person had received the Holy Spirit baptism. Peter had earlier spoken in Acts 2:38 that believing in the name of Jesus would lead to forgiving of sins, and receiving the Holy Spirit. "Then Peter said to them, 'Repent, and let every one of you be baptized in the name of Jesus Christ for the remission of sins; and you shall receive the gift of the Holy Spirit. For the promise is to you and to your children, and to all who are afar off, as many as the Lord our God will call'" (Acts 2:38–39 NKJV). For even though the people of Samaria had believed in the name of Jesus and their sins had been forgiven, they had not received the baptism in the Holy Spirit. Peter and John were sent to them for this purpose; receiving the baptism in the Holy Spirit which was something that was evident for people to know.

In Samaria, when the apostles prayed for them, they received the Holy Spirit baptism and there was something visible that the people around saw or heard that caused Simon to offer the apostles money to pray for him to receive that power. The assumption here is that, that "something" was speaking in tongues. Of course, they could have prophesied or magnified God since that was one of the signs of the baptism on the day of Pentecost. Or, they could have done both. This assumption here becomes possible in Acts 10:1–48. Peter was directed through a revelation to visit the household of Cornelius and present the gospel to the Gentiles. As Peter was speaking, the Holy Spirit fell on them. How did the people see it?

> While Peter was still speaking these words, the Holy Spirit fell upon all those who heard the word. And those of the circumcision who believed were astonished, as many as came with Peter, because the gift of the Holy Spirit had been poured out on the Gentiles also. For they heard them speak with tongues and magnify God. Then Peter answered, "Can anyone forbid water, that these should not be baptized who have received the Holy Spirit just as we have?" And he commanded them to be baptized in the name of the Lord. Then they asked him to stay a few days. (Acts 10:44–48 NKJV)

They heard them speaking in tongues and magnifying God. Thus, speaking in tongues and magnifying God were signs that the Holy Spirit had been poured on the people.

Another important incident is Paul's visit to Ephesus. He saw some disciples there, who had not been baptized in neither water nor the Holy Spirit:

> And it happened, while Apollos was at Corinth, that Paul, having passed through the upper regions, came to Ephesus. And finding some disciples he said to them, "Did you receive the Holy Spirit when you believed?" So they said to him, "We have not so much as heard whether there is a Holy Spirit." And he said to them, "Into what then were you baptized?" So they said, "Into John's baptism." Then Paul said, "John indeed baptized with a baptism of repentance, saying to the people that they should believe on Him who would come after him, that is, on Christ Jesus." When they heard this, they were baptized in the name of the Lord Jesus. And when Paul had laid hands on them, the Holy Spirit came upon them, and they spoke with tongues and prophesied. Now the men were about twelve in all. (Acts 19:1–7 NKJV)

After he had given them the gospel of Christ, he prayed for them to receive the Holy Spirit, and they spoke in tongues and prophesied. In this situation, we realized that speaking in tongues and prophesying were signs that the people had been baptized in the Holy Spirit.

From the incidents that we have discussed, it is apparent that speaking in tongues and prophesying (or magnifying God), with the exception of Acts 8, have been prevalent in all the areas where people were said to have received the Holy Spirit. Classical Pentecostals, therefore, believe that speaking in tongues is the evidence that a person has received the baptism in the Holy Spirit. Prophesy was still experienced in the Old Testament. Speaking in tongues was the new experience which the day of Pentecost brought about.

The Purpose of Speaking in Tongues

Paul shows that when someone speaks in tongues, he speaks mysteries to God, "For he who speaks in a tongue does not speak to men but to God, for no one understands him; however, in the spirit he speaks mysteries" (1 Cor 14:2 NKJV). Paul's explanation here means when someone speaks in tongues nobody understands him, but he would be speaking mysteries of God. He could be magnifying God. He could be speaking the deep truth about God. It is only the Lord, who understands him.

Thus, the one who speaks in tongues will be edifying himself through speaking in tongues, "He who speaks in a tongue edifies himself" (1 Cor 14:4 NKJV). Jude considers edifying yourself as building yourself up in the faith; "But you, beloved, building yourselves up on your most holy faith, praying in the Holy Spirit" (Jude 20 NKJV). Praying in the Holy Spirit here could mean speaking in tongues. What does "edifying himself" or "building yourself" mean? "Edifying himself" means the person's spirit is lifted up since the spirit understands what is going on. The person may be excited and feel happy and confident of the presence of God in his life. His love for the Lord will increase. He feels much more committed to God and has the courage to face life confidently.

The Gift of Diverse Kinds of Tongues Is Different

The gift of speaking in diverse kinds of tongues is considered different from speaking in tongues, which is the sign of the baptism in the Holy Spirit. Perhaps when Paul was saying, "Do all have gifts of healings? Do all speak with tongues? Do all interpret" (1 Cor 12:30–31 NKJV), he was speaking about the gift of speaking in diverse kinds of tongues. This is possible if 1 Cor 12:28, where Paul mentions "varieties of tongues" is taken into consideration. "And God has appointed these in the church: first apostles, second prophets, third teachers, after that miracles, then gifts of healings, helps, administrations, varieties of tongues" (1 Cor 12:28 NKJV). It is quite clear here that he was not talking about the devotional tongues, which he says is to edify oneself in the Lord.

Sometimes one who has this gift of speaking in varieties of tongues realizes that he will be speaking different tongues. There have been testimonies where people claim to speak known languages through the power of the Spirit. It is clear that a person speaking in varieties of tongues changes from seemingly one language to another, but whether these are known languages is difficult to tell. Sometimes after speaking in tongues for a while, it changes to songs. Often, I would see myself singing in the Spirit and then later hearing myself singing in a known language. Paul says in 1 Cor 14:13–15:

Therefore let him who speaks in a tongue pray that he may interpret. For if I pray in a tongue, my spirit prays, but my understanding is unfruitful. What is the conclusion then? I will pray with the spirit, and I will also pray with the understanding. I will sing with the spirit, and I will also sing with the understanding. (NKJV)

There is the potential for the one who speaks in tongues to interpret. Paul tells the Corinthians, "For this reason anyone who speaks in a tongue should pray that he may interpret what he says" (1 Cor 14:13–14 NIV). However, not all who speak in diverse kinds of tongues are able to interpret it. Thus, there is the need for the gift of interpretation.

THE GIFT OF INTERPRETATION

First Corinthians 12:10 reads, "to another the working of miracles, to another prophecy, to another discerning of spirits, to another different kinds of tongues, to another the interpretation of tongues" (NKJV). The gift of interpretation is one of the gifts that the prophet may possess.[4]

The gift of interpretation is the ability to understand and interpret an utterance which is spoken in tongues. The purpose of this gift is simply to provide meaning to a message which has been spoken in an unknown tongue.

When this gift is in operation, one seems to understand the tongues that he speaks in personal devotion. He can speak in varieties of tongues and then appears to understand the meaning of the tongues he has spoken. This is very similar to what Paul says in 1 Cor 14:15, "What is the conclusion then? I will pray with the spirit, and I will also pray with the understanding. I will sing with the spirit, and I will also sing with the understanding" (NKJV).

I remember that something like this happened to me the third day after I was baptized in the Holy Spirit. We were five people praying. After praying for some time, it appeared that I understood the tongues that I was speaking. After this incident, I could often understand the varieties of tongues I spoke. One of the most dramatic incidents which happened in my life in this area was an interpretation, which took place at Tamale

---

4. For some reading on the Gift of Interpretation, see Ahn, *Interpretation of Tongues and Prophecy*.

District Presbytery meeting of the Church of Pentecost.[5] The meeting had been quite stressful. There was a lot of tension as a result of a misunderstanding. Then I heard the Lord speaking to me to prophesy, but I questioned myself, "How can I prophesy in such a meeting?" Then, I felt the Lord saying that someone was going to speak in tongues and he would provide me the meaning, which was the same word of prophecy he had given to me. Soon after this, a sister stood up and spoke in tongues in the meeting. Then, I provided the meaning and the meeting ended successfully, with no further tension. Everyone there appeared to have witnessed the hand of the Lord in the meeting. This was very uncommon in presbytery meetings. After this, I have never witnessed another of such a spectacular interpretation of tongues.

This gives us a clue of what happens when an interpretation is provided for a spoken tongue. It is not like a translation where a message is translated word for word. The moment a person begins to speak in tongues, the person with the gift of interpretation begins to receive the meaning of the tongues within him. Then, he may start delivering the meaning, which may not be word for word but a general meaning. The interpretation that Daniel provided for Belshazzar in Daniel 5 gives a clue:

> "And this is the inscription that was written:
>
> MENE, MENE, TEKEL, PERES.
>
> This is the interpretation of each word. Mene: God has numbered your kingdom, and finished it; Tekel: You have been weighed in the balances, and found wanting; Peres: Your kingdom has been divided, and given to the Medes and Persians." Then Belshazzar gave the command, and they clothed Daniel with purple and put a chain of gold around his neck, and made a proclamation concerning him that he should be the third ruler in the kingdom. (Dan 5:25–29 NKJV)

King Belshazzar of Babylon abused the utensils, which were taken from the temple of God in Jerusalem by drinking from them. As he was in the process of abusing these, some fingers without hands wrote on the walls. When Daniel was brought in to offer interpretation, he did not translate word for word, but gave the general meaning:

> "Mene" meant, "God has numbered your kingdom, and finished it." (v. 26)

---

5. Tamale is the capital town of one of the political regions in Ghana.

"Tekel" meant, "You have been weighed in the balances, and found wanting." (v. 27)

"Peres" meant, "Your kingdom has been divided, and given to the Medes and Persians." (v. 28)

This means that interpretation is not necessarily word for word but provides the general meaning of the words spoken. The gifts of speaking in diversities of tongues and interpretation are equal to prophecy. There is the potential for all who speak in diverse kinds of tongues to pray for interpretation. Paul says in 1 Cor 14:27, "If anyone speaks in tongue, *let there be* two or at the most three, *each* in turn, and let one interpret" (NKJV). Once a person speaks and nobody interprets, that person must pray for the ability to interpret his own tongues. The person may begin by speaking in tongues and then interpret it himself like prophecy. When he grows in the operating of the gifts, it will not be necessary for him to speak in tongues before interpreting. He will be able to receive the message and deliver straight ahead. Sometimes, some people would speak in tongues and then later prophesy. Such speaking in tongues is to prepare or give the person the strength or ability to prophesy. It happens to persons who are new in the prophetic. Once someone is mature in the operation of the gift, he may not need such preparation again. He may be able to receive the message and then utter it straight ahead. The prophet may function in the interpretation of tongues, together with other gifts.

Chapter 5

The Gifts of Revelation

CHAPTER 5 DEALS WITH the gifts of revelation. These are gifts which reveal and explain hidden things. Three gifts will be discussed here. These are the gift of the word of knowledge, the gift of the word of wisdom, and the gift of discerning of spirits. The discussion follows.

THE GIFT OF THE WORD OF KNOWLEDGE

The gift to be considered here, first, is "the word of knowledge," as stated in 1 Cor 12:8 in the King James Version. There have been many attempts to define this gift. Some classical Pentecostals define it as having knowledge about things in the present and the past. I am defining it through the simple verb "know," through which we have the noun form "knowledge." The gift of knowledge is the ability to know truth that is hidden. The information received through the word of knowledge is something which is not possible to know through the normal human way or through natural knowledge. It is not the knowledge that Scripture normally gives, or the knowledge received through a person's relationship with Christ. Rather, the gift can operate as the person studies the Scriptures. The person often receives some insight into the Scriptures as he studies or waits upon the Lord in prayer. Sometimes it drops into the mind smoothly without the person thinking about it. It often offers deep meaning or understanding into a scriptural passage which people find difficult to understand.

One time as I was preparing a message on Mary's visit to Elizabeth, I had a very good insight, which was the manifestation of the word of knowledge. It dropped that Jesus, while he was in the womb of Mary, was already controlling the world. How could this happen? Now the angel had told Zechariah that John would be filled with the Holy Spirit, while still in his mother's womb (Luke 1:15). Jesus who was the baptizer of the Holy Spirit was in Mary's womb as well. Therefore, Jesus who was in the womb of Mary had to ask Mary to go to visit Elizabeth in order for him to baptize John with the Holy Spirit, in fulfillment of the prophetic message, through the angel Gabriel, given to Zechariah. Accordingly, Mary went there for the Lord Jesus in her womb, to baptize John, in the womb of his mother Elizabeth, with the Holy Spirit. Because of the baptism of the Holy Spirit in the womb, John "leaped for joy," as Elizabeth explained (Luke 1:44 NIV). Here, the Holy Spirit was working through the wombs of two women. It was the power of the Holy Spirit that caused John to leap in joy in the womb. What was that leap of joy? It was the baptism in the Holy Spirit of John in the womb of Elizabeth. This is what we the Pentecostals would call the baptism in the Holy Spirit or that one has been touched by the power of God.

It was this filling of the Holy Spirit that sanctified John, set him aside and gave him the audacity to baptize Jesus. Jesus baptized John with the Holy Spirit to give John the authority to baptize Jesus in water, in order to fulfill all righteousness (Matt 3:15). Such encounter of the power of God in the wombs of women would not end there. It would affect the grounds, in this case, the two wombs. Accordingly, "in a loud voice [Elizabeth] exclaimed, 'Blessed are you among women, and blessed is the child you will bear!'" (Luke 1:42 NIV). She knew that Mary was pregnant, although the pregnancy had not come out. She also knew that the one in Mary's womb was the Lord. She exclaimed, "But why am I so favored, that the mother of my Lord should come to me?" (Luke 1:43 NIV). This was the outcome of what had gone on in her womb. This was revealed to me when I was praying and preparing a message.

The purpose of the gift is to reveal hidden things, which are useful for human beings to know at the time to promote the will of God on earth. It can reveal things in the past, present and the future. This type of knowledge is not revealed through curiosity, or for public display. The purpose again is to help accomplish the will of God on earth. God knows everything, but it is not all those things that are important for people to know. The reason is that when some people know some things, they are unable to keep it and they voice them out to cause trouble. For example, Prophet Elisha saw the evil that Hazael, a servant sent by his master Ben-Hadad, the king of Syria, would do to Israel and told him. Elisha fixed his gaze and stared at Hazael, until he was embarrassed. And then Elisha wept. Hazael said, "'Why does my lord weep?' He told him, 'Because I know the evil that you will do to the people of Israel. You will set on fire their fortresses, and you will kill their young men with the sword and dash in pieces their little ones and rip open their pregnant women'" (2 Kgs 8:10–12). The servant Hazael immediately went to kill his king and took over the kingship.

Elisha should not have shared all that he knew. Sharing it caused Hazael to kill his master immediately. We can see how inappropriately such an experienced prophet acted. Therefore, God only reveals a fragment of what he knows to us which is only necessary at a given period.

Sometimes the Lord would reveal the sin of a person through the gift of knowledge as he did with the sins of Ananias and Sapphira (Acts 5:1–10). The gift of the word of knowledge needs to be handled well so as not to cause confusion in families and society in general.

Manifestation

The gift functions through diverse means. It can manifest through dreams, visions, trances and deep insights within one's spirit.

Dreams are the images that we see when we sleep. These images appear involuntarily to our mental sight, as we are asleep. The images may be a series of events, which are well understood, or events which make no sense at all. Everyone dreams. Daniel was a man full of dreams; God revealed the dream of Nebuchadnezzar to him (Dan 2). This was the operation of the gift of knowledge.

Visions are mental images that appear to people while they are still awake, and not sleeping. Not everyone sees visions. However, most of the prophets have visions. For example, Isaiah (6), Jeremiah (1:11–12), Amos (1:1), and Obadiah (1). Ezekiel states, "In the thirtieth year, in the fourth month on the fifth day, while I was among the exiles by the Kebar River, the heavens were opened and I saw visions of God" (Ezek 1:1 NIV). The example of Ananias who prayed for Paul is a very good example of the gift in the New Testament:

> In Damascus there was a disciple named Ananias. The Lord called to him in a vision, "Ananias!" "Yes, Lord," he answered. The Lord told him, "Go to the house of Judas on Straight Street and ask for a man from Tarsus named Saul, for he is praying. In a vision he has seen a man named Ananias come and place his hands on him to restore his sight." "Lord," Ananias answered, "I have heard many reports about this man and all the harm he has done to your saints in Jerusalem. And he has come here with authority from the chief priests to arrest all who call on your name." But the Lord said to Ananias, "Go! This man is my chosen instrument to carry my name before the Gentiles and their kings and before the people of Israel. I will show him how much he must suffer for my name." Then Ananias went to the house and entered it. Placing his hands on Saul, he said, "Brother Saul, the Lord-Jesus, who appeared to you on the road as you were coming here—has sent me so that you may see again and be filled with the Holy Spirit." Immediately, something like scales fell from Saul's eyes, and he could see again. He got up and was baptized, and after taking some food, he regained his strength. (Acts 9:10–19 NIV)

Trances are a state of temporary unconsciousness where images appear to people, or situations in which people may not be in control of what is happening to them. Peter, for example, had this experience:

> About noon the following day as they were on their journey and approaching the city, Peter went up on the roof to pray. He became hungry and wanted something to eat, and while the meal was being prepared, he fell into a trance. He saw heaven opened and something like a large sheet being let down to earth by its four corners. It contained all kinds of four-footed animals, as well as reptiles of the earth and birds of the air. Then a voice told him, "Get up, Peter. Kill and eat." "Surely not, Lord!" Peter replied. "I have never eaten anything impure or unclean." The voice spoke to him a second time, "Do not call anything impure that God has made clean." This happened three times, and immediately the sheet was taken back to heaven. While Peter was wondering about the meaning of the vision, the men sent by Cornelius found out where Simon's house was and stopped at the gate. They called out, asking if Simon who was known as Peter was staying there. (Acts 10:9–18 NIV)

Sometimes, the Lord may grant some people dreams, put some into trances, or give others visions that are related to the past, present or future events. With regards to visions, some images may appear to people while praying with their eyes closed or opened. The vision can be a revelation, which the Lord communicates to a person. Dreams, visions and trances are related to the office of a prophet (Isa 6:1–7; Ps 89:19; Lam 2:9; Mic 3:6; Ezek 1:1–3; 8:1–4; Dan 1:17).

Open vision may be related to angelic visitation. The Lord has been revealing himself to people through angelic visitations. For example, the Lord sent angels to Abraham, Gideon and Daniel (Gen 18:1–2; Judg 6:11–12; Dan 9:20–23). The angels may appear like human beings and suddenly leave the scene immediately they accomplish their mission. The people they deal with mostly do not recognize them until they leave. Some examples are the angels who visited Abraham on their way to destroy Sodom and Gomorrah, and the angel who spoke to Gideon in the wine threshold (Gen 18:1–2; Judg 6:11–12). Angelic visitation is also associated with the office of the prophet (e.g., 1 Kgs 19:5–7; 2 Kgs 1:3, 15; Dan 9:20–23; Zech 1:9–19; 2:3).

When the Lord established the Hebrews as a nation (Israel), he spoke to them in an audible voice (Exod 20:18–20; Deut 4:15, 36; 5:23–24). This assured them that the God they serve was a person. It also created fear in them to worship the God who is alive. Such an audible voice was heard during the baptism and ministry of Jesus (Matt 3:17; 17:5; John 12:28–29). Paul also heard an audible voice like this when he encountered Christ on the way to Damascus (Acts 9:4). Hearing an audible voice is sometimes associated with the office of a prophet (Isa 6:8). A very typical example of hearing a voice is that of Samuel's call:

> The Lord came and stood there, calling as at the other times, "Samuel! Samuel!" Then Samuel said, "Speak, for your servant is listening." And the Lord said to Samuel: "See, I am about to do something in Israel that will make the ears of everyone who hears of it tingle. At that time I will carry out against Eli everything I spoke against his family—from beginning to end. For I told him that I would judge his family forever because of the sin he knew about; his sons made themselves contemptible, and he failed to restrain them. Therefore, I swore to the house of Eli, 'The guilt of Eli's house will never be atoned for by sacrifice or offering.'" (1 Sam 3:10–14 NIV)

Sometimes the gift functions as having a deep insight into something or a word of God dropping into your spirit and mind. This gift operated in Peter on the day of Pentecost. Here, he read meaning into what was happening as the fulfillment of Joel's prophecy.

THE GIFT OF THE WORD OF WISDOM

The gift of the word of knowledge works with the gift of "the word of wisdom" (1 Cor 12:8 KJV). There are divergent views about the definition or description of "the word of wisdom." I consider the word of wisdom as the ability that the Holy Spirit offers a person to understand and explain a revelation and have special insight into difficult situations. The understanding will come in a way that makes difficult and complex issues well understood; it appears as an insight that the Holy Spirit drops in the spirit, heart or mind of a person. It can also come in a form of a dream or vision, where the Lord provides the meaning of a given revelation.

Comparing the word of knowledge to the word of wisdom is that while the word of knowledge reveals what is past, ongoing, or present, the word of wisdom provides the meaning or understanding for such revelations. Thus, while the word of knowledge gives you the ability to know, the word of wisdom provides the ability to understand.

The word of wisdom provided here is not natural wisdom. Natural wisdom is the fruit of the intellectual reasoning process that tries to provide answers to human beings. It comes through experiences and learning. In the Bible, someone like Gamaliel had this type of wisdom. He used this type of wisdom to save the Apostles Peter and John from being executed:

> When they heard this, they were furious and wanted to put them to death. But a Pharisee named Gamaliel, a teacher of the law, who was honored by all the people, stood up in the Sanhedrin and ordered that the men be put outside for a little while. Then he addressed them: "Men of Israel, consider carefully what you intend to do to these men. Some time ago Theudas appeared, claiming to be somebody, and about four hundred men rallied to him. He was killed, all his followers were dispersed, and it all came to nothing. After him, Judas the Galilean appeared in the days of the census and led a band of people in revolt. He too was killed, and all his followers were scattered. Therefore, in the present case I advise you: Leave these men alone! Let them go! For if their purpose or activity is of human origin, it will fail. But if it is from God, you will not be able to stop these men; you will only find yourselves fighting against God." (Acts 5:33–39 NIV)

This is the display of natural wisdom. But for his intervention the two apostles would have been killed. Natural wisdom is good, but it is different from the gift of wisdom.

The gift of the word of wisdom is also not the general wisdom that James speaks about in the Bible:

> Consider it pure joy, my brothers, whenever you face trials of many kinds, because you know that the testing of your faith develops perseverance. Perseverance must finish its work so that you may be mature and complete, not lacking anything. If any of you lacks wisdom, he should ask God, who gives generously to all without finding fault, and it will be given to him. (Jas 1:2–5 NIV)

> But the wisdom that comes from heaven is first of all pure; then peace-loving, considerate, submissive, full of mercy and good fruit, impartial and sincere. (Jas 3:17 NIV)

James was concerned that believers do not understand the purpose of suffering. People often murmur against God and some even lose their faith when they are suffering. James advises that when we encounter such difficulties, we need to pray for the Lord to give us wisdom. This may not be the gift of wisdom, and neither is it the natural wisdom that some people are already endowed with. Rather, it is general wisdom needed to help us go through life's traumas. This is the wisdom, which we need in trials in order to understand their design and purpose. It is the wisdom that will help us perform our routine duties.

There is another kind of wisdom, which the Bible describes as worldly or earthly wisdom, "Who is wise and understanding among you? Let him show by good conduct that his works are done in the meekness of wisdom. But if you have bitter envy and self-seeking in your hearts, do not boast and lie against the truth. This wisdom does not descend from above, but is earthly, sensual, demonic" (Jas 3:13–15 NKJV).

Worldly wisdom is at enmity with God. Paul shows that the Lord will destroy the wisdom of the world. "For it is written: 'I will destroy the wisdom of the wise, And bring to nothing the understanding of the prudent.' Where is the wise? Where is the scribe? Where is the disputer of this age? Has not God made foolish the wisdom of this world?" (1 Cor 1:19–21 NKJV).

The gift of the word of wisdom is different from all these types of wisdom. It may grant a person the ability to understand the meaning of a dream as it manifested in the life of Joseph. Pharaoh dreamed and was worried about it. The Lord gave Joseph the interpretation through the gift of the word of wisdom:

> Then Joseph said to Pharaoh, "The dreams of Pharaoh are one; God has shown Pharaoh what he is about to do: The seven good cows are seven years, and the seven good heads are seven years; the dreams are one. And the seven thin and ugly cows which came up after them are seven years, and the seven empty heads blighted by the east wind are seven years of famine. This is the thing which I have spoken to Pharaoh. God has shown Pharaoh what he is about to do. Indeed seven years of great plenty will come throughout all the land of Egypt; but after them seven years of famine will arise, and all the plenty will be forgotten in the land of Egypt; and the famine will deplete the land. So the plenty will not be known in the land because of the famine following, for it will be very severe. And the dream was repeated to Pharaoh twice because the thing is established by God, and God will shortly bring it to pass. Now therefore, let Pharaoh select a discerning and wise man, and set him over the land of Egypt. Let Pharaoh do this, and let him appoint officers over the land, to collect one-fifth of the produce of the land of Egypt in the seven plentiful years." (Gen 41:25–34 NKJV)

Similarly, Daniel was able to know and interpret the dream of Nebuchadnezzar (Dan 2). In Daniel's situation, it was both the gift of knowledge and the gift of wisdom at work. The gift of the word of knowledge gave him the ability to know the dream, and then the gift of the word of wisdom gave him the ability to understand.

Solomon prayed for wisdom and the Lord granted it to him. His manifestation of wisdom is like the gift of the word of wisdom:

> And the king said, "The one says, 'This is my son, who lives, and your son is the dead one'; and the other says, 'No! But your son is the dead one, and my son is the living one.'" Then the king said, "Bring me a sword." So they brought a sword before the king. And the king said, "Divide the living child in two, and give half to one, and half to the other." Then the woman whose son was living spoke to the king, for she yearned with compassion for her son; and she said, "O my lord, give her the living child, and by no means kill him!" But the other said, "Let him be neither mine nor yours, but divide him." So the king answered and said, "Give the first woman the living child, and by no means kill him; she is his mother." (1 Kgs 3:23–27 NKJV)

This wisdom of Solomon appears to come from above as a gift in operation.

When the gift of wisdom is in operation, God helps a person to speak the right thing at the right time. I do not like citing Jesus when teaching about spiritual gifts, since he was the gift himself. However, here I want to use the operation of this type of wisdom in his ministry. When a woman was caught in the act of adultery and Jesus was questioned, he gave the right answer at the right time. The law of Moses states that adultery merited capital punishment. The Roman government required that capital punishment cases are first referred to the Roman government representative. The religious Jews were against the control of the Romans on their own land and, thus, they wanted to know what the Messiah would say. Jesus' answer:

> So when they continued asking Him, He raised Himself up and said to them, "He who is without sin among you, let him throw a stone at her first." And again He stooped down and wrote on the ground. Then those who heard it, being convicted by their conscience, went out one by one, beginning with the oldest even to the last. And Jesus was left alone, and the woman standing in the midst. When Jesus had raised Himself up and saw no one but the woman, He said to her, "Woman, where are those accusers of yours? Has no one condemned you?" (John 8:7–10 NKJV)

The wisdom exhibited here was super. Nobody was able to throw a stone at her, yet Jesus had fulfilled their demand.

Again, when the Pharisees and the Herodians came together to find something against Jesus to arrest him, they put a question to him concerning the payment of tax. Follow the reading:

> Then the Pharisees went and plotted how they might entangle Him in His talk. And they sent to Him their disciples with the Herodians, saying, "Teacher, we know that You are true, and teach the way of God in truth; nor do You care about anyone, for You do not regard the person of men. Tell us, therefore, what do You think? Is it lawful to pay taxes to Caesar, or not?" But Jesus perceived their wickedness, and said, "Why do you test Me, you hypocrites? Show Me the tax money." So they brought Him a denarius. And He said to them, "Whose image and inscription is this?" They said to Him, "Caesar's." And He said to them, "Render therefore to Caesar the things that are Caesar's, and to God the things that are God's." When they had heard

these words, they marveled, and left Him and went their way. (Matt 22:15–22 NKJV)

This was the display of super wisdom. The gift of "the word of wisdom" gives the right counseling and guidance. It helps a person know the right thing to do without causing havoc.

A prophet needs this gift—wisdom—to guide and lead him.

THE GIFT OF DISCERNING OF SPIRITS

The gift of the discerning of spirits operates in a person who functions as a prophet. First Corinthians 12:10 reads, "to another the working of miracles, to another prophecy, to another discerning of spirits, to another different kinds of tongues, to another the interpretation of tongues" (1 Cor 12:10 NKJV).

The gift of discerning of spirits is the ability given to a person to distinguish and know whether a manifestation is from God or not. There are many sources of manifestations. At least, three are very clear in the Bible. The first is a manifestation that stems from the devil. The devil speaks a lot. When Jesus had fasted forty days and forty nights, the first voice he heard was that of the devil, "Then Jesus was led by the Spirit into the desert to be tempted by the devil. After fasting forty days and forty nights, he was hungry. The tempter came to him and said, 'If you are the Son of God, tell these stones to become bread'" (Matt 4:1–3 NIV; cf. Luke 4:1–13). Here, the devil came directly to tempt him to reject the word of God. In Matt 3:17, after Jesus had been baptized, "And a voice from heaven said, 'This is my Son, whom I love; with him I am well pleased.'" The devil came to challenge that voice.

The devil can speak through evil spirits. For example, in Mark 1:23–24, Jesus was teaching at a synagogue: "Just then a man in their synagogue who was possessed by an evil spirit cried out, 'What do you want with us, Jesus of Nazareth? Have you come to destroy us? I know who you are—the Holy One of God!'" (NIV). Here, it was an evil spirit speaking through the man.

The second source of manifestation is the flesh. When Jesus asked his disciples a question, and Peter answered, Jesus said that it was not flesh and blood that had revealed it but his Father in heaven:

> Jesus replied, "Blessed are you, Simon son of Jonah, for this was not revealed to you by man, but by my Father in heaven." (Matt 16:17 NIV)

> Jesus answered and said to him, "Blessed are you, Simon Bar-Jonah, for flesh and blood has not revealed this to you, but My Father who is in heaven." (Matt 16:17 NKJV)

> Jesus replied, "You are blessed, Simon son of John, because my Father in heaven has revealed this to you. You did not learn this from any human being." (Matt 16:17 NLT)

The implication is that "flesh and blood" often reveal things to people. The expression, "flesh and blood," refers to the natural way of revealing or doing things.

The third source of manifestation is the Spirit of God. This is the focus of what we are discussing. Since there are many sources of manifestation, the Lord will like us to know the source of every manifestation before accepting it. Hence, the need to judge prophecies (1 Thess 5:19–22).

What makes the gift of discerning of spirits more important is that sometimes a person who is truly endowed with the gift of prophecy can also be used by the flesh or the devil. An example of this is the old prophet who said an angel of God had spoken to him, hence deceiving and leading a young person to his death (1 Kgs 13). Later, the Lord spoke through this same old man:

> But the old prophet answered, "I am a prophet, too, just as you are. And an angel gave me this command from the Lord: 'Bring him home with you so he can have something to eat and drink.'" But the old man was lying to him. So they went back together, and the man of God ate and drank at the prophet's home. Then while they were sitting at the table, a command from the Lord came to the old prophet. He cried out to the man of God from Judah, "This is what the Lord says: You have defied the word of the Lord and have disobeyed the command the Lord your God gave you. You came back to this place and ate and drank where he told you not to eat or drink. Because of this, your body will not be buried in the grave of your ancestors." (1 Kgs 13:18–22 NLT)

While "the flesh" deceived him, the Lord also spoke through him. How could you know whether the Lord was speaking to him or the flesh? The above text said, he was lying (18). This means that the old prophet was speaking from the flesh and he knew he was not telling the truth; he deceived the young man. There are many people like this old man in the system.

Another example is King Saul. When he was anointed by the Lord through Samuel, and was filled with the Spirit of God, he prophesied:

> When they arrived at Gibeah, a procession of prophets met him; the Spirit of God came upon him in power, and he joined in their prophesying. When all those who had formerly known him saw him prophesying with the prophets, they asked each other, "What is this that has happened to the son of Kish? Is Saul also among the prophets?" (1 Sam 10:10–11 NIV)

Then later, an evil spirit filled him, to the extent that he wanted to kill David:

> The next day an evil spirit from God came forcefully upon Saul. He was prophesying in his house, while David was playing the harp, as he usually did. Saul had a spear in his hand and he hurled it, saying to himself, "I'll pin David to the wall." But David eluded him twice. (1 Sam 18:10–11; 16:14 NIV)

Yet, later, he was also filled with the Spirit of God, and he prophesied:

> Finally, he himself left for Ramah and went to the great cistern at Secu. And he asked, "Where are Samuel and David?" "Over in Naioth at Ramah," they said. So Saul went to Naioth at Ramah. But the Spirit of God came even upon him, and he walked along prophesying until he came to Naioth. He stripped off his robes and also prophesied in Samuel's presence. He lay that way all that day and night. This is why people say, "Is Saul also among the prophets?" (1 Sam 19:22–24 NIV)

There are many ways to know the source of a manifestation without the gift of discernment. Everyone who knows the voice of God can often know outright the source of some manifestations. The Bible does not contradict itself. Thus, if a person claims to speak from God and goes directly against the word of God, the Christian who knows the word will know outright that the speaker is wrong. A mature Christian can also know the source of a manifestation through his maturity in the Lord. Yet, besides these, the Lord has endowed his church with the gift of discerning of spirits, for the church to know the source of a specific manifestation, when in doubt.

The purpose of the gift of discerning of spirits makes it operate as one of the most difficult gifts of all. It enables a person to identify, understand and interpret the spirit, which is behind a manifestation. Whereas the person with the gift may know the spirit behind a manifestation, others may not. How the rest will understand or accept the submission of such a person becomes a challenge.

Paul still admonishes the Corinthians, "Let two or three prophets speak, and let the others judge. But if anything is revealed to another who sits by, let the first keep silent" (1 Cor 14:29–30 NKJV). Here, Paul was asking the rest of the prophets to judge it.[1]

Believers are supposed to test all things including prophecy to find out if they are from God or not. Paul tells the Thessalonians, "Do not put out the Spirit's fire; do not treat prophecies with contempt. Test everything. Hold on to the good. Avoid every kind of evil" (1 Thess 5:19–21 NIV). While in 1 Corinthians, Paul appears to ask the prophets to test prophecies, in 1 Thessalonians, he directed all to test the manifestation through their knowledge of Scripture and maturity in the Lord. Nevertheless, one with this gift of discerning of spirits has been given the supernatural ability to know this outright.

The Gifts of Discerning of Spirits and Word of Knowledge

The gift of discerning of spirits is similar to the word of knowledge in the sense that both may reveal something that is hidden from the limelight, so that even if an evil spirit is behind a manifestation, the operations of these gifts may bring it out. However, this is the area that brings the difference between the word of knowledge and the discerning of spirits. While the word of knowledge may reveal many other hidden things, the gift of discerning of spirits may be limited to the distinguishing of the source behind a manifestation, even including the operation of the word of knowledge.

One of the typical examples of the operation of this gift was in the ministry of Peter in Samaria. The Lord had used Peter and John to baptize people with the Holy Spirit. Simon who claimed to have accepted the Lord into his life requested that he would receive that same power to baptize people with the Holy Spirit. The Apostle Peter discerned something serious in the life of Simon as follows:

1. See Robeck, "Discerning the Spirit," 32–33.

> And when Simon saw that through the laying on of the apostles' hands the Holy Spirit was given, he offered them money, saying, "Give me this power also, that anyone on whom I lay hands may receive the Holy Spirit." But Peter said to him, "Your money perish with you, because you thought that the gift of God could be purchased with money! You have neither part nor portion in this matter, for your heart is not right in the sight of God. Repent therefore of this your wickedness, and pray God if perhaps the thought of your heart may be forgiven you. For I see that you are poisoned by bitterness and bound by iniquity." (Acts 8:18–23 NKJV)

Here, Peter discerned something more than the request Simon made. He saw that Simon was poisoned by bitterness and held captive by sin. This could be the operations of the discerning of spirits.

Another example is seen in Paul and the deliverance of the girl in Philippi:

> One day as we were going down to the place of prayer, we met a demon-possessed slave girl. She was a fortune-teller who earned a lot of money for her masters. She followed Paul and the rest of us, shouting, "These men are servants of the Most High God, and they have come to tell you how to be saved." This went on day after day until Paul got so exasperated that he turned and said to the demon within her, "I command you in the name of Jesus Christ to come out of her." And instantly it left her. (Acts 16:16–18 NLT)

Did Paul really need the gift of discerning to know that this girl was not of God? I do not think so, since she was a fortune teller. Where the gift was needed was in the area of discerning the words that the girl was declaring, "These men are servants of the Most High God." The words were absolutely right, which made it appear that something good was coming out of the girl, or rather she had believed the message of Paul and needed to be recognized. Some people would have allowed the girl to come and testify about it. But Paul discerned that the evil spirit in her was speaking. This was the gift of discerning of spirits.

How does it operate in a person? The person with this gift will at times have a strong, deep feeling within him concerning a manifestation, then, have an inner awareness of the source of the manifestation. I once attended a Christmas Convention with the then chairman of the Church of Pentecost, Prophet M. K. Yeboah, where someone gave a word of prophecy. Immediately the person started, I had a strong inner conviction that the person was not speaking from God. It was something I had not thought of or desired. It just dawned on me spontaneously and strongly, however, the one who was chairing the meeting was a prophet and a mature person in the Lord, besides the fact that he was the chairman of the church. So I kept quiet. Few minutes later, the prophet stopped the one who was prophesying. I considered it as a confirmation of the discernment that I had.

In another incident, there was a woman who claimed to be a prophetess and performed at Wa central church.[2] I was the district pastor of this church but I had traveled to visit one of the churches in the villages. When I returned, I was informed of "how the Lord had visited the church" through the ministration of a woman (a stranger) who was thought to be a prophetess. Immediately something unusual went through my inner being making me uncomfortable and feeling that the woman was not from the Lord. I told the elder that I did not think the woman was sent by the Lord, however, I would need to see her minister before I could draw my conclusion. When she attended the evening service and I saw her, I had the same experience as before. I did not allow her to minister again. About two weeks later, it came out that this woman had stolen someone's golden jewelry and presented them to another person. By this time, she had run away from the town. This confirmed the discernment I had that she was not of the Lord.

The operation of this gift in a person helps him to identify the type of voices speaking within himself so as to protect him from being deceived by any other voice rather than the Lord's. Remember that when Jesus fasted forty days and nights, the devil came to speak to him (Matt 4:1–11). This implies that the devil can speak to everybody. It also means that the operation of this gift within the body of Christ is absolutely essential. This is one of the gifts that makes a person a prophet. It will help the prophet to identify the type of spirit manifesting at a particular period. Without it, people who claim to be prophets can be deceived themselves, to deceive others.

---

2. Wa is one of the towns in Ghana, where I pastored.

Chapter 6

Gifts of the Word

CHAPTER 6 CONTINUES WITH the constitution of the prophets. Three gifts are dealt with here: the gift of teaching, the gift of exhortation, and the gift of music. We begin with the gift of teaching.

THE GIFT OF TEACHING

One of the gifts that may operate in the prophet is teaching. Teaching is considered a spiritual gift:

> We have different gifts, according to the grace given us. If a man's gift is prophesying, let him use it in proportion to his faith. If it is serving, let him serve; if it is teaching, let him teach; if it is encouraging, let him encourage; if it is contributing to the needs of others, let him give generously; if it is leadership, let him govern diligently; if it is showing mercy, let him do it cheerfully. (Rom 12:6–8 NIV)

Some people prefer to call the gift of teaching "a grace gift" or even "a natural gift." Nevertheless, no matter how a person considers it, Paul does not only see it as a gift from the Lord but a very important gift:

> And in the church God has appointed first of all apostles, second prophets, third teachers, then workers of miracles, also those having gifts of healing, those able to help others, those with gifts of administration, and those speaking in different kinds of

tongues. Are all apostles? Are all prophets? Are all teachers? Do all work miracles? (1 Cor 12:28–29 NIV)

When it comes to the edification of the church, Paul sees teachers or the gift of teaching as the third most important gift in the church.

The gift of teaching is the ability to study, analyze and explain Scriptures clearly and communicate it systematically to the understanding of people. Some people relate teaching to prophecy but the two are completely different. The Evangelical theologian Wayne Grudem rightly observes, "If a message is the result of conscious reflection on the text of Scripture, containing interpretation of the text and application to life, then it is (in New Testament terms) a *teaching*."[1] He continues, "But if a message is the report of something God brings suddenly to mind, then it is a prophecy."[2] Prophecy is spontaneously receiving something from God and bringing it out to people. Prophecy however can manifest within teaching, as the teacher is preparing or delivering his message. The two are not mutually exclusive. Often, I do experience prophetic manifestation as I teach. I may teach on one subject in many places but the prophetic insight makes the presentation different.

The purpose of the gift of teaching is to equip the saints in such a way that they become mature in Christ. The operation of the gift of teaching helps believers not to be tossed back and forth by every wind of deceitful teaching; they will not be influenced when people try to trick them with lies which sound like biblical truth (Eph 4:14–15).

The operation of the gift enables the believers to know the duties of the disciples and to function effectively. A church with the gift of teaching operating within it grows and has many of the sections functioning effectively without manipulations, since each disciple knows his roles. While an evangelist brings people in, the gift of teaching shows the people what to do, sustains them, and ushers them to their respective roles.

The manifestation of the gift in a person is very evident. The person has the desire to acquire the truth in the Bible, by examining a text or a specific topic. He does this by studying and comparing scripture with scripture. He has the desire to read, pursue and compare until he stumbles on what he wants. In the course of his studying, he will not skip over the minutest thing. He will use Bible dictionaries to find meanings, atlases to check places, concordances to find similar texts, and commentaries

---

1. Grudem, *Gift of Prophecy*, 143.
2. Grudem, *Gift of Prophecy*, 143.

to find out what other people say about the same thing. He will use the internet and check other references on the topic.

Once he does these, he can arrange his teaching in an orderly manner for easy communication and consumption by his audience. His presentation is easy to follow and interesting to listen to. A scholar may have knowledge yet have difficulty passing on this knowledge to people. A person who has the gift of teaching will make difficult subjects easy to understand.

One person in the Bible who appears to demonstrate this gift is Apollos:

> Meanwhile a Jew named Apollos, a native of Alexandria, came to Ephesus. He was a learned man, with a thorough knowledge of the Scriptures. He had been instructed in the way of the Lord, and he spoke with great fervor and taught about Jesus accurately, though he knew only the baptism of John. He began to speak boldly in the synagogue. When Priscilla and Aquila heard him, they invited him to their home and explained to him the way of God more adequately. (Acts 18:24–26 NIV)

He was endowed with this gift and he could teach accurately about Christ, although he had not been adequately informed about the way of God.[3] Paul respected him so much that he said, he Paul planted and Apollos watered it:

> What, after all, is Apollos? And what is Paul? Only servants, through whom you came to believe—as the Lord has assigned to each his task. I planted the seed, Apollos watered it, but God made it grow. So neither he who plants nor he who waters is anything, but only God, who makes things grow." (1 Cor 3:5–7 NIV)

Furthermore, Paul respected him so much as to compare Apollos with himself (Paul) as well as Peter:

> Do not deceive yourselves. If any one of you thinks he is wise by the standards of this age, he should become a "fool" so that he may become wise. For the wisdom of this world is foolishness in

---

3. The issue that comes out is whether this was a spiritual gift or something that came out of his learning? Since not all people who learn are able to communicate well, this could be considered a gift. The gift could initially be a natural gift, that is, a talent. It is not uncommon for the Lord to endow more grace to people who are already endowed with specific talents. For he says he chooses people before they are formed in their mothers' womb (Jer 1:3).

God's sight. As it is written: "He catches the wise in their craftiness"; and again, "The Lord knows that the thoughts of the wise are futile." So then, no more boasting about men! All things are yours, whether Paul or Apollos or Cephas or the world or life or death or the present or the future—all are yours, and you are of Christ, and Christ is of God." (1 Cor 3:18–23 NIV)

For Paul to compare him to such pillars of the church as Peter and himself shows the extent of the teaching gift of Apollos. When the situation in Corinth was complicated, Paul thought Apollos was one of the persons who could handle it, although Apollos thought it was not the right time, "Now about our brother Apollos: I strongly urged him to go to you with the brothers. He was quite unwilling to go now, but he will go when he has the opportunity" (1 Cor 16:12 NIV). Many people think Apollos was the author of the book of Hebrews.[4] Taking the strong comparison between the Old and New Testaments, the book was certainly written by a person with the gift of teaching. It is possible that Apollos might have written it. The teaching in the book demonstrates the importance of the gift of teaching to the church.

One of the mistakes of many church leaders is to ask volunteers to come and teach Sunday school children. It is thought that anybody can do it, yet the best people to handle our children for us are those with the gift of teaching.

This gift is one of the gifts, which constitute the prophetic office. It helps the prophet to pass on his message to his generation and beyond.

THE GIFT OF EXHORTATION

The gift of exhortation is one of the gifts that Rom 12:8 brings out: "The one who exhorts, in his exhortation; the one who contributes, in generosity; the one who leads, with zeal; the one who does acts of mercy, with cheerfulness" (ESV).

The gift of exhortation is scarcely mentioned as one of the gifts, but I consider it as an equally important gift, which a prophet may possess. It is the ability to motivate people to action. The one who is endowed with this gift will present messages and statements that warn people or assure them of the promises of God to stimulate them to discharge their duties.

---

4. This issue is picked up later in the book.

The purpose of the gift is for the Lord to grant people the ability to offer counseling or support to the weak, the neglected and the vulnerable. Again, the gift helps people to challenge others to come out of sin. It helps to confront people with the real issues, without dodging. The prophet calls people to repentance and encourages them to follow the ways of the Lord, thus, this gift helps the prophet to function naturally in his ministry.

The gift may operate in three ways. First, is the ability to challenge people to act. Second, is the ability to rebuke those who behave inappropriately. Third, is the ability to encourage the weaker brethren to discharge their God-given duties. We shall discuss these in turns.

In the Bible, Joshua for example, threw a challenge to the people of Israel to follow the Lord:

> Now therefore fear the Lord and serve him in sincerity and in faithfulness. Put away the gods that your fathers served beyond the River and in Egypt, and serve the Lord. And if it is evil in your eyes to serve the Lord, choose this day whom you will serve, whether the gods your fathers served in the region beyond the River, or the gods of the Amorites in whose land you dwell. But as for me and my house, we will serve the Lord. Then the people answered, "Far be it from us that we should forsake the Lord to serve other gods, for it is the Lord our God who brought us and our fathers up from the land of Egypt, out of the house of slavery, and who did those great signs in our sight and preserved us in all the way that we went, and among all the peoples through whom we passed. And the Lord drove out before us all the peoples, the Amorites who lived in the land. Therefore we also will serve the Lord, for he is our God." (Josh 24:14–18 ESV)

The life of the people of Israel depended upon their obedience to the Lord. The Lord had established a covenant with them. Moses specifically told the Israelites their very life as a nation depended upon their obedience, "He said to them, 'Take to heart all the words by which I am warning you today, that you may command them to your children, that they may be careful to do all the words of this law. For it is no empty word for you, but your very life, and by this word you shall live long in the land that you are going over the Jordan to possess" (Deut 32:46–47 ESV). Yet, the people had gotten into idolatry. Joshua had to throw a challenge to them and he did it so effectively that the people responded positively. I know a superintendent of works, who had the talent of exhortation and was able to challenge his workers to do extra work for free.

Paul asked the Romans to offer their bodies to God as a living sacrifice. "I appeal to you therefore, brothers, by the mercies of God, to present your bodies as a living sacrifice, holy and acceptable to God, which is your spiritual worship" (Rom 12:1 ESV). Paul, by drawing attention to God's mercy compelled believers to live a holy life. Thus with this gift, the prophet may throw a challenge to believers to live a life of chastity without forcing it on people.

Elijah confronted the people of Israel to worship the Lord, rather than Baal:

> And Elijah came near to all the people and said, "How long will you go limping between two different opinions? If the Lord is God, follow him; but if Baal, then follow him." And the people did not answer him a word. (1 Kgs 18:20–21 ESV)

> Then the fire of the Lord fell and consumed the burnt offering and the wood and the stones and the dust, and licked up the water that was in the trench. And when all the people saw it, they fell on their faces and said, "The Lord, he is God; the Lord, he is God." (1 Kgs 18:38–40 ESV)

The people of Israel at this time of their history wanted to combine the worship of YAHWEH with the worship of Baal. While they wanted to enjoy the pleasurable nature of Baal worship, they did not want to break their past—that is, the worship of the Lord. They were, therefore, confronted with the challenge thrown in by Elijah, and they responded that YAHWEH is God.

Those endowed with the gift of exhortation are also able to rebuke others when they sin. To rebuke here means to discipline or reprimand. The prophet Nathan rebuked David in a wise way, which demonstrated the gift of exhortation. David had gone in for Uriah's wife and killed him too. The sin was known to people but David thought he had covered it until Nathan came to rebuke him:

> Then Nathan said to David, "You are the man! This is what the Lord, the God of Israel, says: 'I anointed you king over Israel, and I delivered you from the hand of Saul. I gave your master's house to you, and your master's wives into your arms. I gave you the house of Israel and Judah. And if all this had been too little, I would have given you even more. Why did you despise the word

of the Lord by doing what is evil in his eyes? You struck down Uriah the Hittite with the sword and took his wife to be your own. You killed him with the sword of the Ammonites. Now, therefore, the sword will never depart from your house, because you despised me and took the wife of Uriah the Hittite to be your own.' This is what the Lord says: 'Out of your own household I am going to bring calamity upon you. Before your very eyes I will take your wives and give them to one who is close to you, and he will lie with your wives in broad daylight. You did it in secret, but I will do this thing in broad daylight before all Israel.'" (2 Sam 12:7–12 NIV)

Paul had to rebuke a young man who was having sexual relations with his stepmother. The rebuke was very strong:

> Even though I am not with you in person, I am with you in the Spirit. And as though I were there, I have already passed judgment on this man in the name of the Lord Jesus. You must call a meeting of the church. I will be present with you in spirit, and so will the power of our Lord Jesus. Then you must throw this man out and hand him over to Satan so that his sinful nature will be destroyed and he himself will be saved on the day the Lord returns. (1 Cor 5:3–5 NLT)

Paul authorized the leaders of the church to minister disciplinary measures on his behalf, under the power of our Lord Jesus Christ. This means the authority to administer discipline is derived from our Lord Jesus, hence, it should be done in his name and honor. The whole church was to meet and minister this discipline to the person. The gift will allow the prophet not to overlook sin but discipline people with the love of God.

Paul was not one of the original twelve apostles chosen by Jesus, but when Peter was wrong, he rebuked him to the face:

> But when Peter came to Antioch, I had to oppose him to his face, for what he did was very wrong. When he first arrived, he ate with the Gentile Christians, who were not circumcised. But afterward, when some friends of James came, Peter wouldn't eat with the Gentiles anymore. He was afraid of criticism from these people who insisted on the necessity of circumcision. As a result, other Jewish Christians followed Peter's hypocrisy, and even Barnabas was led astray by their hypocrisy. When I saw that they were not following the truth of the gospel message, I said to Peter in front of all the others, "Since you, a Jew by birth,

have discarded the Jewish laws and are living like a Gentile, why are you now trying to make these Gentiles follow the Jewish traditions?" (Gal 2:11–14 NLT)

Paul made Peter aware that he was wrong by openly opposing him, and rebuking him. It is quite interesting that when Paul was talking about, perhaps, a relatively new believer, who had sinned, he did not mention his name in both 1 and 2 Corinthians, but mentioned the name of Peter in this public rebuke. He addressed Peter personally. Paul mentioned this to the church publicly because he thought the attitude of Peter as a mature Christian had caused others to shiver in their faith. Whatever Christians do must lead to edification. Sometimes, it is good to show mercy and other times it is good to rebuke. Both are aspects of exhortation.

The gift also encourages the weaker brethren. A person with the gift of exhortation ministers to people who are going through life's challenges in such a way that brings encouragement to them. They know how to make the message acceptable. They can also appeal to some people to encourage others. Paul encourages the church in Corinth to accept a person who has sinned and had repented:

> Now if anyone has caused pain, he has caused it not to me, but in some measure—not to put it too severely—to all of you. For such a one, this punishment by the majority is enough, so you should rather turn to forgive and comfort him, or he may be overwhelmed by excessive sorrow. So I beg you to reaffirm your love for him. For this is why I wrote, that I might test you and know whether you are obedient in everything. Anyone whom you forgive, I also forgive. What I have forgiven, if I have forgiven anything, has been for your sake in the presence of Christ, so that we would not be outwitted by Satan; for we are not ignorant of his designs. (2 Cor 2:5–11 ESV)

Here, Paul might be talking about the man who committed incest with the stepmother, his father's wife, in 1 Cor 5. In 1 Cor 5, it was a very serious incident. The brother might have repented and Paul wanted the church to forgive him. Paul does not mention his name to leave a bad legacy in the letter. He informs the church that although the brother hurt the people even more than he hurt Paul, the punishment given to him was enough. Thus, the church must receive him so that the devil does not take the upper hand. This was the gift of exhortation at work.

People with the gift of exhortation are very good fund-raisers and preachers who can motivate people to action. People are encouraged and challenged by their ministrations. It is one of the gifts associated with prophets (and evangelists). The gift of exhortation is good for the prophet in his operations.

THE GIFT OF MUSIC

Music is considered as a spiritual gift. When Paul was admonishing the church in Corinth on how to exercise spiritual gifts when they come together, he mentioned hymns as one of them. "How is it then, brethren? Whenever you come together, each of you has a psalm, has a teaching, has a tongue, has a revelation, has an interpretation. Let all things be done for edification" (1 Cor 14:26 NKJV).

In Eph 5:18–21, Paul associated music with the filling of the Spirit, "And do not be drunk with wine, in which is dissipation; but be filled with the Spirit, speaking to one another in psalms and hymns and spiritual songs, singing and making melody in your heart to the Lord, giving thanks always for all things to God the Father in the name of our Lord Jesus Christ, submitting to one another in the fear of God" (NKJV; cf. Col 3:16). Here, music is associated with the filling of the Spirit; it can therefore be considered as a gift from the Spirit.

The gift of music wields the ability to articulate one's love to the Lord. Music is one of the things that is common in all churches. Many churches begin service with songs, pray with songs, praise the Lord with songs, take offertory with songs, preach with musical interludes, and close with songs. Thus, music becomes very important in Christian worship. The Lord will never give an assignment without giving the necessary equipment. Therefore, he bestows the gift of music to people for the benefit of the kingdom.

The purpose of this gift is for the Lord to provide the church with songs. Paul shows that there are different types of songs—psalms, hymns and spiritual songs. "Let the word of Christ dwell in you richly in all wisdom, teaching and admonishing one another in psalms and hymns and spiritual songs, singing with grace in your hearts to the Lord" (Col 3:16 NKJV; cf. Eph 5:19). Here too, songs are linked with teaching the word of God. Thus, one of the best ways of teaching people the word of God is to put it in songs.

Psalms may simply refer to the book of Psalms in the Bible, which tells us about the story of God from different perspectives. The Israelites used it a lot during temple worship, during the synagogue worship, and the time of our Lord Jesus Christ and the apostles. Throughout church history, Christians continue to make music out of psalms with modern lyrics to suit various generations.

A hymn is a well-constructed poem that conveys developed statements of objective Christian belief or God and expressed in metered stanzas. Hymns instruct Christians about matters of faith and also provide objective doctrinal teaching. By virtue of stanzas, a hymn is capable of presenting a developed biblical teaching or theological truth. Some hymns encourage, convict and inspire people. Others become means of revelation, helping worshippers respond to the call of God in various ways.

Spiritual songs are the songs that are received through the immediacy of the Holy Spirit. The song can be a hymn, a canticle,[5] or a chorus. The Holy Spirit does this as a form of new wine to nourish his church.[6]

Since every generation has its culture and challenges, the Lord grants this gift for the church to have songs that relate to the challenges of the periods.

Furthermore, the Lord grants this gift to the church to raise people who can play instruments in worship. In the Old Testament, David who was endowed with this grace had to play to cast out evil spirits:

> Then Samuel took the horn of oil and anointed him in the midst of his brothers; and the Spirit of the Lord came upon David from that day forward. So Samuel arose and went to Ramah. But the Spirit of the Lord departed from Saul, and a distressing spirit from the Lord troubled him. And Saul's servants said to him, "Surely, a distressing spirit from God is troubling you. Let our master now command your servants, who are before you, to seek out a man who is a skillful player on the harp. And it shall be that he will play it with his hand when the distressing spirit from God is upon you, and you shall be well." So Saul said to his servants, "Provide me now a man who can play well, and

---

5. Canticles are the songs in the Bible apart from those in the book of Psalms. These include songs in the following passages: Exod 15:1–18, 21; 1 Sam 2:1–10; Isa 26:9–21; Hab 3:2–19; Luke 1:46–55, 68–79; Luke 2:29–32. They are similar to the Psalms in structure. They tell the story of God's deliverance. They connect God's praise with His miraculous acts. These are often chanted by the Roman Catholics, Eastern Orthodox Churches, Anglicans, and Lutherans. Spiritual songs may include these or any other scripture.

6. Onyinah, *Understanding Worship*, 138–52.

bring him to me." Then one of the servants answered and said, "Look, I have seen a son of Jesse the Bethlehemite, who is skillful in playing, a mighty man of valor, a man of war, prudent in speech, and a handsome person; and the Lord is with him." Therefore Saul sent messengers to Jesse, and said, "Send me your son David, who is with the sheep." And Jesse took a donkey loaded with bread, a skin of wine, and a young goat, and sent them by his son David to Saul. So David came to Saul and stood before him. And he loved him greatly, and he became his Armor bearer. Then Saul sent to Jesse, saying, "Please let David stand before me, for he has found favor in my sight." And so it was, whenever the spirit from God was upon Saul, that David would take a harp and play it with his hand. Then Saul would become refreshed and well, and the distressing spirit would depart from him. (1 Sam 16:13–23 NKJV)

Note that the Spirit of God came upon David before he could play to have the evil spirit departing from Saul. Thus, if even the playing of the harp was a talent, the Lord strengthened it with the pouring of his Spirit on David. The gift is also one of the provisions that the Lord has made for the church to make new instruments.

We can have people who are well trained to write music, sing songs, play instruments and manufacture new musical instruments, but those who are gifted in these and are trained will do better and work with joy than those who have just learned them.

The person who is gifted with music loves singing and finds it easy to learn a song. If this sort of person is a member of a Pentecostal church, he can lead the church in singing choruses without running out of songs. He brings a revival through his song leading. He can lead a choir, teach songs, and lead church worship with inspiration.

The Holy Spirit can inspire a Christian who is gifted with prophecy and music to receive a new song. He does this with ease because the inspiration makes it flow naturally without much of human efforts. A person who is not gifted can write a song but this may take him days and weeks. The one with the gift sings, receives or writes with ease. I was really inspired to receive and write the following song while I was having my morning devotion. Once the song dropped, I could not help but sing and write:

1. He who has called you is the faithful One,

He goes before you, orders your steps.

He will never leave his own people,

to suffer loss.

He will protect you, take care of you.

He who has called you is the Strong Tower.

Do not fear him who is in the world.

The mountains shall be brought low before you.

The crooked shall be made straight before you.

All shall see the glory of the Lord

2. He who has loved you, Unfailing One

He goes ahead of you, prepare the way

Defeat is not seen in his own if they,

look up to Him

He will guide them, and show them the way

Rock of Ages is He in whom you hide

Nothing can hurt you or destroy you

All strongholds shall be pulled down before you

All captives shall be set free before you

The name of God shall be glorified

3. He who has sent you, the Son of God

Always available, to show the way

Victory is assured for you in his name,

when you call him

He will provide you with all your needs.

The Spiritual Rock is that which follows you

You shall lack nothing on your journey

You will drink from Him the living water

You will be fed by Him Mana from above

Lord Jesus Christ shall be lifted up

4. He who is with you, Unchanging One

He knows the future, past and present

He is never taken by surprises,

ready to help.

He assures you his ever presence

He who is with you is the Ageless One

Do not fear him who roars like lion

Breaking chains and shackles that bind people

Setting at liberty those who are oppressed

The Lord Jesus shall be glorified

5. He who has promised, the Mighty One

He carries His people on eagle's wings

He shows strength with His arms to His own in, generations

He puts down the mighty from their thrones

He who has promised is the Mighty Rock

You shall tread on serpents and scorpions

Satan falls down like lighten from heaven

Demons flee at the mention of His name

All shall see the power of the Lord.

This song shows the impact of inspiration on a person. Inspiration makes whatever you are doing easy. The Spirit just flows without hindrance.

The gift of music works with other gifts. It may work with the gift of craftsmanship and the gift of prophecy. For example, the Old Testament mentions the gift of craftsmanship:

> Then the Lord said to Moses, "See, I have chosen Bezalel son of Uri, the son of Hur, of the tribe of Judah, *and I have filled him with the Spirit of God, with skill, ability and knowledge in all kinds of crafts*—to make artistic designs for work in gold, silver and bronze, to cut and set stones, to work in wood, and to engage in all kinds of craftsmanship. Moreover, I have appointed

Oholiab son of Ahisamach, of the tribe of Dan, to help him. Also I have given skill to all the craftsmen to make everything I have commanded you." (Exod 31:1–6 NIV, italics mine)

Take notice here that the Lord filled him "with the Spirit of God." It was the Spirit who gave him the ability, making it a gift from the Spirit. The one who exercises the gift of music and possesses the gift of craftsmanship can manufacture a new musical instrument. In the Old Testament, the Lord bestowed these gifts on people to use in serving him in various areas. David for example could sing and play musical instruments (1 Chr 21:1–7; 23:5).

When the Israelites crossed the Red Sea, Moses and Miriam, who were gifted with music and prophecy, were able to write new songs to the praise of God. The miracle brought great revival to the people; the songs and the accompanying jubilation were the evidence:

> Then Moses and the Israelites sang this song to the Lord:
>
> "I will sing to the Lord,
>
> for he is highly exalted.
>
> The horse and its rider
>
> he has hurled into the sea.
>
> The Lord is my strength and my song;
>
> he has become my salvation.
>
> He is my God, and I will praise him,
>
> my father's God, and I will exalt him." (Exod 15:1–2 NIV)

> Then Miriam the prophetess, Aaron's sister, took a tambourine in her hand, and all the women followed her, with tambourines and dancing. Miriam sang to them:
>
> "Sing to the Lord,
>
> for he is highly exalted.
>
> The horse and its rider
>
> he has hurled into the sea." (Exod 15:20–21 NIV)

It can also be seen that when Deborah and Barak defeated a Canaanite king, they sang to celebrate the victory. It was Deborah the prophetess who led this celebration to exalt the Lord:

> On that day Deborah and Barak son of Abinoam sang this song:
>
> "When the princes in Israel take the lead,
>
> when the people willingly offer themselves—
>
> praise the Lord! Hear this, you kings! Listen, you rulers!
>
> I will sing to the Lord, I will sing;
>
> I will make music to the Lord, the God of Israel." (Judg 5:1–3 NIV)

This is an indication that the gift brings about jubilation in the Lord. It helps God's people to manifest their joy in the Lord through appellations. The gift also helps the people of God to teach, memorize, and keep his word in our hearts. Before the death of Moses, the Lord instructed him to restate the law and statutes to the Israelites. He also told him to write the laws in songs and sing for them to remember to obey the Lord:

> Now write down for yourselves this song and teach it to the Israelites and have them sing it, so that it may be a witness for me against them. (Deut 31:19 NIV)
>
> And Moses recited the words of this song from beginning to end in the hearing of the whole assembly of Israel. (Deut 31:30 NIV)
>
> Moses came and recited all the words of this song in the hearing of the people, he and Joshua the son of Nun. And when Moses had finished speaking all these words to all Israel, he said to them, "Take to heart all the words by which I am warning you today, that you may command them to your children, that they may be careful to do all the words of this law. For it is no empty word for you, but your very life, and by this word you shall live long in the land that you are going over the Jordan to possess." (Deut 32:44–47 ESV)

By this, the Lord had stated part of the purposes of the gift of music—it should be used to teach the word of God.

The gift of music reached its climax in the life of David. David wrote many of the psalms. He selected three musicians namely, Asaph, Heman and Jeduthun to organize and lead music in worship (1 Chr 25:1–7). These people and their families, who numbered 288, were trained and skilled in music with accompanying instruments. David also provided four thousand people to the praise of the Lord with musical instruments, "Four thousand [of the Levites] are to be gatekeepers and four thousand are to praise the Lord with the musical instruments I have provided for that purpose" (1 Chr 23:5 NIV). This is an indication of how music was important in worship in Israel. What needs to be noticed here is that music was associated with prophesying:

> David, together with the commanders of the army, set apart some of the sons of Asaph, Heman and Jeduthun *for the ministry of prophesying, accompanied by harps, lyres and cymbals.* Here is the list of the men who performed this service: From the sons of Asaph: Zaccur, Joseph, Nethaniah and Asarelah. The sons of Asaph were under the supervision of Asaph, *who prophesied under the king's supervision.* As for Jeduthun, from his sons: Gedaliah, Zeri, Jeshaiah, Shimei, Hashabiah and Mattithiah, six in all, under the supervision of their father Jeduthun, *who prophesied, using the harp in thanking and praising the Lord.* As for Heman, from his sons: Bukkiah, Mattaniah, Uzziel, Shubael and Jerimoth; Hananiah, Hanani, Eliathah, Giddalti and Romamti-Ezer; Joshbekashah, Mallothi, Hothir and Mahazioth. *All these were sons of Heman the king's seer.* They were given him through the promises of God to exalt him. God gave Heman fourteen sons and three daughters. *All these men were under the supervision of their fathers for the music of the temple of the Lord, with cymbals, lyres and harps, for the ministry at the house of God. Asaph, Jeduthun and Heman were under the supervision of the king.* Along with their relatives—all of them trained and skilled in music for the Lord-they numbered 288. Young and old alike, teacher as well as student, cast lots for their duties. (1 Chr 25:1–8 NIV, italics mine)

Music and prophecy were very close. Most of the musicians were also people with the gift of prophecy. They received songs and they prophesied. Some of David's songs are very prophetic. For example, Psalm 22 is very prophetic: "My God, my God, why have you forsaken me? Why are you so far from saving me, so far from the words of my groaning? . . . All who see me mock me; they hurl insults, shaking their heads: 'He trusts in the Lord; let the Lord rescue him. Let him deliver him, since he delights in him'" (NIV). This psalm intertwines with the death of Jesus. Someone reading it would think that the writer was there when Jesus was being crucified.

The musicians were also trained. The fact that they were gifted did not take away training. Thus, people with gifts need to be trained. Some of the prophets were inspired through music. Elisha, for example, requested for a musician to play for him, and then as he played, the hand of the Lord came upon him and he prophesied (2 Kgs 3:15). Jesus and his disciples often sang. For example, after the Lord's Supper, Jesus and his disciples sang a hymn (Matt 26:30). Often during the Passover Feast, Pss 113–14 would be sung before the meal, and then Pss 115–18 after the meal. Some people think Jesus and his disciples sang Pss 115–18 or the Great *Hallel* which is Ps 136.[7]

The apostles and the New Testament church also sang during their time and encouraged believers to speak to one another in music and thank the Lord through songs. Paul and Silas were praying and singing hymns when the Lord delivered them from prison through the earthquake (Acts 16:25–27). Those with the gift cannot keep quiet. They sing to the Lord during all periods to remind them of the word of God.

The gift of music therefore helps in worship of the Lord. The congregational singing helps everybody to get involved in worship in a personal and intimate way. Accordingly, singing good songs will lead a Christian to growth and maturity in the Lord. The songs bring better knowledge and understanding of the word, hence, leading to an encounter with the Lord. The operation of the gift of music in the writing of songs reminds us of the word of God so that we shall be careful to obey him.

In sum, we have shown that to become a prophet is to have a composition of gifts including the word of knowledge, the word of wisdom, discerning of spirits, speaking in varieties of tongues and interpretations, music, exhortation, teaching, and prophecy. One may not have all of these but the word of knowledge, the word of wisdom, discerning of spirit and prophecy are essential. These basic gifts will make the prophet's ministration sharper and reliable.

What does the prophet do? In the next part, we focus on the functions of the Old Testament prophet.

---

7. Adams, "What Hymn Did Jesus Sing."

PART 3

The Functions of the Prophet in the Old Testament

We have established the fact that a number of gifts come together to constitute a prophet who is the mouthpiece of God. He is to speak what God says. The Old Testament prophets were the mouthpiece of God, declaring his will primarily to the nation Israel and to the rest of the world. How did they execute this divine assignment? Part 3, which comprises three chapters, discusses the functions of the prophet, all linked together. Chapter 7 shows how the prophet becomes the interpreter of the covenant of God; chapter 8 deals with the prophet as the person who understands the times and speaks into it; and then chapter 9 handles the spiritual authority of the prophet.

Chapter 7

The Man of God's Word

ONE OF THE KEY messages that you need to understand is that the prophets were common people just as we are. They were living in society and following trends of their time. What James said in the New Testament about Elijah is relevant here, "Elijah was a man just like us. He prayed earnestly that it would not rain, and it did not rain on the land for three and a half years. Again he prayed, and the heavens gave rain, and the earth produced its crops" (Jas 5:17–18 NIV). Nevertheless, it must also be understood that the Lord chose the prophets as special vessels and used them to accomplish his purpose in their generations. These prophets were living in the communities as normal people and then speaking to issues such as those presented below.

REMINDS ISRAEL OF THE TERMS OF GOD'S COVENANTS

The basis of the Old Testament prophecies was the covenant relationship between the Lord and Israel. The prophetic traditions were all based on this relationship. God made a covenant with Abraham that he would bless him to become a great nation and also grant him a land (Gen 12:1–3; cf. 15:1–21). The covenant started with a promise in Gen 12 and was executed as a covenant in Gen 15:

> Now the Lord said to Abram, "Go from your country and your kindred and your father's house to the land that I will show you.

> And I will make of you a great nation, and I will bless you and make your name great, so that you will be a blessing. I will bless those who bless you, and him who dishonors you I will curse, and in you all the families of the earth shall be blessed." (Gen 12:1–3 ESV)

> On that day the Lord made a covenant with Abram, saying, "To your offspring I give this land, from the river of Egypt to the great river, the river Euphrates, the land of the Kenites, the Kenizzites, the Kadmonites, the Hittites, the Perizzites, the Rephaim, the Amorites, the Canaanites, the Girgashites and the Jebusites." (Gen 15:18–21 ESV)

This covenant was unconditional. This means there was nothing attached to the covenant; it was based on the love and sovereignty of God. The first part of the covenant was fulfilled in the mission of Moses, when the Lord delivered his people from Egypt. On Mount Sinai, God made a covenant with Israel, an extension of what he made with Abraham:

> You yourselves have seen what I did to the Egyptians, and how I bore you on eagles' wings and brought you to myself. Now therefore, if you will indeed obey my voice and keep my covenant, you shall be my treasured possession among all peoples, for all the earth is mine; and you shall be to me a kingdom of priests and a holy nation. (Exod 19:4–6 ESV)

In this covenant, the Lord promised to set Israel aside as his treasured people, a kingdom of priests and a holy nation. The nation would collectively be considered as a royal and priestly nation; a dynasty of priests with each citizen demonstrating the attributes of a king and priest. This means Israel as a nation was going to be set aside to preserve the knowledge and worship of God for the world. The Lord made Israel aware that this was purely an act of grace, and for the benefit of the world. This is emphasized in the phrase, "for the world is mine and all that is in it" (Ps 50:12). The covenant, however, was based on Israel's obedience to the voice of God: "If you will indeed obey my voice . . . " (Exod 19:4; cf. Josh 1:2–9; 21:43; 1 Kgs 4:20–21; Isa 8:5–8). This extension of the covenant was conditional; the blessing would follow if only Israel obeyed. The Lord accordingly gave Israel his commandment—the torah—and sealed the covenant with blood (Exod 24:1–9).

God's voice had been given to Israel in the form of the law, yet, as time went by, the people of Israel disobeyed the law.

The country was united until it was divided into two countries, after the reign of Solomon, and just at the beginning of the reign of Rehoboam (1 Kgs 12:16–24). The northern kingdom maintained the name Israel, but was sometimes called Samaria or Ephraim, and the southern kingdom was referred to as Judah or the House of David. Jerusalem continued to be the capital of Judah with the temple in Jerusalem. For political reasons, that is, in order that those in the northern kingdom would not go to worship in Jerusalem, and be influenced by the Davidic line's kings, the first king of the north, Jeroboam set his own altars at Bethel and Dan for the purpose of worship (1 Kgs 12:25–33). Thus, those in the northern kingdom would go to either Bethel or Dan to worship. This was against the law that the Lord gave to Israel. This action was referred to as idolatry and prostitution by the prophets.[1]

This implies that from the beginning of the division of the kingdom, the northern kingdom (Israel) rejected the law. Judah, the southern kingdom too kept on disobeying the contents. Some of the kings openly got into idol worship. Therefore, the Lord raised the prophets to remind the people of Israel about the terms of the covenant, and call them to repentance. The prophets kept on reminding them that obedience would lead to blessing, while disobedience would bring about punishment and even lead to captivity. This background is essential for understanding the messages of the prophets. Let us read some of the prophetic utterances on the terms of the covenant:

> Put the trumpet to your lips! An eagle is over the house of the Lord because the people have broken my covenant and rebelled against my law. Israel cries out to me, "O our God, we acknowledge you!" (Hos 8:1–2 NIV)

> The Lord said to me, "Proclaim all these words in the towns of Judah and in the streets of Jerusalem: 'Listen to the terms of this covenant and follow them. From the time I brought your forefathers up from Egypt until today, I warned them again and again, saying, "Obey me." But they did not listen or pay attention; instead, they followed the stubbornness of their evil hearts. So I brought on them all the curses of the covenant I had commanded them to follow but that they did not keep.'" Then the

---

1. It was this act of idolatry that "a man of God came from Judah by the word of the Lord" to prophesy against (1 Kgs 13:1 ESV). This was the prophet whom King Jeroboam attempted to kill and his hand became still. It was this prophet who was later deceived by an older prophet whose deception caused his death (1 Kgs 13:1–32).

Lord said to me, "There is a conspiracy among the people of Judah and those who live in Jerusalem. They have returned to the sins of their forefathers, who refused to listen to my words. They have followed other gods to serve them. Both the house of Israel and the house of Judah have broken the covenant I made with their forefathers." (Jer 11:6–10 NIV)

But they refused to pay attention; stubbornly they turned their backs and stopped up their ears. They made their hearts as hard as flint and would not listen to the law or to the words that the Lord Almighty had sent by his Spirit through the earlier prophets. So the Lord Almighty was very angry. "When I called, they did not listen; so when they called, I would not listen," says the Lord Almighty. "I scattered them with a whirlwind among all the nations, where they were strangers. The land was left so desolate behind them that no one could come or go. This is how they made the pleasant land desolate." (Zech 7:11–14 NIV)

Who handed Jacob over to become loot, and Israel to the plunderers? Was it not the Lord, against whom we have sinned? For they would not follow his ways; they did not obey his law. So he poured out on them his burning anger, the violence of war. It enveloped them in flames, yet they did not understand; it consumed them, but they did not take it to heart. (Isa 42:24–25 NIV)

What the Lord was demanding from them through the prophets was repentance. For example, the Lord spoke through Ezekiel, "Therefore say to the house of Israel, 'This is what the Sovereign Lord says: Repent! Turn from your idols and renounce all your detestable practices!'" (Ezek 14:6 NIV). Isaiah declared, "This is what the Sovereign Lord, the Holy One of Israel, says: 'In repentance and rest is your salvation, in quietness and trust is your strength, but you would have none of it. You said, "No, we will flee on horses." Therefore you will flee! You said, "We will ride off on swift horses." Therefore your pursuers will be swift!'" (Isa 30:15–16 NIV)

Understanding the background to the prophets' messages would help us to understand the gift and the ministration of the prophets. The prophets reminded Israel of the contents of the law when the people had closed their eyes to it.

EXPLAINS THE PRINCIPLES UNDERLYING THE LAW OF GOD

The Lord gave Israel his commandment—the law, the torah (Exod 20). Israelites' devoutness, therefore, was rooted strongly in the torah and the land, and later the temple. The essence of the temple activities and the center of the Jewish piety was the torah.[2] The torah is basically the Pentateuch, the five books of Moses, which is supposed to be the religious teaching or doctrines of Israel. However, the rabbi in the attempt to provide an oral interpretation, that is, a commentary, on the torah for daily guidelines, added more to the torah. The collection of these rabbinic writings, consisting of the Mishnah (text) and the Gemara (commentary), which constitute the basis of religious authority in Judaism, is called the Talmud. The oral interpretations were many, detailed and complicated. Donald Kraybill observes that "pious Jews could discover whether it was lawful to eat an egg laid on Sabbath."[3]

Many times, the people followed the letter of the law of God and changed the real intention of God concerning the law. The prophet would then prophesy to explain the principles underlying the law. For example, Amos had to prophesy to show the people that religious rituals, such as sacrifice and feasts without good treatment of fellow human beings are disgusting to God; God would not listen to such prayers (e.g., Amos 5:21–25):

> I hate, I despise your religious feasts; I cannot stand your assemblies. Even though you bring me burnt offerings and grain offerings, I will not accept them. Though you bring choice fellowship offerings, I will have no regard for them. Away with the noise of your songs! I will not listen to the music of your harps. But let justice roll on like a river, righteousness like a never-failing stream! Did you bring me sacrifices and offerings forty years in the desert, O house of Israel? (NIV)

Ezekiel had to correct the people's wrong notion that they were suffering because of their fathers' sins, and that the curses of the fathers follow them (cf. Exod 20:6). Read Ezekiel's explanation:

> What do you people mean by quoting this proverb about the land of Israel: "The fathers eat sour grapes, and the children's

---

2. Guignebert, *Jewish World*, 62–67.
3. Kraybill, *Upside-Down Kingdom*, 66.

teeth are set on edge"? "As surely as I live, declares the Sovereign Lord, you will no longer quote this proverb in Israel. For every living soul belongs to me, the father as well as the son—both alike belong to me. The soul who sins is the one who will die." (Ezek 18:2–4 NIV)

> He withholds his hand from sin and takes no usury or excessive interest. He keeps my laws and follows my decrees. He will not die for his father's sin; he will surely live. But his father will die for his own sin, because he practiced extortion, robbed his brother and did what was wrong among his people. (Ezek 18:17–18 NIV)

The prophets condemned sin and demanded justice for the poor instead of religious practices:

> For three sins of Israel, even for four, I will not turn back [my wrath]. They sell the righteous for silver, and the needy for a pair of sandals. They trample on the heads of the poor as upon the dust of the ground and deny justice to the oppressed. Father and son use the same girl and so profane my holy name. They lie down beside every altar on garments taken in pledge. In the house of their god they drink wine taken as fines. (Amos 2:6–8 NIV)

> Will not all of them taunt him with ridicule and scorn, saying, "Woe to him who piles up stolen goods and makes himself wealthy by extortion! How long must this go on?" Will not your debtors suddenly arise? Will they not wake up and make you tremble? Then you will become their victim. (Hab 2:6–7 NIV)

The prophets declared to the people that without justice and obedience to the law of God, He would not accept the religious practices of the people:

> "The multitude of your sacrifices—what are they to me?" says the Lord. "I have more than enough of burnt offerings of rams and the fat of fattened animals; I have no pleasure in the blood of bulls and lambs and goats. When you come to appear before me, who has asked this of you, this trampling of my courts? Stop bringing meaningless offerings! Your incense is detestable to me. New Moons, Sabbaths and convocations—I cannot bear your evil assemblies. Your New Moon festivals and your appointed feasts my soul hates. They have become a burden to me; I am weary of bearing them. When you spread out your hands

in prayer, I will hide my eyes from you; even if you offer many prayers, I will not listen. Your hands are full of blood; wash and make yourselves clean. Take your evil deeds out of my sight! Stop doing wrong, learn to do right! Seek justice, encourage the oppressed. Defend the cause of the fatherless, plead the case of the widow." (Isa 1:11–17 NIV)

The prophets taught the people to understand the meaning of God's law. People often tend to major on the outward side of the law of God instead of the core. This has been the trend in all generations. The prophets taught the people to understand the spirit of the law instead of the periphery.

SPEAKS ON CONTEMPORARY ISSUES

Although God had revealed his mind to the people in the written word through Moses, there were emerging issues on a day-to-day basis that were not directly in the written word. The primary task of the prophets was to bring the mind of God to their own generation. It was not really their task to predict the future, although this occurred as they discharged their duty of bringing the mind of God to the people of their generation. God was using the prophets to give them what needed to be done in their practical life challenges. An example of this is an issue cited earlier which Deborah spoke into. This was about a Canaanite king, called Jabin who was attacking Israel through his commander Sisera. The Lord through the prophetess revealed the victory Israel could have if they obeyed the Lord's leading (Judg 4:4–10, 17–22). Another example is the choice of a king, which Israel demanded, and Samuel had to battle with it (1 Sam 8).

Besides, there are indications in the Old Testament that in many cases, people consulted the prophets for guidance. These include the consultation of Saul from Samuel concerning the whereabouts of a missing donkey, and the consultation of Jeroboam's wife from Prophet Ahijah, which ended in the prediction of the death of the sick child (1 Kgs 14:1–18). Nevertheless, in all these cases, if pressed hard, it is found out that the issues were concerning the people of God, what they needed to do, and God's plan for them.

Chapter 8

Access to the Council of God

CHAPTER 8 CONTINUES WITH the functions of the prophets. Here, the prophet will be seen as the man who is able to know and explain the mind of God to people.

OFFERS SPIRITUAL GUIDANCE TO POLITICAL LEADERS

The prophets often spoke to the spiritual and political leaders of God's people. They were God's voice offering guidance to the leadership and demanding that they live and rule more in line with God's word. They spoke for God concerning situations, conditions and whatever God wanted to tell the people in certain moments of history.

During the period of King Ahaz of Judah, he left the God of his ancestors, Jehovah God, and went after the Canaanite gods. His intent was to strengthen his kingdom. Knowing that the Assyrians and the neighboring countries had many gods, he thought he needed more gods to fortify his battlefront. Besides, Syria and the northern kingdom of Israel had decided to depose King Ahaz of Judah. The king was in a very terrible condition. The Lord sent Isaiah to go and assure Ahaz of God's love to David that he would protect Judah and the throne of David (Isa 7:3–14). He said that the kings of Syria and Israel appear like firebrand. Why? They were powerful? They had overcome Judah before. They were more in numbers than Judah. They had planned to depose the king of

Judah and replace him with the son of Tabeel (a stranger who did not come from the Davidic line). Yet, they would not succeed; they would die shortly. The fire has come to its end. Within sixty-five years, the northern Israel would cease to exist. Ahaz was encouraged to rely on God, since both Israel and Syria were relying on human kings and powers. Ahaz should have faith in Jehovah God. This was to provide spiritual guidance for the king and the nation but the king did not accept the message.

Elisha, for example, had to offer several guidance to King Joram of Israel (e.g., 2 Kgs 1:17; 3:1; 9:24). He would reveal the plan of the Arameans (Syrians) to the extent that the king of Aram thought his people were disclosing their plans to the Israelites. But they replied, "'None of us, my lord the king,'" said one of his officers, 'but Elisha, the prophet who is in Israel, tells the king of Israel the very words you speak in your bedroom'" (2 Kgs 6:12 NIV). King Jehoash of Israel had to call Elisha "my father": "Now Elisha was suffering from the illness from which he died. Jehoash king of Israel went down to see him and wept over him. 'My father! My father!' he cried. 'The chariots and horsemen of Israel!'" (2 Kgs 13:14 NIV). This shows the extent to which some of the kings respected the prophets as their spiritual guidance.

FORETELLS THE FUTURE

As has been shown earlier, the basic ministry of the prophet was to speak to current issues, but as they spoke to contemporary issues, future events were also revealed. For example, when King Ahaz, referred to above, failed to accept the message of the Lord through Isaiah to rely on him and not on Assyria and also failed to request for a sign, the Lord spoke to Isaiah that he would give the king a sign:

> Again the Lord spoke to Ahaz, "Ask the Lord your God for a sign, whether in the deepest depths or in the highest heights." But Ahaz said, "I will not ask; I will not put the Lord to the test." Then Isaiah said, "Hear now, you house of David! Is it not enough to try the patience of men? Will you try the patience of my God also? *Therefore the Lord himself will give you a sign: The virgin will be with child and will give birth to a son, and will call him Immanuel.* He will eat curds and honey when he knows enough to reject the wrong and choose the right. But before the boy knows enough to reject the wrong and choose the right, the land of the two kings you dread will be laid waste. The Lord will

bring on you and on your people and on the house of your father a time unlike any since Ephraim broke away from Judah—he will bring the king of Assyria." (Isa 7:10–17 NIV, italics mine)

The sign was the birth of a son. Isaiah boldly declared that a virgin would give birth to a child and he would be called Emmanuel, God with us. The use of the term "virgin" here has been a source of dispute among biblical scholars because of the Hebrew term used, *almah*, which can be translated as young woman, who is marriageable, as well as a virgin. However, this should not be a surprise at all, because our God is all-knowing God. The issue is that Prophet Isaiah used the word under the inspiration of the Holy Spirit for a dual purpose. Firstly, the Lord was giving a sign of a child to King Ahaz, during his lifetime. Isaiah was speaking into a contemporary issue. A sign was normally fulfilled within few years, since it was to strengthen a person's faith. Secondly, the Holy Spirit was also predicting the birth of the Messiah who would be born of a virgin. The prophet needed to use a term that would cover both purposes. Accordingly, he used the right term *almah*.[1]

Since Isaiah was speaking into a contemporary issue, the prophecy was fulfilled in the next chapter, Isaiah 8. The child who was to be born as a sign for Ahaz was born to Isaiah (Isa 8:3–4). This meant the young woman which Isaiah spoke about was his own wife. The name of the son born was Maher-Shalal-Hash-Baz, meaning "Quick to the Plunder, Swift to the Spoil." It denotes that Ahaz's enemies would be plundered and Judah would also suffer.

The second part of Isaiah's prophecy was fulfilled in the birth of our Lord Jesus Christ. The fact that Christ was born of a virgin is clear in the New Testament. Both Matthew and Luke use the Greek term *parthenos*, which is indisputably translated as a virgin (Matt 1:23; Luke 1:27, 34). Mary asked the angel Gabriel a question, "'How will this be . . . since I am a virgin?' . . . 'The Holy Spirit will come upon you and the power of the Most High will overshadow you, so the holy one to be born will be called the Son of God'" (Luke 1:34–35 NIV). Matthew clearly shows that the birth of Jesus was to fulfill the prophecy which Isaiah gave: "All this took place to fulfill what the Lord had said through the prophet: 'The virgin will be with child and will give birth to a son, and they will call

---

1. It could mean a young woman, in this case it was Isaiah's own wife, and then a virgin, who later was understood as Mary.

him Immanuel'—which means, 'God with us'" (Matt 1:22–23 NIV).[2] The birth of Jesus through a virgin was foretold by the prophet over 700 years before he was born. Yet Isaiah was speaking into a present-day issue. This shows the sovereignty of God over the world. He is completely in control and knows the end from the beginning.

Another example of speaking into contemporary issues, which hints about the future, is in the book of Amos. As Amos spoke about the evil that was going on in the land, he touched on the disaster that would befall the people in the future:

> Thus says the Lord: "For three transgressions of Israel, and for four, I will not revoke the punishment, because they sell the righteous for silver, and the needy for a pair of sandals—those who trample the head of the poor into the dust of the earth and turn aside the way of the afflicted; a man and his father go in to the same girl, so that my holy name is profaned; they lay themselves down beside every altar on garments taken in pledge, and in the house of their God they drink the wine of those who have been fined." (Amos 2:6–8 ESV)

> So I will make you groan like a wagon loaded down with sheaves of grain. Your fastest runners will not get away. The strongest among you will become weak. Even mighty warriors will be unable to save themselves. The archers will not stand their ground. The swiftest runners won't be fast enough to escape. Even those riding horses won't be able to save themselves. On that day the most courageous of your fighting men will drop their weapons and run for their lives, says the Lord. (Amos 2:13–16 ESV)

It is realized that while he was addressing the disobedience of the people, he also touched on the disaster of defeat that would follow their disobedience to the Lord.

Another prophet who is typical of touching the future as he speaks about the present is Jeremiah. Jeremiah spoke about the destruction of Jerusalem because of their disobedience (e.g., Jer 16, 20, 21; 29:17–19). However, he also predicted the return of the people of God and was so sure that he had to go and buy a land, signifying that they would return (Jer 25:8–14; 30:3, 11, 24; 31:13, 28; 32:6–15, 37–44).

The hope of the Messiah grew out of the failure of the monarchy (the united kingdom of Israel), the division of the nation, the degradation of the two nations, and their captivity. The prophets emphasized that the

---

2. For the full message of this, see Onyinah, *God with Us*.

disobedience of the covenanted people sent them into captivity (e.g., Isa 5:25; Jer 14:19; Ezek 5:14–15; cf. Dan 9:16). The bitter experience they encountered forced them to pray and rely on their God and out of that began to speak of the restoration of Israel as one nation and the establishment of the kingdom of God. Speaking into these, they foresaw that the beginning of the restoration and the coming of the kingdom of God were to begin with the coming of the Servant of the Lord, the Messiah, who would come from the Davidic line. He would be king over the two nations that have become one. On the one hand, as Clifford Hill, a British theologian and a prophet argues, the king the prophets spoke about was still in their "understanding simply a human being related to the household of David."[3] On the other hand too, the Messiah would be so powerful that he would not only be the king of Israel, but also a light for the nations (Isa 35:4–6; 42:6–9; 61:1). The mission of the newly established nation is to be the light to the Gentiles (Isa 49:6). Thus, the Messiah would bring salvation to the rest of the world, and become a king not only to Israel but the whole world.

Understanding that the prophets were speaking initially to their own situations will throw light on why the Lord sometimes used their situations to speak to the future. Daniel, for example, was praying for his nation, and yet the Lord revealed to him things that were going to take place in the future (Dan 9). The vocabularies of Daniel were limited to get the exact words to describe what was revealed to him but he could communicate the glimpse of what was going to take place in the future. For instance, Daniel could not speak of the computer, internet, mobile telephone, but he could tell us that knowledge would increase (Dan 12:4). From this perspective, then, we need not to take revelations verbatim as we see or read, we need to pray for divine understanding.

INTERPRETS THE SIGNS

One of the major ministries of the prophets was to interpret signs. A sign in the Bible is an event that has spiritual significance. A sign is not a parable but an event the people may know about, may be discussing, but its significance is not perceived until someone with prophetic insight interprets its meaning.[4] It could be natural events such as famine, drought,

---

3. Hill, *Prophecy, Past and Present*, 108.
4. Hill, *Prophecy Past and Present*, 79.

earthquakes, volcanic eruptions, an outbreak of disease, or something of human origins, such as economic problems, military defeats, fire outbreaks, or political situations.

For example, Jeremiah cited a drought that had come upon the land as the act of God as a result of his anger in the face of idolatry, which was considered spiritual prostitution; this he said was polluting the land:

> "If a man divorces his wife and she leaves him and marries another man, should he return to her again? Would not the land be completely defiled? But you have lived as a prostitute with many lovers—would you now return to me?" declares the Lord. "Look up to the barren heights and see. Is there any place where you have not been ravished? By the roadside you sat waiting for lovers, like a nomad in the desert. You have defiled the land with your prostitution and wickedness. Therefore the showers have been withheld, and no spring rains have fallen. Yet you have the brazen look of a prostitute; you refuse to blush with shame." (Jer 3:1–3)

Prophet Haggai gave the reason the people were experiencing economic hardship as living for themselves and leaving the work of God aside:

> You have planted much, but have harvested little. You eat, but never have enough. You drink, but never have your fill. You put on clothes, but are not warm. You earn wages, only to put them in a purse with holes in it." This is what the Lord Almighty says: "Give careful thought to your ways. Go up into the mountains and bring down timber and build the house, so that I may take pleasure in it and be honored," says the Lord. "You expected much, but see, it turned out to be little. What you brought home, I blew away. Why?" declares the Lord Almighty. "Because of my house, which remains a ruin, while each of you is busy with his own house. Therefore, because of you the heavens have withheld their dew and the earth its crops. I called for a drought on the fields and the mountains, on the grain, the new wine, the oil and whatever the ground produces, on men and cattle, and on the labor of your hands." (Hag 1:6–11 NIV)

This implies that for Haggai, the reason the people were experiencing little harvest, and their wages were not enough to feed them was that they were not doing the work of God.

In the New Testament, Jesus accused the religious leaders for failure to interpret the times: "He replied, 'When evening comes, you say, "It will be fair weather, for the sky is red," and in the morning, "Today it will be stormy, for the sky is red and overcast." You know how to interpret the appearance of the sky, but you cannot interpret the signs of the times'" (Matt 16:2–4 NIV). Jesus expected that the religious leaders should be able to use their knowledge of the word of God to interpret the period of the Messiah. The prophets were able to interpret the times.

Chapter 9

The Man with the Presence of God

CHAPTER 9 ENDS THE discussion on the functions of the prophets. Here, the prophet is presented as the one who carries the Spirit of God.

CARRIES THE AUTHORITY OF GOD

The prophets were recognized as carrying the presence of God, and as such, his authority. Through them, the presence of God could be brought upon the nations. They had faith in the Lord in such a way that the nation could have confidence in what they said. However, with exception of Elijah and Elisha, and possibly Isaiah, the rest of the prophets are not seen in the Old Testament as performing miracles such as healing. The canonical prophets (the writing ones) are not seen as healing the sick. However, the Lord fulfilled whatever they said. Their recognition lay in bringing the word of God to the people. For example, Isaiah brought the word of God to Hezekiah that led to his healing (Isa 38:1–22). This means the responsibility of the prophet was not to break the laws of nature but to tell people what God is doing at a point in time. A miracle is often the outcome of things that go contrary to nature, such as Elijah and Elisha raising the dead. Yet, in the cause of fulfilling the prophetic mandate, a miracle may take place, such as Elisha's prayer to cause blindness to the Syrians who wanted to arrest him (2 Kgs 18:8–23).

Apart from Moses, Deborah, and Samuel, the prophets were not specifically leaders. Hill observes, "They carried no responsibility for the Temple, for worship, for the institutional side of religion."[1] They had no political power, no party following, no priestly or pastoral function. "They were not involved in the commercial life of the nation, neither were they rulers of men. They were simply servants of the living God whose task was to declare what he was saying to the people."[2]

THE MAN OF PRAYER

It must also be understood that in the Old Testament, the people were not often gathering for church services, as we do in our day for prayer, to make room for the prophets to speak. Rather the prophets were individuals whose lifestyles were engrossed in prayer. Prayer became the main point of their communication with God. As the Lord gave them the messages, they carried their messages along to the people. Sometimes they would go to where people are and speak, write, or dictate for others to write and read to those concerned, especially the leaders (Jer 17:19–21; 29:1–3; 36:1–2; 45:1–2; Isa 7:3–4).

Their messages were often born out of prayers. They included all types of prayers, such as deepening their relationship with the Lord, guidance, offering thanksgiving and worship, asking for divine protection, interceding for the people, and praying for the nation (e.g., 2 Kgs 19:1–7; Isa 33:2–3; 2 Chr 32:20–23; Isa 62:1; 1 Sam 7:8–9). These types of prayers could be associated with majority of the prophets as we examine their lives. Daniel, for example, was often seen praying for guidance (Dan 2:17–19), for protection (Dan 6:10–11), and interceding for the people (e.g., Dan 9). His prayer of intercession gives a clue of his prayer pattern:

- Worship: "O Lord, you are a great and awesome God! You always fulfill your covenant and keep your promises of unfailing love to those who love you and obey your commands" (9:4 NLT).
- Confession: "But we have sinned and done wrong. We have rebelled against you and scorned your commands and regulations" (9:5–17 NLT).
- Petition: "O our God, hear your servant's prayer! Listen as I plead. For your own sake, Lord, smile again on your desolate sanctuary . . .

---

1. Clifford Hill, *Prophecy Past and Present*, 59
2. Clifford Hill, *Prophecy Past and Present*, 59–60

We make this plea, not because we deserve help, but because of your mercy" (9:17–18 NLT).

Samuel was seen interceding for the people (1 Sam 7:5–6). He considered it a sin not to pray for the people and teach them, "As for me, far be it from me that I should sin against the Lord by failing to pray for you. And I will teach you the way that is good and right" (1 Sam 12:23–24 NIV).

Isaiah, a man of prayer (Isa 6), was often consulted to seek God's mind for the people. Accordingly, he prayed with and for the people (2 Kgs 19:1–2, 5–7; 2 Chr 32:20).

Jeremiah's ministry will be used as a case study to further throw light on the prayer ministry of the prophets, since it shows both his glorious and dark sides. Let us begin by examining Jeremiah's prayer of deepening his relationship with the Lord and for protection:

> A glorious throne, exalted from the beginning, is the place of our sanctuary. O Lord, the hope of Israel, all who forsake you will be put to shame. Those who turn away from you will be written in the dust because they have forsaken the Lord, the spring of living water. Heal me, O Lord, and I will be healed; save me and I will be saved, for you are the one I praise. They keep saying to me, "Where is the word of the Lord? Let it now be fulfilled!" I have not run away from being your shepherd; you know I have not desired the day of despair. What passes my lips is open before you. Do not be a terror to me; Let my persecutors be put to shame, but keep me from shame; let them be terrified, but keep me from terror. Bring on them the day of disaster; destroy them with double destruction. (Jer 17:12–18 NIV)

Jeremiah's prayer here includes worship (a glorious throne, v. 12), prayer for healing and protection (heal me; . . . save me, v. 14) and expression of his own emotions (destroy them with double destruction vv. 17–19). Indeed, Jeremiah needed healing. He felt so rejected and frustrated that the people were not accepting his message. They rather wanted to kill him, saying that if the things he said were true, they would have been fulfilled. As a result, Jeremiah was embittered. He wanted the Lord to act quickly by bringing the destruction he had predicted. Yet Jeremiah knew that his intention was wrong. He told the Lord, "What passes my lips is open before you. Do not be a terror to me" (vv. 16–17). It was only the healing of God that could save him from such bitterness and revenge. Do you know how God answered him? He wanted him to still present the message with mercy attached to it:

> Thus said the Lord to me: "Go and stand in the People's Gate, by which the kings of Judah enter and by which they go out, and in all the gates of Jerusalem, and say: 'Hear the word of the Lord, you kings of Judah, and all Judah, and all the inhabitants of Jerusalem, who enter by these gates. *Thus says the Lord: Take care for the sake of your lives*, and do not bear a burden on the Sabbath day or bring it in by the gates of Jerusalem. And do not carry a burden out of your houses on the Sabbath or do any work, but keep the Sabbath day holy, as I commanded your fathers. Yet they did not listen or incline their ear, but stiffened their neck, that they might not hear and receive instruction. *But if you listen to me, declares the Lord*, and bring in no burden by the gates of this city on the Sabbath day, but keep the Sabbath day holy and do no work on it, then there shall enter by the gates of this city kings and princes who sit on the throne of David, riding in chariots and on horses, they and their officials, the men of Judah and the inhabitants of Jerusalem. *And this city shall be inhabited forever*. And people shall come from the cities of Judah and the places around Jerusalem, from the land of Benjamin, from the Shephelah, from the hill country, and from the Negeb, bringing burnt offerings and sacrifices, grain offerings and frankincense, and bringing thank offerings to the house of the Lord. *But if you do not listen to me, to keep the Sabbath day holy*, and not to bear a burden and enter by the gates of Jerusalem on the Sabbath day, *then I will kindle a fire in its gates, and it shall devour the palaces of Jerusalem and shall not be quenched*.'" (Jer 17:19–27 ESV, italics mine)

The Lord knew the sufferings Jeremiah was going through. He did not accuse him for praying like that, however, he corrected his wrong conception. The Lord always shows love when people repent. He wanted Jeremiah to repeat the message with love. The Lord wanted the people to repent and come back to him, hence, the key word was repentance.

The people did not repent. Accordingly, Jeremiah kept on speaking with God, praying, and when God was not answering Jeremiah as he expected, Jeremiah was greatly depressed. Let us listen to some of his prayers:

> So I prayed, "Lord, hear what I am saying and listen to what my enemies are saying about me. *Is evil the payment for good? Yet they have dug a pit for me to fall in*. Remember how I came to

you and spoke on their behalf, so that you would not deal with them in anger. *But now, Lord, let their children starve to death; let them be killed in war. Let the women lose their husbands and children; let the men die of disease and the young men be killed in battle. Send a mob to plunder their homes without warning; make them cry out in terror. They have dug a pit for me to fall in and have set traps to catch me.* But, Lord, you know all their plots to kill me. *Do not forgive their evil or pardon their sin. Throw them down in defeat and deal with them while you are angry.*" (Jer 18:19–23 GNT, italics mine)

O Lord, you have deceived me, and I was deceived; you are stronger than I, and you have prevailed. I have become a laughingstock all the day; everyone mocks me. For whenever I speak, I cry out, I shout, "Violence and destruction!" For the word of the Lord has become for me a reproach and derision all day long. If I say, "I will not mention him, or speak any more in his name," there is in my heart as it were a burning fire shut up in my bones, and I am weary with holding it in, and I cannot. For I hear many whispering. Terror is on every side! "Denounce him! Let us denounce him!" say all my close friends, watching for my fall. "Perhaps he will be deceived; then we can overcome him and take our revenge on him." *But the Lord is with me as a dread warrior; therefore my persecutors will stumble; they will not overcome me. They will be greatly shamed, for they will not succeed. Their eternal dishonor will never be forgotten.* O Lord of hosts, who tests the righteous, who sees the heart and the mind, *let me see your vengeance upon them,* for you have I committed my cause. Sing to the Lord; praise the Lord! For he has delivered the life of the needy from the hand of evildoers. *Cursed be the day on which I was born! The day when my mother bore me, let it not be blessed! Cursed be the man who brought the news to my father, "A son is born to you," making him very glad. Let that man be like the cities that the Lord overthrew without pity; let him hear a cry in the morning and an alarm at noon, because he did not kill me in the womb; so my mother would have been my grave, and her womb forever great.* Why did I come out from the womb to see toil and sorrow, and spend my days in shame? (Jer 20:7–18 ESV, italics mine)

Jeremiah still maintained his prayer of vengeance (18:19–23), accusing God and showing regrets of his call (20:7–9), yet he knew the Lord was with him (11). He cursed the day he was born and even cursed the man who brought the news to his father (20:14–18), yet this man did nothing to him. Jeremiah was still a prophet of God, yet his actions showed signs of deep depression. People of God can get into a depressive state.

Why did Jeremiah get into such condition? Earlier, he prayed for the people but they did not repent; then, he wanted to take God's place. What do I mean by this? Let us examine his prayer of intercession for the people:

> Though our iniquities testify against us, act, O Lord, for your name's sake; for our backslidings are many; we have sinned against you. O you hope of Israel, its savior in time of trouble, why should you be like a stranger in the land, like a traveler who turns aside to tarry for a night? *Why should you be like a man confused, like a mighty warrior who cannot save?* Yet you, O Lord, are in the midst of us, and we are called by your name; do not leave us. (Jer 14:7–9 ESV, italics mine)

Jeremiah was accusing God in his prayer. The Lord told him to stop praying, "The Lord said to me: 'Do not pray for the welfare of this people. Though they fast, I will not hear their cry, and though they offer burnt offering and grain offering, I will not accept them. But I will consume them by the sword, by famine, and by pestilence" (Jer 14:11–12 ESV). In fact, Jeremiah himself was sinning in his prayer. He told the Lord that he was like a man who was confused, but the mercy of God covered him. Often, many of us (people of God), sin against him in our prayer but one of the good things about the Lord is that he understands us more than we say, thus, his mercies cover us. Although he asked Jeremiah to stop praying for them, he did not stop:

> Have you utterly rejected Judah? Does your soul loathe Zion? Why have you struck us down so that there is no healing for us? We looked for peace, but no good came; for a time of healing, but behold, terror. We acknowledge our wickedness, O Lord, and the iniquity of our fathers, for we have sinned against you. *Do not spurn us, for your name's sake; do not dishonor your glorious throne; remember and do not break your covenant with us.* (Jer 14:19–21 ESV, italics mine)

As Jeremiah disobeyed God and prayed for them, he thought that God had it all wrong by maintaining his decision to withdraw his protection from Judah, and allow the enemy to whip them. This is what I meant by taking the place of God. Consequently, God allowed Jeremiah to experience a bit of what was going on among the people and that bit was too much for him. Beloved, we must obey the Lord's voice, no matter the situation, when he says no, we must accept it and pray for his grace to carry us through. I know this is difficult to accept but your prayer or the prayer of the most powerful prophet cannot change the mind of God. Your prayer will lead you to know the will of God and walk along with him. Answering prayer is different from changing the mind of God. Answering prayer is the act of God responding to the request you have put before him. His response can be yes, no, or wait. Sometimes when you pray and you think you have received no response, it does not mean the Lord has not heard your prayer, but it means that he has not answered your prayer as you expect. You do not need to wander from one prophet to another. You must trust him and still look on to him.

The prophets were in constant communication with the Lord. They worshipped the Lord in their prayers, prayed with the people and for the people. Yet, in all these, they demonstrated that they were human beings who were only being used by God as his mouthpiece.

Let us get back to our topic of prayer as one of the functions of the prophets. You will realize that Jeremiah was in constant communication with the Lord in prayer, so were the other prophets. It was through prayer that the Lord spoke with them and they communicated his message to the people. Prayer is part of the prophetic ministry.

These were some of the functions of the Old Testament prophets. They are clear examples of what every prophet must do. We shall now discuss prophecy in the New Testament.

PART 4

The New Testament Prophet

It has been established that the messenger of the word of God in the Old Testament was the prophet. He was the mouthpiece of God as well as his messenger. This study also assumes that the messenger of God's word in the New Testament is the apostle. The apostle will be handled in detail in the next part. However, if this is the assumption, the question that arises is: Is the prophet still needed in the New Testament? This part deals with this question. It is discussed in two chapters, which are closely connected with each other. The first chapter deals with how the New Testament is linked with the Old Testament in reference to the fulfillment of its prophecies. The second chapter deals with the potential for each person to prophesy.

Chapter 10

The Spirit to Fall on All Flesh

THE OLD TESTAMENT INDICATED that, in the new covenant, the Holy Spirit would fall upon all flesh. The chapter shows how the Old Testament prophecies were fulfilled in the New Testament.

MOSES WISHED THAT ALL OF GOD'S PEOPLE WOULD BE PROPHETS

In the Old Testament, the Spirit of God was upon the corporate nation of Israel (Isa 63:10–14; Neh 9:20; Hag 2:2–4). Paul speaks in 1 Cor 10 that the Israelites were all baptized in the cloud and water unto Moses. God had to select some of them and grant them the special grace to prophesy. While Moses, the leader, was hearing constantly from God, the Lord also called Aaron as a prophet to serve Moses. This means that while there can be an apostolic type of leader who hears from the Lord, the Lord can still call others as prophets to serve him. Most important to our discussion is that when Aaron was serving as prophet under Moses, Moses said a prayer that is significant for our study now—his wish was that all God's people would become prophets.

Moses had been overburdened with the work of leading the people. When he complained to the Lord, he decided to take some of the Spirit on him (Moses) and give it to seventy elders the Lord had asked Moses to choose. Two of the elders did not go to the tabernacle as Moses had instructed them but stayed in the camp; however, when the Spirit came on those in the tabernacle, the two who were in the camp also received the Spirit. The evidence was that they prophesied. Those in the tabernacle also prophesied like those in the camp. When Joshua saw that the two of them who did not go to the tabernacle were prophesying, he went to tell Moses to stop them.

This is how he presented it, "Joshua son of Nun, who had been Moses' aide since youth, spoke up and said, 'Moses, my lord, stop them'!" (Num 11:28).

However, Moses' mind was different. "Moses replied, 'Are you jealous for my sake? I wish that all the Lord's people were prophets and that the Lord would put his Spirit on them!' Then Moses and the elders of Israel returned to the camp" (Num 11:29–30 NIV). Perhaps Joshua's concern was not the fact that they were prophesying but that they had been chosen but did not go to the tabernacle. It is difficult to understand why the two did not go to the tabernacle. For Joshua, that was a bad way to begin their leadership position. He had a point, but for Moses, he wished all of God's people would be filled with God's Spirit and prophesy. Why did Moses say that? He knew that once you have the Spirit of God you would be able to hear from him, know his will, and follow suit. It must, however, be said that we do not hear of the seventy prophesying again in the Old Testament. It appears that in the Old Testament, one of the evidences of God's Spirit falling on a person was for them to prophesy. For example, in addition to the experience of the seventy elders, prophesying was a sign which followed Saul when he was anointed (1 Sam 10:10).

A FORESHADOW: SCHOOL OF THE PROPHETS

It has already been postulated that Samuel established the school of prophets, and that the subjects which were taught included the knowledge of the law and psalmody, with instrumental music, which was associated with "prophesying." Through this group of prophets, the prophetic office continued for a very long time in the Old Testament.

In the books of Samuel, there were two other prophets who became prominent. They were thought to have come from the school of the prophets, since they featured in the book of Samuel and functioned after Samuel. They were Gad (1 Sam 22:5; 2 Sam 24:11) and Nathan (2 Sam 7:2ff.; 12:1–17). Both became helpful to King David in his life and kingship. Elisha often interacted with some of the sons of the prophets. It was one of the wives of the sons of the prophets who appealed to Elisha that her husband died and left her in debt. Elisha's interaction with her indicated that he knew the man before his death. Second Kings 4:1 reads, "The wife of a man from the company of the prophets cried out to Elisha, 'Your servant my husband is dead, *and you know that he revered the Lord.* But now his creditor is coming to take my two boys as his slaves'" (NIV, italics mine).

Accordingly, the Lord used Elisha to perform the miracle of multiplication to settle her debts (2 Kgs 4:1–7). Furthermore, it was one of the sons of the prophets whose borrowed axe got into a river, of which the Lord used Elisha to perform the miracle of the floating iron to bring it back (2 Kgs 6:1–7). The assumption here is that if members of the school of the prophets were able to receive the Spirit and prophesied in the Old Testament, then it was a foreshadow of the outpouring of the Holy Spirit on all flesh in the New Testament. Moses' wish that all should become prophets was partly fulfilled in the school of the prophets but the greater one was to be fulfilled in the New Testament.

PROPHECIES ON THE SPIRIT FALLING ON ALL PEOPLE

When the nation of Israel failed the Lord, the prophets began to prophesy about a time when the Spirit of God would be poured on all flesh. These are some of the prophecies about the pouring out of the Spirit:

> For I will pour water on the thirsty land, and streams on the dry ground; I will pour out my Spirit on your offspring, and my blessing on your descendants. They will spring up like grass in a meadow, like poplar trees by flowing streams. One will say, 'I belong to the Lord'; another will call himself by the name of Jacob; still another will write on his hand, 'The Lord's,' and will take the name Israel. (Isa 44:3–5 NIV; cf. Isa 32:15)

> I will give you a new heart and put a new spirit in you; I will remove from you your heart of stone and give you a heart of flesh. And I will put my Spirit in you and move you to follow my decrees and be careful to keep my laws. (Ezek 36:26–28 NIV)

> I will no longer hide my face from them, for I will pour out my Spirit on the house of Israel, declares the Sovereign Lord. (Ezek 39:29 NIV)

> And I will pour out on the house of David and the inhabitants of Jerusalem a spirit of grace and supplication. They will look on me, the one they have pierced, and they will mourn for him as one mourns for an only child, and grieve bitterly for him as one grieves for a firstborn son. (Zech 12:10–11 NIV)

These prophets prophesied that the Lord would put his Spirit upon the nation of Israel. The coming of the Spirit was going to make it easy for them to follow the Lord and follow him well. Their concentration was on Israel, although Isaiah's prophecy goes beyond that. For example, "One will say, 'I belong to the Lord.' Another will call himself by the name of Jacob; still another will write on his hand, 'The Lord's,' and will take the name Israel" (Isa 44:3–5). These seem to go above the nation Israel. They suggest that others who do not belong to the nation Israel would take names from Israel and the Lord's name upon themselves. Most of these prophets gave clues about what was going to happen. Obviously, it was the Prophet Joel who spoke succinctly on the coming of the Spirit "upon all flesh" as it happened in the New Testament:

> And afterward, I will pour out my Spirit on all people. Your sons and daughters will prophesy, your old men will dream dreams, your young men will see visions. Even on my servants, both men and women, I will pour out my Spirit in those day.... And everyone who calls on the name of the Lord will be saved for on Mount Zion and in Jerusalem there will be deliverance. (Joel 2:28–29, 32 NIV)

Joel shows clearly that the outcome of the outpouring of God's Spirit on people is for them to prophesy, dream dreams and see visions. That is, all people will hear from God. The school of the prophets in the Old Testament could be seen as a foreshadow of the outpouring of the Spirit in the New Testament. In the school of the prophets, "all members" were to prophesy. Some of their predictions as seen in the Bible, such as the taking up of Elijah to heaven by the two different groups (2 Kgs 2:3, 5), were correct. In 1 Sam 19:20–23, the messengers which were sent by Saul to arrest David all fell under the power of the Spirit and prophesied. If a school established could cause the participants to prophesy and even the messengers sent by Saul could also prophesy, it is possible for the Spirit of God to fall on all flesh for all to prophesy in the New Testament.

Peter understands the day of Pentecost as the fulfillment of this prophecy when he relates the outpouring of the Spirit on the day of

Pentecost as the fulfillment of Joel's prophecy. On the day of Pentecost, a sound like a mighty rushing wind came from heaven, filled the entire house where the disciples were sitting; then divided tongues as of fire appeared to them and rested on each of them. The disciples then were all filled with the Holy Spirit and began to speak in other tongues as the Spirit gave them utterance (Acts 2:2-4). The people who had gathered for the festival of Pentecost said, "We hear them telling in our own tongues the mighty works of God" (Acts 2:11 ESV); that is, prophesying. All the signs that appear there—mighty sound from heaven, fire, and prophecy—except one, speaking in tongues, had taken place in the Old Testament. Thus, speaking in tongues was the new addition.

Based on this outpouring of the Spirit, many people accept that the day of Pentecost marks the beginning of the new covenant. What some people get confused with is the nature of the outpouring and its importance for the New Testament believers. Many Pentecostal Christians believe that the outpouring of the Spirit is the baptism in the Holy Spirit with speaking in tongues as the initial evidence. However, other Christians including some Pentecostal scholars have insisted that the Pentecostal Spirit in Acts is the Spirit of prophecy prophesied by Joel. Indeed, the people who gathered on the day of Pentecost said to one another, "We hear them telling in our own tongues the mighty works of God" (Acts 2:11 ESV). This is prophecy. Prophecy was common to the Old Testament saints. The new thing added was speaking in tongues. Nevertheless, what is the significance of speaking in tongues or prophesying? Each one is an evidence that the Spirit of God had come to dwell upon a person. All of them had become the abode of God where they could hear him and be led by him. Peter made it clear to those who had gathered that day that the outpouring was for everyone who would believe. Peter's declaration was so clear and powerful that any attempt to tamper with it is to undermine the authority of the word of God. I quote it here:

> And Peter said to them, "Repent and be baptized every one of you in the name of Jesus Christ for the forgiveness of your sins, and you will receive the gift of the Holy Spirit. For the promise is for you and for your children and for all who are far off, everyone whom the Lord our God calls to himself." (Acts 2:38-39 ESV)

The promise is for everyone whom the Lord our God calls to himself. The person receives the Spirit in the body, making himself the receptacle of the "Almighty." That person can then hear from God (the Almighty) and speak out what God has told him—prophesy, or "forth tell" what God has spoken to him. This is what is called "the prophethood of all believers."

Once the Spirit falls upon all, all have the right to hear from God and obey him. Ezekiel puts it this way, "And I will give you a new heart, and a new spirit I will put within you. And I will remove the heart of stone from your flesh and give you a heart of flesh. And I will put my Spirit within you, and cause you to walk in my statutes and be careful to obey my rules" (Ezek 36:26–28 ESV). The Holy Spirit who dwells in every believer speaks to the believer to walk in the way of God. He guides the believer on a daily basis (John 16:12–13). He may guide him through dreams, visions, observations, or Scripture. This is the promise of God for all believers in the new covenant. What is the other side of this? The next chapter takes it up.

Chapter 11

Every Believer Has the Potential to Prophesy

THE PREVIOUS CHAPTER HAS shown that in the New Testament, the Spirit falls upon all who believe in the name of Jesus. These people can hear from the Lord and receive daily guidance from him. Paul makes it clearer that the New Testament believer does not only have the Spirit upon him but he also has the potential to prophesy. Accordingly, he throws light on this claim in the following passages (1 Cor 14:5, 24–25, 30–31):

> I would like every one of you to speak in tongues, *but I would rather have you prophesy*. He who prophesies is greater than one who speaks in tongues, unless he interprets, so that the church may be edified. (1 Cor 14:5 NIV, italics mine)

> But if an unbeliever or someone who does not understand comes in *while everybody is prophesying*, he will be convinced by all that he is a sinner and will be judged by all, and the secrets of his heart will be laid bare. So he will fall down and worship God, exclaiming, "God is really among you!" (1 Cor 14:24–25 NIV, italics mine)

> Two or three prophets should speak, and the others should weigh carefully what is said. And if a revelation comes to someone who is sitting down, the first speaker should stop. *For you can all prophesy in turn* so that everyone may be instructed and encouraged. The spirits of prophets are subject to the control of

prophets. For God is not a God of disorder but of peace. (1 Cor 14:29–33 NIV, italics mine)

He encourages the believers in Corinth to desire to prophesy (1 Cor 14:1). He wants them to speak in tongues but to go above speaking in tongues to prophesying. Paul is bold to declare plainly that those who prophesy are greater than those who only speak in tongues. He declares, "I would like every one of you to speak in tongues, but I would rather have you prophesy. He who prophesies is greater than one who speaks in tongues, unless he interprets, so that the church may be edified" (1 Cor 14:5 NIV). Why so? Two explanations are given. Prophecy is an indication that you have allowed the Lord to speak to you with the possibility of obeying it. Secondly, Paul is concerned about building the church, that is, things that will edify one another in order to build the church. If you speak in tongues while people are listening, nobody is built up. You only build yourself in Spirit. But if you give a word of prophecy, you edify people and by that the church is built up.

Following Paul, I encourage all believers to desire to hear from the Lord, obey him and also to declare what he has told them. This is possible. By hearing this, you may think that it promotes pride in the use of spiritual gifts. But this is exactly the opposition of what Paul was teaching. Already there was pride and a competitive attitude in the Corinthian church (1 Cor 3). What Paul is doing here is rather to discourage pride by asking every believer to exercise his God-given new covenant right by allowing the Spirit of God to speak to him and to the church. And truly, according to the prophecies concerning the coming of the Spirit, which was strongly clarified by Joel, and as Paul also shows, the potential is there for every believer to prophesy (1 Cor 14:5, 24–31). Once I know that I have this gift of hearing from the Lord from diverse means, then, when we come together:

> What then shall we say, brothers? When you come together, everyone has a hymn, or a word of instruction, a revelation, a tongue or an interpretation. All of these must be done for the strengthening of the church. If anyone speaks in a tongue, two—or at the most three—should speak, one at a time, and someone must interpret. If there is no interpreter, the speaker should keep quiet in the church and speak to himself and God. Two or three prophets should speak, and the others should weigh carefully what is said. And if a revelation comes to someone who is sitting down, the first speaker should stop. For you can all prophesy in

turn so that everyone may be instructed and encouraged. The spirits of prophets are subject to the control of prophets. For God is not a God of disorder but of peace. (1 Cor 14:26–33 NIV)

Do you follow what Paul is saying here? Paul implies that once you can speak from the Lord and I can speak from the Lord, when we come together, I must give way for you to bring what the Lord has given to you, and you must also give me the opportunity to bring what the Lord has given to me. Then, we must each weigh what they claim that the Lord has spoken through them and accept what we find as the true voice of God. In other words, I must not impose what I bring as the final word from God, and you must not bring what you say as the final word, but respect the Spirit of God in all of us, while realizing that because we see in part as through a mirror, we can all make human errors (1 Cor 13:12). All of these must be done in the spirit of strengthening the church, in an orderly way (1 Cor 14:26–33, 40).

In other places, Paul explains the concept of allowing the Lord to speak through people and obeying as being led by the Spirit. He continues that those who allow the Spirit of God to lead them are the sons of God. In other words, those who do not allow the Spirit of God to speak through them and do not obey him are not the children of God (Rom 8:14; see also vv. 9–11). This means allowing the Lord to speak to you and obeying him is mandatory for every believer.

It must be said that beside the fact that every New Testament believer can hear from the Spirit and walk in his ways, the New Testament makes it clear that people possess varied gifts (1 Cor 12:4–12, 28; Rom 12:6; Eph 2:20; 4:11; Acts 13:1; 21:9–11). The gifts listed include prophecy. The understanding is that while each believer can hear from God and there is the potential for all to prophesy, all may not prophesy but will manifest other gifts. That does not mean that every individual cannot hear from God. It means a person who hears from God, and has the potential to declare it (prophesy), may not have the gift of prophecy, and thus will not get the courage to prophesy. However, he will have the courage to manifest other special gifts that God has given to him. Many Spirit-led Christians can testify that they have ever felt the urge to prophesy but did not have the courage to do so. Yet, often what they felt came to pass or someone else said it. Those with the gift of prophecy can do so because a gift includes the ability or the ease to manifest it.

Once after a prayer session, a senior minister of mine who was a bit skeptical about prophecy told me, "Opoku, today I nearly did your thing." I said, "What thing, please?" He said, "Prophecy." I said, "But why did you fail to do so?" He continued, "During the prayer my eyes were opened (had a vision), and I saw someone who appeared like the Lord inviting me to come to dine with him, and then he embraced me." I said then, "You should have spoken if you had a word to say."[1] This might not be directly the tendency to prophesy. I think it was the word of knowledge through a vision. However, it shows that the potential to hear from God is there for everyone, even the one who did not believe.

Now, it has been established that whereas all can prophesy, there are those who have been given the gift of prophecy who are able to prophesy with ease. In another scenario, I was holding a meeting where there was one senior minister around. A sister got up and prophesied. The fellow apostle said that "this sister is full of prophecy; she is an embodiment of prophecy." Ten years after the apostle had said this, I attended a meeting somewhere else, when this same sister also attended, and she prophesied. She said what I had planned to say. I felt she said it so well through the prophetic message that I did not need to say it again. The issue was settled. Those with the gift of prophecy can prophesy with ease.

Nevertheless, not all who possess the gift of prophecy are prophets. It is clear from Acts that while all could prophesy, and some could be termed as having the gift of prophecy (Acts 21:9), others were known as prophets. For example, while Philip's four daughters were said to prophesy, Agabus was addressed as prophet, just in the next verse (Acts 21:8–10): "On the next day we departed and came to Caesarea, and we entered the house of Philip the evangelist, who was one of the seven, and stayed with him. He had four unmarried daughters, who prophesied. While we were staying for many days, a prophet named Agabus came down from Judea" (ESV).

The "prophets group" includes Barnabas, Simeon, Lucius of Cyrene, Manaen, Saul and Agabus (Acts 13:1; 21:10). Ephesians specifically mentions "prophet" as one of the ministry gifts (Eph 4:11). Thus, whereas the New Testament speaks of the prophethood of all believers, it does not rule out the possibility of some operating as prophets. The one who is a prophet must have the gift of prophecy. He needs the gift of the word of

---

1. Soon after this vision, the senior minister died. I think the vision he had was about his death. The Lord was inviting him to come and dine with him. Well, it is a good picture of the Christian death.

wisdom in order to understand revelations. He needs the word of knowledge for him to have visions and intuitions from God. He will need the discerning of spirits to know the sort of spirits operating at a particular time. Other gifts include the gifts of exhortation, speaking diverse kinds of tongues and the interpretations of tongues, the gift of music and the gift of teaching. The gift of exhortation will cause him to motivate others to action, while the gift of teaching will help him present his message clearly to people. The gift of music may help him to receive or write new songs for the church. The gift of speaking diverse kinds of tongues and interpretation are equal to prophecy. One may not have all these gifts but at least the first four—prophecy, wisdom, knowledge and discerning of spirits, are essential for a person to be a gift to the church of God.

The major difference between the Old Testaments prophets and the New Testament prophets is that in the Old Testament, the prophet was the main minister of God's word—the mouthpiece of God. However, the king was the anointed one, the representative of God, holding God's authority. For example, Pss 2 and 45 show the authority of the king as the anointed one. For Ps 2:1–7 reads:

> Why do the nations rage, And the people plot a vain thing? The kings of the earth set themselves, And the rulers take counsel together, Against the Lord and against His Anointed, saying, "Let us break Their bonds in pieces And cast away Their cords from us." He who sits in the heavens shall laugh; The Lord shall hold them in derision. Then He shall speak to them in His wrath, And distress them in His deep displeasure: "Yet I have set My King On My holy hill of Zion." "I will declare the decree: The Lord has said to Me, 'You are My Son, Today I have begotten You.'" (NKJV)

This psalm reminds the people of how the Lord anointed David and his descendants to be kings, in order for them to fulfill the promise given to Abraham to be a blessing to the whole world. The king is the anointed one. The nations must kiss him but not revolt against him. The prophet was working with the king. Ps 45:1–7 reads:

> My heart is overflowing with a good theme; I recite my composition concerning the King; My tongue is the pen of a ready writer. You are fairer than the sons of men; Grace is poured upon Your lips; Therefore God has blessed You forever. Gird Your sword upon Your thigh, O Mighty One, With Your glory and Your majesty. And in Your majesty ride prosperously because

of truth, humility, and righteousness; And Your right hand shall teach You awesome things. Your arrows are sharp in the heart of the King's enemies; The peoples fall under You. Your throne, O God, is forever and ever; A scepter of righteousness is the scepter of Your kingdom. You love righteousness and hate wickedness; Therefore God, Your God, has anointed You With the oil of gladness more than Your companions. (NKJV)

This psalm appears like a song, which was sung during a royal wedding, giving appellations to the king. Statements such as "Mighty One," "Your throne is forever and ever," and "your God has anointed you," point to someone in authority and one who represents God. The prophet, however, was God's mouthpiece.

The main minister of God's word in the New Testament is the apostle. The prophet works with the apostle in the New Testament. They move together. The prophet does not stand alone. This will become clearer when I treat the topic on apostle.

PART 5

The Apostle

This part presents the apostle as the messenger of God in the New Testament. It deals with this in four chapters. The first chapter attempts to identify an apostle. The second chapter deals with the training that goes into the making of an apostle, and identifies other apostles besides the known ones. The third chapter highlights the gifts that come together to constitute an apostle. The final chapter sums up these discussions.

Chapter 12

Identifying an Apostle

THIS CHAPTER ATTEMPTS TO understand who an apostle is. It makes a classification of the apostolic gifts by digging into the Old and New Testaments, to examine the gifts and the works of some apostles.

THE OLD TESTAMENT APOSTLES

In the Old Testament the Lord called people such as Moses, Joshua, Deborah, and Samuel and used them as his messengers to accomplish his purpose. Examining the call of Moses shows the sort of mission that was assigned to him:

> The Lord said, "I have indeed seen the misery of my people in Egypt. I have heard them crying out because of their slave drivers, and I am concerned about their suffering. So I have come down to rescue them from the hand of the Egyptians and to bring them up out of that land into a good and spacious land, a land flowing with milk and honey—the home of the Canaanites, Hittites, Amorites, Perizzites, Hivites and Jebusites. And now the cry of the Israelites has reached me, and I have seen the way the Egyptians are oppressing them. So now, go. I am *sending* you to Pharaoh to bring my people the Israelites out of Egypt." But Moses said to God, "Who am I, that I should go to Pharaoh and bring the Israelites out of Egypt?" And God said, "I will be with you. And this will be the sign to you that it is I who have *sent* you: When you have brought the people out of Egypt, you will

> worship God on this mountain." Moses said to God, "Suppose I go to the Israelites and say to them, 'The God of your fathers has *sent* me to you,' and they ask me, 'What is his name?' Then what shall I tell them?" God said to Moses, "I AM WHO I AM. This is what you are to say to the Israelites: 'I AM has *sent* me to you.'" God also said to Moses, "Say to the Israelites, 'The Lord, the God of your fathers—the God of Abraham, the God of Isaac and the God of Jacob—has *sent* me to you.' This is my name forever, the name by which I am to be remembered from generation to generation." (Exod 3:7–15 NIV, italics mine)

The common word in the commissioning of Moses is "sent": "I am sending you," "I who have sent you," "The God of your fathers has sent me to you," "I AM has sent me to you," "the God of Abraham, the God of Isaac and the God of Jacob—has sent me to you" (Exod 7:10, 12, 13, 14, 15). The Lord called him to send him to deliver his people Israel. Moses was "the sent one" to deliver his people. Moses encountered the Lord, who spoke with him and then sent him. Moses was required to do two things: hear from the Lord and respond to "his sending." He was already constantly hearing from God as he was leading his people.

Moses, however, was working with the high priest Aaron who was assisting him. Although, in a sense Moses was endowed with both graces of hearing and leading, he was limited by the priestly functions of his brother, Aaron. The high priest had to do his part. Thus, although Moses was a man of God, he was limited in a way.

On the other hand, the prophets in the Old Testament were mostly sent only to deliver the word of the Lord to people. For example, Jeremiah was told, "But the Lord said to me, 'Do not say, "I am only a child." You must go to everyone I send you to and say whatever I command you'" (Jer 1:7 NIV). Similarly, Isaiah was told, "'Whom shall I send? And who will go for us?' And I said, 'Here am I. Send me!'" (Isa 6:8 NIV; see also Ezek 2:1–5). Thus, the prophets were called and sent. However, the difference between the sending of Moses (also of Joshua, Deborah and Samuel) was that whereas Moses was sent to lead the people, the other prophets were called to hear and communicate messages to the people. Moses, Joshua, Deborah, and Samuel could also hear from God and lead according to the instructions which they received from the Lord.

After the kingship was instituted, the prophets who emerged, such as Elijah, Isaiah, and Jeremiah, were not leading but hearing from God and communicating the messages to the king and the people. Thus, the role that Moses, Joshua, Deborah and Samuel played was different from the role the other prophets, such as Elijah, Elisha and Isaiah played. Whereas the Isaiah type of prophets were assisting the kings, the Moses type of prophets were leading the people. The Moses type of prophet is what I consider as the apostle. These are the people who could hear from God and lead God's people. Some Old Testament examples cited here are Moses, Joshua, Deborah, and Samuel.

Besides this group, there is another group in the Old Testament who functioned as both prophets and apostles. These people include Joseph and Daniel; Joseph was not labeled as a prophet, but his ability to understand dreams was remarkable. It took a prophetic figure with both gifts of knowledge and wisdom to be able to have functioned in that line. Of course, as a young man, Joseph was often having dreams that were very revelatory, telling of the future (Gen 37). The leadership traits that Joseph exhibited in the house of Potiphar (Gen 39), and at prison (Gen 40), which later landed him in the palace of Pharaoh all show how Joseph was raised as no ordinary person (Gen 41). His role as the man next in authority to Pharaoh shows the administrative ability that he possessed (41). Seeing his abilities to dream, his understanding of revelations, and his leadership, Joseph could be considered within apostolic figures.

Another apostolic figure in the Old Testament was Daniel. Daniel was considered a prophet. However, he also had a very strong leadership ability that caused him to bring his friends—Hananiah, Mishael, and Azariah—together to save a community (Dan 2). His service, control, and tenacity eventually led him to work with three kings, Nebuchadnezzar, Belshazzar, and Darius (Dan 3–6). In all these, Daniel did not compromise his faith, but stood as a great witness of Jehovah (Dan 6:19–28). Daniel could be considered an Old Testament apostolic type. Still another apostolic figure of the Old Testament is Nehemiah. Nehemiah was a man of prayer (e.g., Neh 1:4–11) and of great leadership ability. He led God's people to rebuild the walls of Jerusalem in the midst of great opposition (Neh 4–6). He led them to the public reading of the law of Moses which brought about repentance, restoration of the Feast of Tabernacles, temple procedures, and the renewed commitment to Sabbath observance (Neh 7–13).

Coming back to the call of Moses, who was sent by the Lord, the common Hebrew term, which is translated "sent" (*shalah*), is the commonly Greek translated term for apostle (*apostello*). The term *apostello* means "to send," "to send off" or "away," or "to send forth." The term conveys the impression of sending someone on an assignment as one's representative. In other words, he is the messenger of somebody. Therefore, the New Testament apostle (messenger) identifies as the Old Testament messenger who was divinely called and sent by God to act on his behalf. As the prophet was the main messenger of God in the Old Testament, so is the apostle the main messenger of God in the New Testament.

JESUS, THE APOSTLE

The writer of Hebrews shows that Jesus is an apostle, "Therefore, holy brothers, who share in the heavenly calling, fix your thoughts on Jesus, the apostle and high priest whom we confess" (Heb 3:1 NIV). Here, the New Living Translation uses the term "God's Messenger" for the apostle. This is the only place where the term apostle is directly applied to Jesus. And the usage is very important. The writer was comparing Jesus to Moses. Thus, as Moses was the apostle (messenger) of God so was Jesus. By then, he adds something which makes the apostleship of Jesus higher than Moses. Whereas Moses was an apostle higher than the prophets who were not leaders, he was still limited. In that, he was not a high priest; his brother Aaron was the high priest. Thus, the two important offices were separated. However, in Jesus both offices—apostleship and high priesthood—were combined. The mentioning of Jesus as the high priest was very important because the office of high priest was one of the most distinguished offices that differentiated Christianity from Judaism. The writer shows that in Christ Jesus all the characteristics of the high priest and all the demands and offerings expected to be performed by the high priest in the Old Testament had been fulfilled. Judaism still continued with the office of the high priest after the death of Jesus.

The writer used Moses as an example here because Moses is considered as the greatest prophet, messenger, and originator of the religious affairs of Israel. The goal of the writer of Hebrews is to prove that our Lord Jesus Christ in the new covenant is the greatest messenger—apostle—sent from God, for he functions in a rank and office similar to Moses but superior in power and dignity. So now, we realize that in Jesus' apostleship, we combine the offices of the leader (king), the prophet and the high priesthood. Our Lord Jesus Christ is the apostle par excellence. However, Jesus lived on earth for just a little over thirty years. How could he continue his ministry on earth? He was to call some people to follow in his apostleship.

THE CALL OF THE TWELVE AND MATTHIAS

The first thing to know about the original twelve apostles is that they were all called by the Lord Jesus. Before choosing the twelve apostles, the Lord Jesus had to spend the whole night in prayer, "One of those days Jesus went out to a mountainside to pray, and spent the night praying to God. When morning came, he called his disciples to him and chose twelve of them, whom he also designated apostles" (Luke 6:12-13 NIV). Often, I wonder why the Lord Jesus himself had to spend the whole night in prayer before choosing the apostles. This is an indication that calling people to the apostolic office (or any ministry) must not be taken lightly. It needs prayer. A person cannot assume the office by himself. He must be called by the Lord Jesus and, as will be seen later, be recognized by a body of believers.

However, in the case of the calling of the apostles by Jesus after the all night prayer, he identified one of them as the devil—Judas. Jesus declares, "Then Jesus replied, 'Have I not chosen you, the Twelve? Yet one of you is a devil!' (He meant Judas, the son of Simon Iscariot, who, though one of the Twelve, was later to betray him)" (John 6:70-71 NIV). This means, Jesus knew Judas was inclined to evil and was going to betray him. Why did he have to choose him? It could not mean that Jesus' prayer was not effective. I would think that the whole night's prayer before choosing the apostles and yet choosing Judas meant that Jesus, knowing that Judas would betray him could have excluded him from the selection. But, just as he prayed in the garden of Gethsemane for the will of God to prevail so did he do here (Mark 12:32-42). An important aspect of prayer is knowing the will of God and having the ability to live it.

The names of the twelve apostles appear in all the synoptic gospels, that is, Matt 10:2-4; Mark 3:16-19; and Luke 6:14-16. Interestingly each of the gospel positions the names in three categories of four. The same names appear in each group, but not the same in order. Group 1 has Peter and Andrew, his brother; and James the son of Zebedee and John, his brother. Group 2 has Philip and Bartholomew; Thomas; and Matthew the tax collector. Group three has James the son of Alphaeus and Lebbaeus, whose surname was Thaddaeus or Judas; Simon the Canaanite;

and Judas Iscariot, who also betrayed him. Somehow, in the third group both Matthew and Mark have the name Thaddaeus but Luke has Judas. Matthew describes him as "Lebbaeus, whose surname was Thaddaeus" (KJV). In the Greek version, Luke's description of this apostle is "Judas of James." The King James Version translated it as "Judas the brother of James." Almost all other versions translate it (including the New King James) as "Judas son of James." It is quite possible that the best translation of "Judas of James" is Judas son of James. William Steuart McBirnie, who did special research on the Twelve Apostles, combines the two and calls him Judas Thaddaeus.[1] Judas, the Greek form of Judah, was a common name among the Jews. Concerning this apostle, could it be that because of Judas Iscariot, the authors were trying to bring his other names to clearly differentiate him from "the Iscariot" who betrayed Jesus? Matthew, for example, being among the Twelve brought his other name before bringing what he called his surname to identify him clearly. Luke being distant from the two brought his common name. Luke was emphatic on the name Judas because about two years after he had written the gospel of Luke, he repeated the name Judas among the list of the names of the apostles in the book of Acts (1:13).

It is interesting to note that in listing the apostles, all the authors placed Peter's name first, and Judas Iscariot's name last. People are remembered for what they do. Peter obviously was seen as their leader, whereas Judas's name might have been last because he betrayed his master. Of course, when Jesus rose from the grave and spoke to Peter to take care of his sheep, Peter and the other apostles might have understood it as conferring leadership on him. Accordingly, he was the one who spoke to the apostles (and the other disciples) to select one of the disciples to share the ministry of apostleship with them (Acts 1:15–26). Again, Peter was the one who spoke to the people on the day of Pentecost. These indicate that at the period, Peter might have assumed leadership.

As has been indicated after the death of Judas, the apostles appointed someone to be added to the eleven. The criteria was spelt out in Acts 1:21–22, "Therefore it is necessary to choose one of the men who have been with us the whole time the Lord Jesus went in and out among us, beginning from John's baptism to the time when Jesus was taken up from us. For one of these must become a witness with us of his resurrection" (NIV). For Peter and the eleven, the criteria was a person who had

---

1. McBirnie, *Search for the Twelve Apostles*, 195–96.

been with them (Christ and the apostles) from the beginning. Then, the person was to become a witness of his resurrection. The witness here was very important. Matthias was chosen through the casting of lots (Acts 1:23–24).

The question that arises from the selection of Matthias is, "Did the apostles consider the number of apostles to be limited to twelve?" It is quite possible from the way Peter spoke and how the whole exercise ended that the apostles appeared to have mystified the number twelve. If this was their opinion, it is clear that the Holy Spirit debunked that prejudice through the calling of Paul, and possibly the two brothers of Jesus—James and Jude (1 Cor 9:5; 15:7–8; Acts 1:6–11, 14).[2]

THE CALL OF PAUL

The New Testament gives indication about people who were functioning as apostles, besides the Twelve and Matthias.[3] Paul was outstanding among all of them, perhaps even more than the Twelve because of his letters. He was not modest about his office. He often called himself an apostle (Rom 1:1; 1 Cor 1:1; Gal 1:1; Eph 1:1). He also emphasized that his apostolic call was of equal status as those apostles who were considered the leaders of the church (Gal 1:17–24; 2:9–14; 1 Cor 9:1–5). Since he is one of the apostles whose call has been described vividly, it is better we discuss him. He will be used as a case study to find out how those people whose apostolic calling was not chosen by the earthly Jesus was done. Paul tells us that he was called by God. In Gal 1:13–17, he narrates:

> For you have heard of my previous way of life in Judaism, how intensely I persecuted the church of God and tried to destroy it. I was advancing in Judaism beyond many Jews of my own age and was extremely zealous for the traditions of my fathers. But when God, who set me apart from birth and called me by his grace, was pleased to reveal his Son in me so that I might preach him among the Gentiles, I did not consult any man, nor did I go up to Jerusalem to see those who were apostles before I was, but I went immediately into Arabia and later returned to Damascus. (NIV; cf. Acts 9:3–16)

---

2. The possible call of Jude to apostleship (Jude, the natural brother of Jesus) is taken up later in the book.

3. These will be discussed shortly.

Paul considers his call by God on the road to Damascus as a call by grace. This call by grace included the revelation of Christ in him in order for him to preach Christ among the Gentiles. Although in Acts 9:1–5, Luke, the writer, does not tell us everything that the Lord said, Paul tells us in other instances that he was called and sent by Christ Jesus. He clarified this, when he was explaining himself to the Jews before the Roman commander in Jerusalem:

> "What shall I do, Lord?" I asked. "Get up," the Lord said, "and go into Damascus. There you will be told all that you have been assigned to do." My companions led me by the hand into Damascus, because the brilliance of the light had blinded me. A man named Ananias came to see me. He was a devout observer of the law and highly respected by all the Jews living there. He stood beside me and said, "Brother Saul, receive your sight!" And at that very moment I was able to see him. Then he said: "The God of our fathers has chosen you to know his will and to see the Righteous One and to hear words from his mouth. You will be his witness to all men of what you have seen and heard. And now what are you waiting for? Get up, be baptized and wash your sins away, calling on his name." When I returned to Jerusalem and was praying at the temple, I fell into a trance and saw the Lord speaking. "Quick!" he said to me. "Leave Jerusalem immediately, because they will not accept your testimony about me." "Lord," I replied, "these men know that I went from one synagogue to another to imprison and beat those who believe in you. And when the blood of your martyr Stephen was shed, I stood there giving my approval and guarding the clothes of those who were killing him." Then the Lord said to me, "Go; *I will send you* far away to the Gentiles." (Acts 22:10–21 NIV, italics mine)

Here, Paul was emphatic that God chose him to know his will, to see Christ (the Righteous One), and hear from him. He was to declare what he had seen and heard to all. He was also specifically sent to the Gentiles.

When Paul was defending himself before King Agrippa, he repeated his calling and made some additions to what he said already about his call:

> Then I asked, "Who are you, Lord?" "I am Jesus, whom you are persecuting," the Lord replied. "Now get up and stand on your feet. I have appeared to you to appoint you as a servant and as a witness of what you have seen of me and what I will show you. I

will rescue you from your own people and from the Gentiles. *I am sending* you to them to open their eyes and turn them from darkness to light, and from the power of Satan to God, so that they may receive forgiveness of sins and a place among those who are sanctified by faith in me." (Act 26:15–18 NIV, italics mine)

Here, Paul declared that the Lord said, "I am Jesus, whom you are persecuting", and added that "I am sending you to them." Thus, it was the Lord Jesus who had called him, revealed himself to him, for him (Paul) to know him well and know his will, and send him to speak of what he had seen and known.

This is the apostle. The one who has been called by Christ, known him through revelation and sent by him to build his church. The knowledge of Christ, hearing from him, and authorization from him gives the apostle the authority to speak the word of God with confidence and clarity.

The apostle, therefore, must have a clear sense of God's call upon his life. The call may not come like that of Paul, however, it may be a divine encounter that will help him to hold on to during times of challenges. Divine encounters include angelic visitations, dreams, visions, and hearing of audible voices. I have interacted with many Christian leaders who, though not using the title apostle, have clear evidence of apostolic ministry on their lives, in which they also are functioning. Thus, a person may not use the title apostle but the encounter he might have had with the Lord and his ministry would demonstrate that he is an apostle. The divine encounter helps you to know the One who has called you and sent you. The divine encounter is also crucial for the person to hang on during times of difficulties.[4]

Certainly, the Lord has a different way of calling each individual. For Moses, it was through the burning bush. With Samuel, it was through an audible voice at night. In the case of Paul, it was through a shining light on the way to Damascus. Yours may be different, but the apostle must have a call of Christ in his life.

Apostles are bound to face challenges in ministry because of the awareness of God's call upon their lives and the willingness to follow his will. Often our human will is against the will of God. The knowledge of

---

4. For the story of my personal encounter, read Antwi, *Myth or Mystery*, 149–60.

God's will and clarity of thoughts in promoting the kingdom principles often land apostles in challenges.

Is the call alone enough for ministry? The next section discusses this.

Chapter 13

The Making of Apostles

The previous chapter has shown that the Lord Jesus called some persons to be apostles. But that alone does not make an apostle. This chapter continues with the making of the apostle.

THE TRAINING OF THE TWELVE

Just like the prophet, the Lord does not just call the person. He trains him through various means. Luke shows the difference between the disciples and apostles. He shows that Jesus chose the apostles out of the disciples, "When morning came, he called his disciples to him and chose twelve of them, whom he also designated apostles" (Luke 6:13 NIV). A disciple is a learner; he is like an apprentice, a follower, an adherent, but "an apostle is a person who has been sent, commissioned."[1] The apostle represents the one who sent him. He is given authority by the sender. Jesus had many disciples but he selected only twelve and designated them apostles; King James Version uses ordination in Mark 3:14. Furthermore, Mark adds something which is significant, "And he ordained twelve, *that they should be with him*, and that he might send them forth to preach" (Mark 3:14 KJV, italics mine).

What is the purpose of "being with him"? He was to train and equip them. They were to be with him so that they would constantly hear him, know and understand his teaching, manner of life, give an account of his

---

1. Hendriksen, *Luke*, 326

ministry and life, and be qualified to equip others. The ultimate purpose was to know him and be like him in order for them to carry on his ministry after his death.

In both Matthew and Luke, immediately after calling the first disciples (Matt 4:18—7:29; Luke 5:1—6:41),[2] he gave his sermon on the mount. He wanted them to understand his ministry. The most important thing for an apostle is to know Christ and understand his ministry. Once you know him, you can be his witness.

Training Follows Calling

Training is very important and demands time. Calling is by grace; training is by choice. A person can be called without training. The call often precedes training; a person who is called without training will not be sharp. In the Old Testament, we have pointers of how God trained some of the people he called. For example, right from his adulthood, Moses had the intention that God wanted to use him for something. He advised a Hebrew who was struggling with a fellow Hebrew in the wrong way. That was a sense of awareness that he was a leader. He wanted to deliver his people from slavery, but he was doing it the wrong way. He killed an Egyptian who was beating up a Hebrew (Exod 2:11–15). God had to train Moses, in the wilderness, among others things, to teach him patience for forty years. Meanwhile, he had been trained in the palace of Pharaoh as a statesman, royal, military commander, and in the best knowledge of the period. He was eighty years, when he was finally called to be a leader and at which time the training had prepared him for this leadership position.

Knowing the Person Jesus

Jesus needed to train the apostles to be like him. He needed to help them know who he was through his teachings and miracles. Knowing who he was would help them trust, follow and obey his commandments. Then they could be true representative of him. They passed the test when he examined them, "who do you say I am?" in Matt 16:

> When Jesus came to the region of Caesarea Philippi, he asked his disciples, "Who do people say the Son of Man is?" They

---

2. The names of the first disciples mentioned here are some of the apostles.

replied, "Some say John the Baptist; others say Elijah; and still others, Jeremiah or one of the prophets." "But what about you?" he asked. "Who do you say I am?" Simon Peter answered, "You are the Christ, the Son of the living God." (Matt 16:13–16 NIV)

By this time, the apostles were clear in the mind that Jesus was the Messiah. There was no doubt about this. The training had not ended. It was only part of it.

Knowing That Suffering Could Be God's Will

After this, Jesus took the training to another level. He told the apostles about his purpose of coming to the world, which was to redeem humanity through his death to be preceded by suffering (Matt 16:23–26). Peter who had just known the person of Christ, and had been elevated to be given the keys to heaven, took Jesus aside and rebuked him (Matt 16:17–22). He did not see the need of suffering; he did not understand why the Christ had to suffer; he might not have properly understood the meaning of the keys of heaven given to him. Perhaps he was thinking of an earthly kingdom. Jesus rebuked him and accused him of being Satan. That is, Satan had influenced his thoughts. Then, Jesus again told him that he had not denied himself. The implication is that the "self" that had not been denied was being used by Satan. It is clear from this that knowing Christ is progressive. You may know him up to a certain level but you will have to know him and "the fellowship of His suffering" (Phil 3:10 KJV). The believer must follow the example of Christ in everything. He must be willing to suffer for Jesus' sake. Jesus was teaching the apostles that suffering could be part of God's will and especially for the one sent by God.

Relying Wholly on the Lord

The next thing Jesus taught his apostles was full reliance on God as they work for him. He had given to them authority to cast out evil spirits, heal every disease and affliction, as they preach the good news (Matt 10:1–14). Matthew did not show us the outcome of this mission trip that they undertook. However, from the report Luke gives concerning the sending of the seventy-two, we believe that this trip was successful (Luke 10:17–20). It would appear that the apostles had gone to relax, trusting that once the authority had been vested in them, they could always "perform," without the needed preparation. Jesus taught them the lesson of the need for continuous reliance on God through prayer and fasting, as they seek to do God's work (Matt 17:19–21). It happened that in his absence, they attempted to heal an epileptic boy without success. They thought that once they had experienced some successful healing and casting out of evil spirits, it would always work for them without preparation. They were quite disturbed by their failure, and accordingly asked Jesus why they failed to cast out the evil spirit. In response, Jesus told them the need for faith and then added the need for preparation in prayer and fasting.[3] Believers cannot work with old weapons; we always need to depend upon him daily to sharpen us and our weapons for the battles ahead. One other lesson we can learn from hindsight in this failure experience is that healing and miracles depend upon the sovereign will of God. It is the Lord who heals.

Do not Accept the Praise of Human Beings

Another great lesson Jesus taught the apostles was to educate them not to accept the praise of people. People have the tendency of offering praises to those who lead them. Some of these do not come from good motives. Others, however, may come from genuine reverence. The apostle must learn not to allow himself to be hailed by praises and flattery words.

Jesus taught this through practical demonstration. He had fed five thousand people with five loaves of bread and two fish. They also gathered twelve baskets of the pieces of the five barley loaves leftover by those who had eaten (John 6:1–13). When the people saw this miracle, they wanted to make Jesus a king by force (John 6:14–15). Jesus withdrew himself to the mountainside. Later, Jesus decided to give them some hard teaching including the eating of his flesh and the drinking of his blood. "On hearing it, many of his disciples said, 'This is a hard teaching. Who can accept it?'" (John 6:60 NIV). From that time, many of the disciples left Jesus and no longer followed him.

Jesus turned to the apostles and asked them if they would also leave. Peter's response was very important. "Simon Peter answered him, 'Lord, to whom shall we go? You have the words of eternal life. We believe and

---

3. Matthew 17:21 is in the King James Version but not in many other versions. The understanding is that Matt 17:21 is not in the ancient manuscript of Matthew. It is thought that one of the ancient Christian "scribes" might have added it. That also implies "fasting and prayer" was the popular belief at the time.

know that you are the Holy One of God'" (John 6:68–69 NIV). Peter had confirmed that Jesus was the Holy One of God; that is, the expected Messiah. They do not need to go anywhere and to anybody again; they would stay with him. They had come to know that people can praise for a moment and, later, oppose you. The apostle must not depend upon the praises, which come from people.

Leadership is Servanthood and Service

While with Jesus, the apostles were fighting for places of prominence. Surprisingly as they were closest to the greatest challenge of their time, the death of Jesus, they were disputing on who was the greatest among them. The whole thing started when James and John used their mother to lobby for them (Matt 20:20–23). After Jesus rebuked them, by saying that they did not understand what they requested for, and what it implied—suffering—he said something in v. 23, which I want us to pick up. "Jesus told them, 'You will indeed drink from my bitter cup. But I have no right to say who will sit on my right or my left. My Father has prepared those places for the ones he has chosen'" (Matt 20:23 NLT). Jesus shows here that he was under the authority of the Father, who makes the decision about leadership. It is a very difficult passage to understand. Nevertheless, the lesson about this is that leadership is not given as rewards or even on experience basis. Rather, it is reserved for those who have maintained their commitment and faithfulness to Jesus regardless of trials and challenges. It is for those the Father had known, equipped and prepared. The leader must keep on preparing and training people for leadership, but finally it is the Father who chooses.

Matthew recorded that the apostles were indignant and worried about the request, "When the ten other disciples heard what James and John had asked, they were indignant" (Matt 20:24–25 NLT). Luke adds something which is interesting, "Then they began to argue among themselves about who would be the greatest among them" (Luke 22:24 NLT). Jesus used the occasion to explain the role of true leadership to people. It is to serve. Instead of lording it over people, the leader must become the servant of all; he must serve. I must say that if leadership is in the hands of those who wish to serve and help institutions, societies, nations or humanity, it is rewarding and a blessing to all. However, if it is in the hands of those who are moved by selfish, personal, ethnic, racial or national ambition, it can ruin and destroy institutions, societies, countries and humanity at large.

Before his arrest, trial and death, Jesus demonstrated to his apostles the need to serve. He washed their feet and told them to do same for one another:

> When he had finished washing their feet, he put on his clothes and returned to his place. "Do you understand what I have done for you?" he asked them. "You call me 'Teacher' and 'Lord,' and rightly so, for that is what I am. Now that I, your Lord and Teacher, have washed your feet, you also should wash one another's feet. I have set you an example that you should do as I have done for you. I tell you the truth, no servant is greater than his master, nor is a messenger greater than the one who sent him. Now that you know these things, you will be blessed if you do them." (John 13:12–17 NIV)

By this, Jesus set the pace that all his disciples, including the apostles should humble themselves and serve in whatever role their Master asks them to play.

Jesus taught that the apostle must be a servant; he must serve others. Apostleship is not an office of lordship.

THE TRAINING OF PAUL

After Christ called Paul, he was trained and recognized as an apostle before functioning as such. The Lord did not tell Paul immediately what to do. He sent him to Ananias, a respected disciple, who told Paul why the Lord had called him. Paul asked the Lord, "'Who are you, Lord?' Saul asked. 'I am Jesus, whom you are persecuting,' he replied. 'Now get up and go into the city, and you will be told what you must do'" (Acts 9:5–6 NIV). The Lord could have told him straight away what to do but before he spoke to Paul specifically about what he destined for him, he wanted Paul to be mentored by the other disciples. The first disciple the Lord referred him to was Ananias. Ananias prayed for him to receive the Holy Spirit and baptized him. He might have also told him some aspects of the will of God for Paul. Acts tells the story:

> But the Lord said to him, "Go, for he is a chosen vessel of Mine to bear My name before Gentiles, kings, and the children of Israel. For I will show him how many things he must suffer for

> My name's sake." And Ananias went his way and entered the house; and laying his hands on him he said, "Brother Saul, the Lord Jesus, who appeared to you on the road as you came, has sent me that you may receive your sight and be filled with the Holy Spirit." Immediately there fell from his eyes something like scales, and he received his sight at once; and he arose and was baptized. (Acts 9:15–18 NIV)

After Ananias ministered to Paul, he (Paul) also spent some days with the disciples in Damascus. Why? Despite Paul's knowledge of the Lord in the Old Testament and his learning, he still needed some training from the disciples. The referral to Ananias and his stay with the disciples were to humble Paul and to allow him to be mentored by the disciples.

Another disciple who became of great help to Paul was Barnabas. Paul needed to come to Jerusalem to learn from the apostles. The Lord caused him to leave Damascus through persecution to Jerusalem. In Jerusalem, the disciples did not want to accept him. It was Barnabas who introduced him to the apostles and other disciples:

> When he came to Jerusalem, he tried to join the disciples, but they were all afraid of him, not believing that he really was a disciple. But Barnabas took him and brought him to the apostles. He told them how Saul on his journey had seen the Lord and that the Lord had spoken to him, and how in Damascus he had preached fearlessly in the name of Jesus. So Saul stayed with them and moved about freely in Jerusalem, speaking boldly in the name of the Lord. He talked and debated with the Grecian Jews, but they tried to kill him. When the brothers learned of this, they took him down to Caesarea and sent him off to Tarsus. (Acts 9:26–30 NIV)

Paul needed to stay with the disciples to learn from them. He recounts his story to the Galatians that three years after his conversion, he went to Jerusalem to visit Peter and stayed with him for fifteen days (Gal 1:18). When some Grecian Jews wanted to kill Paul, he finally went to stay in his hometown Tarsus (Acts 9:26–30). Barnabas went to bring Paul for the believers in Antioch to benefit from his ministry.

Before the Holy Spirit spoke to separate Barnabas and Paul for the work to which he had called them, they had been working together in missions already:

> Then news of these things came to the ears of the church in Jerusalem, and they sent out Barnabas to go as far as Antioch.

> When he came and had seen the grace of God, he was glad, and encouraged them all that with purpose of heart they should continue with the Lord. For he was a good man, full of the Holy Spirit and of faith. And a great many people were added to the Lord. Then Barnabas departed for Tarsus to seek Saul. And when he had found him, he brought him to Antioch. So it was that for a whole year they assembled with the church and taught a great many people. And the disciples were first called Christians in Antioch. (Acts 11:22–26 NKJV)

Sometimes the Holy Spirit confirms what he has already started doing. Barnabas had seen the gifts in Paul. He was the one who introduced him to the apostles at Jerusalem. Thus, the call to apostleship is not a situation where someone stands up and makes himself. He must be called by the Lord, trained by others and recognized by a body.

THE CALL AND TRAINING OF OTHER APOSTLES

Besides the original twelve apostles, we have discussed the appointment of Matthias and Paul. Besides these, the New Testament shows that some other people were apostles. Our attention will now turn to them.

James and Jude

We will discuss the first of these, that is, James, the natural brother of Jesus. When Jesus was alive, the gospels present his brothers as not believing in him (John 7:5; Mark 3:21, 31–35). But when he died and resurrected, we realized that James was one of those to whom he revealed himself. Paul is the one who tells the story:

> For what I received I passed on to you as of first importance: that Christ died for our sins according to the Scriptures, that he was buried, that he was raised on the third day according to the Scriptures, and that he appeared to Peter, and then to the Twelve. After that, he appeared to more than five hundred of the brothers at the same time, most of whom are still living, though some have fallen asleep. *Then he appeared to James, then to all the apostles*, and last of all he appeared to me also, as to one abnormally born. (1 Cor 15:3–8 NIV, italics mine)

Paul mentions those to whom the Lord Jesus revealed himself, when he resurrected. He specifically mentioned James. I believe that this revelation had great impact on James and transformed him into a great apostle of the Lord. In his book, "To twelve tribes that had scattered among the nations," James identified himself as "a servant of God and of the Lord Jesus Christ" (Jas 1:1 NIV). Consequently, after the resurrection he joined the apostles and the other disciples. Luke shows that the brothers of Jesus and his mother, Mary, were among those who gathered in the Upper Room to pray (Acts 1:14). Thus, when Matthias was chosen, James and his brother Jude were there. When the Holy Spirit descended, they were also with them and they received the baptism of the Holy Spirit together with the rest.

When Paul went to Jerusalem, he had to see those who were considered pillars of the church, and James was among them. The way Paul writes it shows that James was very influential and possibly the leader, "James, Peter and John, those reputed to be pillars, gave me and Barnabas the right hand of fellowship when they recognized the grace given to me. They agreed that we should go to the Gentiles, and they to the Jews" (Gal 2:9 NIV). James' name appears first. In addition, it seems the leadership of James somehow intimidated Peter. Paul shows that when Peter visited Antioch he (Peter) was eating with the Gentiles because he knew in Christ that they were all one. But when certain Jews came from James to join them, he withdrew, an attitude which Paul describes as hypocrisy (Gal 2:11–13). Thus, James was somehow wielding some sort of authority. Besides, James was the one who appeared to chair the Council of Jerusalem in Acts 15. The effort he put in to write a letter to the Jews who were scattered also shows an apostolic responsibility. The fact that the letter made it into the canon of Scripture, the first after those which were considered to be Paul's shows the respect the people had for James. With all these, we can conclude that James was an apostle of Christ.

Jude, the natural brother of our Lord Jesus (Jude 1) too, can be considered an apostle. In Acts 1–2, Jude could be one of the Lord's brothers who were there (see Acts 1:14). This aside, when Paul was describing those the Lord Jesus revealed himself to when he resurrected as quoted above, after he mentioned James, he continued "then to all the apostles." He had already mentioned the Twelve, the five hundred, James, so who were the "all apostles" here? It could be a repetition of the Twelve but it could also give a signal that there were others who were considered apostles we are not very sure of including Jesus' brothers, who were among those who gathered on the day of Pentecost.

In 1 Cor 9, Paul was talking about his apostleship and the rights of apostles. He begins, "Am I not free? Am I not an apostle?" (v. 1). In v. 5, when talking about the rights of the apostles, he mentioned the Lord's brothers, "Don't we have the right to take a believing wife along with us, as do the other apostles and *the Lord's brothers* and Cephas? Or is it only I and Barnabas who must work for a living?" (1 Cor 9:5–6 NIV, italics mine). Here, included in the list of apostles were the Lord's brothers. He mentions the Lord's brothers, indicating that they were more than one and they were apostles since he was speaking about the rights of apostles. Since it was the Lord's brothers, Jude was included.

What crowns Jude's apostleship is his letter in which he makes it clear that he was the brother of James (v. 1). This, of course, is the Apostle James and it implies that Jude was the natural brother of our Lord Jesus Christ. He sees himself as "a servant of Jesus Christ" (v. 1). It is a short letter, yet with deep theological reflections refuting a false teaching. It was one of the books quoted by Clement of Rome, a first-century church father, and other Christian leaders in the second century including Clement of Alexandria, Tertullian, and Origen.[4] The fact that the book found its way in the canon of Scripture shows the respect that the people had for Jude. Apart from Mark and Luke, who were both found to be companions of apostles, no other books were accepted in the canon of Scripture, except those that were considered by the time to be the writings of an apostle. In the letter, he senses the call of God to write (v. 2). Jude can be considered one of the apostles of our Lord Jesus Christ.

Barnabas

Undoubtedly Barnabas was one of the finest brothers in the New Testament. He first appeared in the New Testament in Acts 4:36–37, where he sold a land he owned and brought the money to the apostles. His real name was Joseph but because of his character of encouraging people, he won the accolade Barnabas (son of encouragement), which eventually substituted his name. As Luke describes his nature and work in Antioch before the arrival of Paul, he said, he was "a good man, full of the Holy Spirit and faith." He continued that "and a great number of people were

---

4. See Blum, "Jude," 381.

brought to the Lord" (Acts 11:24 NIV). Thus, his ministry in Antioch was very fruitful. Barnabas, as mentioned already, was the one who introduced Paul to the other apostles, encouraged him to use his gifts, and also mentored him (Acts 9:26–28; 11:25–26). Luke calls both of them apostles (Acts 13:3; cf. 14:4, 14).

When the news reached the church in Jerusalem that the brethren in Antioch had received the word of God, it was Barnabas who was sent to minister to the people (Acts 11:22–24). When the news reached the apostles that Samaria had received the word of God, it was Peter and John who were sent to see the brethren (Acts 8:14). The fact that Barnabas was sent to Antioch shows the impression that the apostles had for him. Significantly, it was in Antioch that the believers of Christ were first called Christians.

In Acts 13:2, it was Barnabas and Saul that the Holy Spirit chose to be set apart for the work to which he had called them (Acts 13:2). Barnabas's call to apostolic ministry was through the Holy Spirit. Barnabas was often mentioned first until later the trend changed to Paul and Barnabas. During the missionary work, both Barnabas and Saul were addressed as apostles (Acts 14:4, 14). When Paul wanted to ascertain some recognition with the apostles in Jerusalem, as a result of a revelation he received, he went with Barnabas, and the three apostles who were considered pillars of the church (James, Peter, and John) extended the right hand of fellowship to both of them (Paul and Barnabas, Gal 2:9). The three of them agreed that they would minister to the Jews while Paul and Barnabas go to the Gentiles, which implied that the two of them were the apostles to the Gentiles (Gal 2:1–10). Paul and Barnabas were at the center of the Jerusalem council (Acts 15) because of their apostolic ministry. That is, they undertook the apostolic ministry with success until he and Paul parted company.

Barnabas was the one who took Mark when Paul was fed-up with his indecisiveness and dumped him, only for Paul to accept him later because he found him to be helpful (Acts 15:36–40). If Barnabas had not tolerated him, Paul would not have benefited from him later. He requested that Mark be brought to him in Rome, because he was very helpful (2 Tim 4:11). Barnabas was the apostle who continued to encourage people to come out of weaknesses to higher height. It was this Mark who blessed us with the gospel according to Mark. Barnabas's effort was not in vain. Paul openly called Barnabas an apostle (1 Cor 9:5–6)—an apostle who had to do the work of God without using his rights for the people to take care of him.

As scholars dispute the authorship of Hebrews, some have suggested it was the work of Barnabas. However, this has not been accepted. Surely Barnabas was one of the apostles. He was called by the Holy Spirit, he mentored Paul and encouraged him and others, went on apostolic tour, he ministered to the church in Antioch and a great number of people were added to the church.

Timothy and Silas

In Paul's ministry, he always worked with teams. He was specific in some of his writings in telling us the kind of person he was working with. He showed us those who were coworkers, fellow prisoners, helpers and apostles as he was. Luke who recorded Paul's apostolic activities in Acts also helped us know the persons that Paul worked with by describing them as a disciple, a prophet or an apostle. Most of the apostles who are discussed below fall under those Paul worked with.

Paul addressed Timothy and Silas as apostles (1 Thess 1:1; 2:6). To the Thessalonians, Paul said, as apostles of Christ, "we could have been a burden to you" (1 Thess 2:6). The "we" he used here was concerning three of them who wrote the letter. He had told them in 1:1 that it was three of them, Paul, Silas and Timothy who wrote to them. Both Timothy and Silas were with Paul, when he established churches in Philippi, Thessalonica, and Corinth (2 Cor 1:19; Acts 16:1—18:11).

Timothy, for example, was sent to visit and minister to the churches in Macedonia (Phil 2:19–24; 1 Thess 3:1–6). He had to stay in Ephesus to teach and lead them for some time (1 Tim 1:1–3; 4:11–16). Timothy had to accompany Paul in his travel through the Aegean Sea and then to Jerusalem (Acts 19:21–22; 20:4; Rom 16:21). Timothy was indeed a coworker, team player and an apostle with Paul.

Silas was a Christian leader before he accompanied Paul. He was one of the brothers, with a prophetic gift, who was sent by the apostles and elders in Jerusalem, to accompany Paul and Barnabas to read the letter, which was the outcome of the Council of Jerusalem to the Gentiles (Acts 15:22, 32). He was said to say much to encourage and strengthen the people during this assignment. Paul selected him to join his apostolic team after he parted company with Barnabas (Acts 15:40—18:5, 2 Cor

1:19; 1 Thess 1:1; 2 Thess 1:1). During this period, Paul and Silas were imprisoned in Philistia. It was here that an earthquake shook and opened the prison doors as they were praying and singing hymns (Acts 16:25–30). In his travel with Paul and Timothy to Thessalonica, they suffered hostility (Acts 17:5–9). He (Silas) and Paul had to be sent to Berea for safety but their hecklers followed them up. For the fact that Paul and Silas were often attacked showed Silas played an active role in their apostolic journey.

In 1 Pet 5:12, Peter shows that it was Silas who assisted him to write, "With the help of Silas, whom I regard as a faithful brother, I have written to you briefly, encouraging you and testifying that this is the true grace of God. Stand fast in it" (NIV). Peter regards him as a faithful brother and this letter shows that at that period, they were together. Thus, he was an apostle who had received training from both the apostles in Jerusalem and Paul. Silas could be considered an apostle.

Titus

One of the closest associates of Paul who was not directly mentioned as apostle but could be one was, Titus. When Paul was going to Jerusalem the second time as a result of a revelation he received, he went with Barnabas. Paul wanted to seek the consent of the apostles in Jerusalem once again so that their efforts would not be in vain. He added that he also went with Titus (Gal 2:1–5) and this shows that Titus was playing a very important role in Paul's ministry. As he wanted to seek the consent of the apostles concerning his ministry, he needed to take him (Titus) along.

Paul delegated Titus to represent him and minister to the church in Corinth, which appeared to be a troublesome church. He was able to cool the waters and brought a good report to Paul (2 Cor 7:5–7). When the Lord opened the door for Paul to minister in Troas, he had no peace and had to leave because Titus was not there (2 Cor 2:12). Strong as Paul was, he needed a person of equal status to do ministry with. Titus was one of them.

In 2 Cor 8:23, Paul called Titus "my partner and coworker" (2 Cor 8:23). Calling him "my partner and coworker" here is very significant. Titus was in the company of some brothers who had been sent to the Corinthians. Paul described the brothers as the representative of the churches, and an honor of Christ. However, Titus was a partner and coworker, someone who was doing the same work as Paul.

One time, Titus had to be left in Crete to appoint elders (or bishops) in the churches (Titus 1:4–5, 7). Later, the bishops claimed to be the successors of the apostles. Although Paul did not address him directly as an apostle, his description of him shows that he had an apostolic ministry. Concluding his discussion on Titus, Francis A. Sullivan, a Catholic priest and theologian, stated, "One can surely feel justified in concluding that in making Titus his 'partner and coworker,' Paul transmitted to him a share in the mission he himself had received from the risen Christ."[5] Thus, it will not be out of place to assume that Titus was an apostle.

Apollos

Another colleague of Paul who was not directly addressed as apostle but whose ministry portrayed him as an apostle of high caliber was Apollos.

Apollos was first described as someone who taught accurately about Jesus, but only knew the baptism of John (Acts 18:26). Then a couple, Priscilla and Aquila, who were disciples of Paul (Acts 18:24–26), schooled him in the way of God, which could mean that they taught him about the ministry of the Lord Jesus. Later, he was presented as joining the team of Paul. What brings his apostolic ministry to bear on the front is the way Paul involved him in a discussion in 1 Corinthians.

In 1 Cor 1:12–13, Paul laments, "What I mean is this: One of you says, 'I follow Paul'; another, 'I follow Apollos'; another, 'I follow Cephas'; still another, 'I follow Christ.' Is Christ divided? Was Paul crucified for you? Were you baptized into the name of Paul?" (NIV). He then continued in 3:6, he planted and Apollos watered. His point was to show that they were all God's fellow workers. For Paul to compare the works that he and Peter were doing to that of Apollos might mean Apollos might have been performing apostolic ministry that was recognized by many people. In addition, it always shows that his ministry was of high standard. In 1 Cor 16:12, Paul wanted him to go to Corinth but he refused, perhaps he did that because of the controversy which was going on in Corinth. He said he would go when there was opportunity. That could mean he would go when the dust settled down. In Titus 3:13, however, Paul indicated

---

5. Sullivan, *From Apostles to Bishops*, 46.

that Apollos was on the way to Crete with Zenas. That implies that Apollos was working with Paul.

Apollos has highly been tipped as the author of the book of Hebrews. Theologians who propose him instead of Paul and Barnabas include Martin Luther.[6] Taking into consideration the nature of the book, the quality of Greek as scholars assert, it needed an apostle of "weight" like Paul's type who could have written such a letter with strong Old Testament typologies of Christ and theological implications. The qualities given to Apollos perfectly fit him in well without holes:

> Meanwhile a Jew named Apollos, a native of Alexandria, came to Ephesus. He was a learned man, with a thorough knowledge of the Scriptures. He had been instructed in the way of the Lord, and he spoke with great fervor and taught about Jesus accurately, though he knew only the baptism of John. He began to speak boldly in the synagogue. When Priscilla and Aquila heard him, they invited him to their home and explained to him the way of God more adequately. (Acts 24–26 NIV)

Apollos might have left us with this quality of Scripture, which depicts Christ in the Old Testament more than any other book. Apollos could be a man of high apostolic ministry.

Priscilla and Women Apostleship

It is important for us to discuss the ministry of Priscilla as a possible apostolic in nature. Our Lord Jesus Christ did not choose any woman among his twelve apostles. Nevertheless, he had a radical approach in dealing with women during his early ministry;[7] some women were sometimes following and supporting his ministry (Matt 27:55; Luke 8:1–3).[8] It must, therefore, be considered that with the way and manner Jesus was working

---

6. Barclays, *Book of Hebrews*, 10.

7. He made it known publicly that a woman who had been bleeding had touched him; he also allowed the woman who anointed her to wipe his feet with her hair (Mark 5:24–34; Luke 7:36–50).

8. "After this, Jesus traveled about from one town and village to another, proclaiming the good news of the kingdom of God. The Twelve were with him, and also some women who had been cured of evil spirits and diseases: Mary (called Magdalene) from whom seven demons had come out; Joanna the wife of Cuza, the manager of Herod's household; Susanna; and many others. These women were helping to support them out of their own means" (Luke 8:1–3 NIV).

and training his apostles, it would have been very difficult to have some women among them always following him in his travels. Interestingly, at the crucifixion, when the apostles ran away, it was some of these women who occasionally followed him who stayed to watch the end of Jesus on earth. Consequently, when Jesus resurrected, it was a woman who carried the message to the apostles (John 19:10–18). Furthermore, when the disciples met at the upper room, there were some women among them (Acts 1:14). However, none of these women was labeled an apostle.

One woman, nonetheless, who has apostolic functions in the New Testament is Priscilla. Priscilla worked closely with the husband Aquila that the husband was never mentioned without her. In fact, six times that their names appear in the Bible, the name of Aquila is mentioned first in three of the references and Priscilla first in the other three. Both were tent makers as Paul was. Paul stayed with them for many days (Acts 18:18). They accompanied Paul to Syria, but stopped in Ephesus. Here, they heard Apollos taught the word of God accurately but without the full knowledge of Christ. They brought him home and explained the way of the Lord more accurately. In other words, they mentored him. Here, it was possibly Priscilla led the couple (Acts 18:26).[9]

Paul informs us of how they risked their lives for him (Rom 16:4). There was a church at their house in Rome (Rom 16:3–5); also there was a church at their house in Ephesus (1 Cor 16:8; cf. 16:19). Paul had not been to Rome by the time he was writing a letter to the church in Rome. It had always been Paul's ambition to preach the gospel where Christ was not known. He did not want to build on someone's foundation (Rom 15:20). Could it be possible that Priscilla and Aquila might have started the church in Rome or might have been founding members of the church and, thus, Paul had the desire to visit to the church in Rome? Thus, since Priscilla and Aquila and Paul had always been players, he considered their work as his own. Paul finally addresses them as his coworkers (Rom 16:3). In Paul's last letter—2 Timothy—he mentions Priscilla before Aquila (4:19). Clearly Priscilla and Aquila had been doing the work of missions with Paul.

Some scholars have suggested Priscilla to be the author of the book of Hebrews. Significant among them is Ruth Hoppin who argues that Priscilla solely qualifies to be the author of the book. She suggests that

9. Many of the versions, including RSV, NIV ESV and GNB bring Priscilla first; however, other versions, including KJ and NKJV bring Aquila first. It might depend upon the Greek manuscript which was used by the translators of a specific version.

she is the one person who could meet all the qualifications for the authorship of the book.¹⁰ Hoppin and others, such as Gilbert Bilezikian, and Lee Anna Starr contend that either her name was deliberately deleted to protect the book from suppression or it was deleted to suppress female authorship.¹¹ Although the search for the author for the book of Hebrews will continue, this claim raises the status of Priscilla.

The Apostolic Constitution names Aquila and Nicetas as the first bishops of the church in Asia Minor (*Apostolic Constitution* 46). In addition to this, the churches that canonize saints such as the Catholic and Orthodox have canonized Priscilla and Aquila, and commemorate them on July 8, a day which tradition set their martyrdom.¹² Besides, the American Orthodox church regards Aquila as an apostle, labeling him, "Apostle Aquila of the seventy."¹³ If Priscilla was considered an equal partner with her husband in all their ministry, trained Apollos, opened and housed churches at their home, was a coworker of Paul, then Priscilla may be considered an apostolic figure in the New Testament—a woman apostle.

PAUL'S ASSOCIATES WHO MAY NOT BE APOSTLES: EPAPHRODITUS, ANDRONICUS, AND JUNIAS

There are a few people who, some suggest, could be apostles, which we need to discuss. The first is Paul's fellow worker Epaphroditus. Philippians 2:25 reads, "But I think it is necessary to send back to you Epaphroditus, my brother, fellow worker and fellow soldier, who is also your messenger, whom you sent to take care of my needs" (NIV). Paul commended him as "my brother," "fellow worker" and "fellow soldier." Then, he added "also your messenger." As the result of the use of the term messenger (*apostolos*) here, which means apostle, some people think Epaphroditus was an apostle by calling. Nevertheless, the context does not fit in so well as such. Epaphroditus was from Philippi, and the Philippians had sent him to send some gifts to Paul. As he discharged this work, he really felt

---

10. Hoppin, *Priscilla's Letter*.

11. Starr, *Bible Status of Woman*, 392–415; Bilezikian, *Beyond Sex Roles*, 200–201.

12. Catholic New Agency, "Sts. Aquila and Priscilla," https://www.catholicnewsagency.com/saint/sts-aquila-and-priscilla-531.

13. Orthodox Church in America, "Apostle Aquila of the Seventy," https://www.oca.org/saints/lives/2010/07/14/101950-apostle-aquila-of-the-seventy.

seriously sick. On recovery, Paul wanted to send him back to his people, possibly with the letter. Paul had to commend him for his faithfulness, zeal and commitment. I do not see in "also your messenger" the call to apostleship.[14]

In Rom 16:7, Paul called Andronicus and Junias (a woman), outstanding among the apostles. Paul's statement here is not clear as to whether the two were apostles who stood out among the other apostles or they were highly respected among the apostles. I will go for the latter, which implies that the couple and their works, as believers, were highly appreciated among the apostles.

14. See also discussion on Paul's two ways of using the term apostle in Barnett, "Apostle," 47.

Chapter 14

The Constitution of an Apostle

THE PREVIOUS CHAPTER HAS shown how the Lord calls and trains the apostles. This chapter continues by showing us how to recognize an apostle through his gifts.

EMBODIMENT OF GIFTS

Our analysis so far has helped us identify some apostles besides the original Twelve and Paul. The question is, how did we arrive at this? The New Testament gives clues of who an apostle is. In other words, apostleship is not just conferring the name apostle on a person; rather, it is the embodiment of gifts in a person that makes him an apostle. We should be able to get traits of these graces and enablement as we interact with the ministries of the apostles, especially that of Paul. What I am doing in this section is to attempt to let us identify the constitution, the nature, or the makeups of an apostle. Through this exercise, we should be able to identify an apostle from the other gifts.

From Paul's letters, we recognize that one of the differences between spiritual gifts and ministry gifts (Eph 4:11–12) is that whereas every Christian is endowed with a spiritual gift or gifts, a great number of gifts come upon a person to make them a gift to the church. Paul throws light on this in Eph 4:11–13:

> It was he who gave some to be apostles, some to be prophets, some to be evangelists, and some to be pastors and teachers, to

prepare God's people for works of service, so that the body of Christ may be built up until we all reach unity in the faith and in the knowledge of the Son of God and become mature, attaining to the whole measure of the fullness of Christ. (NIV)

Similarly in 1 Cor 12:27–30, Paul's teaching appears to say that certain people are gifts to the body of Christ while others possess certain spiritual gifts:

> Now you are the body of Christ, and each one of you is a part of it. And in the church God has appointed first of all apostles, second prophets, third teachers, then workers of miracles, also those having gifts of healing, those able to help others, those with gifts of administration, and those speaking in different kinds of tongues. Are all apostles? Are all prophets? Are all teachers? Do all work miracles? Do all have gifts of healing? Do all speak in tongues? Do all interpret? (1 Cor 12:27–30 NIV)

Verse 28 begins with, "And in the church God has appointed first apostles, second prophets," which indicates that the list which includes apostles, prophets, teachers, and workers of miracles are gifts that God has placed in the church. Stated in another way, God has placed gifts of apostles, prophets, teachers and miracle workers in the church. In the next sentence ("also having gifts of healing"), the trend changes from the persons being the subject matter of gifts to the gifts as the subject. The gifts stated are healing, helps, administration, and different kinds of tongues. The understanding then is that while some people are gifts themselves, others possess certain gifts. This implies that the person with a ministry gift is himself a gift to the body of God. Ephesians 5:11–12 show the ministry gifts are apostles, prophets, evangelists, pastors and teachers. The most important thing, however, is that all are to use whatever gift they possess or are, for the building of the church.

What then is the apostle? As it was in the case of the prophet, a number of gifts come together on an individual for him to be identified as apostle. The apostle must have a balanced ministry. That is, having both the ministry to evangelize and to teach or having the grace to hear from God and also to lead. Sometimes, if the apostle is ministering, he may be considered as a teacher, other times, he may be taken as an evangelist, and still other times, he may be measured as a prophet or a pastor. Thus, the apostle can operate in many spiritual gifts. The depth of his operation will identify him as an apostle and by that bring out the differences between the manifestation of the apostolic gift and the other offices.

A CALL

Already, it has been established that the apostle must be called by the Lord. Once the Lord calls a person, he will endow him with grace to execute his task. The call itself is the greatest gift that every apostle has. The call, which comes with an assignment attached which appears in a form of instructions, gives the person an assurance of what the Lord wants him to do. The person who has been called knows it; it is imprinted in his mind. He always has a divine awareness of his task.

TEACHING THE WORD

The Lord has called the apostle. The apostle has heard from him and should be able to tell others of what he has heard. The gift of teaching is one of the gifts that comes along with apostleship. The original apostles specified the ministration of the word as a core duty of the apostle. They declared, "Brothers, choose seven men from among you who are known to be full of the Spirit and wisdom. We will turn this responsibility over to them and will give our attention to prayer and *the ministry of the word*" (Acts 6:3–4 NIV, italics mine). The apostle should be able to divide the word of God with clarity.[1] We cannot have an apostle without the word. Every messenger carries the message of his master (Acts 26:16; 1:22).

LEADERSHIP AND ADMINISTRATION

Apart from the call, one of the gifts that an apostle has is leadership. Paul shows in Ephesians that the church is built on the foundation of apostles and prophets, with Christ Jesus as the Cornerstone; "Consequently, you are no longer foreigners and aliens, but fellow citizens with God's people and members of God's household, built on the foundation of the apostles and prophets, with Christ Jesus himself as the chief cornerstone" (Eph 2:19–21 NIV). Then, again, Paul indicates that the administration or governance of God's grace has been given to him (Eph 3:2), and further

---

1. See chapter 6, under the gift of teaching.

explains that he had been tasked "to make plain to everyone the administration of this mystery" (Eph 3:9 NIV). I understand the foundation here as the solid teaching of the apostles and prophets, with the chief cornerstone as the thrust of their message which is Christ and what he has done for humanity. The leader must know where he is going and then ask people to follow him. Paul was shown what to do and he saw to it that it was done. Thus, the management (with wisdom and knowledge) of running the church is what we consider here as administration. Paul says that this management with "wisdom and knowledge" has been given to him. In 1 Cor 4:1–2, Paul puts it this way, "Let a man so consider us, as servants of Christ and stewards of the mysteries of God. Moreover it is required in stewards that one be found faithful" (NKJV). The apostles are stewards who manage the household of God. They are the storekeepers of the treasures of God. They are to provide for the needs of the family. They are to give instructions, guidance and directives as will help the well-being of the family. The office is a position of high trust.

Jesus told the Apostle Peter that he was going to build his church on "this rock," and would give him the keys to heaven and earth. Matthew 16:16–19 reads:

> Simon Peter answered, "You are the Christ, the Son of the living God." Jesus replied, "Blessed are you, Simon son of Jonah, for this was not revealed to you by man, but by my Father in heaven. And I tell you that you are Peter, and on this rock I will build my church, and the gates of Hades will not overcome it. I will give you the keys of the kingdom of heaven; whatever you bind on earth will be bound in heaven, and whatever you loose on earth will be loosed in heaven." (NIV)

Many interpretations have been given on this statement, "You are Peter, and on this rock I will build my church." One of the most convincing interpretations is that Jesus was referring to the statement made by Peter that "you are the Christ, the Son of the living God" (Matt 16:16 NIV). While this could be a probable interpretation, it does not also rule out the possibility that the church was going to be built through the leadership of Peter. Giving the keys to Peter was a sign that leadership had been invested into Peter by Jesus. Peter would represent the twelve apostles who were called directly by Jesus, when he (Jesus) was physically on earth. Their call, training, and commissioning in Matt 28:18–20 are evidence that the apostles had been given the responsibility to do the foundational work of the church. While Peter stands for the twelve, Paul stands for those apostles called after the death, resurrection, ascension, and glorification of Jesus. Paul's calling, training, commissioning by the Lord, and the church in Antioch are evidence that he had been given the responsibility to manage God's church. Apostleship goes along with leadership and administration.[2]

SIGNS, WONDERS, AND MIRACLES

When Paul was defending his apostleship to the Corinthians, he said, "The things that mark an apostle—signs, wonders and miracles—were done among you with great perseverance" (2 Cor 12:12). By this, Paul is telling us that there are some things, which follow an apostle. Accordingly, in Acts 14:3, Luke reports, "So Paul and Barnabas spent considerable time there, speaking boldly for the Lord, who confirmed the message of his grace by enabling them to do miraculous signs and wonders." (Acts 14:3 NIV).

He was an apostle and was fully aware of these things. The things he mentions here are signs, wonders, and miracles. Many people try to differentiate these phenomena. James Gyimah, a pastor with an apostolic gift, in the Church of Pentecost, gives an explanation of signs, wonders and miracles, which will be of interest here. For him:

- A sign is that which shows that somebody or something is present or exists or something may happen—a pointer.

- A wonder is a feeling of surprise and delight caused by something beautiful, unusual or unexpected.

- A miracle is a remarkable or unexplainable event—a surprising or welcoming act or an event which does not follow the known laws of nature and therefore thought to be caused by God.[3]

What these point to is that some visible things will happen through the apostolic ministry to the extent that at least some of the people around will know that indeed God is with this person. Paul told the Corinthians, "My message and my preaching were not with wise and persuasive words, but with a demonstration of the Spirit's power, so that your faith might not rest on men's wisdom, but on God's power" (1 Cor 2:4–5 NIV).

---

2. More light will be thrown on leadership and apostleship later in this book.
3. Gyimah, "Ministry of Apostles and Prophets," 361.

The gifts of confirmation such as faith, miracles and healing follow the apostle's ministry.

The Gift of Faith

The gift of faith is the ability to have unshaken trust in God to do something beyond the ordinary. This is different from the saving faith (Eph 2:8–9). In order to be saved, a person needs to believe in Jesus. This is what we call the saving faith. Christians also need to walk by faith. Second Corinthians 5:7 reads, "We live by faith, not by sight" (NIV). The Christian life is a life of faith. We do not see the God we believe in. The book of Hebrews says, "And without faith it is impossible to please God, because anyone who comes to him must believe that he exists and that he rewards those who earnestly seek him" (Heb 11:6 NIV). A person cannot be a good Christian without exercising some amount of faith in life. Faith enables people to stand trials and go through challenges in their lives without much complaint. They are able to believe that all things work together for the good of Christians (Rom 8:28). Yet, besides this faith is the gift of faith. This gift gives a person the strong assurance of the things hoped for; the real conviction of things not seen as real (cf. Heb 11:1). The person with this gift believes that God can do things, which others do not believe are possible. He has the strong conviction, without entertaining fear that those things are possible. This gift is well displayed in the life of King David. When David heard what Goliath was saying, he was worried and was very sure that God would deliver him to Israel. When King Saul was worried for David, he (David) was very sure that the Lord would deliver Goliath to him:

> But David said to Saul, "Your servant has been keeping his father's sheep. When a lion or a bear came and carried off a sheep from the flock, I went after it, struck it and rescued the sheep from its mouth. When it turned on me, I seized it by its hair, struck it and killed it. Your servant has killed both the lion and the bear; this uncircumcised Philistine will be like one of them, because he has defied the armies of the living God. The Lord who delivered me from the paw of the lion and the paw of the bear will deliver me from the hand of this Philistine." Saul said to David, "Go, and the Lord be with you." (1 Sam 17:34–37 NIV)

If you examine David's statement, he had no doubts in his spirit that the Lord would deliver Goliath to him. Even when Goliath threatened David, he was still not afraid. Listen to David:

> David said to the Philistine, "You come against me with sword and spear and javelin, but I come against you in the name of the Lord Almighty, the God of the armies of Israel, whom you have defied. This day the Lord will hand you over to me, and I'll strike you down and cut off your head. Today I will give the carcasses of the Philistine army to the birds of the air and the beasts of the earth, and the whole world will know that there is a God in Israel. All those gathered here will know that it is not by sword or spear that the Lord saves; for the battle is the Lord's, and he will give all of you into our hands." (1 Sam 17:45–47 NIV)

He knew the Lord was going to deliver Goliath to him, he would kill him and cut off his head. When Goliath moved forward to attack him, he ran to meet him. When Goliath fell down, he ran and stood over him and cut off his head (1 Sam 17:51). A person without faith would have thought that Goliath was even playing tricks for David to come closer for him to attack David and kill him. Yet, David moved forward to attack him. The gift of faith generates such strong assurance in the person who has been granted the gift.

I remember when I was leading the Church of Pentecost to put up a convention center, it was so natural for me. I saw the convention center as a need. The proposal was that we were not going to raise funds, neither were we going to levy church members. We were going to put up the center through the prudent management of the regular monthly money that was coming to the church. Some people really registered their doubts about this and could not see how we were going to raise money for such a project. Eventually the church was able to put up a center that cost us an equivalent of $40,000,000 without taking money from banks and without appealing for funds from members. At the time we were taking the decision, it was so normal to me that I was not thinking of it as a gift of faith as such. It was after the project had been commissioned that other people drew our attention to the fact that the putting up of the center was led by the mighty hand of God.[4] The gift of faith might have been in operation.

---

4. Just Google Pentecost Convention Centre Ghana.

The Gift of Miracles

The gift of miracles is the ability to perform acts with the power of the Holy Spirit, which are beyond human capacity and are contrary to natural laws. It is the Lord who really causes miracles to take place in the cause of his sent one's ministries. One of the purposes of the gift of miracles is for the people around to know that the Lord has sent the person. During the earthly life of Jesus, many miracles followed him for the people to know that the Messiah had arrived. Miracles often cause people to listen to the word of God and to give them the opportunity to believe in God (Matt 12:13–22; Luke 13:10–17). Yet, miracles do not guarantee faith in Jesus. This is clearly displayed in the lives of the Pharisees. The more they saw the miracles of Jesus, the more they wanted to kill him. They wanted to kill Jesus because he was performing miracles and many people were believing in him (John 11:46–50). Yet, miracles strengthen other people's faith to accept that indeed the Lord is God (1 Kgs 18:39). The power to perform miracles is of the Lord and not of the individual. Miracles take place at the sovereign will of God.

The Gifts of Healing

The gifts of healing is linked with the gift of miracles. However, whereas the gift of miracles deals with all aspects of miracles, the gifts of healing directly deal with healing. The gifts (*charisma*) of healing is the ability to heal diseases of all kinds with the power of the Holy Spirit. The use of the plural form to describe this gift is generally understood to signify the possibility for healing diverse forms of diseases (1 Cor 12:9, 28, 30). There are different forms of healing, such as natural healing which takes place through the body's instincts and environmental resources. Many may fall sick without going to the hospital or taking any medicine, yet the body may heal itself. Other healings include medical healing, which takes place through preventive and therapeutic means. This is mainly administered through medical doctors. God has endowed people with knowledge in the medical field to do this job. Still another type of healing is emotional or inner healing, where the focus is on past psychological and emotional traumas. Here, too, people who are trained can administer counselling resulting in healing of various traumas and fears. Emotional healing brings comfort and emotional stability to individuals who go through emotional battles.

Another type of healing is divine healing where the focus is on the power of the Holy Spirit to cure diseases. People who are endowed with this gift are expected to pray for the sick to have majority of them healed in Jesus' name. The gift is given for the benefit of the church, and it operates through the sovereign will of God and not through the individual's own will. In other words, the individuals who possess this gift do not have the healing power within themselves to heal people wherever they go. It is not a gift to be used to display one's power, but it is part of the gifts that the Lord has given to build up the body of Christ. The Lord is the source of all these types of healings. The gifts of healing in operation can heal any type of disease by the power of the Holy Spirit.

The gift of faith links both the gifts of healing and miracles together. Consequently the emphasis on the issue of faith in Jesus' healing ministry (Matt 15:21–28; Matt 9:23–26; Luke 8:50; Mark 6:1–6) and those of the apostles Peter and Paul (Acts 3:16; 14:9–10) has caused some Christians to infer that if a person could only generate enough faith, healing and miracles would always occur. Nevertheless, there is a balancing theme, which pervades the New Testament. Sometimes, a miracle occurs where there was little or no faith in order to instill belief in Jesus, as the Son of God (e.g., Matt 8:26). Faith was frequently spoken of as the result, rather than the precondition of the healing power of Jesus (cf. Matt 9:18, 22; Matt 15:31). Although the gospels point out that Jesus "did not many mighty works" (Matt 13:58 KJV; see also Mark 6:5) in his hometown because of unbelief, nowhere is the failure to be healed attributed to the lack of faith on the part of the sick person. This means that while it is essential for us to have faith in God and his ability to heal, healing is solely his sovereign will.[5] The implication is that the focus is not on the person who has the gifts of healing but on the Lord who heals.

Besides the Lord Jesus Christ, in the New Testament Apostle Peter (and John), Philip, and Apostle Paul were those who exhibited this type of gift. With Peter and John's ministries, the cripple was healed as Peter commanded him when they were going to the temple (Acts 3:1–10). Generally, it was said that the apostles performed many miraculous signs and wonders (Acts 5:12). On Peter alone, it was said that sick people were brought out into the streets so that his shadow might fall on them, leading to healing (Acts 5:15–16). Through Peter's ministry, a paralytic (Aeneas) got up from bed (Acts 9:32–35), the dead was brought back to life (Acts

---

5. Onyinah, "Divine Healing," 295–339.

9:36–43), and he himself had angelic visitation leading to freedom from prison (Acts 12:6–19). Philip's ministry in Samaria resulted in miracles; evil spirits were cast out, the paralyzed and cripples were healed. Many accepted the Lord (Acts 8:6–8).

In Paul's ministry, the man crippled from birth sprang up and walked (Acts 14:8–10); a false prophet went blind for preventing someone from hearing the word of God (Acts 13:6–12); the dead was raised up (Acts 20:7–12); sick people were healed by handkerchiefs and aprons that had touched him (Acts 19:11–12); there was deliverance from prisons through earthquake (Acts 16:15–30); and evil spirits were cast out (Acts 16:6–10; 19:12).

It should be noted that in all these it was the Lord who was working through them. They did not have power on their own to perform these miracles. They could not also claim to heal people. They worked hard to stop people from making them heroes and worshipping them. For example, Barnabas and Paul worked hard in Ephesus to stop the people from worshipping them:

> When the crowd saw what Paul had done, they shouted in the Lycaonian language, "The gods have come down to us in human form!" Barnabas they called Zeus, and Paul they called Hermes because he was the chief speaker. The priest of Zeus, whose temple was just outside the city, brought bulls and wreaths to the city gates because he and the crowd wanted to offer sacrifices to them. But when the apostles Barnabas and Paul heard of this, they tore their clothes and rushed out into the crowd, shouting: "Men, why are you doing this? We too are only men, human like you. We are bringing you good news, telling you to turn from these worthless things to the living God, who made heaven and earth and sea and everything in them. In the past, he let all nations go their own way. Yet he has not left himself without testimony: He has shown kindness by giving you rain from heaven and crops in their seasons; he provides you with plenty of food and fills your hearts with joy." Even with these words, they had difficulty keeping the crowd from sacrificing to them. (Acts 14:11–18 NIV)

Barnabas and Paul did all they could to let the people focus on the Lord. They showed themselves as just vessels being used by the Lord. Apostles do not take glory for themselves. Christ becomes their Master and their focus in ministry. They do not advertise miracles since it is the Lord who confirms their message with miracles at his own will.

The apostles could not do miracles with their own will and power. The examples shown above mean that the miracles the apostles performed in the name of Jesus were limited; they were not as many as some people think. For example, despite the extraordinary miracles that the Lord did through Paul, he could not heal his closest associates when they were sick. He had to ask Timothy to stop drinking only water because of his stomach and frequent illnesses (1 Tim 5:23). He left Trophimus sick in Miletus (2 Tim 4:20–21). Epaphroditus was sick and almost died but God did have mercy on them (Phil 2:25–27). All of these show that the apostles could not heal by their power. They were very much limited. They were human beings just as we are, who availed themselves to be used by the Lord at his will. It was the Lord who healed or performed miracles through them as a confirmation of his word.

I believe that these gifts—"a call," "teaching," "leadership and administration or governance," healing, miracles and faith may be the basic gifts of the apostolic office. There could be many other gifts that follow, I think these form the foundation of the gift of apostleship. Once a person has a call, endowed with teaching and leadership, together with one of the "signs, wonders and miraculous gifts" (healing, miracles and faith), the person has traits of apostleship. These basic gifts make the apostle a person of *charisma* who attracts following. He carries a lot of authority and "awe," and it is not difficult to identify him as a leader among leaders.

Consequently, apostles may have special operations tailored after the other ministry gifts, such as prophets, evangelists, teachers, and pastors. In practical ministry, it is realized that all apostles do not function in the same direction. Peter's ministry was different from John. Yet, both were called by Jesus as apostles. Peter's ministry appears to be like an evangelist (e.g., Acts 2–3), John's ministry depicts a prophet (e.g., the book of Revelation), and a teacher (e.g., the Gospel of John). From a similar perspective of varieties of ministries among the apostles, Bill Hamon, the founder of Christian Ministries International,[6] has proposed that there are apostolic-apostles, prophetic-apostles, evangelistic-apostles, pastoral-apostles, and teacher-apostles.[7] Although many people have their reservations about the New Apostolic Reformation, this proposal could be a very practical way of explaining the diversities in the operations

---

6. Bill Hamon is one of the pastors who is associated with the unpopular New Apostolic Reformation. See Geivett and Pivec, *God's Super-Apostles*, 5. Yet, the practicality of what I present here is similar to Hamon's assumption cited in the next footnote.

7. See Hamon, *Apostles and Prophets*, 223–25.

of the apostles.[8] Accordingly, I adopt it and throw more light on it. There can be apostles whose ministry is typically apostolic; they move around, establish churches, train and plant leaders to take charge like Paul did. There can also be apostles like John who can be seen as prophetic-apostles. Such people do prophesy and sometimes function like prophets. There can be evangelistic-apostles like Peter, whose ministry appear more as an evangelist, even though they are apostles. There can be pastoral-apostles like James, the natural brother of Jesus, who happened to pastor the church in Jerusalem. There can also be the teacher-apostles like Apollos, who became one of the centers of controversy in the church at Corinth (1 Cor 3:1–9).[9] This is to say that apostles do not have the same ministry, however, they are called and sent by the same Lord. Who then is an apostle? This is the subject of the next chapter.

---

8. Peter Wagner also proposes four types of apostles: Vertical—those who head apostolic network; Horizontal—have authority over other apostles either for a defined, prolonged period of time or for a season or a particular assignment; Hyphenated—apostles who have other gifts and offices; Market place apostles—the apostles who ministered outside the church. Wagner, *Apostles and Prophets*, 41–73. I think Hamon's proposal gives a possible explanation to the varieties of ministries among the apostles than Wagner's proposal. Hamon, *Apostles and Prophets and the Coming Moves of God*, 41–73.

9. The apostleship of Apollos is discussed in chapter 13.

Chapter 15

Who Then Is an Apostle?

THE DISCUSSION THUS FAR has sought to identify who an apostle is. By so doing we have discovered that there were apostles in the Old Testament. Although prophets were the messengers of God in the Old Testament, there were people who exhibited apostolic gift by leading the people of God. Most prominent among them was Moses. Others include Joshua, Deborah, Samuel and Nehemiah. The prophets such as Isaiah, Nathan, Elisha, assisted kings but they were not leading. The Moses type of leaders, hearing from God and directing people, were identified as apostles in the Old Testament. Yet, the Moses type of leaders were still limited in that they needed to work also with the high priests.

The Lord Jesus operated as the apostle par excellence. In him combined the offices of the leader (king), the prophet and the high priesthood. He exemplified the next messenger of God in the New Testament for us. Consequently, he chose twelve apostles, trained, empowered and then commissioned them.

The selection of the Twelve by the Lord Jesus inspired the eleven apostles to choose an additional apostle to fill the vacuum created by the death of Judas. It would appear, at the period, that the total number of the apostles was going to be mystified and limited to twelve. However, the Lord Jesus demystified this by calling two other apostles whose apostolicity cannot be challenged by Christians of all ages; these are Paul and James. Paul who championed the Gentile mission and James who championed the Jewish mission.

I argued that besides these two well-recognized and acceptable apostles, there were others whose ministries demonstrated that they were apostles. These included Jude, Barnabas, Apollos, Silas, Timothy, and Titus. Some of these including Jude and Barnabas might have seen Jesus in the flesh, others such as Timothy, Titus and Apollos had not.

We did not accidentally propose some individuals in Scripture to be apostles, but the New Testament gives pointers on what constitute an apostle. As we dug out these indicators, we discovered some graces associated with apostleship. They included "a call," "teaching ability," "leadership and administration or governance," and "signs, wonders and miracles." The apostle, I assert, should have these gifts as a base to launch him into ministry.

Who then is an apostle? The criteria that Peter, the apostles and the disciples who met to select Matthias set down for inclusion into the apostleship was a person who had been with them (Christ and the apostles), from the beginning of John's baptism until the time Jesus was taken up. Then, the person was to become a witness of his resurrection (Acts 1:23–24). Thus, their primary aim was to get a person who would become a witness together with them of the resurrected Jesus. From this perspective, then, an apostle must have seen the resurrected Jesus in order for him to become a witness of his resurrection. Paul's call to apostleship throws more light on the importance of seeing Jesus in order to become his witness. He saw the resurrected Jesus who sent him to declare what he had seen and heard to the Gentiles. Thus, "being with Jesus," or "seeing Jesus" is not just seeing Jesus or being with him in the flesh. Rather, it is seeing and knowing the resurrected Jesus in order to witness about him. It can be said of the twelve apostles that it was not just being with and seeing Jesus in the flesh that made their calling complete. It was seeing the resurrected Jesus that made the eleven complete. In other words, a member of the twelve apostles could walk with Jesus, talk with him, eat with him without knowing him as the Son of God and the Savior, in order to witness about what he had seen and experienced. Thus, seeing the resurrected Jesus makes the difference.

For example, Thomas, one of the apostles who had not seen Jesus after the resurrection, still did not believe him, until Jesus revealed himself to him. After seeing Jesus, he called him, "My Lord and my God" (John 21:24–29). There was a complete change from disbelief to acknowledging Jesus as both Lord and God. Thomas never became the doubting Thomas again. The difference was the revelation of Jesus in his spirit.

James the brother of Jesus knew Jesus physically but he was not an apostle. What transformed him was the revelation of the resurrected Jesus. From there, James did not see Jesus just as his brother but as his Lord. He saw himself as a servant of Jesus (Jas 1:1). A person could know Jesus physically but that might not matter too much. The two disciples on the road to Emmaus knew Jesus very well, but they could not recognize him when he was walking with them (Luke 24:45). They considered him a visitor in Jerusalem. What made the difference for them was the moment their eyes opened and they saw the resurrected Jesus.

Mary Magdalene who visited the tomb of Jesus could not recognize Jesus either, although she knew him very well. She thought Jesus was the gardener, until he revealed himself to her (John 20:10–18). Once Jesus opened her eyes to see him as the resurrected one, "she turned toward him and cried out in Aramaic, 'Rabboni!' (which means 'Teacher')" (John 20:16 NIV).

Until Jesus reveals himself to you, you may see him as a normal person like the natural brothers of Jesus, as a stranger like the two disciples who walked with Jesus on the road to Emmaus, or as a gardener like Mary Magdalene who visited Jesus on the tomb. Thus, the most important aspect of the call to apostleship is to know the person of Jesus clearly through a revelation. Then, you can know him as "my Lord and my God" so that you can positively proclaim what you have seen and heard.

I would, therefore, venture to say that the selection of the Twelve by the Lord Jesus and their training was to open the way for us to know the type of ministry that had begun in the New Testament. The calling of Paul who had not seen Jesus in the flesh set a clearer paradigm for us to know what Jesus intended for us to know about the type of messengers (apostles), he had chosen for the New Testament; Jesus wanted to continue his work through the apostles. The apostle, therefore, is the one who has seen Jesus in revelation, heard clearly from him, is empowered with gifts of the Spirit, and has thereby been sent to discharge all these, with the Lord confirming his ministry with signs, wonders and miracles. The apostle may be given special capabilities to execute with excellence an aspect of the kingdom's business, including establishing churches, Bible Colleges, and parachurch organizations. People who had the grace to begin such kingdom oriented organizations as the following may possess the apostolic gift: Bible Society, Child Evangelism Fellowship, Operation Mobilization, Mercy Ships, Wycliffe Bible Translations, Gideon's International, Scripture Union, International Fellowship of Evangelical Students,

Youth for Christ, Youth with a Mission, Prison Fellowship, Langham Partnership International, Samaritan's Purse, Full Gospel Business Men's Fellowship International, and World Vision International. Thus, it is not a question of whether there is an apostle today or not but whether a person has heard from Jesus and has been sent by him to do something and to see the Lord confirming his word through the person's ministry with signs.[1]

The next chapter, therefore, discusses the functions of the one sent by God, the apostle.

---

1. The question of why there was no one titled apostle in church history after the death of the New Testament period apostles is handled in part 7.

PART 6

The Functions of an Apostle

This part discusses the functions of apostles. This is remarkably different from the functions of the prophets in the Old Testament. However, there are some similarities. The functions are presented in thirteen topics under four chapters. It begins with chapters 16–20. The chapters are closely linked with one another; they are divided for easy reading. Chapter 21 attempts to draw similarities as well as dissimilarities between apostles and prophets. It is not necessarily part of the functions of the apostle as such.

Chapter 16

Foundation Layers

APOSTLES ARE FOUNDATION LAYERS. They begin a work and build on it. This chapter discusses this topic under three headings: the ability to lay sound foundation in doctrines; the ability to begin a new church, the ability to grow a church and the ability to supervise churches.

THE ABILITY TO LAY SOUND FOUNDATION IN DOCTRINES

One of the main works of the apostle is to speak the word of God with clarity. Using the building as an analogy, Ephesians brings out a powerful truth of the church, "Consequently, you are no longer foreigners and aliens, but fellow citizens with God's people and members of God's household, built on the foundation of the apostles and prophets, with Christ Jesus himself as the chief cornerstone. In him the whole building is joined together and rises to become a holy temple in the Lord" (Eph 2:19–21 NIV).

The statement seems to bring out the teaching and practices of the apostles and prophets which become the basis upon which the church is built. The apostle is like a good builder who puts up a very solid foundation and puts up his building. Some scholars think that the "prophets" here basically refers to the Old Testament prophets.[1] Whereas the divine

---

1. For brief discussion on this see, Patzia, *Ephesians, Colossians, Philemon*, 201; see also Clarke, "Ephesians 2:20."

revelation communicated by the Old Testament prophets form the basis of the Christian doctrines, here, Paul may be referring to the apostles and prophets in the New Testament. This becomes more likely if we consider that in the next chapter Paul writes, "In reading this, then, you will be able to understand my insight into the mystery of Christ, which was not made known to men in other generations as it has now been revealed by the Spirit to God's holy apostles and prophets" (Eph 3:4–5 NIV). Here, Paul indicates that the mystery of the church revealed to the apostles and prophets by the Spirit of God was not revealed "to men in other generations." Thus, the use of "prophets" here refers to the New Testament prophets. In addition, Paul was writing to Gentile Christians who did not know much about Old Testament prophets. Prophets here might be referring to prophets such as Judas and Silas who, when sent by the church in Jerusalem, strengthened the newly converted Gentiles (Acts 15:32; cf. Acts 13:1–4).

The point, however, is that apostles can share the basic word of God with clarity and set the foundation for a church. They do not entertain false doctrines.

THE ABILITY TO BEGIN A NEW CHURCH

Apostolic ministry includes founding or establishing local churches on the sure foundation of Christ Jesus (1 Cor 3:9–16; Rom 16:20; Eph 2:20–22). It is not very clear in the New Testament whether all the twelve apostles chosen directly by Christ planted new churches. Extrabiblical information, however, shows that some of them planted churches. William Steuart McBirnie has shown this in his inspiring accounts of the untold stories about the twelve apostles.[2] The ministries of Paul and Barnabas who were called to be apostles after the death of Christ (Acts 13:1–4) show that planting and growing a church is one of the real signs of the apostle. Before the Holy Spirit sent Paul and Barnabas, they had the apostolic call, yet they were not considered as such by the church. The presentation of Luke, who wrote the Acts of the Apostles, shows this:

> Now in the church that was at Antioch there were certain prophets and teachers: Barnabas, Simeon who was called Niger, Lucius of Cyrene, Manaen who had been brought up with

---

2. McBirnie, *Search for the Twelve Apostles*. See also Lockyer, *All the Apostles of the Bible*.

Herod the tetrarch, and Saul. As they ministered to the Lord and fasted, the Holy Spirit said, "Now separate to Me Barnabas and Saul for the work to which I have called them." Then, having fasted and prayed, and laid hands on them, they sent them away. (Acts 13:1–3 NKJV)

Luke mentions in Acts 13:1–3, "certain prophets and teachers," which is an indication that the people who had gathered to pray were considered as either prophets or teachers. Consequently, when the Holy Spirit spoke that they should separate Barnabas and Paul for the work to which he had called them, they prayed for them and released them to begin their ministry. When they began ministering, people saw them as apostles (Acts 14:4, 14). One lesson that can be learnt here is that some may initially be considered as prophets or teachers but later recognized as apostles. What happens at times is that since the apostleship is a combination of gifts, one of the gifts may operate initially to show that one's ministry could be, for example, prophetic, while later the dominant aspect which is apostolic might show up. Paul and Barnabas were considered among the prophets and teachers before they were sent out. When they went out, their ministry demonstrated that they were apostles.

Furthermore, another lesson that can be picked is that the two were already working together before the Holy Spirit spoke to the church in Antioch to send them:

> And the hand of the Lord was with them, and a great number believed and turned to the Lord. Then news of these things came to the ears of the church in Jerusalem, and they sent out Barnabas to go as far as Antioch. When he came and saw the grace of God, he was glad, and encouraged them all that with purpose of heart they should continue with the Lord. For he was a good man, full of the Holy Spirit and of faith. And a great many people were added to the Lord. Then Barnabas departed for Tarsus to seek Saul. And when he had found him, he brought him to Antioch. So it was that for a whole year they assembled with the church and taught a great many people. And the disciples were first called Christians in Antioch. (Acts 11:22–26 NKJV)

Sometimes the Holy Spirit confirms what he had already started doing. Barnabas saw the gifts in Paul; he was the one who introduced Paul to the apostles at Jerusalem. When some Grecian Jews wanted to kill Paul, he finally went to stay in his hometown Tarsus (Acts 9:26–30).

Barnabas went to bring Paul for the believers in Antioch to benefit from his ministry. This is an indication that the Holy Spirit confirmed what the Lord had already been using the brothers to do. For Paul, the Lord spoke to him the very day he revealed himself to him. He was being trained in the ministry as he moved around. He needed a support base for his ministry. He was also waiting for the right time. The commissioning by the Holy Spirit in Antioch was significant for both of them.

Sometimes, many people launch into something which they have not been trained for, not comfortable with, not skillful or not interested in by claiming that the Lord has sent them. God has his ways of doing things and calling people. Yet, he allows people to have hints of his will, trains them and gives them the support base. People who do not have this may have shipwreck of their ministries. Apostles keep on opening churches but they have a support base for their ministry.

Apostolic Ministry Brings a Harvest

When the Holy Spirit sent Paul and Barnabas, they preached the gospel and planted churches in the cities of Pisidian Antioch, Iconium, Lystra, and Derbe. The Scripture records that "a great multitude both of the Jews and of the Greeks believed" (Acts 14:1 NKJV). In Derbe, for example, it was reported that "they won a large number of disciples" (Acts 14:21 NIV). After the separation of Paul and Barnabas, it was still reported that there was success in the preaching of the gospel. For example, in Berea it was recorded that "many of them believed, and also not a few of the Greeks, prominent women as well as men" (Acts 17:12 NKJV). Eventually churches were established in cities including Philippi, Thessalonica, Athens, Corinth, and Ephesus. When God calls, he confirms.

The Apostle and the Evangelist

The establishing of churches by the apostle sometimes makes people think that he is an evangelist. The evangelist is the person who is given the ability by the Lord to present the gospel message so clearly and simply that people usually respond. One of the gifts a person may have as an evangelist is the gift of exhortation.[3] The evangelist may also have one of the gifts of confirmation, such as miracles, healings, or faith. In

---

3. For the discussion on the gift of exhortation, see chapter 6.

addition, music is one of the gifts which people with the evangelistic gift may possess.[4] These gifts, bestowed on a person, make him present the gospel in a simple, passionate, and interesting way, and sometimes with miracles following. People often respond to the evangelist's message. The evangelistic gift is necessary for the apostle to begin a church. He must present the gospel clearly for people to accept. However, whereas an evangelist may not be able to nurse a church and grow it, the apostle has the God-given ability to do these.

THE ABILITY TO GROW A CHURCH

Teaching and Pastoring

A church grows through teaching the word of God, setting in place good leadership, encouraging, fellowshipping, training, praying, and encouraging members to witness about their faith. Church growth is the work of the pastor. The pastor has a God-given ability to shepherd a church. He may also have the gift of serving (or help), showing mercy, and leadership. The gift of service or help is the ability to give assistance in any practical way that brings strength or encouragement to others (1 Cor 12:28; Rom 12:7). The person endowed with this gift serves people freely without expecting any reward. He serves both young and old, rich and poor, those in position and those without. They serve both believers and unbelievers. They can bring people to Christ through their services. While Paul was in prison and many people deserted him, he spoke of Onesiphorus who served him and was not ashamed of him. He appears to be a person with the gift of serving:

> You know that everyone in the province of Asia has deserted me, including Phygelus and Hermogenes. May the Lord show mercy to the household of Onesiphorus, because he often refreshed me and was not ashamed of my chains. On the contrary, when he was in Rome, he searched hard for me until he found me. May the Lord grant that he will find mercy from the Lord on that day! You know very well in how many ways he helped me in Ephesus. (2 Tim 1:15–18 NIV)

Those with this gift often serve as deacons and pastors. They enjoy visitations and catering for the needs of people, however, they may not

---

4. For the discussion on the gift of music, see chapter 6.

be very good preachers. Once, an elder of a church approached me and asked that I see his pastor and speak to him on his behalf. His request was that he preferred serving to preaching. Thus, he would appreciate it if the pastor limited his duties to serving and assisting people. I consider him as someone who was gifted with the grace of serving.

The gift of showing mercy is the ability to work joyfully with those whom the majority ignores or the marginalized, such as the sick, oppressed, homeless, orphans and the troublesome (Rom 12:8). This gift of showing mercy is linked with the gift of serving. The difference, however, is that those with the gift of showing mercy are happy to serve those whom the majority have neglected. They can move among the mentally derailed people and serve them with joy. They work with those who are bedridden with joy. I was quite curious to find out from a nurse who chose to work among the aged who were bedridden. She informed me of her conviction to gladly assist the aged without being overwhelmed by their challenges. She is a typical example of a person endowed with the grace of showing mercy to people. In the Bible, one person who could be said to have this gift was Titus. He was able to work peacefully with the troublesome Corinthian church. He comforted Paul in his difficult periods, and he was a good worker (2 Cor 2:13; 7:5–16).

The gift of leadership is one of the gifts needed by the pastor. The gift of leadership here is the ability to preside over a church and direct its affairs (Rom 12:8; 1 Cor 12:28).[5] The pastor may have these four gifts: teaching, service, showing mercy and leadership.

Sometimes, a pastor without the gift of teaching may not be able to break the word of God simply and systematically for people to understand. The pastor-teacher is the one who shepherds the church with the clear teaching of the word of God.[6] People often associate the apostle with the pastor-teacher because of the various gifts in which they operate. The apostle possesses a number of these gifts in order to oversee churches. He has the ability to teach and build a good foundation for new converts. The leadership and administrative gifts enable him to set leaders in place to have oversight of the work, even in his absence, and by that helps the church to grow.

---

5. See chapter 17 for discussions on this.
6. For discussion on the gift of teachings, see chapter 6.

Once, there was a district[7] supervised by a pastor, which was being closed down because the churches were not growing. The superintendent minister called the apostle who had oversight of the pastors in the area and recommended that the pastor be changed and another person brought in to take over the churches. The new pastor who came there had the apostolic gift, although he had not been labeled as such. Within a few years, the churches grew, and many local assemblies were opened. The place was turned into an area center (like a diocese), which was headed by a man with apostolic ministry to have oversight of the pastors, who had come in to shepherd the local churches. The man with the apostolic gift changed the situation. Apostles can grow churches.

Appointing Church Officers to Help the Church Grow

When Paul and Barnabas went out for missions, they started appointing elders to help in the administration of the churches. Before this period, we had not heard of elders assisting in the governing of the churches. Acts 11:30 records the first time the term "elders" was used in connection with the church. It was a term that was used in the time of Moses. It literally denotes "aged men." But later when it was used in connection with the seventy leaders chosen to assist Moses (Num 11:16, 24), it was used with regard to an office. The elders exercised authority over the people and represented them in affairs where all the people could not be present (Exod 3:18; Deut 27:1; Ezra 10:8).

The usage in Acts 11:30 does not give us the sense in which the term was used. It is not clear here whether the term "elders" was used in connection with an office or aged men. The background was that some donations were being collected and sent to the believers in Jerusalem. Acts 11:29–30 show that "the disciples, each according to his ability, decided to provide help for the brothers living in Judea. This they did, sending their gift to the elders by Barnabas and Saul" (NIV). The statement could indicate that the donation was either entrusted to the aged and experienced men in the church for distribution among the members, or it was entrusted to the church officers for distribution. The most important

---

7. A district in this case is the situation where a number of local churches or congregations come together as one unit under one pastor. In this case, church officers such as elders, deacons and deaconesses take care of the local churches. A district may have one to twenty small congregations.

issue is that the gifts were sent to the elders, thus the elders played an important role there.

It was in Acts 14:23 that the appointment of elders was first mentioned in connection with the church. "Paul and Barnabas appointed elders for them in each church and, with prayer and fasting, committed them to the Lord, in whom they had put their trust" (Acts 14:23 NIV). The term here in Greek is *presbúteros*. The English word "presbytery" is translated from this term. The term used indicates the plurality of elders in the church and such was the usage in most of the places it was used (Acts 20:28; 1 Tim 5:2; Acts 14:23; 1 Tim 5:17). In Acts 14:23, it is apparent that it was the apostles, who identified the gifts in them and appointed them for leadership in the local church. The service was so important that they had to fast and pray. It appears that always this type of service was organized as a public gathering; people should have nothing against the body (Tit 1:5–9; 1 Tim 3:1–8).

Later, it was seen that elders assisted the apostles in the government of the church (e.g., Acts 15:2, 4). The elders were also the overseers (bishops) of the local assemblies (e.g., 1 Tim 3:1; Tit 1:5).

It has been established already in the New Testament that not all the apostles were seen in the planting of new churches, however, majority of them were involved in growing and establishing new converts in the faith once delivered to the saints known as the foundational truths. Some of them did this through writing letters, praying for people to receive the Holy Spirit and assisting in directions on doctrinal truth (1 Pet 1:1; Jas 1:1; Jude 1–3; Heb 13:22–23; Acts 8:9–25; Acts 15). These are all activities that help a church to grow. It is the apostle who champions these.

THE ABILITY TO SUPERVISE THE CHURCH

Apostolic ministry includes playing a general oversight of the churches, more especially the churches that the apostolic team has established. No doubt this might have necessitated Paul to say, "If to others I am not an apostle, at least I am to you, for you are the seal of my apostleship in the Lord" (1 Cor 9:2 ESV). Paul had established the church in Corinth. The apostle exercises spiritual control over the work he has established, nevertheless, the original apostles played a general oversight of the churches. Right from the beginning of the church, when Philip's ministry touched Samaria, the apostles sent Peter and John to visit and pray for them to receive the Holy Spirit baptism (Acts 8:14). Peter paid a visit to the saints in Lydda (Acts 9:32). Again, from Lydda, Peter visited Joppa and prayed for a disciple, Tabitha, who was dead and through the power of God brought her back to life. John's message in 3 John about his intended visit to discipline a man called Diotrephes shows that he was fond of visiting the churches (3 John 9). From Acts chapter 13 to 21, Paul (and team) was seen as visiting the churches and strengthening them.

Where the apostles were not able to visit themselves, personal representatives were sent, such as Barnabas sent to minister in Antioch (Acts 11). Paul had to send his representative to minister and strengthen most of the churches he established (e.g., 1 Cor 16:10; Titus 3:12–13).

Another area where the apostles play their supervisory roles is in the areas of writing letters. They could even write to churches that they had not established, even Paul (e.g., Rom 1:11–13; Col 1:6–7). Jude's letter shows that it was his duty to write at the time (Jude 3). We do have the epistles of the Bible as we have now because the apostles wrote to strengthen, encourage or settle cases. Thus, visitation, personal representation and writing of letters are important parts of the apostolic ministry.

Chapter 17

Government of the Church

THIS CHAPTER CONTINUES THE functions of the apostle. Four topics are discussed here: the ability to administer the affairs of the church; the ability to deal with challenges in the church; the ability to train leaders; and the ability to go through satanic oppositions.

THE ABILITY TO ADMINISTER THE AFFAIRS OF THE CHURCH

One of the most important aspects of the apostle's work is the administration of the church. The apostle directs the affairs of the church, and sets things in order. Thus, the apostle must be gifted with administration and leadership. Paul uses three Greek words to explain this aspect of the apostle's role. First, is the term *proisteni* in Rom 12:8, when he was dealing with gifts. KJV translates it as "he that ruleth"; the NKJV renders it as "he who leads"; the ESV "the one who leads"; the NIV "if it is leadership"; and the NLT translates it "leadership ability." *Strong's Exhaustive Concordance* translates it as "to stand before (in rank), to preside." The term is applied to the father who manages his household well (1 Tim 3:4–5, 12). In addition, in 1 Tim 5:17, Paul uses the term when he exhorted church members to respect the elders who work among them. Thus, from these translations, the term denotes governing a church or presiding over church issues.

The second term is *kubernesis* which Paul uses in 1 Cor 12:28, when he talked about spiritual gifts. KJV uses the term "government" to represent it; NKJV uses "administration"; ESV "administrating"; NIV "administration"; and NLT "leadership." Besides the noun form, *kuberneetees* which appears in Acts 27:11 and translated as governor and in Rev 18:17 as shipmaster, the term does not appear anywhere else in the New Testament. The literal translation from *Strong Exhaustive Concordance* is to "steer, pilotage, directorship in the church." Thus, here the term may denote those who direct the affairs of the church. The third term is *oikonomia* which Paul uses in Eph 3:2. Both the KJV and NKJV render it as dispensation; ESV stewardship; NIV administration; and NLT special responsibility. The term is used in Luke 16:2–4 for the manager or steward who was to render an account to his master. In Eph 1:10, it is used to describe the plan of the fullness of God's time. Also in Col 1:25, it is used to describe the responsibility or stewardship of God's grace given to Paul. KJV uses dispensation to render the term in both verses. *Strong Exhaustive Concordance* translates it as "administration (of a household or estate)." *Oikonomia* can be understood as the management of or the handling of treasures entrusted to someone. From these translations, the apostle can be understood as the one who has been given the responsibility to administer the treasures of God's household. The apostle, therefore, should be able to hold on to the true word of God and preach it. Paul declares:

> For this reason I, Paul, the prisoner of Christ Jesus for the sake of you Gentiles—Surely you have heard about the administration of God's grace that was given to me for you, that is, the mystery made known to me by revelation, as I have already written briefly. (Eph 3:1–3 NIV)

> I became a servant of this gospel by the gift of God's grace given me through the working of his power. Although I am less than the least of all God's people, this grace was given me: to preach to the Gentiles the unsearchable riches of Christ, and to make plain to everyone the administration of this mystery, which for ages past was kept hidden in God, who created all things. (Eph 3:7–9 NIV)

Most of the apostles had to defend the faith through writing to the believers in various cities to hold on to the right doctrines of Christ. Jude, for example, had this to write:

> Jude, a servant of Jesus Christ and a brother of James, To those who have been called, who are loved by God the Father and kept by Jesus Christ: Mercy, peace and love be yours in abundance. Dear friends, although I was very eager to write to you about the salvation we share, I felt I had to write and urge you to contend for the faith that was once for all entrusted to the saints. For certain men whose condemnation was written about long ago have secretly slipped in among you. They are godless men, who change the grace of our God into a license for immorality and deny Jesus Christ our only Sovereign and Lord. Though you already know all this, I want to remind you that the Lord delivered his people out of Egypt, but later destroyed those who did not believe. (Jude 1–5 NIV)

Jude shows that it was a responsibility to write. The church was being deceived by some false teachers and, therefore, needed to be reminded to contend for the faith. The apostle shows that in the scriptures such people who engaged in false teaching and evil practices were condemned and punished. Then, he gave examples of the disobedient Israelites, the unfaithful angels, and the people of Sodom and Gomorrah. He took the pain to teach the people about these.

The concern here is how Jude took time to see to it that the right things were taught in the church. He considered it as his responsibility. After Paul had recounted all his problems, he ended by saying, "Besides everything else, I face daily the pressure of my concern for all the churches. Who is weak, and I do not feel weak? Who is led into sin, and I do not inwardly burn?" (2 Cor 11:28–29 NIV). The apostle is to administer the church in all aspects.

The apostle settles cases within a church. Paul shows in his writings that he often addressed cases the churches were encountering. For example, in 1 Corinthians, he wrote, "Now for the matters, you wrote about . . ." (7:1). In Philippians, he had to plead with Euodia and Syntyche to agree with each other in the Lord (Phil 4:2). The very minor issues in the church were his concern.

As has been discussed already, the apostles had to settle perhaps the most controversial issue which cropped up in the New Testament church. This was the issue which arose between the Jewish and Gentile Christians concerning the Mosaic law (Acts 15).

The apostle is able to place the right person in the right church. In Titus 3:12–14, Paul was rescheduling his workers, what others call transfer or posting, "As soon as I send Artemas or Tychicus to you, do your best to come to me at Nicopolis, because I have decided to winter there. Do everything you can to help Zenas the lawyer and Apollos on their way and see that they have everything they need" (NIV). The apostle positioned his pastors so well as to have the churches move forward. In the Church of Pentecost where transferring of pastors take place, often these result in practical growth, both in membership and finances.

The whole well-being of a church is placed in the hands of the apostle. This links us with the next point.

THE ABILITY TO DEAL WITH CHALLENGES IN THE CHURCH

The apostle has the God-given ability to deal with specific problems that arise in a church, such as emerging teaching and practices, false doctrines and sin. While the Holy Spirit is actively working, the devil will also continue to stir up a church with emerging trends, false doctrines and sins.

The apostle has the ability to examine an issue and prescribe the right antidote. An example of this is when a great number of Gentiles accepted Christ Jesus as their Lord. The Jewish Christians felt that the Gentile Christians should observe the Mosaic laws. Of course the laws were given to Moses by the Lord and Israel was to observe them together with aliens who live with them (Exod 12:45–49; Num 15:15–16; 9:14; Lev 22:18). In most aspects of the law, it was stated that it should be "a lasting ordinance" for the generations to come (e.g., Exod 12:24; 27:21; Lev 16:31; 23:21, 31, 29; 24:3; Num 15:15; Gen 17:9–14). One of the most important laws was on the issue of circumcision. It was the first covenantal law given to Abraham and confirmed to Moses (Gen 17:9–14; Exod 4:24–26; Lev 12:3). Here, we are with Gentiles coming to enjoy the treasures of the "God of Israel." Why should the Gentiles not observe the laws that the God of Israel set for them (Israel)? As Paul and Barnabas preached the gospel to the Gentiles, this issue became no small matter. The issue of the Gentile Christians observing the law was brought before the apostles and elders in Jerusalem. As the discussion went on, "Then some of the believers who belonged to the party of the Pharisees stood up and said, the Gentiles must be circumcised and required to obey the law of Moses'" (Acts 15:5 NIV). These were believers who had accepted Christ from among the Pharisees. They could not understand why the lasting ordinance of the Lord could not be brought to bear on the

Gentiles. The apostles had to consider "the whole word of God" and allow the Holy Spirit in them to solve the new challenge that had cropped up.

Peter was the first to throw some light on this. He showed that God had called the Gentiles and given them the Holy Spirit and he accepted them just as he accepted the Jews. They should not put "on the necks of the disciples [Gentile disciples] a yoke that neither we nor our fathers have been able to bear" (Acts 15:8–11). By this, Peter through the Spirit has said that the law was like a yoke, which was difficult to bear, and that the Jews themselves, whether old or new generations, were not able to observe it. After Peter had spoken, Paul and Barnabas reported their ministry and the outcome to the apostles and elders.

James continued that the prophets agreed with what Peter said since they also prophesied that the Gentiles would bear the name of God. That is, the Gentiles would be called by God into his kingdom. Thus, they "should not make it difficult for the Gentiles who are turning to God" (Acts 15:15–19 NIV). By this, James was saying that they should not ask the Gentiles to observe the laws of Moses. They should find the most essential ones and ask them to observe them. For the apostles and elders who met in Jerusalem in Acts 15, these were the most essential laws which they wanted the Gentiles to observe:

> It seemed good to the Holy Spirit and to us not to burden you with anything beyond the following requirements: You are to abstain from food sacrificed to idols, from blood, from the meat of strangled animals and from sexual immorality. You will do well to avoid these things. (Acts 15:28–29 NIV)

How could the eleven apostles chosen by Jesus and others, such as Matthias, James, Paul and Barnabas, reduce the law into only four issues? They did this as the Holy Spirit in them threw light into the spirit of the written word. The Scripture interprets itself. For example, while the Old Testament established the covenant of circumcision, it had also stated that "the Lord your God will circumcise your hearts and the hearts of your descendants, so that you may love him with all your heart and with all your soul, and live" (Deut 30:6–7; cf. 10:16; Jer 31:33; 32:39–40; Ezek 11:19; 36:26–27 NIV). Based on this, the apostles could say that both Gentiles and Jews are saved by grace and that God knows the hearts and accepts people (Acts 15:8, 11). Paul had to teach consistently that circumcision was nothing, it was only the heart that was important (Gal 6:15; Rom 2:29; Col 2:11; Phil 3:3). The issue was a very big one. It needed the grace of God for the Jewish Christians to understand it. From time to time, such challenges will appear which do not have direct answers from the Bible. That is when God uses the apostles "to interpret the times" from his word.

In addition to the fact that the apostle is able to handle new challenges, he is also able to deal with sin and other related issues within a church. Some examples of these are found in the way Paul handles problems in the epistle of 1 Corinthians. The church in Corinth was a dishonored church. Some of the members were using the grace of God to entangle themselves in sinful lives, to the extent of one member having an ongoing affair with his stepmother. Others got drunk, ate on the Lord's table and ate at the feast of idols.

Still others had challenges with marriage and others thought that there was no resurrection. The church was divided on four of the vessels the Lord had used to minister among them (1 Cor 1:12). While these were going on, the Corinthians still had to boast in the use of spiritual gifts and their leaders. Paul wrote to address these issues.

For some of the issues, he had direct answers from the word of God or from the Lord. He had to put sanctions on the person who had been living an immoral life with the stepmother by handing him over to Satan (1 Cor 5). He had to sternly warn those who were eating the Lord's Supper unworthily (1 Cor 11:27–34).

With others, he had to use his own mind having been sanctified by the Holy Spirit and full of the word of God. For example, see 1 Cor 7:10–13:

> To the married I give this command (*not I, but the Lord*): A wife must not separate from her husband. But if she does, she must remain unmarried or else be reconciled to her husband. And a husband must not divorce his wife. To the rest I say this (*I, not the Lord*): If any brother has a wife who is not a believer and she is willing to live with him, he must not divorce her. (NIV, italics mine)

As an example, Paul was able to address the issues that came from the churches through the ability that the Lord had given to him.

Reading the book of James shows that he dealt with social challenges in the church. Some factions had entered the church, with favoritism rearing its face. Some of the believers had fallen into worldliness, taken the grace of God for granted and were playing double lives. James addressed the situation, saying:

> That man should not think he will receive anything from the Lord; he is a double-minded man, unstable in all he does. (Jas 1:7–8 NIV)

> Therefore, get rid of all moral filth and the evil that is so prevalent and humbly accept the word planted in you, which can save you. (Jas 1:21 NIV)

> What good is it, my brothers, if a man claims to have faith but has no deeds? Can such faith save him? Suppose a brother or sister is without clothes and daily food. If one of you says to him, "Go, I wish you well; keep warm and well fed," but does nothing about his physical needs, what good is it? In the same way, faith by itself, if it is not accompanied by action, is dead. But someone will say, "You have faith; I have deeds." Show me your faith without deeds, and I will show you my faith by what I do. You believe that there is one God. Good! Even the demons believe that—and shudder. You foolish man, do you want evidence that faith without deeds is useless? (Jas 2:14–20)

The Apostle James is also a clear example of how the apostle does not compromise with the gospel. They deal with sin and worldliness head on.

One of the issues that the apostles dealt with in the New Testament was false doctrines. Peter, Paul, John and Jude had to deal with false teachers and doctrines (2 Pet 2:1–22; 2 Cor 11; 1 John 3; Jude). There were people who sometimes characterized by greed twisted the Christian message for their own benefits. Sometimes they succeeded in raising opposition against the apostles (e.g., 2 Cor 12:20). Paul had to strongly warn the Galatians, "But even if we or an angel from heaven should preach a gospel other than the one we preached to you, let him be eternally condemned!" (1:8 NIV). The apostle boldly handles challenges that arise in the church.

THE ABILITY TO TRAIN LEADERS

One of the important roles of the apostle is to train people. The apostle must be able to identify potentials, tap and equip them. Ephesians 4:11–12 bring this out clearly, "He Himself gave some to be apostles, some prophets, some evangelists, and some pastors and teachers, for the equipping of the saints for the work of ministry, for the edifying of the body of Christ" (NKJV). This shows that equipping the saints is a main duty of those with the ministry gifts, led by the apostle. People must be trained, appointed and released for ministry. Once a person leaves, another one must be identified and trained. The training should be ongoing so that if one person is not in, another should fill in the vacuum.

When Paul and Barnabas were sent forth by the Holy Spirit to do the work that he had assigned them, they started appointing and training leaders straight away as they established churches (Acts 14:21–23). Along the line, they broke the relationship. However, both continued with their apostolic ministry. As they broke relations, they did not carry on alone but continued to recruit people. Paul recruited Silas. As it has been indicated earlier, Silas was initially addressed as a prophet (Acts 15:32), but later he was addressed as an apostle (1 Thess 1:1; 2:7). What had possibly happened was that Paul trained him or mentored him to mature in his apostolic gift.

When they moved further, they recruited Timothy into the apostolic team:

> Then he came to Derbe and Lystra. And behold, a certain disciple was there, named Timothy, *the* son of a certain Jewish woman who believed, but his father *was* Greek. He was well spoken of by the brethren who were at Lystra and Iconium. Paul wanted to have him go on with him. And he took *him* and circumcised him because of the Jews who were in that region, for they all knew that his father was Greek. (Acts 16:1–3 NKJV)

We see here that Timothy was spoken well of by his local church. People who are called into the ministry must begin from the local church. Becoming a pastor without the blessing of your local church is not very healthy. Many people think that Timothy was only a pastor, but later we find the name of Timothy added to the list of apostles (e.g., 1 Thess 1:1; 2:7). Timothy and Silas were addressed as apostles together with Paul. The first letter to the Thessalonians was not only written by Paul, but also by the apostles Silas and Timothy.

In Troas, Luke might have joined the team of Paul. Until this time, Luke had written the book as if he were not there. From Acts 16:10 following, the "we" passages begin: "Now after he had seen the vision, immediately we sought to go to Macedonia, concluding that the Lord had called us to preach the gospel to them" (Acts 16:10 NKJV). The implication is that Luke is informing the readers that he had joined the team at Troas (Acts 16:8–10). Thus, he would also come under the training of Paul.

In Corinth, Paul met Aquila and Priscilla (Acts 18:1–4). When he went to Syria he recruited them for some time and then left them in Ephesus (Acts 19:18–19). In Acts 19:22, Paul had already discipled Erastus to the point that he could send Timothy and Erastus back to Macedonia. If Erastus is the same mentioned in the Epistle of Romans, then he became very active in Paul's ministry. "Erastus, the treasurer of the city, greets you, and Quartus, a brother" (Rom 16:23 NKJV, see also 2 Tim 4:20). Paul might have recruited him from Corinth. In Acts 20, Paul had recruited many people in his team. Luke reports this, "And Sopater of Berea accompanied him to Asia—also Aristarchus and Secundus of the Thessalonians, and Gaius of Derbe, and Timothy, and Tychicus and Trophimus of Asia. These men, going ahead, waited for us at Troas" (Acts 20:4–5 NKJV).

We do not have the full details of how Barnabas trained John Mark, but it appears that Barnabas was able to train Mark, who was rejected by Paul. This is seen in the fact that later, about twelve years, Paul accepted Mark back and made good compliments about him. In Paul's letter to Colossians, written possibly in Rome, he writes, "Aristarchus my fellow prisoner greets you, with Mark the cousin of Barnabas (about whom you received instructions: if he comes to you, welcome him" (Col 4:10 NKJV). Again in Phlm 23, Mark was one of the people who were listed as Paul's fellow workers. In five years after this, that is, about seventeen years after the incident which separated Paul and Barnabas concerning Mark, Paul requested him (Mark) to be brought to him, because he was useful to him (2 Tim 4:11). Generally, Mark was one of the gifts to the church in early days. He was closely associated with Peter. It was in the house of the mother of Mark, Mary, where the believers prayed; the place where Peter went first when he was released from prison through divine intervention (Acts 12:12–13). As indicated already, the gospel according to St. Mark was said to be written by this Mark. This is evidence that Barnabas might have done a good job on John Mark, not allowing the church to lose him. Training is a very important aspect of apostolic ministry.

THE ABILITY TO GO THROUGH SATANIC OPPOSITIONS

One of the signs of the apostolic ministry, which may sound strange to some people is that apostolic ministration stirs satanic strongholds, and thereby invites confrontation, both physically and spiritually. This confrontation includes false accusation, insults, beating, stoning, murder, mystification, poverty and riches. These stirrings may come through diverse ways, such as through unbelievers, religious people, traditional Christians who think they know the best, and Christians who are living in the flesh.

As the Lord was using Peter and the apostles, they were arrested, beaten up, put into prison, and some executed (Acts 4:1–4; 5:18, 40; 12:1–4). The twelve apostles never took it easy. James, the brother of John was executed (Acts 12:1–4). McBirnie as well as Sean McDonald have shown that all the apostles, with the exception of John suffered martyrdom.[1]

You would think that while the Lord is performing miracles with people like these, disaster must never take place, but that was exactly the opposite. In fact, whenever God raises an apostle, there are almost always some stirrings from the devil.

As Paul and Barnabas continued to make disciples of Christ, the devil also increased his attacks. There were severe persecutions. In Pisidian Antioch, for example, the Lord used them to bring many converts to Christ (Acts 13:43). Yet the Jews stirred persecution against them (Acts 13:50). What surprised me in Antioch was that while the Jews incited trouble for Paul and Barnabas, the disciples were not worried, they supported them and were rather filled with joy and the Holy Spirit. In other words, they did not say that if these men of God face persecution, they might not come from God. They saw that they were being persecuted because they were doing the right thing.

In Lystra, some "Jews from Antioch and Iconium came there; and having persuaded the multitudes, they stoned Paul and dragged him out of the city, supposing him to be dead" (Acts 14:20 NKJV). The tactic they used was to form mobs and start a riot against them (e.g., Acts 17:5–9; 18:12–17; 19:23–41). Stoning was not easy. It took the grace of God to sustain Paul during this period.

As the true apostle ministers, false teaching, miracles and revelations increase. In 2 Cor 11, Paul shows how false apostles and teachers

---

1. McBirnie, *Search for the Twelve Apostles*; McDowell, *Fate of the Apostles*.

masquerade the true apostles, and then attack them subtly. They appear as doing the right thing and even accuse the true apostle of doing the wrong thing, while they milk the church. In Paul's case, for example, he was accused of not being a burden to the people by soliciting their money to take care of himself (2 Cor 11:8–11). Some of the major persecutions that the true apostle encounters come from false teachers and prophets who often are hit hard and would like to fight back. The devil is often behind such actions. Paul tells the Corinthians:

> And I will keep on doing what I am doing in order to cut the ground from under those who want an opportunity to be considered equal with us in the things they boast about. For such men are false apostles, deceitful workmen, masquerading as apostles of Christ. And no wonder, for Satan himself masquerades as an angel of light. It is not surprising, then, if his servants masquerade as servants of righteousness. Their end will be what their actions deserve. (2 Cor 11:12–15 NIV)

Wherever the gospel is breaking down the stronghold of Satan, he will incite persecution against Christians. Christians need to understand this and stand.

The devil will continue to attack true apostles of Christ always. He does this through activities, such as false accusation, false teaching, misinterpretation, creating physical attacks, and causing confusion.

At my first pastoral station at Wa in Ghana, I organized a one-week teaching and fasting prayer meeting which was well attended. A well to do woman who had just accepted Christ also attended. At the end of the meeting, she visited and presented a guinea fowl as a gift to me. As we were living outside the main building, I chained this guinea fowl, getting ready to slaughter it for a meal. However, within few minutes, lots of guinea fowls came around quacking and then surrounded the one that had been chained. Suddenly an old man in the vicinity approached me to say that the guinea fowl belonged to him. He lost one of his guinea fowls, that was why the others had come around; they had seen one of their own that was lost. The implication was that I, the pastor, had stolen a guinea fowl. I told the old man how I came to own the guinea fowl and then invited the woman to come and explain that it was a gift. Ultimately what had happened was that the woman saw someone selling the guinea fowl and bought it. When she identified the person who sold it to her, it turned out to be one of the sons of the old man. One of this man's sons had stolen the father's guinea fowl and sold it. This is an example of satanic stirring, something that will cast a snare on the man of God so that his message will not be accepted.

On the other hand, some Christians may do the wrong thing and claim they are suffering for Christ. This should not be the case for true apostles of Christ. Peter tells us that suffering must be in the Lord. In other words, we must not attribute our suffering for doing the wrong thing to the Lord. Peter explains:

> So be happy when you are insulted for being a Christian, for then the glorious Spirit of God rests upon you. If you suffer, however, it must not be for murder, stealing, making trouble, or prying into other people's affairs. But it is no shame to suffer for being a Christian. Praise God for the privilege of being called by his name. (1 Pet 4:14–17 NLT)

Persecution does not mean doing the wrong thing and being attacked. You must walk the will of God. There cannot be a move of God without persecution. Though the devil will continue to stir troubles for the ministers of God, the Lord will continue to hold them up.

Chapter 18

Spiritual Authority

THIS CHAPTER CONTINUES WITH the functions of the apostles. It focuses on spiritual authority with three headings: the ability to strengthen one's relation with his Master, the ability to impact spiritual gifts, and the ability to receive revelation and theologize.

THE ABILITY TO STRENGTHEN HIS RELATIONSHIP WITH THE LORD

The apostle strengthens his relationship with the Lord through prayer and worship. One of the reasons that Jesus called the apostles was for them to be with him (Mark 3:13). Being with him so they could see him do what he did and learn from him. One of the ministries of Jesus here on earth was prayer. He would often leave the masses and hide to pray (Mark 1:35; Luke 5:16; 6:12–16; Matt 26:36–46). Obviously the apostles must have learned this habit of praying from their Master.

Right after the ascension of Christ, the apostles gathered in the upper room to pray (Acts 1:13—2:13). It was during these prayers that the Holy Spirit eventually descended. In Acts 6:4, when there was murmuring among the believers about the distribution of food among widows, they handed over the work to the chosen deacons and said they would give attention to prayer and the ministry of the word (Acts 6:4). In Acts 10, Peter was seen fasting and praying, when the Lord sent him to the house of Cornelius. In Acts 13, the teachers and prophets were worshipping the

Lord and fasting, when the Holy Spirit spoke to them. Eventually, the two people sent by the Holy Spirit, Saul and Barnabas, were later recognized as apostles (Acts 14:14). When Paul said in 2 Cor 12:8 that three times he pleaded with the Lord to take away the messenger of Satan who tormented him, some consider it as special times of prayer. When John said, he was in the Spirit in the Lord's Day (Rev 1:10), it could be understood that he was praying or better still fasting and praying.

We do not have the life stories of the rest of the apostles, but it would appear that fasting, prayers, and worshipping were part of the apostolic practices. Since Jesus found it necessary to isolate himself in prayer, so must the apostles. It is in such special times with the Lord that deeper insight into his word and revelations may be received.

Generally, the Christian life needs to be a life of prayer, thus the apostle who oversees the church must take lead in such spiritual exercise. Fasting, praying, and studying God's word draw a person closer to the Lord and keep him humble. It is through these that a person's spiritual authority emanates. Spiritual authority derives from a person's measure of surrender to the Lord. It is not a matter of just callings or giving of titles such as pastor, prophet, bishop, or apostle. The more you get closer to the Lord, the more you see your nakedness. The more you see your nakedness, the more you humble yourself and seek gold from the Lord to cover your nakedness and clothe yourself with his righteousness. His righteousness on a person grants them that ability to lead battles.

THE ABILITY TO IMPART SPIRITUAL GIFTS

The apostle has the grace to impart spiritual gifts to people. Paul was a very good example. Having ministered in Corinth and Galatia, he was aware that these churches were endowed with spiritual gifts (1 Cor 1:7; Gal 3:5). He states:

> I always thank God for you because of his grace given you in Christ Jesus. For in him you have been enriched in every way—in all your speaking and in all your knowledge—because our testimony about Christ was confirmed in you. Therefore you do not lack any spiritual gift as you eagerly wait for our Lord Jesus Christ to be revealed. (1 Cor 1:4–8 NIV)

> Does God give you his Spirit and work miracles among you because you observe the law, or because you believe what you heard? (Gal 3:5 NIV)

Reading the epistles of 1 and 2 Corinthians shows how the church in Corinth was endowed with gifts. One of the points of conflicts in Corinth was the misuse of spiritual gifts. Paul had to write to direct them toward the right way of using spiritual gifts. Similarly, he asked the Galatians to remind themselves of how the Lord granted them the Spirit and performed miracles among them. They had resorted to giving way to the flesh. They needed to walk in the Spirit as they also exercise spiritual gifts (Gal 3:2–3; 5:16–17).

Being an apostle, he was aware that the Lord had granted him grace to impart spiritual gifts. This divine awareness was evident in the ministry of Paul. He told Timothy to fan into flame the gift of God which was imparted into him through the laying on of his hands (2 Tim 1:6–7). The implication of this is that Paul had laid his hands on Timothy and he knew that by so doing he had imparted some spiritual gifts into his life. Perhaps, Paul had witnessed the manifestation of these gifts in the life of Timothy, but Timothy was not being effective as Paul expected him to be. Therefore, he needed to stir him up. It could also be that as Paul was in prison and sensed he could die at any time, it was a general exhortation to Timothy to be more effective in the exercise of his spiritual gifts. The lesson here is that Paul as the apostle has the grace to impart as well as stir up the gifts in people.

Paul tells the Romans, "I long to see you so that I may impart to you some spiritual gift to make you strong" (Rom 1:11 NIV), possibly because no known apostle had visited the church physically.[1] Therefore, Paul desired so much to be with the Romans physically, lay hands on and teach them, so that they would be imparted with spiritual gifts. The rationale for them to be imparted with spiritual gifts was for the testimony of the Lord Jesus to be more confirmed in their midst.

Initially, in the New Testament, it was the apostles who were leading people to receive the baptism in the Holy Spirit. For example, Peter and John were sent to visit the new church in Samaria to pray for them to receive the Holy Spirit (Acts 8:14–17). Peter was sent to the house of Cornelius to share the gospel. Through that the Holy Spirit was poured

---

1. Some theologians think Paul was not talking about spiritual gifts or charismatic gifts, but such interpretation is very weak since both *pneumatikos* and *charisma* were used in Rom 1:11 as they were used in 1 Cor 12:1, 30. See Hendriksen, *Romans*, 51–52.

on the household (1 Cor 10). Paul had to pray for the church in Ephesus to receive the baptism of the Holy Spirit; they spoke in tongues and prophesied (Acts 19:5-7).

Once a church is endowed with a genuine apostle, there will be manifestation of spiritual gifts in the church. People will be imparted. The testimony of Christ will be confirmed in their midst. As a young pastor at Wa, Ghana, my senior pastor, who was a prophet by calling, visited me. Witnessing the manifestation of the gifts in the church, such as prophecies, sharing of revelations, exuberant songs, and explosions of joy, he declared, "Opoku, you have a breakthrough."

In another instance, when I was the regional head of the Eastern "A,"[2] with its headquarters at Koforidua, in Ghana, there came a time that all the pastors who had the gift of prophecy in my jurisdiction were transferred. I said to myself, "Here I am as a pastor ordained into the apostleship by the Church of Pentecost. I need to pray to have some of the pastors here to be imparted with spiritual gifts, since as a Pentecostal church the spiritual gifts need to operate in our midst." I summoned the pastors under my supervision for a prayer meeting. I laid hands on them in prayer as a sign of imparting spiritual gifts into their lives. Two of them prophesied immediately and two others received revelations in vision forms and shared. The apostle has been endowed with the grace to impart others with spiritual gifts. Imparting others with spiritual gifts releases them for the work of the ministry. They themselves would be strengthened and equipped to go out and witness Christ with boldness and power.

THE ABILITY TO RECEIVE REVELATION AND THEOLOGIZE

The apostle has God-given ability to receive revelations and also do local theology without "syncretism."[3] Paul is an example here. He did not sit under the ministry of our Lord Jesus Christ when he was on earth, yet he claimed to have worked more than all the apostles. He writes:

> For I am the least of the apostles and do not even deserve to be called an apostle, because I persecuted the church of God. But

---

2. This was one of the administrative regions of the Church of Pentecost.
3. Syncretism is used here to signify the pollution of the Word of God, which goes against the general principles in the Bible.

> by the grace of God I am what I am, and his grace to me was not without effect. No, I worked harder than all of them—yet not I, but the grace of God that was with me. (1 Cor 15:9–10 NIV)

He wrote to the church in Ephesus, telling them how he was given the revelation of the church:

> Surely you have heard about the administration of God's grace that was given to me for you, that is, the mystery made known to me by revelation, as I have already written briefly. In reading this, then, you will be able to understand my insight into the mystery of Christ, which was not made known to men in other generations as it has now been revealed by the Spirit to God's holy apostles and prophets. This mystery is that through the gospel the Gentiles are heirs together with Israel, members together of one body, and sharers together in the promise in Christ Jesus. (Eph 3:2–6 NIV)

Christ gave special insight of the church to Paul that the church comprises both Jews and Gentiles. He showed him that there is no difference between Jews and Gentiles, slave and free, and male and females (Gal 3:26); in Christ Jesus, all are one. This was a new revelation, yet it was built upon the foundation of the Old Testament. Some of the prophets in the Old Testament prophesied that the Lord was going to bring the Gentiles into his kingdom. For example, Joel prophesied that the Lord would pour out his spirit on all people, including sons and daughters, slaves, and then men and women (Joel 2:28–29). Isaiah also prophesied that the Lord's Servant was going to be a light to the Gentiles (Isa 42:6; Luke 2:32). Paul gave a clearer picture about this act of the Lord; in Christ Jesus, all people are one. Apostles have deeper insight into the word of God to be able to interpret new issues and address them within the framework of Scripture.

This tendency of being able to bring the word of God into contemporary issues makes the apostle different from the other gifts. Whereas the prophet may have a vision or dream on an issue, the apostle may have revelation within his very personality without having a direct vision or picture of it. This is another aspect of the gift of the word of wisdom where the person clearly understands a scripture passage or interprets contemporary issues from a biblical perspective.

Jesus told his apostles that he would not tell them all that he had, but the Spirit would:

> I have much more to say to you, more than you can now bear. But when he, the Spirit of truth, comes, he will guide you into all truth. He will not speak on his own; he will speak only what he hears, and he will tell you what is yet to come. He will bring glory to me by taking from what is mine and making it known to you. (John 16:12–14 NIV)

The implication of this is that the Holy Spirit will continue to pick up what is Christ's, and make it clear to the apostles at the right time. As the church of God is being built continuously, the Holy Spirit will continue to reveal things to the apostles. Jesus shows in Matt 13:52, "Therefore every scribe who has become a disciple of the kingdom of heaven is like a head of a household, who brings out of his treasure things new and old" (NASU). Jesus gives the apostle the ability to understand or receive a "new" revelation and how it is related to the biblical principle. The apostle is like the owner of a store who can bring out of his shop both new and old things. And he will be able to do this without pollution. The "old" are things that are written in the word of God, that is, the Bible. These are stored in people's mind. This means the apostle must read, study, memorize and meditate on the word of God. By so doing, the word of God becomes part of him. Whether he remembers it or not, since the word has become part of him, his *psyche* (soul) will bring it out when it is needed.

The "new" are the revelations that the Holy Spirit will bring to him concerning new trends. Since the apostle knows the written word of God, the Holy Spirit will combine both within him in such a way as to give an interpretation that will perfectly fit into the situation. There is the need for the Lord always to raise up apostles to lead the kingdom business.

Chapter 19

Broader Perspective of God's Kingdom

CHAPTER 19 CONTINUES WITH the functions of the apostle. Two topics are treated here; the ability to care for the poor and the vulnerable, and the ability to promote unity in the body of Christ.

THE ABILITY TO CARE FOR THE POOR AND THE VULNERABLE

The administration of the church includes taking care of the poor and the needy. In a church, there are the rich and poor people as well as the vulnerable and neglected people. The apostle is not only concerned about these people but he also defends their cause.

In Acts 6, when the Grecian Jews complained to the apostles that their widows were being overlooked in the distribution of food, the apostles requested them to appoint deacons to take care of the physical needs of the people. Two things that we can learn from this story are first, that the apostles or rather the church was assisting the widows which shows that assisting the needy is important in a church. Second, the apostles were listening to the people; they took the complaints made by the Grecian Jewish Christians into serious consideration. Apostles must open their eyes to the things that go on in a church.

In Acts 11:29, when there was famine in Judea, the disciples, each according to their abilities provided help for the brethren. They did this through Barnabas and Saul who were later identified as apostles. This act is an aspect of social justice within the Christian community.

When Paul went to see the apostles in Jerusalem as a result of a revelation he had, the one thing they requested from him was to continue taking care of the poor. Galatians 2:10 reads, "All they asked was that we should continue to remember the poor, the very thing I was eager to do" (NIV). Paul's writings show that he was concerned about the poor. For example, in Rom 15:25–27, he writes, "Now, however, I am on my way to Jerusalem in the service of the saints there. For Macedonia and Achaia were pleased to make a contribution for the poor among the saints in Jerusalem" (NIV). He was still serving the poor in society. Again, his writings show that the widows who were over sixty had been placed on a list. He instructed that proper attention must be given to widows:

> Give proper recognition to those widows who are really in need. (1 Tim 5:3 NIV)

> No widow may be put on the list of widows unless she is over sixty, has been faithful to her husband, and is well known for her good deeds, such as bringing up children, showing hospitality, washing the feet of the saints, helping those in trouble and devoting herself to all kinds of good deeds. (1 Tim 5:9–10 NIV)

Paul was concerned about how people should be handled in the church. They must be handled with care and respect. Advantage must not be taken of such needy people, neither should one use his position to treat others harshly. He admonishes Timothy, "Do not rebuke an older man harshly, but exhort him as if he were your father. Treat younger men as brothers, older women as mothers, and younger women as sisters, with absolute purity" (1 Tim 5:1–2 NIV). It is always wrong for pastors and other church leaders to treat sick, poor, or needy people harshly and without dignity.

The Apostle James also warns church leaders not to show partiality in our dealing with people. He writes:

> My brothers, as believers in our glorious Lord Jesus Christ, don't show favoritism. Suppose a man comes into your meeting wearing a gold ring and fine clothes, and a poor man in shabby clothes also comes in. If you show special attention to the man wearing fine clothes and say, "Here's a good seat for you," but say to the poor man, "You stand there" or "Sit on the floor by my

feet," have you not discriminated among yourselves and become judges with evil thoughts? (Jas 2:1–4 NIV)

The foregoing shows how the apostle must be concerned about the needy and the vulnerable in society. Showing concern and addressing their needs are marks of Christ, who is our Master.

The apostles saw to it that money was shared equally among the believers. Luke reports in Acts:

> All the believers were one in heart and mind. No one claimed that any of his possessions was his own, but they shared everything they had. With great power the apostles continued to testify to the resurrection of the Lord Jesus, and much grace was upon them all. There were no needy persons among them. For from time to time those who owned lands or houses sold them, brought the money from the sales and put it at the apostles' feet, and it was distributed to anyone as he had need. Joseph, a Levite from Cyprus, whom the apostles called Barnabas (which means Son of Encouragement), sold a field he owned and brought the money and put it at the apostles' feet. (Acts 4:32–37 NIV)

In the New Testament church, the apostles were seeing to it that the believing community was distributing wealth among themselves. Barnabas who became an apostle was one of the first to sell his land and brought the proceeds to the apostles' feet to be shared with others. Bringing it to the apostles' feet did not mean that the money was for the apostles. No! Rather they were to be shared among all. Barnabas is a very good example of the Christian giver. Everybody is to exhibit this grace.

Another way the apostle helps the weak is to help them work with their own hands to survive. Someone may assist another with money for few days, but he cannot do it always. Paul had to use himself and those of his colleague as an example for the brothers and sisters in Thessalonica to work hard in order to survive:

> In the name of the Lord Jesus Christ, we command you, brothers, to keep away from every brother who is idle and does not live according to the teaching you received from us. For you yourselves know how you ought to follow our example. We were not idle when we were with you, nor did we eat anyone's food without paying for it. On the contrary, we worked night and day, laboring and toiling so that we would not be a burden to any of you. We did this, not because we do not have the right to such help, but in order to make ourselves a model for you to follow.

> For even when we were with you, we gave you this rule: "If a man will not work, he shall not eat." We hear that some among you are idle. They are not busy; they are busybodies. Such people we command and urge in the Lord Jesus Christ to settle down and earn the bread they eat. And as for you, brothers, never tire of doing what is right. (2 Thess 3:6–13 NIV)

The Apostle Paul was also teaching that the Christian must not be a beggar; he must work hard to earn his living. Christian generosity must not be taken for granted to the extent where others will not work. What Christian generosity means is to do whatever one can to help his neighbor survive, whether in cash or kind. You can help another to survive through the provision of a job. The individual Christian must also work with his hand. The apostle is to lead in this teaching.

THE ABILITY TO PROMOTE UNITY IN THE BODY OF CHRIST

The apostle is a father-type figure who promotes unity in the body of Christ; he is able to network denominations and parachurch organizations. Paul admonishes the Ephesians:

> Make every effort to keep the unity of the Spirit through the bond of peace. There is one body and one Spirit—just as you were called to one hope when you were called—one Lord, one faith, one baptism; one God and Father of all, who is over all and through all and in all. But to each one of us grace has been given as Christ apportioned it. (Eph 4:3–7 NIV)

Paul recognizes that there is one body and one Spirit, but some people have been apportioned special grace to function in unique aspects of the body of Christ. Therefore, we must all endeavor to unite and do the work of the ministry. This is the basis for church unity and network. The one with the apostolic gift sees the need for denominations to bury their differences and come together as one army to do the King's business.[1]

In Acts 11:16–33, when news reached the apostles that the believers who had scattered had preached the good news to win some new converts, they sent Barnabas to visit. They were trying to network the church in Jerusalem with the believers who had accepted Christ in different

---

1. See Fife's concept of apostles, Fife, *Holy Spirit*, 123.

cities. It was during Barnabas's assignment in Antioch that he sent for Paul to assist him.

In Paul's writing there is evidence of how he networked the churches. For example, the following Scriptures show how he was able to network the churches in Macedonia, Achaia, Galatians, and Jerusalem:

> Now, however, I am on my way to Jerusalem in the service of the saints there. For Macedonia and Achaia were pleased to make a contribution for the poor among the saints in Jerusalem. They were pleased to do it, and indeed they owe it to them. For if the Gentiles have shared in the Jews' spiritual blessings, they owe it to the Jews to share with them their material blessings. So after I have completed this task and have made sure that they have received this fruit, I will go to Spain and visit you on the way. I know that when I come to you, I will come in the full measure of the blessing of Christ. (Rom 15:25-29 NIV)

> Now about the collection for God's people: Do what I told the Galatian churches to do. On the first day of every week, each one of you should set aside a sum of money in keeping with his income, saving it up, so that when I come no collections will have to be made. Then, when I arrive, I will give letters of introduction to the men you approve and send them with your gift to Jerusalem. If it seems advisable for me to go also, they will accompany me. After I go through Macedonia, I will come to you—for I will be going through Macedonia. Perhaps I will stay with you awhile, or even spend the winter, so that you can help me on my journey, wherever I go. (1 Cor 16:1-6 NIV)

> And now, brothers, we want you to know about the grace that God has given the Macedonian churches. Out of the most severe trial, their overflowing joy and their extreme poverty welled up in rich generosity. For I testify that they gave as much as they were able, and even beyond their ability. Entirely on their own. (2 Cor 8:1-3 NIV)

Paul's special area of ministry was among the Gentiles, but he was bringing the Gentile churches to unite with the church in Jerusalem through their services.

Although Peter was known to be the apostle of the Jews, his first letter was written to "God's chosen people who are living as foreigners in the provinces of Pontus, Galatia, Cappadocia, Asia, and Bithynia" (1 Pet 1:1 NLT). His concern was for all Christians. The apostle does not think of his special ministry or church alone but he thinks of the entire body of Christ.

Professor Cecil Mel Robeck Jr. is an example of an apostle who is concerned about unity in the body of Christ. He is a North American Assemblies of God ordained minister, who is also a professor of church history and ecumenics. Although the Assemblies of God as a denomination does not accept the apostolic office in this present age, the ministry of Mel Robeck depicts him as an apostle. In my discussions with him, he has shared how he had a divine encounter in which he saw Jesus, and then Jesus commissioned him. Visiting his website shows that

> he has worked on ecumenical issues for nearly 40 years with the World Council of Churches, the Vatican, the World Alliance [now Communion] of Reformed Churches, and other groups. He serves as a Consultant to the Chairman of the Lausanne Committee for World Evangelization for long-term relations with the Vatican. For the past 23 years Robeck has served on the steering committee of the Global Christian Forum. He also participated with Pope John Paul II in worship events in Rome and Assisi. For 30 years he has met annually with the Secretaries of Christian World Communions and he appears regularly as a panelist on broadcasts of the American Religious Town Hall Meeting.[2]

The passion he has for ecumenism is an indication that the Lord has spoken to him to promote church unity. His publications on ecumenics are enormous. These centered on the Holy Spirit, the unity in the Pentecostal perspective, the church and potential contributions the Pentecostal Movement can make to the world Christian movements.[3] Although his church does not sponsor him on this special ministry, the Lord found his own ways of sponsoring him. If the Lord calls, he will provide the needed resources. The One who provided for the needs of Elijah through a widow will certainly provide for all the needs of his chosen ones.

---

2. http://fuller.edu/faculty/crobeck/; originally assessed on April 8, 2017. However, currently see https://www.fuller.edu/wp-content/uploads/2018/05/Mel_Robeck_CV_2018.pdf.

3. See Robeck, "Ecumenism," 286–307; "Evangelism and Ecumenism One Hundred Years after Edinburgh, Part I," 33–39; "Evangelism and Ecumenism One Hundred Years after Edinburgh, Part II," 39–44; "Fuller's Ecumenical Vision," 19–22, 28; "Roman Catholic–Pentecostal Dialogue"; "Christian Unity and Pentecostal Mission," 182–206; "Pentecostal Ecumenism," part 1 ,113–32; "Pentecostal Ecumenism," part 2, 5–17; Smith, *Pentecostal Power*, 249–76.

In Ghana, a typical example of an apostle of ecumenism is Jude Hama, a former director of Scripture Union in Ghana. I worked with him for over ten years without knowing his church affiliation. The day I found his church, I was surprised. He also works toward the promotion of the body of Christ. The unity in the body of Christ is paramount in the operation of the apostle.

Chapter 20

The Apostle Works in Teams

THIS CHAPTER ENDS THE functions of the apostle. One of the outstanding marks of the apostles in the New Testaments is that they work in teams. Since Scripture shows that the church is built on the foundation of the apostles and prophets, one may immediately arrive at the conclusion that the team would be made up of an apostle and a prophet. That is not necessarily so. The apostle works in teams of all types of people and gifts, including prophets.

You will hardly find in the New Testament an apostle functioning alone. Therefore, we will set out to see how this teamwork comes out in the New Testament.

The first group to be considered for teamwork are Apostles Peter and John. They were together going to the temple, when the "crippled beggar" was healed (Acts 3:1–9). Furthermore, we found out that Peter and John were sent to Samaria. "Now when the apostles who were at Jerusalem heard that Samaria had received the word of God, they sent Peter and John to them, who, when they had come down, prayed for them that they might receive the Holy Spirit" (Acts 8:14 NKJV). One apostle could have been sent but the two great apostles were sent, which shows the desire for teamwork.

Linked with the teamwork of Peter and John was the teamwork of the three who were considered pillars—James, Peter, and John. When Paul and Barnabas went to Jerusalem privately to meet the apostles, three of them met Paul and Barnabas, and extended the right hand of fellowship to them (Gal 2:1–10). Any one of them could have done his alone or privately but they came together to extend the right hand of fellowship. When Peter was released from prison, he went to the place where some of the believers were praying, and after he had told them what had happened, he instructed them, "'Tell James and the other brothers what happened,' he said. And then he went to another place" (Acts 12:17). This was a sign of good relations and teamwork.

The next group to be considered for teamwork is Barnabas and Paul. Barnabas was sent to Antioch. He was doing well, but he realized that he needed his friend Paul to join him. Therefore, he sent for Paul:

> News of this reached the ears of the church at Jerusalem, and they sent Barnabas to Antioch. When he arrived and saw the evidence of the grace of God, he was glad and encouraged them all to remain true to the Lord with all their hearts. He was a good man, full of the Holy Spirit and faith, and a great number of people were brought to the Lord. Then Barnabas went to Tarsus to look for Saul, and when he found him, he brought him to Antioch. So for a whole year Barnabas and Saul met with the church and taught great numbers of people. The disciples were called Christians first at Antioch. (Acts 11:22–26 NIV)

He saw the need for teamwork. They stayed there for a year teaching the people. As it was earlier on pointed out, it was in Antioch that the Holy Spirit said to set apart Barnabas and Paul for the work which he had called them (Acts 13:1–3). They had already started teamwork before the Holy Spirit sent them. For Paul, the Lord was confirming what he had told him earlier when he was called (Acts 9:15–16 NIV). However, the most important aspect here is that he was not going alone. He was going with Barnabas.

Another team was the messengers who were sent to deliver the message from the Jerusalem Council, Prophets Judas and Silas (Acts 15:22). The Council of Jerusalem had to choose two people to join Paul and Barnabas. One person could have joined them but they thought it appropriate to select two, for two are better than one. The two prophets chosen went to strengthen the believers with their teaching and encouragement (Acts 15:32).

The discussion has shown that the team could be a team of apostles or prophets. Thus, the important aspect here is teamwork. This becomes very important if we consider how the apostles were working with the elders. The elders were appointed by the apostles. "So when they [Barnabas and Paul] had appointed elders in every church, and prayed with fasting, they commended them to the Lord in whom they had believed" (Acts 14:23 NKJV). Again, Paul instructed Titus that the reason he left him in Crete was to set things in order and appoint elders (Titus 1:5).

The elders could appoint the apostles, prophets and teachers. As Paul encouraged Timothy to rekindle his gifts imparted to him, he revealed that the impartation was done by the presbytery. Paul stirs Timothy, "Do not neglect your gift, which was given you through a prophetic message when the body of elders laid their hands on you" (1 Tim 4:14 NIV). Paul does not tell us the occasion, but it is possible that this was the period where the elders commissioned or sent Timothy for the mission that the Lord had called him to. The lesson here is the elders laid their hands on Timothy, a man later recognized as an apostle, and ordained or commissioned him. Elders and apostles work in teams.

In Antioch, it was the prophets and teachers who appeared like the local presbytery that sent Barnabas and Saul (Acts 13:1–3). Immediately Barnabas and Paul began their ministry they were addressed as apostles (Acts 14:14). Now we realize that the apostles were moving in teams and appeared independent, nevertheless, the elders sent them. Thus, they were interdependent. A general rule within the body of Christ is that every member of the body is responsible for their own lives, and there are areas in which no one else can dictate to individuals. Individuals must be led by the Spirit. Nevertheless, none of the members is completely independent from the other members of the body of Christ. This is clearly demonstrated in the functioning of the apostles and the presbyteries.

When there arose a problem in the apostolic team of Paul and Barnabas with some believers, they had to bring it to the apostles and elders in Jerusalem (Acts 15:2). Although the church in Jerusalem did not send Paul and Barnabas, they had to come there for clearance. The important point for me here is the interdependence of each group—apostles and elders. If we continue, it reads, "Now the apostles and elders came together to consider this matter" (Acts 15:6 NKJV). One of the lessons that we need to learn in Acts 15 is the important role that the presbyteries play in the government of the church. Five times, the phrase the "apostles and elders" is used in this story (Acts 15:2, 4, 6, 22 and Acts 16:4). We must not lose sight of this or minimize it. In order for harmony as well as check and balances to continue in the local churches, the apostles and elders must cooperate.

Apostles do not have to rule the church alone. They must employ the services of the elders. They must move in teams of apostles, prophets, evangelists, pastors, and teachers. Since the Lord has a variety of gifts, he will also use these gifts within the team to lift up his name.

Early in my Christian life, the Lord taught me the importance of teamwork. I had fasted for six days seeking the baptism of the Holy Spirit, but did not receive it until there was another boy of my age who joined me to pray on the seventh day. Early in pastoral ministry, when I prayed with one of the brothers of the church that I pastored, the Lord revealed the archangel Michael to him and passed God's message through him to me. In another encounter, the Lord revealed the angel Gabriel to a young girl who passed the message to me. The message was that I had decided to give the name Caleb to our second baby to be born, but I should not, since the immediate past one who had died was also Caleb. She continued that indeed my wife, who was pregnant, would give birth to a baby boy. Although I had this idea, I had not shared it with anybody including my wife but the angel revealed this to the young girl, Florence Oye, a teenager of about fourteen years. I prayed that the Lord should reveal the angel to me and let him tell me the message himself. For this reason, I invited the girl together with an elder to pray with them, in the elder's guest room, where I used to go for some personal meditations in fasting and prayers. My real secret desire for organizing the prayer was to see the angel, since Gabriel is one of the angels whose name is mentioned in the Bible. I did not share this with any of them.

During the prayers, the girl said the angel had appeared to her in an episode like an open vision. She behaved as if the angel was standing in our midst; shivering, she pointed to him and asked whether we could see him. Then, she said the angel was saying that I had prayed that the Lord should reveal him (the angel) to me and present the message to me as well. However, according to the girl, the Lord said he was not going to reveal the angel to me because that was how he had chosen to work with me.[1] I understood this move as the Lord showing me the importance of teamwork. God can do whatever he wants; he can work with one person but somehow, he often works with teams.

---

1. This story may sound like fiction to some people, but since I experienced it practically, it spoke to me strongly and showed me the presence of God in my life and ministry. Indeed, my wife, who was pregnant at the time, gave birth to a baby boy, as the girl said. The first one was born on Saturday around 5:00 a.m., so was this one too born on Saturday around 5:00 a.m.

As mentioned already, in Acts 15:39–41, Paul broke fellowship with Barnabas, yet he did not go alone, he chose to get along with Silas, while Barnabas went with Mark. Again, here, both apostles showed us the importance of teamwork.

From another perspective, why did Paul have to break with Barnabas? Was the break from the Lord? I would think that it was the recurrence of the dictates of the old nature, which often causes people to take unsatisfactory decisions. Why should I say this? Paul himself discourages division among the people of God (Rom 16:17; 1 Cor 3:3–4). We do not know what the church would have received if they had worked together as the Holy Spirit directed them. We lost the records of the latter part of Barnabas's apostolic missions. I, however, believe that God still causes all things to work together for good to those who love him (Rom 8:28). Despite what happened, the remarkable thing here is that none of them went alone, they still chose to work in teams.

In addition, what they did best in the break is that they still related to each other, there is no record of the two of them fighting or accusing each other. Rather as already mentioned, there is a record of Paul speaking well of Mark, and even said he should be brought to him because he was useful to him (Col 4:11; 2 Tim 2:11). Paul's acceptance of Mark was to show that he had accepted the fact that when Barnabas took him up, he did the right thing.

I consider teamwork to be the biblical type of foundation of leadership God has put in place, which if followed, helps the church to stand the test of time. Teamwork has been the Lord's model. After all, God works in the form of the Trinity: God the Father, Son, and the Holy Spirit. Our Lord Jesus stressed the need for unity and teamwork at John 17:

> My prayer is not for them alone. I pray also for those who will believe in me through their message, that all of them may be one, Father, just as you are in me and I am in you. May they also be in us so that the world may believe that you have sent me. I have given them the glory that you gave me, that they may be one as we are one: I in them and you in me. May they be brought to complete unity to let the world know that you sent me and have loved them even as you have loved me. (John 17:20–23 NIV)

Teamwork shows that we need the support of one another. No matter how good a person is, he will have his own limitations. The human being has its own limitations. Despite the gifts of the Apostle Paul, individuals wrote his letters for him (Rom 16:21; 1 Cor 16:21). The Lord did not heal Moses of stammering, rather he asked Aaron to assist him (Exod 4:10–17). Ecclesiastes advises that two are better than one. Even if one falls down the other will lift him up, and better still, a cord of three is difficult to break (Eccl 4:9–12).

Teamwork helps in accountability. Since the apostle is a very gifted person, failure to work in teams and be accountable to a body may cause him to be puffed up. In a way, Paul and Barnabas were accountable to the church in Antioch that sent them. Peter and John were accountable to the church in Jerusalem. As has been said, although Paul and Barnabas were not directly under the church in Jerusalem, they had to bring the challenge they encountered for the decision or advice of the apostles and elders in Jerusalem. Paul came to see the apostles in Jerusalem because of a revelation he had. God will want us to be accountable to one another.

Why should the apostles work in teams? God has invested authority in the apostles and also the prophet. Working in teams helps them to be accountable to others. Barnabas and Paul were accountable to the church in Antioch. Peter and John were accountable to the church in Jerusalem. God demands that you become another's keeper. Teamwork is a must for every apostle and prophet.

Chapter 21

The Difference between Apostles and Prophets

THE APOSTLES AND THE prophets are both messengers of God and share very similar graces. This chapter attempts to bring out the differences between the apostles and prophets so that you can distinguish them in their operations and support them. These differences have already been featured in previous chapters; this chapter outlines them for the purpose of clarity.

SIMILARITIES

There are some similarities between apostles and prophets.

Both Are Called Messengers of God

They are both messengers of God, but whereas the prophet was the main messenger of God in the Old Testament, the apostle is the main messenger of God in the New Testament. In the Old Testament there were some apostolic figures who were not labeled as apostles. These included Moses, Joshua, Deborah, and Samuel. These leaders could see and hear from God and lead God's people in their generation. Yet, the focus of the Old Testament after Samuel was the prophets. The reason was that when kingship was instituted, God supported the kingship with the prophet who could hear from God and direct the king.

The apostle and prophet are both specially called by God (e.g., Jer 1:4–5; Isa 6:8–9; Acts 9:1–9). We have accounts of how some of the prophets in the Old Testament were called. These include prophets such as Samuel, Isaiah, Jeremiah, and Elisha. We do not have accounts of how the prophets in the New Testament were called. However, we do have stories of how the majority of the apostle were called. Thus, as the prophets in the Old Testaments were called specially by the Lord, so were the apostles in the New Testament called by the Lord.

Links between Call and Ordination for Prophets and Apostles

While both prophets and apostles are called by the Lord, some prophets and apostles were not physically ordained in the Bible. In the OT, the Lord allowed the Prophet Samuel to anoint Saul as a king and later anoint David as king. A king was anointed to lead or rule the people of God and have authority over them on behalf of God. But when it comes to the prophets, we only have the account of Elisha who was anointed a prophet (1 Kgs 19:16–21).[1] The purpose of the physical anointing was for the people around to know that the Lord has set a person aside to be used for his service. It was supposed to be a symbol of a spiritual exercise that has taken place.

Most of the people who were used mightily by God were not physically ordained or anointed. These people included Moses, Elijah and Samuel. Nonetheless, God called these people, commissioned and used them. Although not anointed, the ministries of Moses, Samuel and Elijah were spectacular. This means the ordination or anointing of oil is a symbol of what had taken place in a person inwardly. Or, put in another way, the oil symbolizes what is taking place in a person. While the physical oil or ordination was important, the most important part was the anointing of the Lord that was to be demonstrated in the life of the person.

In the New Testament while the Twelve were called and ordained or appointed as apostles (Mark 3:13–14), others such as Paul and James

---

1. This is the only place where we hear of the anointing of a prophet. It is assumed that Elijah would anoint him.

were not directly ordained.[2] These are some apostles whose ordination accounts we do not have. Yet, the Lord used them. John P. Lathrop, a North American Pentecostal Pastor, observes that "the details of Philip's call [to evangelist] are not given to us at all. . . . It is possible that circumstances revealed what was in him."[3] Often, circumstances bring out the gifts that are in people. People even begin to call others apostles, prophets, or evangelists, before these are officially conferred on them.

This does not mean that there is no need for ordination of officers. Ordination is seen in both Old and New Testaments. Interestingly, Moses, Samuel and Elijah were all not ordained by people, however, they were all asked to ordain others. Joshua was to be anointed in place of Moses, Elisha in place of Elijah, and Saul as well as David as kings were both anointed by Samuel. Paul had to ordain Timothy. Thus, while some may not be ordained, others may be ordained. The Lord is not limited, and we must not limit the move of God. What we need to recognize is the hand of God in situations.

Both have Revelations from God

The call of God comes with a revelation, where the Lord directs a person to do a specific thing for him. The revelation will continue from different perspectives to direct both the apostle and the prophet. The measure of a person's surrender will determine how the Lord will use him. Someone may be an apostle or prophet but may not surrender fully to the Lord's will. This will impair the way the Lord will continue to use him. The prophetic books are examples of how God continues to direct the prophets and his messengers after the call. Some of them were so available to the Lord that he continued to direct and use them for the benefit of his people and society at large. Others, however, could be used only for a brief period of time. The measure of one's surrender indeed determines the way the Lord uses him.

In the Acts of the Apostles, we see how the Lord was directing the apostles. Peter, for example, had been given the keys to the kingdom of heaven, but when he used one of the keys on the day of Pentecost, he waited for a long time without doing missions to use the other keys for

---

2. It may be argued that Paul was later ordained by the church in Antioch (Acts 13) or perhaps was ordained by Ananias in Acts 9.

3. Lathrop, *Apostles, Prophets, Evangelists, Pastors, and Teachers*, 58.

Gentiles to enter the kingdom. Philip led the missions to Samaria before Peter and John joined in. Peter needed revelation before visiting the home of Cornelius to open the way for the Gentiles to enter the kingdom.

Peter was an apostle, but the Lord directed him through revelations (Acts 10). In a vision, the Lord taught him that what he, the Lord, accepted as clean, Peter should not call unclean (Act 10:13–16). As Peter was thinking of the vision, the Holy Spirit said to him, three men were looking for him so he should go down to meet them without hesitation (Acts 10:19–20). In Act 16, Paul saw in a vision a man asking him to come to Macedonia and help (Acts 16:8–10). He and his team concluded that the Lord wanted them to visit Macedonia. Thus, God speaks to both apostles and prophets.

Both are Foundation Layers

Both the apostle and the prophets can lay a good foundation in churches. The apostle can build and so can a prophet. They can both teach sound doctrines, grow churches as well as identify and train leaders. Some examples of prophets who trained others are Samuel and Elisha. Paul is a very typical example of an apostle who trained many people.

DISSIMILARITIES

There are however some basic differences between the two gifts. The differences in gifts do mainly come in frequency.

Differences in Basic Gifts

The basic gifts which constitute the prophet are the "call," prophecy, gift of interpretation of diverse kinds of tongues, the word of knowledge, the word of wisdom, and discerning of spirits. Many prophets possess these as the basic gifts. As have been shown already, the prophet may possess other gifts, but at least those mentioned here are the basic ones for a person to really function in the prophetic office.

The basic gifts which constitute the apostolic office are the "call," the gift of teaching, leadership and administration, and the gifts of confirmation (the gift of faith, the gift of miracle or the gifts of healings). The apostle may possess the gift of the word of knowledge or the word of wisdom, but at least those suggested here may form the basic apostolic calling. While the prophet may not have the gift of leadership to be able to lead a team, the apostle must possess that. The gift of leadership is that which makes the apostle.

There are some apostles who still have strong prophetic ministry. In the New Testament, the Apostle John is one of such apostles. He was the one who wrote the book of Revelation. In the Old Testament, Moses was like the apostle; we see this in his strong leadership ability. However, the Lord is not limited. A majority of those in the prophetic ministry who exhibit high leadership tendencies and break new ground in missions may be apostolic in calling.

Difference in Operating the Gifts of Revelation

When it comes to revelations, many of the prophets see vision, dream, and hear the Lord in the form of prophecy. This is very clear in the call of prophets such as Samuel, Isaiah, Ezekiel, Elisha, Daniel, and Zechariah. Daniel specially had the enablement to re-dream the dream of Nebuchadnezzar and interpreted it (Dan 2:19-45). In the New Testament, Agabus was one of such prophets (Acts 11:27-28; Act 21:10-11). The way some of them received constant revelations show the way the prophetic gift operates.

Apostles may see visions and have dreams, but often they perceive or feel within their beings what the Lord wants to do. The Lord's will may dawn strongly upon an apostle like possession. The Lord's will becomes clear in his mind for him to know what the Lord intends to reveal. For example, the Spirit compelled Paul to go to Jerusalem, but there was persecution ahead. He states, "And see, now I go bound in the spirit to Jerusalem, not knowing the things that will happen to me there, 'except that the Holy Spirit testifies in every city, saying that chains and tribulations await me" (Acts 20:22-24 NIV). In Acts 27:10, when Paul was being sent to Rome with other prisoners, sailing had become dangerous. Paul had a perception. He opines, "Men, I perceive that this voyage will end with disaster and much loss, not only of the cargo and ship, but also our lives" (NKJV). This is a major difference between the Old Testament messenger of God and the New Testament messenger of God. In the New Testament the revelation is within the body of the messenger, while in the Old Testament the messenger was a "voice."

BASIC IN FUNCTIONS

When it comes to the functions of the prophets in the Old Testaments, basically they were helping the leaders or the kings to govern the people of God. They were to explain the contents of God's way to the people and warn them of the repercussion of failure to obey God's covenant. Besides the apostolic figures including Moses and Samuel, the prophets were not leading the people. They were the voice of God for the people. The watchmen of God's people.

On the other hand, the apostles carry the word of God and also lead. The word has settled in the bodies of the apostles so that they use their bodies to carry the word of God to the people. They combine the ministry of the prophets and that of the Lord Jesus Christ. They receive the revelation of Christ and become receptacles of the revelation. They do not have other leaders ahead of them, when it comes to ministering to the people of God. They govern the administration of the church and they are stewards of God's treasure.

All said and done, there is no sharp line of demarcation between the gifts of God. There are however a combination of gifts. An apostle may function as an evangelist, pastor, teacher, or prophet. Similarly, a prophet may function as an apostle, teacher or pastor. The gifts of God are in the control of the Lord himself. Apostle John was available when he was needed to receive the revelation for the people of God. He states:

> I, John, your brother and companion in the suffering and kingdom and patient endurance that are ours in Jesus, was on the island of Patmos because of the word of God and the testimony of Jesus. On the Lord's Day I was in the Spirit, and I heard behind me a loud voice like a trumpet, which said: "Write on a scroll what you see and send it to the seven churches: to Ephesus, Smyrna, Pergamum, Thyatira, Sardis, Philadelphia and Laodicea." (Rev 1:9–11 NIV)

The most important things for a person to do is to avail himself as a vessel of honor for the Lord to use. What the Lord needs from you is to avail yourself to be used whenever he needs you.

PART 7

From Apostles to Bishops

THE TASK OF THIS part is to find out why the leadership of the church dropped from apostles to bishops. The approach is to draw from the New Testament and make a brief survey from church history to find out how the apostles dropped to give way to bishops as the managers of the church. For continuity sake, some of the issues that were featured in the previous chapters will be summarized here to make a point. I dig out from available first and second centuries' books to find out the roles of church officers during those periods. Then I select a few church fathers and analyze the type of gifts they had, and how the community recognized them. The part is divided into five chapters. Chapter 22 shows how the apostles led the New Testament church. Chapter 23 finds out what happened after the apostles. Chapter 24 examines the works of the church fathers to find out how they considered their roles and those of the apostles. Chapter 25 draws conclusions from the discussions made so far, and then chapter 26 appeals for apostles and prophets in our generation.

Chapter 22

The New Testament Church Was Led by Apostles

The office of the apostle is not a concern to many of the Protestant churches that believe that the operations of the spiritual gifts ceased after the demise of the original apostles. However, it becomes an issue for discussion, when it comes to the very aggressive evangelicals and more especially some Pentecostals who believe that there has been a restoration of the spiritual gifts. A classical Pentecostal denomination like the Assemblies of God does not officially recognize the office of the apostle. Yet, there are some Pentecostals who do not only recognize them but also ordain apostles. What can we deduce from the New Testament and church history about the office and ministry of the apostle? Read on.

It has been shown that in the Old Testament, the minister of God was the prophet. In the New Testament, the minister of God was the apostle. The Lord chose twelve out of the disciples and ordained them as apostles. When Jesus died, rose, and ascended to heaven, the apostles led by Peter chose Matthias to be added to the apostles to maintain the number twelve. The call of Paul as an apostle was confirmed by the original apostles. James, the natural brother of Jesus, was also identified as apostle, and thus defying the idea that the apostles were limited to twelve. Jude, the natural brother of Jesus, although not mentioned directly as apostle, exhibited apostolic prowess. It has already been shown that the apostolic work continued in the ministry of Paul and his associates, some of whom were identified as apostles. These included Barnabas, Timothy, Silas, Titus, and Apollos.

The New Testament indicates that the apostles were working together with the elders. Together, they handled difficult cases, with the apostles playing general oversight of the work. In Acts 6:1–7, when murmuring arose in the church, the apostles quickly asked the people to select seven men full of the Holy Spirit on whom they laid their hands to pray for as helpers. In Acts 8:14–25, when the apostles in Jerusalem heard that the Samaritans had received the word of God for the first time, they sent Peter and John to minister baptism of the Holy Spirit to them. In Acts 15:1–35, when there was a great concern about the role of the Gentiles in the Mosaic law, the apostles and the elders had to settle it. Against this backdrop, it can be assumed that besides the apostles' roles of ministering the word of God and prayer, they were also playing a general oversight of the churches. As has been pointed out already, reading through the Acts of the Apostles and the epistles, we see that the apostles were visiting the churches, as well as sending their personal representatives to strengthen, encourage and bring reports to them (Acts 9:32–42; Acts 13–20; Rom 1:10–13). The epistles are evidence of how they wrote letters to strengthen, encourage and instruct them, and in some cases settle disputes. They teamed up with the elders to execute their duties.

This becomes clearer in the ministry of Paul. Paul was called by the Lord Jesus Christ in a revelation as an apostle. He is the one apostle whose apostolic ministry has been more intricately recorded than any other. For the fact that the Lord allowed his ministry to be put down shows that his apostolic ministry could be used as an example of how apostles work with others. We have already seen how he teamed up with others who were considered apostles in his apostolic missions. We now need to know how he worked with the other officers. This will help us to know the use of the terms presbytery and overseers, which eventually developed to episcopacy.

OTHER COWORKERS OF PAUL

Paul was very much appreciative of his coworkers and those who assisted him in his ministry. In his letters, he was always appreciative of them. By so doing, he has helped us to know the majority of the officers he worked with and how he related with them.

Paul considered Euodia, Syntyche, and Clement as "loyal yokefellow" who contended at his side in the cause of the gospel (Phil 4:2-3). For Sosthenes, he called him "brother." Sosthenes was the official of the Jewish synagogue at Corinth who became a Christian. When the people wanted to kill Paul and did not get him, Sosthenes was beaten up (1 Cor 1:1; Acts 18:17). In the book of Philemon, Philemon was addressed as "dear friend" and "fellow worker," Apphia addressed as "our sister," and then Archippus as "fellow soldier" (Phlm 1-2). Epaphras was described as "fellow prisoner," and then Mark, Aristarchus, Demas and Luke as "fellow workers" (Phlm 23-24). Mark is again addressed as one who was helpful to him (2 Tim 4:11). Tychicus, a Christian from Asia, was also highly commended. He had done some travels with Paul (Acts 20:4). Paul sent him to Ephesus, Colossae and Titus (Eph 6:21-22; Col 4:7-9; 2 Tim 4:12; Titus 3:12). He described him as "a dear brother, a faithful minister and fellow servant in the Lord" (Col 4:7 NIV). Trophimus was a member of Paul's team from Ephesus in Asia who traveled with him for a while (Acts 20:4; 21:29). Paul had to leave him sick in Miletus (2 Tim 4:20).

Again, here, mention needs to be made of Aquila and Priscilla. In Rom 16:1-16, many of Paul's coworkers were acknowledged. Some notable ones are Aquila and Priscilla who were old friends of Paul from Acts 18:1-3. They worked closely with Paul in his early missions and they became leaders of the church in Ephesus (Acts 18:18-28; 2 Tim 4:19). In Romans, they had moved to Rome and served as church leaders there. Paul commended them as fellow workers who risked their lives for him. Phoebe was mentioned specifically as a deaconess. Paul commended her as a deaconess of the church in Cenchrea (Rom 1:1). Others who were acknowledged included Epenetus, the "first covert in the province of Asia"; Mary, who "worked very hard" for them; Urbanus, "fellow worker in Christ"; Apelles, "tested and approved in Christ." Still others included Herodian, relative of Paul; members of the household of Aristobulus; Tryphena and Tryphosa, women who "work hard in the Lord"; Persis, another woman who worked very hard in the Lord"; and then Rufus, "chosen in the Lord," and his mother who was also a mother to Paul. It is worth reading Rom 16:1-16 to refresh yourself on some of Paul's coworkers.

It is amazing how Paul remembers all those who worked with him and acknowledges each one of them for what they had done. The apostle works in teams, and he does not forget his teammates who cooperate to build the kingdom of God. It is always important to acknowledge those who work with you, and all who assist you to accomplish your work.

HOW PAUL CAME ABOUT HIS LEADERS

As the Apostle Paul works around, he works with local leaders too. Some scholars have questioned the role Paul played in the selection of these leaders.[1] For me, this is not a problem at all. As a pastor who has planted many churches, I do not plant a church without finding leaders to take care of it. It would be ridiculous for Paul to begin a church without setting leaders to take charge of the work that he has done. Acts 14:23 shows an example of what was happening, "Paul and Barnabas appointed elders for them in each church and, with prayer and fasting, committed them to the Lord, in whom they had put their trust" (NIV). His command to Titus in Crete shows that where he could not do this, he requested his associate to do that. Titus 1:5 reads, "The reason I left you in Crete was that you might straighten out what was left unfinished and appoint elders in every town, as I directed you" (NIV). This means that it was the principle of Paul to appoint leaders in places where he established churches and saw to it that everything was done well. Titus was to straighten out what was left unfinished.

To Timothy (and similar to Titus), he gave the qualifications of such leaders (1 Tim 3:1–16; Titus 1:5–9). Paul further told Timothy that he wrote to him so that he would know what to do in case he (Paul) delayed his visit to him (1 Tim 3:15). He admonished Timothy in 1 Tim 5:22 that he should not be hasty in laying hands on people, which is an indication that the ordination of officers was an ongoing activity. This implies that Paul expected that the appointing of leaders for the churches would continue. Our concern now is the type of leaders who were being appointed.

First, in Acts 14:23, Luke shows that elders, Greek *presbúteros*, were appointed. Similarly the directive given to Titus, in Titus 1:5, was to appoint elders. However, in v. 6, when he was given the qualifications, he used the term overseer or bishop *(epískopos)*. In 1 Tim 3:1–7, the qualifications listed were concerning the appointment of overseers (or bishops), Greek *epískopos*. Contrary to this, in the same book, 5:17, when Paul was instructing about the double honor that should be given to the leaders

---

1. Sullivan, *From Apostles to Bishops*, 51; Schillebeeckx, *Church with a Human Face*, 77–78.

who direct the affairs of the church, he used elders, *presbúteros*. In Ephesus, when Paul asked to speak to the leaders, Luke reported that he sent for the elders, *presbúteros* (Acts 20:17). But when Paul was speaking to them, he said, "Keep watch over yourselves and all the flock of which the Holy Spirit has made you overseers" (*epískopos*, Acts 20:28 NIV). Thus, here Paul used both terms elders and overseer or bishop. It would therefore appear that the terms overseers (bishops) and elders were used interchangeably.

Other officers which were appointed were deacons *(diákonos)*. The original apostles were the first to appoint deacons in Acts 6:1–7. These were people who assisted manual duties. In 1 Tim 3:8, Paul listed the qualifications of deacons. The conjunction, likewise, bringing the two verses (7 and 8), together shows that it was an ongoing practice. The term was also used to describe Phoebe who was serving in the church of Cenchrea. It was possible the term "deacon" was created as an office of the church.

HOW DID PAUL APPOINT THE ASSOCIATES?

Paul's coworkers who stand out are Timothy and Titus, and in a way, Barnabas. He gave orders to Titus and by implication Timothy to appoint church leaders. How were these closest associates themselves appointed? In the case of Barnabas and Paul, the Holy Spirit directed, through prophecy that they should be set aside for the work, which he had given to them (Acts 13). The prophets and teachers who had gathered fasted and prayed for them. This could be said to be the official ordination or commissioning of the two apostles. Essentially, in Acts 9:1–19, the Lord had already chosen Paul and set him aside for this task; Ananias prayed for him. What about the numerous associates?

Apart from Timothy, we do not have the records of Paul appointing or ordaining the associates he worked with. In the case of Timothy, 1 Tim 4:14 indicates that a body of elders laid their hands on him as if he was being commissioned to do some work. Similarly, 2 Tim 1:6 reveals that Paul laid his hand on him. Thus, Timothy, at least, had two types of laying on of hands, one by Paul, and the other by the body of elders. Into what office, ministry or position was he prayed for? The Scripture is silent about this. However, he might have been ordained or commissioned to do specific work.

On the others who accompanied Paul in his missions, can we assume that similar prayers like that which was done for Timothy might have been said for them as they joined Paul in his missions? Apparently, this type of prayer, which could be called ordination, might have been said for both Timothy and Titus, thus, possibly giving them the authority to appoint other officers.

Chapter 23

After the Death of the Apostles

THE DIDACHE

WE DO NOT HAVE records of how Peter and the other apostles ordained officers, thus, we were limited to Paul. Now we want to find out what happened when Paul left the scene. Since these accounts are not written in the Bible, we will have to use the available literature of the period. One of the books, which is helpful is the *Didache*. It has two titles.[1] First, it is entitled "The Teaching of the Twelve Apostles," and second, "The Teaching of the Lord to the Gentiles by the Twelve Apostles." The second title is an indication that it was written by some second-generation Jewish Christians who adopted their practices for non-Jewish Christians. The specific date of writing is not settled among scholars. It is considered to be written between AD 100 and 120, and possibly from Syria.[2] Since it was not accepted into the canon of Scripture, it must be considered a book that may throw light on what was happening during the period. In the *Didache*, the terms "apostle" and "apostles" are mentioned three times in one discourse, while the terms "prophet" and "prophets" are used sixteen times in four discourses. Another term that is used alongside apostles and prophets in three discourses is teacher and the plural form teachers. This can be an indication that by this time, although apostles and teachers were in a way recognized in the church, prophets were becoming more prominent in the system.

---

1. The one used here is the *Didache* or the Teaching of the Lord to the Gentiles by the Twelve Apostles, translated and edited by J. B. Lightfoot.

2. Sullivan, *From Apostles to Bishop*, 81.

The *Didache* had to take time to instruct how to receive visiting apostles, prophets and teachers. The instructions show that these were visitors who claim to function in those offices, however, their operations were generating a sort of confusion within the churches. Let us consider the passage below:

> Whosoever therefore shall come and teach you all these things that have been said before, receive him; but if the teacher himself be perverted and teach a different doctrine to the destruction thereof, hear him not; but if to the increase of righteousness and the knowledge of the Lord, receive him as the Lord. But *concerning the apostles and prophets*, so do ye according to the ordinance of the Gospel. Let every apostle, when he cometh to you, be received as the Lord; but *he shall not abide more than a single day*, or if there be need, a second likewise; but if he abide three days, he is a false prophet. And when he departeth let the apostle receive nothing save bread, until he findeth shelter; but if he ask money, he is a false prophet. *And any prophet speaking in the Spirit ye shall not try neither discern*; for every sin shall be forgiven, but this sin shall not be forgiven. *Yet not every one that speaketh in the Spirit is a prophet*, but only if he have the ways of the Lord. From his ways therefore the false prophet and the prophet shall be recognized. *And no prophet when he ordereth a table in the Spirit shall eat of it; otherwise he is a false prophet. And every prophet teaching the truth, if he doeth not what he teacheth, is a false prophet.* And every prophet approved and found true, if he doeth ought as an outward mystery typical of the Church, and yet teacheth you not to do all that he himself doeth, *shall not be judged before you; he hath his judgment in the presence of God*; for in like manner also did the prophets of old time. *And whosoever shall say in the Spirit, Give me silver or anything else, ye shall not listen to him*; but if he tell you to give on behalf of others that are in want, let no man judge him. (11:1–12, italics mine)

The instructions concerning the teachers was that the teacher should be received if he teaches "all these things that have been said before," which implies the right teachings, which had already been taught to the believers. If the teacher lives by what he says, he should be listened to. If he does not follow what he says, he should not be accepted.

An apostle was to be received like the Lord as all the apostles and prophets in the gospel; he could stay for a day, and not more than two days. Once he exceeds two days, he should be considered as a false prophet. If he departs, nothing should be given to him except bread, that is, food. If he requests money, he should be considered a false prophet.

The instruction concerning the prophets were quite complicated. "And any prophet speaking in the Spirit ye shall not try neither discern." This may imply that the prophetic messages from the prophets were not to be judged. However, it continues, "Yet not everyone that speaketh in the Spirit is a prophet, but only if he have the ways of the Lord." It appears that recognized prophets were not to be judged. Judgment was to be left for the Lord. This becomes clearer as it directs later that an approved prophet, "shall not be judged before you; he hath his judgment in the presence of God." An approved prophet here could be a member of the local church, who was well known. Furthermore, it says that "no prophet when he ordereth a table in the Spirit shall eat of it," which means a prophetic message should not favor the prophet. If he asks for money or anything, do not give to him, but if he makes a request for someone else, it can be given to the person. Any prophet who teaches the truth and does not do it should be considered a false prophet. Thus, it harmonizes with Jesus' teaching that by their fruits you shall know them.

Considering the instruction not to judge an approved prophet and the claim that "not every one that speaketh in the Spirit is a prophet" shows that there was tension between the desire to accept prophecy just as it is and the instruction to judge prophecy. Later, the *Didache* gave warning to the people that "in the last days the false prophets and corrupters shall be multiplied, and the sheep shall be turned into wolves, and love shall be turned into hate" (16:3). It is quite possible that already the prophetic ministry was posing challenges to the people. The mentioning of false prophets and the type of lives they were living shows that during the period that the *Didache* was written, false prophets were around and the writers had to draw from ongoing examples from the churches. The instruction here shows that the leadership was willing to address the challenges. Meanwhile, there was the fear not to interfere in the true move of God among his people. It is in the struggle to bring a balance that the instruction not to judge an approved prophet might have been given. Yet, such instruction has the potential to manipulate a system. No doubt, few years later, there was confusion, which eventually led to the decline of the prophetic.[3]

---

3. See chapter 31, especially the discussion on Montanism.

Currently, Christians have the sound teaching of Jesus, Paul and John concerning how to judge prophecy. For Jesus, you shall know false prophets by their fruits. Paul sets down the guidelines on the operations of prophecy and how to test it within the assembly of believers. Everything is to be done in a fitting and orderly manner and it should be done toward edification of the Church (1 Cor 14:5–6, 26, 40). Prophets are to speak with the intention of allowing others to speak and exercise their gifts in the church (1 Cor 14:26, 30–31). The assembly of believers should allow the prophets to speak but also judge the utterance (1 Thess 5:19–22). Prophets were to allow others to judge their messages (1 Cor 14:29).

Coming back to the issue of apostleship, it is clear that the term "apostle" was mentioned here, it is apparent that the functions do not depict the type of apostles we see in the New Testament. In the New Testament, as discussed already, once an apostle established a church, the church was under his control and nurturing. The apostle had an oversight of the work and exercised authority over the people. Difficult issues were referred to the apostles for their counsel. The apostles who were being addressed here were not of such caliber. Those apostles as have been described here could not be apostles who had the call of the apostolic ministry. They are portrayed as itinerant teachers who were moving from one place to another.

In another instance, the *Didache* gives instructions to the prophets and teachers, which is relevant for our purpose:

> But every true prophet desiring to settle among you is *worthy of his food*. In like manner a true teacher *is* also *worthy*, like *the workman, of his food*. Every firstfruit then of the produce of the wine-vat and of the threshing-floor, of thy oxen and of thy sheep, thou shalt take and give as the firstfruit to the prophets; for they are your chief-priests. But if ye have not a prophet, give them to the poor. If thou makest bread, take the firstfruit and give according to the commandment. In like manner, when thou openest a jar of wine or of oil, take the firstfruit and give to the prophets; yea and of money and raiment and every possession take the firstfruit, as shall seem good to thee, and give according to the commandment. (13:1–7)

The instruction was concerning how to take care of a person who was considered a true prophet and had settled in a local church. Such prophets desired to be taken care of; similarly, a true teacher was to be taken care of. The prophets were to be considered as chief priests who should receive first fruits and money. In the absence of prophets, first fruits were to be given to the poor.

Here, it is realized that the attention had been taken from the apostle to the prophet. The prophet was to be considered as the chief priest. Still at another point, some directions were given concerning the appointment of bishops and deacons alongside prophets, and teachers. The direction follows:

> Appoint for yourselves therefore bishops and deacons worthy of the Lord, men who are meek and not lovers of money, and true and approved; for unto you they also perform the service of the prophets and teachers. Therefore despise them not; for they are your honourable men along with the prophets and teachers. (15:1–2)

It shows that by this time, attention was being taken away from the apostles, and in most cases prophets and teachers were leading the local churches. Here, the instruction was for the churches to consider appointing bishops and deacons to work alongside the prophets and teachers. Significantly, the term used is *epískopos* (bishops), not *presbúteros* (elders). They were to be respected as people who were carrying similar duties as prophets and teachers.

Special privilege was given to the prophets, rather than the teachers. For example, the *Didache* recommends that the leaders of the congregations say a special prayer during the Eucharist, that is, on the Lord's Supper Day. However, the prophet was given the privilege to pray as he ought; "But permit the prophets to offer thanksgiving as much as they desire" (10:7). Thus, the prophet was the man of the Spirit who did not need to be limited. The prophet has assumed a higher position here.

Generally, from the *Didache*'s perspective then, those who were leading the church were the leaders whom the apostles had set in place, thus the bishops and the elders. The apostolic had been diminished or was dying swiftly. There were prophets and teachers, but the prophets were highly respected as people of the Spirit.

THE SHEPHERD OF HERMAS

The other book which is available is the *Shepherd of Hermas*, which was written in AD 125.[4] It was written by a lay member of the church

---

4. Editors of Encyclopaedia Britannica, "Shepherd of Hermas."

in Rome. He claims to have received messages, visions and instructions from heavenly messengers.[5] His work shows that the prophetic ministry was still active in some people.

Hermas's work comprises five visions, twelve commandments (mandates), and ten parables (similitudes). The messages are quite complex, because they are metaphors, however, the thrust is a call for the true transformation of the servants of God. The book ministers to people who are searching for salvation. It demonstrates that the process of God's work of salvation passes through human weaknesses; for the writer himself had to pray for forgiveness. It directs people to live the righteous life by repenting of their sins, and preserving the holiness of the church.[6] It also provides hope for people who think they cannot make it.

In one of the interpretations of the vision to Hermas, the message centered on apostles, bishops, teachers and deacons. It will be appropriate to cite it:

> Hear now concerning the stones that go to the building. The stones that are squared and white, and that fit together in their joints, these are the apostles and bishops and teachers and deacons, who walked after the holiness of God, and exercised their office of bishop and teacher and deacon in purity and sanctity for the elect of God, some of them already fallen on sleep, and others still living. And because they always agreed with one another, they both had peace among themselves and listened one to another. (17:1–6)

The message touched on apostles, bishops, teachers and deacons who walked after the holiness of God. It appears that he was talking about the apostles of the past. However, he also showed that they "exercised their office of bishop and teacher and deacon in purity," and concluded that "some of them already fallen on sleep, and others still living." The phrase "others still living" shows that he was talking about some of them who were still functioning in these offices including apostles. Nevertheless, for the fact that he left the term "apostle" out when he was talking

---

5. The book was accepted by some church leaders, including Irenaeus, Clement of Alexandria, and Origen, as even inspired, but others, including Tertullian, rejected it. The Muratorian Canon rejected it as inspired. The Muratorian Canon is considered the oldest possible known list of most of the books of the New Testament. Hill, "Debate over the Muratorian Fragment," 437–52.

6. Purity is mentioned twelve times, holiness and holy twenty seven times (including holy angels).

about those "exercising their offices," it may appear that at the period the apostolic office was not functional. In addition, in four other places, he referred to apostles and teachers of the past who discharged their duties faithfully and had fallen asleep (101:16; 102:12; 103:5; 111:2). This gives an indication that he might have been speaking about the apostles of blessed memory.

The presentation here also shows that the office of the bishop was developing, as he uses the phrase "exercised their office of bishop and teacher and deacon." Initially he used the term *epískopoi* (plural), but when he was talking about the office, he used the singular term, bishop. Earlier in his vision, he had been instructed to collect two books, which were later read alongside the elders who presided over the church. He used the term elders two times and both were in the plural form. The term used was *presbuteroi*, plural (8:14–16; 11:16). Nevertheless, when talking about an office, he used the term bishop. This is a signal that the office of the bishop was developing gradually.

Hermas, however, spoke extensively about prophets. His messages condemned people who consult prophets for oracles and prophets who responded to such things. He compared that to soothsaying; the Spirit of God, he said, did not need consultation (49:14–16). He rather promoted prophetic utterance within the community of God's people (49:31). Generally, he admonished people not to be deceived by such prophets. Furthermore, he stressed that the life and works of a prophet would truly show his source. He prescribed that the true prophet was gentle, humble, and considered his neighbor as superior to himself, shunned worldliness, and denied himself (49:25–27). He recommended that the prophet's message be directed toward the multitude (49:31). His conclusion was very sharp:

> Thus, also the empty prophets, whenever they come unto the spirits of righteous men, are found just such as they came. I have given thee the life of both kinds of prophets. Therefore test, by his life and his works, the man who says that he is moved by the Spirit. But do thou trust the Spirit that cometh from God, and hath power; but in the earthly and empty spirit put no trust at all; for in it there is no power, for it cometh from the devil. Listen [then] to the parable which I shall tell thee. (49:50–56)

This is an indication that at his time, the focus was on the prophet, and the apostolic was fading away.

CONCLUSION

Drawing conclusions from the two ancient documents, it is clear that after the death of the twelve apostles, Paul, and his colleagues, nobody had the audacity to ordain another as an apostle. The apostles, especially the accounts of Paul, show that they appointed bishops or elders and deacons. The officers that they chose became the officers of the church. These officers ordained others as bishops and deacons. The term "bishops" became more prominent than the term "elders," although sometimes both were used interchangeably. The *Didache* directs that some people could be ordained into the offices of bishop and deacon. This shows that the ordination of people as bishops and deacons was a practice that was ongoing in the period. Besides these officers, there were some itinerant ministers who were considered as prophets and teachers. Few of them were called apostles and along the line, the term apostle faded away. The prophets and the teachers were featuring, with the prophet becoming a key figure. There is no indication that the prophets were ordained but the charismatic nature of the prophetic ministry made them acceptable in the church community to the extent that they used to officiate the Lord's Supper. They appeared to be accepted more than the bishops and the deacons. However, the bishops who had been ordained by the apostles and their representatives appeared to control the churches. Ultimately, the bishops who were leading the churches became the representatives of the apostles. Does that mean that there was no apostle functioning again? The next chapter picks it up.

Chapter 24

From the Church Fathers

THE TASK OF THIS section is to find out how the leaders of the church after the apostles considered themselves. For the sake of space, few of these leaders have been considered for our purpose.

CLEMENT OF ROME

One of the church leaders who needs to be considered is Clement. He is the link between the apostles and the bishops. Clement is mostly known in church history because of a letter that is generally accepted as his work that was sent to the church in Corinth.[1] Some think that he is the Clement who was mentioned at Phil 4:3, as one of the coworkers of Paul. Indeed, his letter demonstrated that he knew both Paul and Peter and their ministries (*1 Clement* 3:12–15).[2]

---

1. The archbishop's translation from the ancient Greek copy of the epistle, which is at the end of the celebrated Alexandrine MS. Another letter was ascribed to him, but generally that one has not been accepted as his work.

2. This quote from his letter shows that he had been close to them and knew their works and the incidents that led to the death. "Let us set before our eyes the holy Apostles; Peter by unjust envy underwent not one or two, but many sufferings; at last being martyred, he went to the place of glory that was due unto him. For the same cause did Paul in like manner receive the reward of his patience. Seven times he was in bonds; he was whipped, was stoned; he preached both in the East and in the West; leaving behind him the glorious report of his faith: And so having taught the whole world righteousness, and for that end traveled even to the utmost bounds of the West; he at last suffered martyrdom by the command of the governors, And departed out

The letter was written by the church of Rome to the church in Corinth about the year AD 96. The letter was written in response to schisms that had caused some of the presbyters of the church to be deposed (1 Clement 1:13; 20:15, 19; 22:14). In the letter, Clement asserted the authority of the presbyters as the governing body of the church, based on the proposition that it was the apostles who appointed them. Clement's concern was to demonstrate that the bishops and the deacons were really to be accepted as the leaders of the church with all dignity. To prove this, he declared that bishops and the deacons were the first fruits of the apostles:

> The Apostles have preached to us from the Lord Jesus Christ; Jesus Christ from God. Christ therefore was sent by God, the Apostles by Christ; so both were orderly sent, according to the will of God. . . . And thus preaching through countries and cities, they appointed the first fruits of their conversion to be bishops and ministers over such as should afterwards believe, having first proved them by the Spirit. Nor was this any new thing: seeing that long before it was written concerning bishops and deacons. For thus saith the Scripture, in a certain place: I will appoint their overseers in righteousness, and their ministers in faith. . . . So likewise our Apostles knew by our Lord Jesus Christ, that there should contentions arise, upon account of the ministry. And therefore having a perfect fore-knowledge of this, they appointed persons, as we have before said, and then gave direction, how, when they should die, other chosen and approved men should succeed in their ministry. Wherefore we cannot think that those may justly be thrown out of their ministry, who were either appointed by them, or afterwards chosen by other eminent men, with the consent of the whole church; and who have with all lowliness and innocency. (1 Clement 19:2–18)

Clement's letter draws a distinction between the apostles and the people they ordained as bishops and deacons; the apostles appointed bishops. The apostles knew that contentions would arise and, therefore, prepared the way to deal with them by appointing bishops and deacons as their representatives who must be respected and adhered to in all matters. Clement, however, used the term presbyters in connection with the leaders who governed the church (1 Clement 19:20; 20:24; 22:14). It appears that whenever he wanted to make a stress on the appointment then

---

of the world, and went unto his holy place; being become a most eminent pattern of patience unto all ages," 1 Clement 3:12–15).

he used bishops and deacons, perhaps because he knew Paul used it in Phil 1:1. In addition, he wanted the schismatic church to accept the bishops and deacons as representing the apostles. He however did not speak of one bishop who was presiding over the church. He spoke of bishops and deacons.

Clement was not considered an apostle. However, the little known of him through his letter portrayed him as such. Although he did not say he was ordained by one of the apostles, his emphasis on apostolic succession and his confidence to write such a letter to a church in controversy confer apostolicity on him. For the fact that he was able to write to settle schisms against church leaders (including bishops and deacons) reveals that he was held in high esteem as someone possibly above them "in rank." His action is considered among scholars to be the first of such actions to be written outside one's sphere of operation; for churches were under the control of their own bishops and deacons. By this action, he considered himself to have the right to intervene. The possible impartation he received from his association with both Peter and Paul, which made him lead the church in Rome to write such qualitative letter, was incredible. For his letter was said to be widely read in the churches and almost achieved canonical status. Still some regard his letter as Scripture. The introduction to *1 Clement* in the archbishop's translation from the ancient Greek copy of the epistle, below, tells it all:

> Clement was a disciple of Peter, and afterwards Bishop of Rome. Clemens Alexandrinus calls him an apostle. Jerome says he was an apostolical man, and Rufinus that he was almost an apostle. Eusebius calls this the wonderful Epistle of St. Clement, and says that it was publicly read in the assemblies of the primitive church. It is included in one of the ancient collections of the Canon Scripture.

Accordingly, Clement can be said to have functioned in the apostolic office.

IGNATIUS OF ANTIOCH

One of the churches that features in the Acts of the Apostles is the church in Antioch. This was the place where the believers were first called Christians and the place where Barnabas and Paul were first sent out for "the work which the Holy Spirit had called them" (Acts 11:19–26; 13:1–3 NIV). One of the key leaders of the church in Antioch was Ignatius.

Ignatius was a great influential leader, and a theologian who contributed immensely to the development of Christian doctrines after the apostles. He is accredited with seven letters to the churches and to Polycarp, another church leader.[3] His writings demonstrate that he represented Christianity as being transformed from its Jewish origin to the Greco-Roman world. His writings show the gradual development of the bishopric (episcopal) authority. His letters show that by the year 115, the church in Antioch as well as the church in Ephesus each had one bishop as well as presbyters.[4] He claimed at times that the Holy Spirit was speaking to him, like prophecy:

> Some, it is true, suspected that I spoke thus because I had been told in advance that some of you were schismatics. But I swear by Him for whose cause I am a prisoner, that from no human channels did I learn this. It was the Spirit that kept on preaching in these words: "Do nothing apart from the bishop; keep your bodies as if they were God's temple; value unity; flee schism; imitate Jesus Christ as he imitated his Father." (Ignatius, *To the Philadelphians* 7:2)

He also had the desire to work with teams. For example, he had to counsel Polycarp to convey a council to make an appointment (Ignatius, *To Polycarp*, 7:2). The desire that the Lord placed upon him to write letters to strengthen the churches, the desire to preserve doctrine of Christ, the claim to hear from the Spirit, and the ability of setting structures for the church all show that he was indeed functioning within the apostolicity.

POLYCARP, BISHOP OF SMYRNA

Polycarp is one of the church fathers who has been specially accorded respect from church history up to today, possibly because of the bold confession of his faith during his martyrdom. He was the bishop of Smyrna around AD 100 and died around 107. Tradition places him as a disciple of Apostle John. Irenaeus says that the apostles in Asia appointed him as a bishop.[5] He lived in the era of the church when it was being transitioned

---

3. The Seven Epistles of St. Ignatius of Antioch.
4. Sullivan, *From Apostles to Bishop*, 104.
5. Irenaeus, *Against Heresies*, Book 111, 3:4.

from the original apostles to the second generation, and championed the fight against the heresies that plagued the church in the turbulent second century.

Irenaeus who claimed he saw him as a young man said, he was very bold and passionate and turned many from the heresy of Marcion, especially when he visited Rome. Irenaeus's records of the encounter between Polycarp and Marcion is relevant for our purpose:

> And Polycarp himself replied to Marcion, who met him on one occasion, and said, "Dost thou know me?" "I do know thee, the first-born of Satan." Such was the horror which the apostles and their disciples had against holding even verbal communication with any corrupters of the truth; as Paul also says, "A man that is an heretic, after the first and second admonition, reject; knowing that he that is such is subverted, and sinneth, being condemned of himself." (Irenaeus, *Against Heresies*, 3.4)

Polycarp's core rationale of visiting Rome was to visit the bishop of Rome, Anicetus, to settle a dispute over the date of celebrating Easter. Although they were not able to come to an agreement initially, they did later on. Later generations however picked up the controversy again.[6]

His main epistle is a letter that he wrote to the Philippian church as they requested him to give some directive concerning a presbyter who had mishandled the community fund. He writes, "Both you and Ignatius wrote to me, that if any one went [from this] into Syria, he should carry your letter with him; which request I will attend to if I find a fitting opportunity, either personally, or through some other acting for me, that your desire may be fulfilled" (Polycarp, *To the Philippians* 13:1). His reply was very mature and sounded Pauline, "I am deeply grieved, therefore, brethren, for him (Valens) and his wife; to whom may the Lord grant true repentance! And be ye then moderate in regard to this matter, and 'do not count such as enemies,' but call them back as suffering and straying members, that ye may save your whole body. For by so acting ye shall edify yourselves" (Poly. *Phil* 11:4; cf. 2 Cor 2:6–11). Commenting on this epistle, Irenaeus does not consider it just a reply to the question, but "This is also a very powerful Epistle of Polycarp written to the Philippians, from which those who choose to do so, and are anxious about their salvation, can learn the character of his faith, and the preaching of the truth" (Irenaeus, *Against Heresies* 3:4).

---

6. See report of this meeting, in Sullivan, *From Apostle to Bishop*, 152.

The person and call of Polycarp comes out by the community of people he lived with. The report on his martyrdom tells us how his perpetrators considered him:

> While he spoke these and many other like things, he was filled with confidence and joy, and his countenance was full of grace, so that not merely did it not fall as if troubled by the things said to him, but, on the contrary, the proconsul was astonished, and sent his herald to proclaim in the midst of the stadium thrice, Polycarp has confessed that he is a Christian. This proclamation having been made by the herald, the whole multitude both of the heathen and Jews, who dwelt at Smyrna, cried out with uncontrollable fury, and in a loud voice, *This is the teacher of Asia, the father of the Christians, and the overthrower of our gods, he who has been teaching many not to sacrifice, or to worship the gods*. Speaking thus, they cried out, and besought Philip the Asiarch to let loose a lion upon Polycarp. But Philip answered that it was not lawful for him to do so, seeing the shows of wild beasts were already finished. Then it seemed good to them to cry out with one consent, that Polycarp should be burnt alive. For thus it behooved the vision which was revealed to him in regard to his pillow to be fulfilled, when, seeing it on fire as he was praying, he turned about and said prophetically to the faithful that were with him, I must be burnt alive.[7] (italics mine)

Although he was threatened with death if he failed to deny his faith, he was still filled with confidence and joy, and his face was full of grace. When it was confirmed that Polycarp had confessed to be a Christian, the whole multitude said, as captured above, "*This is the teacher of Asia, the father of the Christian, and the overthrower of our gods, he who has been teaching many not to sacrifice, or to worship the gods.*" What a sound testimony about a Christian leader! Already he had seen a vision of his pillow being burnt, of which he prophetically interpreted that he would be burnt alive. Thus, he was a bishop with the prophetic gift.

In sum, Polycarp's ministry shows that he was an apostle. His desire for teamwork that sent him to Rome, despite the authority that he wielded as a bishop, is one of the qualities. The respect accorded him by another church to speak into their situation and the quality of the letter he wrote that became a guide for some of the churches are other signs. The apostolic includes the prophetic insight, which he demonstrated. His ability to refute Marcion and his heresy and even winning some of his

---

7. *The Martyrdom of Polycarp.*

people for the Lord shows his true knowledge of the Lord and a clear understanding of the word. All these portray him as a great apostle of the Lord.

IRENAEUS, BISHOP OF LYON

Irenaeus is one of the most distinguished church fathers. He was the bishop of Lyon and also considered as one of the first theologians of the church. He writes that he saw Polycarp in his early youth and described him as "a man who was of much greater weight, and a more steadfast witness of truth" (*Against Heresies* 3:4). As heresy beset the church of the second century from many angles, the church needed people of apostolic figures to lead them. Irenaeus is said to have stood up to the challenge. His writings were of great importance to the development of the Christian doctrine. Those that are preserved include the five volumes of *Against Heresies*, and the *Demonstration of Apostolic Preaching*. In *Against Heresies* series, Irenaeus offered a detailed theological refutation of the Gnostic teaching. Although his purpose of writing the volumes of *Against Heresies* was to refute the teaching of the heretics, the work has been accepted as a very good systematic theological treatise of the church.

He is accredited for being the first Christian writer to list the four gospels by names as divinely inspired in his argument against the Gnostics. He is accredited for being the first Christian author to affirm that the Gospel of John was written by the Apostle John.[8] In addition, he is acknowledged for being the first to assert that the Gospel of Luke was written by Luke, the companion of Paul.[9] He writes, "It is not possible that the Gospels can be either more or fewer in number than they are. For since there are four zones of the world in which we live, and four principal winds, while the church is scattered throughout all the world, and the 'pillar and ground' of the Church is the Gospel and the spirit of life; it is fitting that she should have four pillars, breathing out" (*Against Heresies*, 3.11). In the era where the Gnostics were creating challenges for Christianity, he affirmed the teaching of the centrality of Christ and by that conveyed the truth that all things are summed up in Christ. He writes:

---

8. Brown, *Introduction to the New Testament*, 368.
9. Brown, *Introduction to the New Testament*, 267.

> "All things," he says, "were made by Him"; therefore in "all things" this creation of ours is [included], for we cannot concede to these men that [the words] "all things" are spoken in reference to those within their Pleroma. For if their Pleroma do indeed contain these, this creation, as being such, is not outside, as I have demonstrated in the preceding book. . . . John, however, does himself put this matter beyond all controversy on our part, when he says, "He was in this world, and the world was made by Him, and the world knew Him not. He came unto His own [things], and His own [people] received Him not." But according to Marcion, and those like him, neither was the world made by Him; nor did He come to His own things, but to those of another. And, according to certain of the Gnostics, this world was made by angels. (3.11:1–2)

He affirmed the humanity as well of the divinity of Christ, by showing that Christ alone was able to truly teach the divine things and to redeem us. He took human flesh through Mary by the work of the Holy Spirit in order to regenerate us:

> Vain also are the Ebionites, who do not receive by faith into their soul the union of God and man, but who remain in the old leaven of [the natural] birth, and who do not choose to understand that the Holy Ghost came upon Mary, and the power of the Most High did overshadow her: wherefore also what was generated is a holy thing, and the Son of the Most High God the Father of all, who effected the incarnation of this being, and showed forth a new [kind of] generation; that as by the former generation we inherited death, so by this new generation we might inherit life. (5.1)

Irenaeus had the greatest task of affirming in his writing, and as a bishop in his teaching, that the apostles entrusted their messages to the bishops to whom they handed over the churches. There were no secret messages besides those given to the successors of the apostles. He stated that the church in Rome had been associated with "the two most glorious apostles, Peter and Paul." In the Roman church, "the apostolic tradition has been preserved continuously by [faithful men] who exist everywhere" (3.1:2). There was no secret message besides what their successors had given to them. He stresses that the bishops were the successors of the apostles:

> It is within the power of all, therefore, in every Church, who may wish to see the truth, to contemplate clearly the tradition of the apostles manifested throughout the whole world; and we are in a position to reckon up those who were by the apostles instituted bishops in the Churches, and [to demonstrate] the succession of these men to our own times; those who neither taught nor knew of anything like what these [heretics] rave about. For if the apostles had known hidden mysteries, which they were in the habit of imparting to "the perfect" apart and privily from the rest, they would have delivered them especially to those to whom they were also committing the Churches themselves. For they were desirous that these men should be very perfect and blameless in all things, whom also they were leaving behind as their successors, delivering up their own place of government to these men; which men, if they discharged their functions honestly, would be a great boon [to the Church], but if they should fall away, the direst calamity. (3.1:1)

By this, Irenaeus reiterates that the bishops took over from the apostles. In fact, he shows that the apostles appointed them. His concern was to let the people know that the apostles transmitted their teaching message and the governing of the church to the bishops, and if there had been any secret message, they would have known. By this, Irenaeus drew a clear line between the apostles and the bishops; the apostles possessed the message; the bishops are the recipients of the apostolic message. From this standpoint, Irenaeus demonstrated that the bishops were the right people who could effectively teach the apostolic message and carry on the work of the apostles.

How Irenaeus did his pastoral work together with his academic work was remarkable. He functioned as a teacher and a pastor, a bishop who was overseeing his flock. His writings and person demonstrate that he had a complete mastery of the message handed over to him and he knew his Master, Christ. He made very good use of the association he had with Bishop Polycarp who had imparted his life. His great works helped to preserve the teaching of the apostles in the second century and served as a primary source for others to build upon. He can be seen as one of the apostles in his generation.

This next chapter draws a conclusion from the discussion made in this part.

Chapter 25

Deductions on Apostleship from Ancient Literature

WHAT THEN IS THE conclusion drawn from the New Testament, the ancient literature, and the church fathers examined so far? It is quite clear from the analysis made from the examples of the selected church fathers that they did not consider themselves as apostles. Neither did they consider their ordination by the original apostles (or their representatives) as a call to apostleship. They were very much aware that they were ordained as bishops and were the successors of the apostles, and they were content with it. Nonetheless, from the ancient literature examined, there were some people moving around as apostles and prophets (some as teachers as well), who were not treated as the original apostles and prophets. The presentations do not show that these were people of authorities, like those who had established churches, and were playing general oversight over them. Along the line, the apostles faded out leaving the prophets. Those types of prophets, with the controversies which they were creating, forced the leadership of the church to bring guidelines which eventually smoked them out of the system.

ANCIENT LITERATURE

Taking into consideration the heresies in the second and third centuries, which the church fathers had to confront, it was absolutely essential that they maintained the office into which they were ordained. They needed to emphasize that the bishops were the successors of the apostles in order to refute the heretics who claimed to have received some secret messages from the apostles. We can, therefore, deduce from these that the church fathers were led by divine wisdom.

Nonetheless, it does not mean that some of the bishops were not really operating in the apostolic. Their ministries really portrayed some of them as apostles. Their abilities to play that leadership role with charisma coupled with the pioneering roles in many areas show their apostolicity. They exhibited conscientiousness and confidence that they had succeeded the apostles and as such knew their message and articulated this without ambiguity. The revelatory aspect of some of them as indicated in Ignatius and Polycarp showed the continuity of the charismata in them. The combination of the apostolic message and the charismata or the Spirit's manifestation was that which helped them to solve new problems which emerged in the local churches. Thus, although the term "apostle" was not conferred on them, they were operating in the apostolic.

From the analysis in the New Testament and the writings of the earliest post-Christian period such as the *Didache*, the *Shepherds of Hermas* and the writing of Clement, it could be recognized that initially the terms "bishops" or "elders" were used to describe the leaders of the local churches. However, the writings of Ignatius, Polycarp, and Irenaeus show that a local bishop had been appointed for local churches distinct from the presbyters. This should not be a surprise. Whenever, there are more than one person in a group, there is a need to choose a leader. Even in marriage where the husband and the wife are suitable helpmeets, the husband is supposed to be the head (Eph 5:21–24). Although the New Testament does not specify one person overseeing a local church, there could be one person who was always considered as such. It is apparent from Acts 15 that the original apostles might have given that leadership role to James, who concluded the Jerusalem Council by saying, "it is my judgement" (NIV). In the King James version, it is stated, "Wherefore my sentence is." The Greek is *krino*, which according to *Strong Exhaustive Concordance* could be interpreted as: "Properly to distinguish, decide (mentally or judicially)." This shows an aspect of chairmanship from James, which does not appear in the presentation of Peter (Acts 15:7–12). This seems to convey the notion that by that period, the apostles might have considered James as the leader of the church in Jerusalem. The reason could be the fact that James was the natural brother of our Lord Jesus, and that Jesus revealed himself to him after his resurrection (1 Cor 15:7).

APOSTOLIC SUCCESSION IN THE CATHOLIC CHURCH

Therefore, the advancement of one person as a bishop to preside over a church in a city and its surroundings was a natural outcome. The Catholic Church, then, must be appreciated for the development of the episcopacy (government of a church by bishops) in the early church. However, in the process of this development, the Catholic Church came out with some issues, which continue to pose challenges to Protestant Christians.[1] The church asserted that the "ordination confers a teaching office by which bishops can teach with authority in the name of Jesus Christ, and, as a college united with its head, can proclaim the doctrine of Christ with infallibility."[2] The second ecumenical council of the Catholic Church, referred to as Vatican II, held in 1962, which sought to address relations between the Catholic Church and the contemporary world, affirms this teaching in many ways. For example, it says, "The sacred synod teaches that the bishops have by divine institution taken the place of the apostles as pastors of the church in such wise that whoever hears them hears Christ and whoever rejects them rejects Christ and him who sent Christ."[3] The document further states:

> Although the individual bishops do not enjoy the prerogative of infallibility, they do . . . in authoritatively teaching matters to do with faith and morals, they are in agreement that a particular teaching is to be held definitely. This is still more clearly the case when, assembled in an ecumenical council, they are for the universal church, teachers of and judges in matters of faith and morals, whose definitions must be adhered to with obedience of faith.[4]

It continues, "Thus apostolic preaching, which is expressed in a special way in the inspired books, was to be preserved in a continuous line of succession until the end of time."[5]

This recognition offers the foundation of the Catholic's belief that through the ordination of a bishop, "the grace of the Holy Spirit is given, and a sacred character is impressed, in such a way that bishops, eminently and visibly, take the place of Christ himself as teacher, shepherd and

---

1. Protestant is used here in the largest sense, which includes Pentecostals.
2. Quoted in Sullivan, *From Apostles to Bishop*, 12.
3. Quoted in Sullivan, *From Apostles to Bishop*, 10.
4. Quoted in Sullivan, *From Apostles to Bishop*, 10.
5. Quoted in Sullivan, *From Apostles to Bishop*, 11.

priest, and act in his person."[6] This is a practice, which might have fully developed in the fourth century. The *Apostolic Constitution*, a document dated in the fourth century, shows this sort of practice. For example, it instructs:

> Ye, therefore, at the present day, Bishops, are to your people *priests* and *Levites*, ministering to the holy tabernacle, the holy catholic church; who stand at the altar of the Lord your God, and offer to him reasonable and unbloody sacrifices, through Jesus, the great High Priest. Ye are to the laity, *prophets, rulers, governors, and kings; the mediators between God and his faithful people*, who receive and declare his word, well acquainted with the Scriptures. *Ye are the voice of God*, and witnesses of his will, who bear the sins of all, and intercede for all; whom, as ye have heard, the Word severely threateneth, if ye hide from men the key of knowledge, who are liable to perdition, if ye do not declare his will to the people that are under you. (*Apostolic Constitution*, 25, italics mine)

Summing up the role of the bishop in the *Apostolic Constitution*, Killian McDonnell and George T. Montague, who are both Roman Catholic priests, state:

> The whole order converges on the bishop, to whom a variety of titles are given: Father, Lord, Master, Levitical Priest, Director, King, Mediator, Agent of the Word, Ambassador, Witness, Pontiff, Teacher, President, Prophet, Medical Doctor. Finally, the bishop is "the mouth piece of God," 'to be venerated as one of the gods.' The bishop appropriates the charisms of the prophet, teacher, and healer. Like the charism of the apostles, the episcopacy is itself a charism.[7]

Thus, the ordination of a bishop comes along with charisms. Put another way, you cannot be a bishop without the spiritual gifts. Here, the manifestation is not the issue but the office, which is the evidence of charisms. A Belgian Roman Catholic priest and theologian, Edward Schillebeeckx opines that by this, the collegial and prophetic authorities have been "incorporated into (or supplanted by) the ministry of the presbyter and the (apostolic) authority of the one local overseer (*episkopos*);

---

6. Quoted in Sullivan, *From Apostles to Bishop*, 13
7. McDonnell and Montague, *Christian Initiation and Baptism*, 255.

the charisma of the few."[8] It is one of the beliefs, which, he pleads, could be changed.

DIFFERENCE BETWEEN CATHOLICS AND PROTESTANTS

The teaching by the bishops with authority and as pastors of the church do not pose challenges to the Protestant Christians. Again, the bishops as the successors of the apostles also do not pose challenges. These beliefs rather affirm the church's apostolicity in doctrine and practices. Where the difference comes out is the understanding of apostolicity. The statement, which says, "as a college united with its head, can proclaim the doctrine of Christ with infallibility," is also reflected in the Vatican II and in a way, grants some aspects of infallibility to the individual bishops. Herein lies the difference. Protestant understanding of apostolicity has been the acceptance of Scripture alone as the source and criterion of apostolic faith. Thus, the Protestant's main difference on the Catholic Church has been the church's doctrine, which "regards the Church's traditions as providing authentic interpretation of Christian revelation."[9]

In connection with this, a tradition, which the Pentecostals, even members of the Charismatic Renewal Movement within the Catholic church,[10] struggle with, is the baptism of the Holy Spirit and charism deposited in the bishop, which are imparted during Christian initiation (e.g., baptism and confirmation). That of the bishop being a charism himself is not a challenge. This is similar to Eph 4:11, which considers apostles, prophets, evangelists, pastors and teachers as gifts to the church. The struggle has been the belief that initiation bestows or includes the baptism of the Holy Spirit. For Pentecostals, the baptism of the Holy Spirit must manifest with speaking in tongues. The charism must manifest as prophecy or healing the sick.

Our interest now, however, should be the Catholic Church's strong stance on apostolicity. This could mean that, for them, the bishop is just like the apostle, and when pushed forward Christ's direct representative in person. The only difference is between the titles bishop and apostle.

---

8. Schillebeeckx, *Church with a Human Face*, 121.

9. Sullivan, *From Apostles to Bishop*, 7.

10. McDonnell and Montague's book *Christian Initiation and Baptism in the Holy Spirit* is an evidence of this.

The functions are very similar or the same since the Catholic Church also accepts the progressive revelation of the episcopal. Within the general framework of the Protestant's belief of considering Scripture alone as the source and criterion of apostolic faith, some see some limitation with the individual original apostles. Peter, for example, had to be rebuked by Paul (Gal 2:11–14). The advice given to Paul by the council of apostles and elders led by James, which led to Paul's arrest in Jerusalem needs to be explored further. Below is the highlight:

> The next day Paul and the rest of us went to see James, and all the elders were present.... What shall we do? They will certainly hear that you have come, so do what we tell you. There are four men with us who have made a vow. Take these men, join in their purification rites and pay their expenses, so that they can have their heads shaved.... The next day Paul took the men and purified himself along with them. Then he went to the temple to give notice of the date when the days of purification would end and the offering would be made for each of them. When the seven days were nearly over, some Jews from the province of Asia saw Paul at the temple. They stirred up the whole crowd and seized him. (Acts 21:18–27 NIV)

Thus, the apostle may be endowed with many spiritual gifts, yet he may have his own limitations. Even a council of apostles may still have some limitations.

SOME APOSTLES IN CHURCH HISTORY

Although Protestants generally do not accept this, the unofficial socialization of some of the founding fathers of Protestant denominations and their views is not incompatible with the official stance of the Catholic Church. In other words, some of such leaders operated as apostles, and thus left legacies for their denominations which are difficult to overlook. From our discussions then, we can positively say that throughout church history, there have been apostles, people of charisma, of leadership ability, people who could hear from God and initiate new ministry and administer it successfully to promote the kingdom business. Significantly, these persons should include John Wycliffe, Martin Luther, John Calvin, and John Wesley. Many people hesitate to recognize the office of the apostle but the discussions have shown that God's minister of the New Testament has been the apostle. Who can say with confidence that Martin Luther was not an apostle? Thus, there have always been apostles to carry on the kingdom work after the demise of the original apostles. The next chapter will propose the need for apostles in our generation.

Chapter 26

The Need for Apostles and Prophets

THIS RESEARCH HAS DEMONSTRATED that God always speaks to people. God's messenger for the Old Testament was the prophet, and his messenger for the New Testament is the apostle.

APOSTOLICITY CONTINUES

A survey through the lives of some church fathers and available literature after the death of the original apostles shows that the church fathers considered themselves as the successors of the apostles. We could not come across God coming out with a new order besides that which had been climaxed in the apostles—that is, the Holy Spirit combining with the human personality to communicate the voice of God to people. The church fathers, who had been ordained as bishops, did not ordain some people as apostles neither did they recognize themselves as apostles. Yet, the study has shown that some of them operated as apostles. Thus, the divine system of the apostle becoming the mouthpiece of God in the New Testament has not changed. Some people think that the canonization of Scripture is complete of itself.[1] Thus, there is no need for people to operate in the charismata again, since the Scripture is complete of itself. This standpoint is very difficult to accept. Why? Because, besides the discussions thus far, we have the Scripture, yet denominations keep on

---

1. For some reading on cessation, see Ruthven, *On the Cessation of the Charismata*; Grudem, *Are Miraculous Gifts for Today*.

making constitutions and guidelines for the people of God. The people who interpret Scriptures to draw guidelines for people of God to follow should be people of apostolic caliber, who can process the new within the framework of Scripture in order to get it right. In other words, the people who process the new within the framework of the old should be messengers of God who are in tune with the Holy Spirit to lead the church of God. That is, apostles. The apostles continue to be the messengers of God in this generation. Thus, the New Testament system still operates in the current generation.

If a new system had emerged besides the apostolic, then that might have been considered as the way God speaks to his people after the New Testaments. Clearly, in many denominations, bishops or arch-bishops and superintendents function as apostles, and truly some of them operate in the apostolic office. However, it appears there is a collective fear within many denominations to adopt or accept the name apostle. The term apostle should not bring fear into people. It is interesting to observe that the Greek term for pastor (shepherd), besides its use in natural significance to describe shepherds of animals (Matt 9:36; 25:32; Luke 2:8, 15, 18, 20; John 10:2), is used in reference mainly to our Lord Jesus (Matt 26:27; John 10:11, 14; Heb 13:20; 1 Pet 2:25). It is only used directly to describe leaders of the church in Eph 4:11, but people find it easier to use it for themselves.[2] This is to say that the term "pastor" should be heavier in its application to people than the term "apostle."

People have always wanted to deify others who are used by the Lord. Our Lord Jesus had to nullify the minds of people during his earthly ministry that John was greater than all the people who had been born by women (Matt 11:11). In other words, John was greater than prophets such as Moses, Elijah, and Isaiah. The people found it difficult to accept this. In the book of Revelation, John the apostle had wanted to bow down to the angel who was sent to reveal things to him. The angel had to warn him that he was only a fellow servant as John himself (Rev 22:8–9). As mentioned already in this book, James encouraged his audience by writing, "Elijah was a man just like us. He prayed earnestly that it would not rain, and it did not rain on the land for three and a half years. Again, he prayed, and the heavens gave rain, and the earth produced its crops" (Jas 5:17–18 NIV). James wanted to tell us that we should respect the people the Lord used in the Bible as normal people like us who availed

---

2. The role of the shepherds work for church leaders is implied in the usage in Acts 20:28 and 1 Pet 5:1–2.

themselves to the Lord. They were not super humans. The apostles must be respected as men who availed themselves to be used by the Lord in their generation, but they should not be deified. Therefore, if we also avail ourselves, the Lord will raise some among us in our generation to lead in his kingdom business. From this perspective, then, and from our study, there has not been a messenger of God higher than the apostle in calling, I dare to propose that the church of God should recognize and pray for the Lord to raise more apostles and prophets in our generation. I was overwhelmed when I stumbled on a profound statement by Eric S. Fife. Fife was a former missionary director of InterVarsity Christian Fellowship, and an English pastor. Writing in 1978, he said:

> Many Christians are of the opinion that the apostolic gift has passed away and that there are no apostles today. For many years, I subscribed to that view but now I am less convinced. Few men would have the temerity to claim that they are apostles. During my ministry, however, I have met at least some men who seem to be performing the work of an apostle, as far as is possible in the changed circumstances of the twentieth century.[3]

Thus, throughout Fife's tour around the world, he recognized that some people were operating in the apostolic. However, few people could have the boldness to declare or claim that calling upon their lives. It is quite remarkable that an Evangelical in the 1970s could arrive at such a conclusion.

One may ask if people are already operating in the apostolic in various denominations and institutions, why then the need for the recognition? To this question, another may ask, and why not the recognition? I have come to realize that there is power in corporate recognition and prayer for empowerment. The twentieth century was termed as the year of the re-emergence of the outpouring of the Holy Spirit. The charismata, which laid dormant, had now been reactivated. In the New Testament, the charismata were being managed by the apostles who were themselves endowed with the same grace and were operating at a higher level than the rest. Paul said, "I thank God that I speak in tongues more than any of you" (1 Cor 14:18–19 NLT). Peter and Simon had to go and pray for the believers in Samaria to receive the baptism of the Holy Spirit (Acts 8:14–17). Paul told the church in Rome, "I long to see you so that I may impart to you some spiritual gift to make you strong—that is, that you

---

3. Fife, *Holy Spirit*, 123.

and I may be mutually encouraged by each other's faith" (Rom 1:11–12 NIV). Thus, the apostle must be involved in the charismata and direct how they should be used.

From the Bible, it is apparent that whenever there is a great work to be done, God raises people of apostolic ability to lead such crusades. In the Old Testament, God's messengers, such as Moses, Deborah, Samuel, and Nehemiah discharged such duties. In church history, too, as mentioned already, we have God's messengers including John Wycliffe, Martin Luther, John Knox, John Calvin, John Wesley, William Carey, Hudson Taylor, and Watchman Nee of China playing such roles. The modern challenges are many such that it needs God to raise apostles and prophets leading the Christian fraternity. Below is the preview of some of the modern challenges.

THE KNOWLEDGE REVOLUTION

In his book *Faith at the Speed of Light*, Ron Luce declares, "Exponential is a fundamental description of the times we live in."[4] This is how Luce describes the knowledge revolution that has shaken the entire world in these few years. Luce observes that because of the knowledge revolution, "the opportunities for exponential change and impact are everywhere."[5] The opportunity, however, must be utilized. The rule of the competition, according to a research he highlights, is whoever learns fastest wins.[6] Thus, while some are exploding, others are converging with one another to survive, and still others are dying.

On the use of modern technology by people, he points out that, currently there are about three and a half billion people online, but by 2025 it is estimated to be six billion people online, mostly using mobile devices.[7] This trend alone shows that what took thirty years to achieve will be doubled within six years. He directs attention to a research that shows that by 2030, it is estimated to have "a trillion Internet-connected devices known as the Internet of Things."[8] Looking back, he points to five hundred companies, which diminished according to experts'

---

4. Luce, *Faith at the Speed of Light*, 24.
5. Luce, *Faith at the Speed of Light*, 24.
6. Luce, *Faith at the Speed of Light*, 26.
7. Luce, *Faith at the Speed of Light*, 26–27.
8. Luce, *Faith at the Speed of Light*, 27.

research, because they could not change quickly enough to catch up with the modern trend.[9]

The impact of the knowledge revolution is that now self-driving cars are available. Automobile usage is estimated to go from ownership to "usership" as a subscription on-demand for electric self-driving service, saving the average person in the US $5,600 per year, per person. Five thousand autonomous Lyft rides have already been taken in Las Vegas in the United States.[10] He announces that about "250,000 Lyft users sold their cars, a hint that owning cars [is] going away since an owned car is used only 4% of time but a fleet car is used 80% of the time."[11] He hints that scientists are mapping all twenty-three million genes in a person to know every disease a person will ever get. The expected result is, "if you can see the disease you will get, especially cancer, heart disease and dementia, and start early preventive medicine, predicted immediate lifespan increase average to 100 years old."[12] Currently he explains that medical prevention rather than treatment is adding ten to twenty years onto life. With this sort of progress in science, he indicates, "scientists now believe the first person to live to 1000 years is now alive on the earth because of longevity growth."[13]

He touches on artificial intelligence (AI) where computers think faster and interact with humans, and people do not even realize it is a computer. The AI are infused with moral decision-making power. For example, he states, a self-driving car equipped with AI will have to decide when an accident is imminent, should it hit head on a car with a mother and three small children, or an elderly man crossing the road.[14] He briefs us that with chip implants in the brain, which will control epilepsy and other behaviors and boost intelligence to make a "superhuman" is on the way. He says this approach is called "upgrading Minds to make higher cognition possible, process information quicker, recall memory enhancement, intelligence augmentation and make direct interface between man

9. Luce, *Faith at the Speed of Light*, 28.

10. Lyft rides is the arrangement with a nearby driver in your community who will pick you up and take you where you want to go. Lyft is the app you use to get a ride in minutes. Just tap request and a driver is there. It is believed that by asking for a Lyft, you assist your community to reduce traffic and take cars off the road.

11. Luce, *Faith at the Speed of Light*, 29

12. Luce, *Faith at the Speed of Light*, 29.

13. Luce, *Faith at the Speed of Light*, 29.

14. Luce, *Faith at the Speed of Light*, 33.

and machines."[15] The good thing is that the AI will adopt the ethics of the person who programs its software; it will learn from that person by watching their decisions. He asks this question, "Should followers of Christ be the ones in the front of the line to make sure biblical ethics are adopted by Artificial Intelligence?"[16]

As the knowledge revolution goes on, he reminds us, "Christianity in Europe is in a nose dive," "the average age of a church attendee is 61 years old in Great Britain"; "an estimated 515 Roman Catholic churches in Germany have closed their doors in the past 10 years and Catholic leaders project that two-thirds of their 1,600 churches in the Netherlands will be closed by 2020."[17] In Great Britain, Islam has overtaken Anglicanism as the dominant religion as more people attend mosques than the Church of England.[18] All the data indicate Islam will soon overtake France as the dominant religion because so many church buildings there are being purchased by Muslims. In addition, construction of new mosques is exploding to make room for all their adherents.[19]

He delights that after decades of churches in America closing down, eclipsing those newly planted, today they celebrate approximately four thousand churches that are birthed in the United States, five hundred more than are closed. However, he regrets the research also shows that 84 percent of churches are declining or experiencing a growth rate below the population growth rate for their communities.[20]

He hails the revival that is going on in many African countries. However, many of the leaders caught up in the revival thirty years ago have questioned openly, "If I were a youth today, would I be attracted to this revival?" Again, hearing of the abysmal demise of the unprecedented revival in South Korea in the twentieth century makes people alarmed. In the revival that broke out in Korea in 1970 and 1980, Christianity grew from 2.0 percent in 1945 to 29.3 percent in 2010. Luce points out, "The

---

15. Luce, *Faith at the Speed of Light*, 33–34
16. Luce, *Faith at the Speed of Light*, 33.
17. Luce, *Faith at the Speed of Light*, 43–44. The book was published in 2019. When I checked this in January 2020, it was reported that 55 percent of parishes had been closed down. The weekly said research warned that, with the majority of church funds devoted to maintaining buildings, the "biggest wave of church closures" was still to come. Luxmoore, "As Dutch Parishes Close," lines 17–23.
18. Luce, *Faith at the Speed of Light*, 51.
19. Luce, *Faith at the Speed of Light*, 51.
20. Luce, *Faith at the Speed of Light*, 52.

tragic reality is that today among the youth there are only 1.7% identified as Christians, actually less than before the revival."[21]

For this reason, in the past ten years, ten thousand churches have closed, simply because the old people died and there were no young ones to replace them. If this could happen in South Korea, could it not happen elsewhere if care was not taken and strategic plans put in place to arrest the trend?[22]

Quite compelling are the trends of global religions; he draws our attention to the rapid growth of Islam, possibly because of birth rate, and the slowing growth of Christianity. He opines that if current momentum continues, by 2050, Pew Research predicts for the first time in history that Islam will be almost equal to all forms of Christianity (Catholic, Orthodox, and Protestants). Then after this, Islam will dominate the world religion between 2050 to 2070. He posits this question: "What will that world look like? Syria? North Africa [or Dubai]?"[23]

Luce's main concern is this: "Given the eminent diminishing number of young Christians world-wide, and the explosive impact of the Knowledge Revolution, what is the best possible actionable plan to change the trajectory of the Church?"[24]

A PLEA

It is against this backdrop that I think there is the urgent need for the Lord to raise up apostles and prophets for us in this generation. The old order alone cannot face these modern challenges. There should be new disciples who really understand the old system, that is, Scripture very clearly. These people should be able to receive new revelation from the Lord and then interpret the new with the old in the background. This brings us to Matt 13:52, "And He said to them, 'Therefore every scribe who has become a disciple of the kingdom of heaven is like a head of a household, who brings forth out of his treasure things new and old'" (Matt 13:52 NASB). The disciple of the kingdom must know the old. He must also be ready to receive the new. He should not be limited to either the old or the new only. He must know both very well. Then, the disciple

---

21. Luce, *Faith at the Speed of Light*, 45.
22. Luce, *Faith at the Speed of Light*, 45.
23. Luce, *Faith at the Speed of Light*, 51.
24. Luce, *Faith at the Speed of Light*, 54.

must be able to apply the old and the new to new situations that emerge. Thus, we need people who are truly endowed with the apostolic ministry; people who can receive revelation and handle modern challenges. The Lord is ever ready, but he is looking for people who are ready and willing to pay the price.

The apostolic ministry is confirmed with signs and wonders; we are looking for the apostles who will move in signs and wonders not by human power but by divine authorizations. Apostles confront contemporary challenges but do not compromise; we are looking forward to apostles and prophets who will confront contemporary challenges of LGBTI+ and its complications. Apostles move in teams; we are looking for apostles who will be working with others in harmony to confront the contemporary challenges. Prophets understand the times, interpret the times, and move with the apostles; we are expecting prophets who will hear from the Lord and interpret the times for God's people to move to the battlefield.

WHO CALLS APOSTLES?

On the one hand, I believe that already there are apostles and prophets in the system. On the other hand, Jesus makes this call: "If anyone is thirsty, let him come to me and drink. Whoever believes in me, as the Scripture has said, streams of living water will flow from within him" (John 7:37–38 NIV). In other words, if a church desires that the Lord should grant them apostles and prophets, he will do so. It is not difficult to recognize apostles and prophets. You will know them by their fruits and works. Churches may have to draw their own criteria for recognizing apostles and prophets. They may have to look at the Scripture to find out the criteria or improve on the criteria proposed in this book. It is true that often, acknowledging the gifts and talents of people encourages and challenges them to excel in their roles. I am looking at the situation where denominations will have a place within their structures for apostles and prophets, and prayerfully look for people who operate in these gifts, ordain and allow them to function as such.

I do not recommend the situation where some groups of clergies come together and confer apostleship or bishopry on others who pay for these. This practice needs to be discouraged. The independent churches that have come together to form networks need to be strengthened to move beyond encouraging one another to making such ministers accountable. These organizations need to work toward achieving sanity in Christian and religious circles while promoting the course of Christ globally. Such networks should seek to encourage the Christian community to be a model of ethical behavior. They need to ensure that pastors who abuse their members are held responsible, and where possible, name and shame abusers. Apostles are to live high standards of life that indicate that indeed they are the messengers of the Almighty One. By this, the world will know that they are the followers of Christ.

PART 8

Receiving Revelations

This part highlights how a person can receive revelation. The first chapter shows developments of receiving revelation, and the second chapter deals with hindrances to hearing from God.

Chapter 27

How to Receive Revelation

THE STUDY ASSERTS THAT there are apostles and prophets in our generation and that we need to pray for the Lord to raise more of them for us. Both apostles and prophets receive revelations from the Lord. This chapter shows how one receives a revelation and brings it forth. Receiving a message also is considered as receiving a revelation. There are five stages I want you to observe here in this chapter.[1]

PROMPTINGS

The first step of receiving a revelation is what I term as "prompting." Here the person having the revelation just has some sense of God's special presence. Ezekiel calls it the "hand of the Lord upon me." For example, in Ezek 37:1–2, Ezekiel declares, "The hand of the Lord was upon me, and he brought me out by the Spirit of the Lord and set me in the middle of a valley; it was full of bones" (NIV; cf. Ezek 1:3; 3:14–17; 33:22).

At this time, there is no revelation. The Lord is prompting the person to be aware that there is something ahead. Some people term this experience as enlightenment or light. It is a sort of indescribable little light, which appears in a person's spirit. This is only a starting point of receiving a message or revelation from the Lord. The light flashes and moves out very swiftly. Sometimes several of these will appear before a

---

1. For some reading on this from different perspectives, see Nee, *Ministry of God's Word*; and Nee, *Spiritual Man*.

person can grasp what the Lord wants to say. .For the young Samuel, it took three turns of God's audible voice before he realized that the Lord was speaking to him (1 Sam 3:8–10). Ezekiel was often quick to realize that the hand of the Lord was upon him. Moses saw a visible light like fire burning without consumption (Exod 3:1–2). The Lord has a way of dealing with each individual.

Apostle Dr. M. K. Ntumy, a former chairman of the Church of Pentecost often said, he would feel like someone tapped him on the shoulder. That is what I consider as "a prompting." Often, in my prayers, when I feel a special presence of the Lord, I receive deeper understanding to the meaning of my prayers and songs while enjoying the Lord and feeling as if the Almighty One (the Lord) was physically present. Often following this, I would feel extreme sadness or happiness. This leads to the sort of message ahead. Once I get there, I know that the Lord wants to speak to me in diverse forms.

IDEAS

What follows this light is a drop of idea or a thought. For example, when Moses saw the light, he decided to go and see what was happening. That is, the light begins to be translated into an idea or a thought. By this time, the revelation settles only in ideas but not in words. The person feels something within him, but it is not clear—the thought here is obscure. It cannot be shared with others. In fact, you, the bearer, are still not sure of what the message is. It is like what the Prophet Isaiah heard: "A voice said, 'Shout!' I asked, 'What should I shout?'" (Isa 40:6 NLT). Here, the prophet has got nothing to say. The prompting is there, the idea is following but he did not really know exactly what to say. Many people prophesy here out of emotion but Isaiah was right by requesting for what to say. The most important aspect here is "turning aside to see." That is, the Moses experience. Let us examine the Moses' experience a bit:

> Now Moses was tending the flock of Jethro his father-in-law, the priest of Midian, and he led the flock to the far side of the desert and came to Horeb, the mountain of God. There the angel of the Lord appeared to him in flames of fire from within a bush. Moses saw that though the bush was on fire it did not burn up. So Moses thought, "I will go over and see this strange sight—why the bush does not burn up." (Exod 3:1–3 NIV)

When Moses saw the light, he decided to find out what was happening. This is the idea level. The one begins to think that something is happening which he needs to follow. The person feels like shouting but has got nothing to shout about. Here, many Pentecostals speak in tongues and shout without following the light or the thoughts to know what the Lord wants to say. Without following it, the revelation may drop. It was when Moses followed that he had the revelation of the "I am." It was when Isaiah followed it that he was told, "Shout that people are like the grass. Their beauty fades as quickly as the flowers in a field" (Isa 40:6). Ezekiel explains his situation. Ezekiel 21:33:

> In the twelfth year of our exile, in the tenth month on the fifth day, a man who had escaped from Jerusalem came to me and said, "The city has fallen!" Now the evening before the man arrived, *the hand of the Lord was upon me*, and he opened my mouth before the man came to me in the morning. So my mouth was opened and I was no longer silent. *Then the word of the Lord came to me*: "Son of man, the people living in those ruins in the land of Israel are saying, 'Abraham was only one man, yet he possessed the land. But we are many; surely the land has been given to us as our possession.' . . . As for you, son of man, your countrymen are talking together about you by the walls and at the doors of the houses, saying to each other, 'Come and hear the message that has come from the Lord.' My people come to you, as they usually do, and sit before you to listen to your words, but they do not put them into practice. With their mouths they express devotion, but their hearts are greedy for unjust gain. Indeed, to them you are nothing more than one who sings love songs with a beautiful voice and plays an instrument well, for they hear your words but do not put them into practice. When all this comes true—and it surely will—then they will know that a prophet has been among them." (Ezek 33:21–33 NIV, italics mine)

Ezekiel first had the hand of God upon his life. His mouth that was closed was opened, and then he received the word of God. The prompting came as the hand of God upon him, then the Lord opened his mouth and gave him a message.

When the idea comes and the bearer is not in good standing with the Lord, he will find it difficult to grasp what the Lord is communicating. In other words, sin in the life of the person can blur the light. If one's mind is not based on the word of God too, he finds it difficult to understand it. The thoughts of the person living in sin cannot accept the light or idea from the Lord. It is here that the devil accuses believers who live in sin. In some cases, a Christian will not directly be living in sin but may still pollute his thoughts. How does a Christian's thoughts become polluted? Spending much time in profanity, jokes, or comedy weakens one's thoughts. Similarly, occupying one's thoughts with the cares of the world does the same.

When the idea comes and the person is living in sin, he will not have the courage to follow up. If even he wants to follow up, many other thoughts may appear. Eventually the sinful thought may master that person, thus overpowering the light that shines. His sinful thoughts will accuse him so strongly that he may not be able to push them out to receive the revelation. Thoughts are powerful. Therefore, Paul says that:

> The weapons we fight with are not the weapons of the world. On the contrary, they have divine power to demolish strongholds. We demolish arguments and every pretension that sets itself up against the knowledge of God, and we take captive every thought to make it obedient to Christ. And we will be ready to punish every act of disobedience, once your obedience is complete. (2 Cor 10:4–6 NIV)

The best thing for every Christian is to put aside every act of disobedience. When the Christian does this, he can allow the Spirit of God to lead, direct and reveal things to him.

On the other hand too, if even the Christian is not living in sin, but has not trained his thoughts to be obedient to Christ, "the thoughts" will still master his thinking to the point that his mind cannot translate the light of God into fully blown ideas. Often, the thought becomes so weak in such situations that the person will still be thinking of past or present events as the light shines. The thought or idea will not pick the light rightly. Thus, receiving the revelation goes beyond not living in sin; the outer person of the Christian must be broken. The Christian must be obedient to the Lord. If the outer person or the "self" is dealt with, the Christian is able to have his thoughts serve him. This is the condition where the believer is able to push his thoughts behind him and focus on the Lord and his kingdom. This is where the fruit of the Spirit is demonstrated as evidence of self-control.

Other things that can break the flow of the revelation include noise—calling by name, receiving a telephone call, too much talking around the place. In fact, once you get into the condition of prompting and receiving ideas, if someone calls you the revelation may break, sometimes it may come later, if the Lord wants to really give you something. However, from personal experience, I have observed that on other occasions, the issue may not come again. For example, if a person is receiving a prophetic message in a church praying setting and someone raises a wrong song or disturbs the praying, the message may drop. The message may come later or not. If it is a vision and someone taps the receiver, calls him by name, the vision may break, and you may not have it again. Yet, besides all these a person may train himself in such a way that he could live within a noisy place and still hear from the Lord. Thus, a person can receive a revelation in such conditions which others may not be able to receive it.

Dangers of Unbroken Christians

There is a danger here for the Christians who are living in sin and those who have not been broken. The Scripture shows that "the gifts and the calling of God are irrevocable" (Rom 11:29–30 ESV). That is to say that God's gifts and his call are never withdrawn. In other words, once God grants a gift, he does so permanently. Since the gift will not be withdrawn, the one living in sin may still have lights within him. The problem comes in the translation of the light into thoughts. His unbroken nature will saturate his thoughts and manufacture his own words on the light. That is where people give prophecy from their own mind or on issues that are circulating. This is where some "apostles and prophets" manifest from the flesh.

There is the need for the believer to pray and read so that the word of God captures his thoughts. This means bringing your thoughts to the obedience of Christ. Here, the Spirit of life in Christ Jesus works automatically in the believer (Rom 8:2), offering them self-control. Thus, his thoughts will quickly pick a light when it flashes. Once the thought picks light, the individual will have the idea that God wants to do something. Yet, at this moment the person may not know exactly what the Lord wants him to say or do. The idea may drop that the Lord wants to show you something concerning the church, or speak to you concerning something that is going on, give you a song, and even tell you the type of song. However, you may still not receive the fully blown revelation as yet.

BURDEN

The next step is considered the burden period. The person has the prompting and the idea that God wants to speak to him or has something for him. Yet he is not sure of what the Lord has for him. These two things place a heavy burden on the person. The challenge is to find out what God has for him so that he will be able to carry it out clearly. This situation is what is being termed as a burden. Yet, the real burden is the message that comes out of these two steps—prompting and idea. Thus, the term "burden" here is the message (prompting and idea) that the prophet has. Read through the texts below:

> The burden against Babylon which Isaiah the son of Amoz saw. (Isa 13:1 NKJV)
>
> This is the burden which came in the year that King Ahaz died. (Isa 14:28 NKJV)
>
> The burden against the Wilderness of the Sea. (Isa 21:1 NKJV)
>
> The burden against Nineveh. The book of the vision of Nahum the Elkoshite. (Nah 1:1 NKJV)
>
> The burden which the prophet Habakkuk saw. (Hab 1:1 NKJV)
>
> The burden of the word of the Lord to Israel by Malachi. (Mal 1:1 NKJV)

What the New King James translates "burden" is translated in the New International Version, Revised Standard Version, and English Standard Version as "oracle"; the Good News Bible and the New Living Translation translate it as "message." *Strong Exhaustive Concordance* translates the Hebrew term *massaw* as "a burden, specifically tribute, figuratively an utterance, chiefly a doom, especially singing." In the Bible, the term *massaw* is used in various ways.

It is used to express the sort of burden that a donkey carries, "If you see the donkey of one who hates you lying down under its burden, you shall refrain from leaving him with it; you shall rescue it with him" (Exod 25:5 ESV).

Massaw is also used to express the task that is placed on the Levites, "This is the service of the clans of the Gershonites, in serving and bearing burdens" (Num 4:24–25; see also vv. 15, 19 ESV). Here, it shows the specific duty that has been assigned to specific clans. Along this line, Moses told the people of Israel, "How can I bear by myself the weight and burden of you and your strife?" (Deut 1:12-13 ESV). By this, Moses was saying that he alone could not hear and try the numerous cases that the people brought to him. They were too heavy for him to carry. By implication he used the term burden to show the sort of responsibility placed on him by leading the people of Israel. Combining the three different usages, the term *massaw* is used in the case of the prophet to show the responsibility that God places on him by giving a message or revelation. The revelation becomes a heavy burden to carry. By this time, the burden has developed to be understandable. The person would have some understanding of what the Lord would like him to do. This becomes clear in his spirit.

Where there is no burden, there is no revelation, no message, no ministry, no prophet or apostle. The burden makes the prophet or apostle aware of his revelation and knows what God wants him to say or do so clearly that nothing seems to deter him from doing it.

The Formation of the Burden

As has been shown, the starting point of a revelation is the prompting—a flashing light or an enlightenment that becomes an idea or a thought. The idea or thought then becomes a burden. If one's old nature has been dealt with, he is able to translate the burden into an understandable task. There cannot be a burden without the light and a thought (idea). Thus, the burden is formed by adding understanding to the prompting and the idea.

The burden will only be off-loaded after the task has been discharged successfully. Once it has not been discharged, the bearer can never be free. You need words to release the burden, and the words must be clear. If the right words are not used, the burden will remain. Thus, finding the right and appropriate words is very important. This brings us to the next step—the formation of words.

The Divine Words

There are two types of words to express the burden. First, is what I call the divine words or the words which are supplied by the Holy Spirit. The divine words are words that are received through your human spirit, which is married to the Holy Spirit. The Holy Spirit dwells within the human spirit. Thus, the divine words are received within the spirit of the person.

Others call it words within; they are short, simple and sharp. The divine words alone may be strong for human consumption yet they are well understood by the receiver. He knows it is from the Lord and not through his making. But, at this stage he cannot give out the divine message because people may not fully understand these divine words. Sometimes, the receiver himself is not very clear of what follows or the full import of the message, yet the message is clear to him.

This is sometimes difficult to understand. I will give a personal experience here. In January 1981, the then church secretary of the Church of Pentecost, Apostle Joseph Egyir Paintsil spoke at a Witness Movement leaders' end-of-year meeting. I was a participant. We entered into a prayer, which I eventually received a divine message. The message was: "Set your house in order for the time has come for me to call you." These words were very clear to me. I did not make them up. But, I did not understand clearly what the Lord wanted to say. I could not utter them, I needed to wait, follow up to get the human words. This, I did not do. The message was to Apostle Paintsil. Less than two months after this meeting, Apostle Paintsil was called to glory; he died. I believe that if I had given this message, short as it is, Apostle Paintsil would have understood it. Yet, it is appropriate that the divine message must not be given at once. The receiver must wait to get the continuation of the revelation. The most important aspect of the revelation, however, is to get the divine words. The reception of the divine words increases a burden in the person.

The Relationship between Burden and the Divine Words

In normal human communication, we often discharge our ideas in speech. But this is different in the spiritual realm. Paul shows that we do not discharge the burden with human words. Rather, it should be discharged with words taught by the Lord. In 1 Cor 2:13, Paul shows that "this is what we speak, not in words taught us by human wisdom but in words taught by the Spirit, expressing spiritual truths in spiritual words" (NIV).

Paul is saying that when it comes to spiritual things, we do not use human philosophy, ideas or eloquence, but we must allow the Holy Spirit to impart us. The Holy Spirit brings to us words taught by himself; thus, the Spirit must bring out the language and expressions. This is the "divine words," but Paul does not end here. He continues by saying that you must express spiritual truth in spiritual words. The Holy Spirit must lead in the illustration given, the expression of the human language or the additions (human words), and also inspire a person to say these (the delivery). The Holy Spirit must lead in every aspect of the delivery. The words added must all be led by the Spirit. However, the human being is actively involved. How? We shall come to it but, for now, we are on the divine words.

The Formation of the Divine Words

The words which are supplied by the Holy Spirit are the divine aspect of the message. How do we receive these? They can be words that are very new to a person. However, they come through one's personal knowledge of the Lord and the word of God. The divine words are often biblical words. Thus, the knowledge of Scripture is very important in the prophetic ministry. It can also be part of a song you know, a message you have heard or preached, or something "spiritual" that you have observed somewhere else. It flashes quickly in your spirit. As a person waits upon the Lord in prayer, reading and singing, the Holy Spirit may drop a word to him.

To receive it, a person will have to be in the Spirit. Being in the Spirit here means the person must have complete mastery of his thoughts. To get into this position, one may pray in tongues and with his understanding until he begins to enjoy the prayer. As he prays in tongues and with his understanding, the understanding may be the meaning of the praying in tongues. This may lead to joy in the Spirit, where the person begins to give special appellations to the Lord by exalting him—saying wonderful things about him. Or, it can lead to sadness, where the person will be quite disturbed in his spirit. This will depend upon the type of message to be received. On the other hand, too, a person can easily get into the Spirit if he has been reading or studying the Bible, reading good Christian books, singing Christian songs, listening to Christian tapes or watching Christian programs or videos. These prepare the Christian and set his mind on spiritual issues. When the Lord Jesus Christ revealed himself to Apostle John in Revelation, the apostle was already in the Spirit, "On the Lord's Day I was in the Spirit, and I heard behind me a loud voice like a trumpet" (Rev 1:10–11 NIV).

If a person keeps on accusing others, gossiping, joking with divine things, watching bad films and pictures such as pornographic pictures and videos, he quenches the Spirit. His personal spirit gets very dull. He feeds his soul with evil desires, and becomes very active in the soulish realm. Thus, his thoughts have mastery over him; he can prophesy but his prophecy will completely come from the soulish realm. This will be based on what he has watched, heard and discussed with people. His dreams and perceptions may come from the soulish realm, that is, the things he has fed his soul with, and he will minister death to people. This sort of ministry was taking place during the time of Jeremiah. For example, after Jeremiah had ministered life to people by foretelling the doom that was ahead which needed repentance from the people, one of the prophets who was living in the soulish realm countered his prophecy and brought complete death to the nation:

> Then the prophet Hananiah took the yoke off the neck of the prophet Jeremiah and broke it, and he said before all the people, "*This is what the Lord says*: 'In the same way will I break the yoke of Nebuchadnezzar king of Babylon off the neck of all the nations within two years.'" At this, the prophet Jeremiah went on his way. (Jer 28:10–11 NIV, italics mine)

This man was supposed to be a prophet of the Lord, not Baal. But he was living in the flesh. He had allowed the soul to take over. He might be afraid of persecution, wanting self-glory, or was enjoying the soulish life.

Similarly, during the kingship of Ahab, some of prophets of the Lord joined hands with other prophets and were prophesying according to their own imaginations. One of such prophets was Zedekiah:

> Then Zedekiah son of Kenaanah went up and slapped Micaiah in the face. "Which way did the *spirit from the Lord go when he went from me to speak to you*?" he asked. Micaiah replied, "You will find out on the day you go to hide in an inner room." The king of Israel then ordered, "Take Micaiah and send him back to Amon the ruler of the city and to Joash the king's son and say, 'This is what the king says: Put this fellow in prison and give him nothing but bread and water until I return safely.'" Micaiah declared, "If you ever return safely, the Lord has not spoken through me." Then he added, "Mark my words, all you people!" (1 Kgs 22:24–28 NIV, italics mine)

Zedekiah appears to be full of the Spirit of God. He slapped Micaiah. He was completely in the flesh, using carnal means to deal with the things of the Spirit. The king went to that war and never returned. He brought death to the people. Many people promise blessing but bring death to people.

It will take a very long time for a Christian who has muddled himself with filth to be quickened up to receive a message from the Lord. He needs repentance and the cleansing of the mind with the word of God to set himself up to receive from the Lord. In dealing with husbands at Ephesians, Paul says, "Husbands, love your wives, just as Christ loved the church and gave himself up for her to make her holy, cleansing her by the washing with water through the word, and to present her to himself as a radiant church, without stain or wrinkle or any other blemish, but holy and blameless" (Eph 5:25–27 NIV). The aspect that is relevant for us here is "cleansing her by the washing with water through the word." When the Christian muddles himself with filth, he needs cleansing by the washing with water which is the word of God. This will bring him back to relations with the Lord.

The divine words are short but rich in content. They are life-releasing. However, they must not be released at this time. Many people prophesy at this time. Such people are those who may prophesy two or three times in a meeting; they do so, because they do not wait to add "words without"[2] (human words) to divine words. Once a person does not wait for the completion of the revelation, his burden will not be released. He will still have the burden, since he has not been able to release the burden with the right spoken words.

Difference between Divine Words and Human Thoughts

If a person is not careful, he may take the human thoughts as divine words. But they are two different things. The human thoughts or ideas come from a person's own anxieties and thinking, not from the Holy Spirit. My personal experience shows a clear difference between the two. For example, when I start my devotion in prayer, all the things that I need to do in the day or week will be dropping in my mind. These are thoughts going through my mind, and I begin to write them as they drop into my mind until I do not hear anything again. Then I begin to enjoy my prayer

---

2. I call this "words without" in the sense that although they are human words, they are words that do not come from the carnal person. They are sanctified by the Holy Spirit within the Christian who allows the Holy Spirit to lead him.

and singing. As I continue praying, the Lord will bring some promptings leading to a revelation either of an instruction or a song. They are divine words.

What we have discussed so far shows that there is a combination of the divine and human. The divine is the prompting, and the light or an idea, which lead to a burden. Following the burden are the divine words, which are words supplied by the Holy Spirit or the words within. The "human" first sets in as the idea or thought. The "human" will need to put additional words into the words supplied by the "divine" to make the message meaningful. At this stage, where the person has received the divine message, his burden increases, and he is looking for a way of discharging it.

The burden here now is the prompting of the Spirit, plus the translating of the prompting into an idea plus the divine words. These three constitute the prophet's burden, for now. This burden must be released with the human words. This becomes our focus, next.

THE HUMAN WORDS

The second type of words, which are needed in the reception and delivery of a revelation, are the human words. The human words are the spoken words that the receiver will add to the divine words received. These human words come from the receiver himself to carry his message out to the people. He can make it short or long depending upon his maturity, knowledge of the word of God and experience. Thus, the human words are the expansion of the divine words. The divine words are objective; they come from the Holy Spirit directly and are received within the spirit of a person. The human words are subjective; they come from the person himself and received through the soul of the person. Yet, it is the human words that make the divine words understandable.

For example, declaring that "Jesus is the Son of God" is a divine language. We do not fully understand Jesus as the Son of God without seeing Jesus first as the Son of Man. Jesus as the Son of Man helps us to see Jesus being conceived by Mary and born as a human being. Then, we see Herod attempting to kill all firstborns of the Jews, while Joseph the human father of Jesus runs away with him to Egypt. We see Jesus growing and being baptized in water and receiving the Holy Spirit. We hear the Father declaring Jesus as his beloved Son. We see Jesus healing the sick, casting out demons, demons shouting that they know Jesus as the Son of God, wanting to know if he had come to destroy them. We see the crucifixion of Jesus, his resurrection, ascension, and glorification. These experiences help us to see Jesus as a different person. We then understand why Jesus is the unique Son of God. These human experiences help us to understand the divine message that Jesus is the Son of God, otherwise, we could not have understood why Jesus is the Son of God, while all of us are also the children of God. Thus, the human words or examples here help us to understand the divine message.

The Need for the Human Words before Release

When a person receives the divine words, the burden becomes strong like fire within a person. But releasing then will result in a lack of better understanding. This is the period where the person needs the human words and it is the burden that helps to bring out the human words. However, the human words do not come out from human wisdom, philosophy or "the things of men" (Matt 16:23). The human words come through the person's experience in life, maturity in the Lord, knowledge of Scripture and how to apply the Scripture to life situations. The Holy Spirit enables a person to apply these.

If the person is not mature and remains under the anointing, at this stage, he may pollute the divine words with the human words. He may add things that are "human" and do not come from the Lord. Thus, here too the Holy Spirit must bring to memory the human words through the person's knowledge of Scripture, life experiences, and maturity. Once a person gets it wrong here, the human words (spoken words) will be human and polluted. Once a person gets it right here, he releases the message with life. Jesus declares, "The Spirit gives life; the flesh counts for nothing. The words I have spoken to you are spirit and they are life" (John 6:63 64 NIV).

Two Types of Revelations

There are two types of messages or revelations. First, is the spontaneous message of prophecy that a person will receive and deliver. The message, however, goes through similar processes as explained above. The Lord is not limited so the process may not always be the same as explained.

However, what has been explained can be a general overview of what happens in receiving a prophetic message or a revelation. Second, is the deep revelation that may take one, two, or ten days, weeks, months or years to receive. The revelations that most of the apostles have fall under this category. It does not mean some apostles do not receive revelations under the first category; they may.

In this type of deep revelation, the prompting comes, the idea follows, but the divine words may take some days or weeks. After the "divine word" has been received, it may take some days, weeks, months or years to receive enough human words to cover it or explain it. An example of this is when God called Abraham to leave his country in Gen 12:1–3:

> The Lord had said to Abram, "Leave your country, your people and your father's household and go to the land I will show you. I will make you into a great nation and I will bless you; I will make your name great, and you will be a blessing. I will bless those who bless you, and whoever curses you I will curse; and all peoples on earth will be blessed through you." (NIV)

This appears like the divine words. It was condensed. In chapter 15, more light was thrown on the revelation:

> As the sun was setting, Abram fell into a deep sleep, and a thick and dreadful darkness came over him. Then the Lord said to him, "Know for certain that your descendants will be strangers in a country not their own, and they will be enslaved and mistreated four hundred years. But I will punish the nation they serve as slaves, and afterward they will come out with great possessions. You, however, will go to your fathers in peace and be buried at a good old age. In the fourth generation your descendants will come back here, for the sin of the Amorites has not yet reached its full measure." When the sun had set and darkness had fallen, a smoking firepot with a blazing torch appeared and passed between the pieces. On that day the Lord made a covenant with Abram and said, "To your descendants I give this land, from the river of Egypt to the great river, the Euphrates—the land of the Kenites, Kenizzites, Kadmonites, Hittites, Perizzites, Rephaites, Amorites, Canaanites, Girgashites and Jebusites." (Gen 15:12–21 NIV)

Here, there is an extension of the message, making it even clearer. This is more understood than the first one given to Abraham. This second one is like the human words added to the divine one given earlier. There is always the need to wait to have the human words for clearer understanding of a message.

The Bible is the inspired word of God. Yet we realized that the authors have their preference in words. Let us cite the example of the gospel writers who wrote about the same thing. Matthew often speaks of the kingdom of heaven. The expression is found in Matthew only; thirty-two times. As a Jew, he was concerned about the coming kingdom of God through the Messiah. His concern was about the first coming and the rejection of the promised Messiah, the King of Israel (Matt 23:37–39).

Mark often uses the term straightaway or immediately about forty times. The Lord Jesus is presented as the suffering servant of God (Mark 10:45), who performed mighty works. Unlike Matthew, Mark was not concerned about the genealogy of Jesus, but the servant of God who was made a ransom for people. Luke presents Jesus as the Son of Man; about twenty-six times in the book. He speaks of his humanity in contrast to his deity to show that he was a perfect man, who is the true representative of the whole human race (Luke 19:10). The profession of Luke is seen in his writings, especially in Acts. As he describes the crippled man who got healed, he shows that immediately, his feet and ankles were made strong (Acts 3:7). As a medical doctor, he knew his feet and ankles had to be strong before he could walk. Mark would not have explained that detail.

John shows that Jesus Christ was the Son of God who gave himself for people so that all who believe in him would have eternal life (John 3:16). John's concern was to present Jesus as the savior of the world. To accomplish this, he selected certain miracles and items to demonstrate his purpose.

Now, if these gospel writers added their human words to the gospel without making it impaired, then we can also add human words to divine words without contaminating the revelation of God. However, the man who adds to the divine has the responsibility of living the life of Christ. The old nature must be dealt with, and Christ must be seen in his life, otherwise, he will pollute the word of God.

The Formation of Human Words in People

In order to have the human words, which are sanctified, the word of God must be born in the person. The word must be personified in us just as the word of God was personified in Christ. God wishes to speak through the human body. Right from the beginning, he created human beings in his image. He has ever since been choosing people to speak through them. The tendency of speaking through people shows God's willingness to indwell in humanity to manifest himself. The coming of Christ into the world as a human being is a demonstration of what God wants from us, being like him, in everything we do. He affirms this through the coming of the Holy Spirit to dwell in us. By the indwelling of the Spirit, God is able to "integrate" himself in us so that when we think and speak, the word of God comes to pass. This is to say that our thoughts must not only agree with God's word; not just coincide with his, but they should be God's thoughts—God's word.

At this level, praying for wealth does not come in, neither is praying against the enemy a thought; rather prayer is centered on being an integral part of the building of God's kingdom on earth. How does God work this out in us? This is the period where the cross of Christ deals with the old nature. The Lord deals with the individual through daily trials, which the Holy Spirit arranges in his life. This is the difficult aspect for people to accept. The Holy Spirit will arrange it in such a way that sometimes the Christian will not understand why even he is going through such trials, but it will be a way that the cross of our Lord Jesus will deal with the old nature. This helps to purify the person in such a way that he will be mature and think as Christ thinks.

The claim that the Holy Spirit will arrange trials in the life of a person should not be a surprise. After the Lord Jesus Christ had fasted forty days and forty nights, he was led by the Spirit to be tempted by the devil (Matt 4:1). Our Lord Jesus was victorious in his earthly life's trials and temptations. Through those activities, the human Jesus knows that to be tempted by the devil is a serious issue. He familiarized himself with human beings; accordingly, the author of Hebrews writes:

> In bringing many sons to glory, it was fitting that God, for whom and through whom everything exists, should make the author of their salvation perfect through suffering. Both the one who makes men holy and those who are made holy are of the same family. So Jesus is not ashamed to call them brothers. He says, "I will declare your name to my brothers; in the presence of the congregation I will sing your praises." And again, "I will put my trust in him." And again he says, "Here am I, and the children God has given me." Since the children have flesh and blood, he too shared in their humanity so that by his death he

might destroy him who holds the power of death—that is, the devil—and free those who all their lives were held in slavery by their fear of death. For surely it is not angels he helps, but Abraham's descendants. For this reason he had to be made like his brothers in every way, in order that he might become a merciful and faithful high priest in service to God, and that he might make atonement for the sins of the people. Because he himself suffered when he was tempted, he is able to help those who are being tempted. (Heb 2:10–18 NIV)

Jesus had to take a body, go through pain, and suffer as a human being in order to bring us salvation. He has a message. He is the author of salvation. By going through temptations himself, he taught us that when we pray, we should tell the Father, "And lead us not into temptation, but deliver us from the evil one" (Matt 6:13 NIV). He knows the import of temptation. The message has been borne in him.

The Christian will likewise go through temptations and trials. Unlike Jesus, the Christian may be successful in some areas and fail in other areas. The Lord will use both victories and defeats in his dealings with us. He is not saying that the Christian should fail, yet he will use that failure to work out his message in him. The success brings human words of encouragement to people. The word of God is borne through that. What the person goes through becomes the word of God in him. The failure also becomes the word of God, just as the failure of Abraham by listening to his wife, Sarah, and taking Hagar has become a lesson for us.

The weakness in a person causes a person to pray. By praying the person may have a touch from the Lord, and by so doing comes out sharpened and ready to be used by the Lord. He has a message that has been borne in his body. As Paul kept on praying on his weaknesses, he had a message of grace:

> Three times I pleaded with the Lord to take it away from me. But he said to me, "My grace is sufficient for you, for my power is made perfect in weakness." Therefore I will boast all the more gladly about my weaknesses, so that Christ's power may rest on me. That is why, for Christ's sake, I delight in weaknesses, in insults, in hardships, in persecutions, in difficulties. For when I am weak, then I am strong. (2 Cor 12:8–10 NIV)

Through the message of grace, Paul can go through more trials and do the work of God by winning new converts for Christ and teaching others from his personal examples. He has learned humanity. This is how the message is borne in us. If you expect to have greater ministry, you must expect to go through greater dealings of the cross. As you go through trials you will know Christ the more, his grace that supplies our needs and then his ability to carry his people through. Each revelation reveals a special facet of Christ to you. The more you know Christ, the more divinely sanctified human words are created in you. In fact, all revelations lead to Christ. The absence of Christ in a revelation leads to nothing but "self."

At this time, as I write and pray, this song dropped:

> Closer draw yourself to me
>
> To the mountain of Glory
>
> Sin will not have dominion over you
>
> Earthly pleasures will grow dim and shameful
>
> You will know Christ and his resurrection power
>
> At work in you to share in his suffering and shame
>
> to my glory.

If people are not broken, and Christ does not take the center of their lives, then, they pollute the word of God. They are not broken, so they add human elements to the word. The channels are faulty. There is bad water in the pipe, or the tank. The tank is not cleansed. If a person speaks against his fellows, even leaders and begin to prophesy, he ministers pollution. The person brings out what he has gone through. Jokes, watching bad films, getting involved in filthy things and wickedness all pollute the word. This is where Psalm 1 comes in:

> Blessed is the man who does not walk in the counsel of the wicked or stand in the way of sinners or sit in the seat of mockers. But his delight is in the law of the Lord, and on his law he meditates day and night. He is like a tree planted by streams of water, which yields its fruit in season and whose leaf does not wither. Whatever he does prospers. (vv. 1–3 NIV)

Every revelation must be based on the Scripture. It must not contradict God's word that is already in existence. The special facet of Christ revealed in your revelation, which must have come through your trial must break your "self," the old nature, or that aspect of you that you had not been able to give up. Sometimes, I see some people who want to be used by the Lord and yet fear to go through trials. It is not possible. The will of God often goes against the will of human beings. Consequently, once you want to follow God's will, you will be broken, otherwise, you will be people pleasers.

Once you are broken and know the Scripture, you have human words to add to the divine words. These sanctified human words will keep your message alive and bring life to the people. Once human words are added to the divine words, the burden becomes very high. It is boiling up in you and keeping it becomes difficult. This is the time where the word of God is delivered at the highest level. When this is done people break down in repentance, they change from bad habits, shed tears, and Christ is formed in them. Preaching to get people to understand is what Watchman calls preaching the word of God at the lowest level.[3] We must go above ministering for understanding to where people will act on the message. Getting people to act on a message is ministering the word at the highest level.

THE DELIVERY OF THE MESSAGE

Once you have got the divine message, and clothed it with human words then you are ready to deliver the message. It must be delivered at the right time and at the right place. The delivery brings life. Jesus says at John 6:63, "The Spirit gives life; the flesh counts for nothing. The words I have spoken to you are spirit and they are life" (NIV). Delivering the message with the release of the Spirit will cause people to repent, act and bring them close to the Lord.

Churches do not often make room for revelations, yet they are an important part of our services. Paul admonishes, "What then shall we say, brothers? When you come together, everyone has a hymn, or a word of instruction, a revelation, a tongue or an interpretation. All of these must be done for the strengthening of the church" (1 Cor 14:26 NIV). Time must be given for people to share what they have from the Lord.

Once the revelation is given out, the burden is released. If after the delivery of the message the burden is still there, it means the person did not use the right human words; the words were wrong. In such a case, if it was prophecy, the person may give two or three prophecies in a session. When it happens that way, it is a sign that the person may have failed

---

3. Nee, *Ministry of God's Word*, 83–89.

to clothe the divine message with the right words and illustration. If it is preaching, and the person had clothed the divine words with human words, it could mean that the Spirit was released along with the delivery of the word.

If a person struggles to find the right words during the delivery, it means the message is not ripe. Once the message is delivered rightly the person becomes like a balloon or football that has been deflated because the burden is released, whether it was prophecy or preaching. The person feels happy and settled in his spirit. Some time ago, I preached a revelatory message once and never had the urge to preach it again. This may mean that the revelation must have been delivered well. Other times, I may preach a message again and again, without feeling bored about it. It could mean that the message has still not gone to the people or I might not have put the right clothes on it. On the other hand, once the Lord gives a revelation to a person, he may preach and preach until the people grasp it.

Once the burden is released, the "prophet" has discharged his duty faithfully. The prompting, the idea, the burden, the divine words, and the human words have all come together to be delivered to the recipients. The Lord will follow up with the rest.

Chapter 28

Hindrances to Hearing from the Lord

THIS CHAPTER BRINGS ATTENTION explicitly to some of the issues mentioned already and others, which may hinder one from receiving a message from the Lord or hearing from him. The story of Eli and Samuel is one of the incidents that shows that the Lord always speaks but people do not hear. The Lord spoke to Eli through Eli's knowledge of him, but he did not take it. He spoke to him through the man of God, and then finally through Samuel. God spoke to Eli's sons through the people around them, and their father, but they failed to listen until their death. What are the hindrances to hearing the voice of the Lord?

IGNORANCE

From Samuel's experience, we realize that ignorance can cause defects in hearing the voice of the Lord. Ignorance, it is said, is a disease, and Plato, one of the greatest philosophers, added, "It is the greatest disease."[1] But the worse thing is that people who are ignorant do not know that they are. They think they are wise, and will not listen to others. The wise, however, know that they are limited in many ways and seek the counsel of the multitude. This is why someone has said, "Ignorance is the curse of God, knowledge the wing wherewith we fly to heaven."[2] The Almighty One was speaking to Samuel but he thought it was Eli who was calling

---

1. http://www.hermes-press.com/ignorance.htm.
2. http://creatingminds.org/quotes/ignorance.htm5.

him. This shows that we need to read and study to understand how God speaks to people. Hearing the voice of God once is not enough. Once you can avail yourself through the study of God, his word, and his creation, you make yourself available to be used by him in many ways.

Samuel was to address these shortfalls later in his life, by mentoring a group of prophets (1 Sam 10:5).

Ignorance can limit the way the Lord will like to use a person. Peter was given the keys to the doors of heaven and earth, but the works of Paul are more numerous than Peter. Paul used his scholarship to write about half—thirteen out of the twenty-seven books of the New Testament to benefit the church. Most of the missionary journeys of the New Testament were done by Paul who could minister to both Jews and Greeks.

Paul emphatically declares, "Study to shew thyself approved unto God, a workman that needeth not to be ashamed, rightly dividing the word of truth" (2 Tim 2:15 KJV). Do not limit yourself with ignorance. Continue to know God and his word more through studying. Do not satisfy yourself by saying that studying kills spirituality. The Bible was written by people who had studied and were spiritual. Both studying and praying are necessary. Keep yourself abreast with time through reading, studying, listening to the radio, watching the TV, and making good use of the internet, and social media in general.

THE PRESSURE OF THE PEOPLE

The pressure of the people can cause some prophets to prophesy without hearing from God. Later in the book of Samuel, we realized that after Saul had been appointed by the Lord through Samuel to be a king, the pressure of the people caused Saul to disobey the voice of the Lord (1 Sam 13:6–10). Samuel had told him to wait for him to offer the sacrifice, but the pressure from the people caused him to offer the sacrifice. When people are giving us pressure, we may decide to act without waiting for the voice of God. Once people are pushing you for an action, you may hear the voice of the masses and prophesy, or prophesy through a charged atmosphere. That will not come from the Lord.

The masses can cause leaders to respond to them instead of listening to the Lord. It is very important for every leader or Christian to know when God is speaking and when people are putting pressure on them.

Listening to God brings relief and lasting peace. Listening to human beings may bring temporary relief but lead to many disasters in future.

SIN

Sin is a vice that keeps people from hearing the voice of God. The two sons of Eli kept on disobeying the Lord, and as such could not hear him. They continued to sin, and rejected the warnings from their father until the Lord decided to take their lives. Once you live in sin even sacrifice cannot atone for you. The sins of Eli's sons did not only cause them to lose contact with the Lord but it also brought disaster on the whole family. Their sins had gone past forgiveness:

> And I declare to him that I am about to punish his house forever, for the iniquity that he knew, because his sons were blaspheming God, and he did not restrain them. Therefore I swear to the house of Eli that the iniquity of Eli's house shall not be atoned for by sacrifice or offering forever. (1 Sam 3:13–14 ESV)

The implication of "could not be atoned for by sacrifice or offering forever" is that Eli might have prayed on the issue. However, the Lord was saying that the judgement had already been passed. It could be deduced from the message given to Samuel that Eli had prayed toward the first message that was given to him by the unnamed man of God (1 Sam 2:27–36). Perhaps, he wanted to know if God had answered his prayer of plea; that is why the Lord said "could not be atoned for." In the first message, which was given by a man of God, the Lord did not swear and did not say that sacrifice and offering could not atone for Eli's family (1 Sam 2:27–36). But in the message to Samuel, the LORD emphasized that the iniquity could not be atoned for by sacrifice or offering. It appears that he thought prayer and offering could help, but the Lord said he had decreed and nothing could stop it.

We should not get to the point of "could not be atoned for." We must not take God's grace for granted. Once we know that the blood of Christ cleanses us, we may be tempted to keep on sinning and expect that the blood will atone for us. Moses got to a time when he prayed three times and the Lord said he had received enough from him:

> And I pleaded with the Lord at that time, saying, "O Lord God, you have only begun to show your servant your greatness and your mighty hand. For what god is there in heaven or on earth

who can do such works and mighty acts as yours? Please let me go over and see the good land beyond the Jordan, that good hill country and Lebanon." But the Lord was angry with me because of you and would not listen to me. And the Lord said to me, "Enough from you; do not speak to me of this matter again. Go up to the top of Pisgah and lift up your eyes westward and northward and southward and eastward, and look at it with your eyes, for you shall not go over this Jordan. But charge Joshua, and encourage and strengthen him, for he shall go over at the head of this people, and he shall put them in possession of the land that you shall see." (Deut 3:23–28 ESV)

The author of the book of Hebrews cites a word of caution to believers about reaching the point of no mercy:

> For if we go on sinning deliberately after receiving the knowledge of the truth, there no longer remains a sacrifice for sins, but a fearful expectation of judgment, and a fury of fire that will consume the adversaries. Anyone who has set aside the law of Moses dies without mercy on the evidence of two or three witnesses. How much worse punishment, do you think, will be deserved by the one who has spurned the Son of God, and has profaned the blood of the covenant by which he was sanctified, and has outraged the Spirit of grace? For we know him who said, "Vengeance is mine; I will repay." And again, "The Lord will judge his people." It is a fearful thing to fall into the hands of the living God. (Heb 10:26–31 ESV)

This passage warns against willful sin. This exhortation is to believers, not unbelievers. Backsliding Christians begin to drift through neglect or carelessness. Often, they begin by avoiding the Lord's voice and committing a sin. Then, they start to doubt the reality of the word of God. As they entertain doubts about the word of God, they continue to grow dull toward the reading, studying and hearing of God's word. Once these are going on in their lives, the next step is to continue by deliberately remaining in sin—they begin to find ways of justifying what they are doing. Thomas Nelson's definition of temptation is most appropriate to understanding what is meant by a deliberate sin, "sin's call to our basic needs and desires to be satisfied in self-serving or perverted ways. It is also a call to practice self-deception, finding ways to justify doing as we please, even though we know in our heart of hearts that it is wrong."[3] Once people

---

3. *Word in Life Study Bible.*

begin to deliberately sin, they also despise their spiritual heritage. They begin to condemn spiritual things and see them as not important. This is a willful sin. This situation is similar to what the Apostle John says in 1 John 1:4–10:

> Everyone who makes a practice of sinning also practices lawlessness; sin is lawlessness. You know that he appeared to take away sins, and in him there is no sin. No one who abides in him keeps on sinning; no one who keeps on sinning has either seen him or known him. Little children, let no one deceive you. Whoever practices righteousness is righteous, as he is righteous. Whoever makes a practice of sinning is of the devil, for the devil has been sinning from the beginning. The reason the Son of God appeared was to destroy the works of the devil. No one born of God makes a practice of sinning, for God's seed abides in him, and he cannot keep on sinning because he has been born of God. By this it is evident who are the children of God, and who are the children of the devil: whoever does not practice righteousness is not of God, nor is the one who does not love his brother. (ESV)

The Christian will not deliberately break God's law. Christians may sin, but what this passage is saying is that true Christians will not deliberately and repeatedly practice sin or disobey the Lord. The one who keeps on sinning does not abide in the Lord. The seed of God in the Christian will not allow him to keep on disobeying the Lord.

The iniquity of Eli's family had gone to the extent that it "could not be atoned for by sacrifice or offering forever"; it is considered a deliberate sin. His sons Hophni and Phinehas kept on blaspheming God. They did not listen to their father, neither did they repent and yet they were the serving priests. They were not going to be punished alone because their sin affected Eli's family. Why so, since Eli had not deliberately sinned? What was the sin of Eli?

Eli's sin was that he honored his sons more than God. He had been informed of what the children were doing. He corrected his children but they slighted his correction (1 Sam 2:22–26). What Eli should have done was to remove them from office, but he failed to do so because he loved them more than the Lord. This was Eli's sin; he honored the children more than the Lord. If people abuse their office, whether they are your children, brothers or friends, they must be dealt with.

Disciplining loved ones is part of mentoring. Failure to discipline was part of Eli's sin. Since the sons of Eli had not repented of their sins, they should have been removed from office. Or, they should not have been allowed to perform the priestly function again. The sins of Eli's sons could not be atoned for because they were not ready to repent. When people are not ready to change, atonement does not work. The New Testament shows that once people repent of their sins, the Lord forgives:

> If we confess our sins, he is faithful and just to forgive us our sins and to cleanse us from all unrighteousness. (1 John 1:9 ESV)

> Let it be known to you therefore, brothers, that through this man forgiveness of sins is proclaimed to you, and by him everyone who believes is freed from everything from which you could not be freed by the law of Moses. (Acts 13:38–39 ESV)

With the Lord, once someone is willing to confess and change, he is willing to forgive. Do not keep on sinning until you come to the point of no return.

Eli's children were not right before the people and the Lord. They were not prepared to change. Even they were snobbish to their own father, the high priest. Their punishment affected the whole of Eli's family. We must not do things that will affect our entire family, the church and our nation. Often, the sin of one person can affect the entire family or church.

The Lord requires obedience more than sacrifice. Samuel rightly told Saul:

> So Samuel said, "Has the Lord as great delight in burnt offerings and sacrifices, As in obeying the voice of the Lord? Behold, to obey is better than sacrifice, And to heed than the fat of rams. For rebellion is as the sin of witchcraft, And stubbornness is as iniquity and idolatry. Because you have rejected the word of the Lord, He also has rejected you from being king." (1 Sam 15:22–23 NKJV)

Obedience to the Lord is more important than "all night prayers," fasting, sacrifice, praise and worship. What the Lord requires of us and for us is to obey. You may pray and pray, fast and fast, study and study, but if there is no obedience to the word of God, the Lord will not hear you. You must hear God before he hears you.

Once you live in sin, you will not hear the voice of God. Sin opens the chance for the devil to accuse you. The devil will continue to accuse you and distort the voice of God in your life. The dreams and visions you see may stem from the sins you have committed and get you so complicated that you will not know the difference between the voice of God, the voice of the devil and the voice of your sins. You must come out of any known sin if you want to hear the voice of God daily.

IMMEDIATE ANSWER

Sometimes people do not hear the voice of God because they want an answer without paying the price. They may want an immediate answer but the Lord will want them wait for his timing. While Samuel had asked Saul to wait, the people wanted an immediate action (1 Sam 13:7–8). It is always better to hear from God before taking an important step. Sometimes, it takes a few minutes, other times too, days, months or years. It took the Prophet Jeremiah ten days before he heard from the Lord, when he was approached by his people (Jer 42:1–7). Wait until you hear from him. A move without God is catastrophic.

The other side of demanding an "immediate answer" is being too expectant. We think the Lord must speak! We must hear him! But hearing from the Lord does not only come from prophecy. Prophecy is only one of the avenues. Putting too much pressure on people to prophesy may cause them to bring us a human message. Samuel was not expecting, yet God revealed himself to him. In the ancient world, people had to sleep in the temples of deities for what they called incubation. In such situations, they were expecting the deities to brood over them with messages. Samuel was not doing so; the Lord spoke to him in his own timing and it was at night.

Once you approach "a prophet" to prophesy in your hearing, he may give you what you want. Remember you are responsible for hearing the voice of God yourself.

HAVING ALREADY DETERMINED RESULTS

People may not hear the true voice of God because they already have in mind what they want to hear. Once you condition your mind of the type of result you want from the Lord, you may not hear him speak, or your mind will speak to you. Samuel nearly made such a mistake. When the people asked for a king, Samuel thought the Lord would say "no," and found it difficult accepting the "yes" answer from the Lord (1 Sam 8:4–7, 18–22).

Furthermore, later, in the life of Samuel, when the Lord sent him to anoint one of the sons of Jesse, he nearly anointed the wrong one. He looked at his appearance and at his physical stature (1 Sam 16:6–7). You must come to the Lord with an open heart, ready to obey him. I think this is one of the greatest hindrances to hearing the voice of the Lord. Often many people, in a way, have the answers already, and anything less than what they expect will not be taken as from the Lord. A typical example is the case of Ahab in the book of 1 Kgs 22:1–26 (see also 2 Chr 18:1–34). He wanted to hear only the message of "yes to war" from the prophets, and this was confirmed for him. When the prophet of the Lord Micaiah was brought in, and his message was different from those of the false prophets, the king could not accept it; Micaiah even had a slap on the cheek and was eventually put into prison:

> Then Zedekiah son of Kenaanah went up and slapped Micaiah in the face. "Which way did the spirit from the Lord go when he went from me to speak to you?" he asked. Micaiah replied, "You will find out on the day you go to hide in an inner room." The king of Israel then ordered, "Take Micaiah and send him back to Amon the ruler of the city and to Joash the king's son and say, 'This is what the king says: Put this fellow in prison and give him nothing but bread and water until I return safely.'" Micaiah declared, "If you ever return safely, the Lord has not spoken through me." Then he added, "Mark my words, all you people!" (1 Kgs 22:24–28 NIV)

Nonetheless, Micaiah's message proved right. The king died in the war. Why should the Prophet Zedekiah do that? The king had his own answer, and the prophets wanted to sing the song of the king. If you have a predetermined answer, you may not hear the voice of the Lord. This does not mean that we must not use our minds to reason. We need to think and use the sanctified common sense. The Lord wants us to use our reasoning ability. But we should not ask the Lord to speak on an issue to which we have already determined an answer. We must be open for his voice. Being open to his voice does not mean that someone is instructing you on what to do, but being ready to accept what the Lord will give to you, within your inner being.

These are some of the hindrances to hearing from God. Once we open up to the Lord and shun sin, the Lord is always available to speak to us.

PART 9

Limitations of Apostles and Prophets

This part deals with the challenges that go along with prophecy. It discusses how to identify both good and false manifestations. It has been divided into three chapters. The chapter deals with how to identify good prophets. The second deals with prophetic flaws, and the last deals with how to test prophecy. The life of Samuel will be used a lot here since he serves the purposes of both good and bad examples.

Chapter 29

Identifying a True Prophet

WHEN THE LORD IS working with people, others see it. Good servants of the Lord, such as apostles, prophets, evangelists, and teachers, are not made out of the blue. The Lord prepares them in chambers. These people avail themselves to God behind the scenes before God brings them out. People begin to see the hand of God in their lives.

Once you see someone claiming to be an apostle or a prophet, imposing himself on others, you must know that he is a deceiver. A person does not even need to say "I am a prophet" or "I am an apostle" to be recognized. The gift of an apostle or a prophet is evident for people around. There were outstanding things in the life of Samuel, for example, which showed that the Lord was making him a prophet; everything he said proved to be reliable (1 Sam 3:19–21). No one can objectively doubt the apostleship of Paul. The following are some of the things, which are evident about an apostle or a prophet. Since we have good examples of the lives of Samuel and Paul, most of the lessons will be drawn from their lives.

PRESENCE OF GOD

An apostle or a prophet carries the presence of God. The young man Samuel is a very good example. At the period that he emerged, the word of the Lord was rare. People were only occasionally hearing from God. They desired to see a prophet of God—someone who often hears and speaks from the Lord. A man of God had spoken to the priest Eli, yet the people knew there was no prophet. When Samuel emerged, they knew the Lord was with the young man:

> The Lord was with Samuel as he grew up, and he let none of his words fall to the ground. And all Israel from Dan to Beersheba recognized that Samuel was attested as a prophet of the Lord. The Lord continued to appear at Shiloh, and there he revealed himself to Samuel through his word. (1 Sam 3:19–21 NIV)

There was evidence in the life of Samuel that the Lord was with him; the people knew of it (1 Sam 3:19a; 2:21). The presence of God is an awe that surrounds people, which is difficult to explain. People around such persons see it; this awe makes the presence of such people either enjoyable or fearful. Enjoyable in the sense that people know they will experience the presence of God, fearful because their presence makes it difficult for people to sin. "The man of God" will not need to blow his own horns. It is evident to people around. I have many examples of this situation. I will cite one. As a young man around thirty-six years, I was waiting to board a plane in Nigeria, two people (male and female) came to me and asked a question, "Please who are you?" I said, "Why do you ask me this question?" They pleaded with me, "Please, you just tell us." I told them I was a pastor. Then one of them (the female) said, "I told you people so." Then, I said, "Why?" She continued, "We had been arguing among ourselves, about your identity. Some say, you are a pastor and others say you are a minister of the government. This is why I want to find out." Why were they arguing among themselves? Possibly, they had seen some indescribable aura which caused them to think I was no ordinary person. That might be the presence of God. I had not told them anything. This is the presence of God I am talking about—something about people that makes them no ordinary persons.

GOD'S ENDORSEMENT OF THE PERSON

The emphasis in 1 Sam 3:19b is very important. The Lord "let none of his words fall to the ground" (NIV). God speaks to the prophet and through him. Once God has spoken through him, he would fulfill what he has said. However, the statement here is suggesting that not only did God fulfill his word through Samuel, but the Lord did not allow any words uttered by Samuel fall to the ground. This is to say that God fulfilled whatever Samuel spoke out of his own mind, even when it was without any direct instruction from the Lord. This is wonderful. God had honored him and "respected" him. This was an aspect of Samuel's ministry, which was later seen clearly in his life. For example, when Samuel was giving his farewell message to the people of Israel, he said he would pray for the Lord to send rains:

> Now then, stand still and see this great thing the Lord is about to do before your eyes! Is it not wheat harvest now? I will call upon the Lord to send thunder and rain. And you will realize what an evil thing you did in the eyes of the Lord when you asked for a king." Then Samuel called upon the Lord, and that same day the Lord sent thunder and rain. So all the people stood in awe of the Lord and of Samuel. (1 Sam 12:16–18 NIV)

God had not asked him to pray for rain, but he requested the Lord to do that, and it did rain. The Lord did not allow any of his words to fall to the ground.

Paul caused blindness to Elymas as he distracted the governor of Paphos from hearing the word of God. Paul spoke and it worked, eventually the governor believed the gospel message (Acts 13:8–12). Some people walk with the Lord to the extent that he does not allow what they say fall to the ground.

RECOGNITION BY MANY PEOPLE

The people knew that God was raising a prophet in Samuel (1 Sam 3:20; 4:1). His ministry was felt by the entire nation. It is the Lord who raises a prophet or an apostle. Peter realized that God had granted Paul special grace such that some of the revelations given to him were difficult to understand (2 Pet 3:15–16).

We do not manufacture prophets or apostles. Once God is raising a person or raises a person, people see it. When there is pressure to appoint or call one, the wrong one may be appointed. People see those who are prophets. A young man called James Osei Amaniampong of Kumasi-Ghana, prophesied during a visit of the then chairman of the Church of Pentecost, Apostle James McKeown. He recognized that the Lord was raising a prophet for the church. He called him and told him among other things that he had confirmed the message he (Apostle McKeown) was going to speak on. He wished many prophecies would toe that line.

When people register their doubts about a person, it is an indication the person might not be genuine. It must be considered that this is not always the case. There are some people who will never be satisfied with others. However, generally some people may not agree with others in many things, but it is often difficult to doubt the presence of God in a person's life.

CONSTANT REVELATION FROM THE LORD

The Lord speaks to Christians. Some of the purposes of the Holy Spirit are to lead and direct the Christian. Yet, when it comes to the apostolic and prophetic offices, the Lord continues to reveal himself to them (1 Sam 3:21). It is not only a once for all experience. Here, again Samuel and Paul will be used as an example.

Samuel was addressed as a seer, a person who was favored with visions from God (1 Sam 9:11; cf. 9:9). But before his emergence, it was said that there was no open vision. The Lord was seeking a person he could trust and endow with the grace of "open vision." When he caught Samuel, he kept on revealing things to him (1 Sam 9:15–17). Examining the ways and manners the Lord directed him to call Saul as a king showed how clear his vision was:

- He was aware that Saul was looking for the father's donkeys;
- He was sure that the donkeys had been found;
- He was sure that the Lord had called him to be king over Israel;
- He had kept part of the cooked meat for him; and
- He was sure that he would meet a group of prophets and the Spirit would fall upon him (1 Sam 9:15–27; 10:1–8).

What a seer Samuel was to his generation! Samuel was also recognized as a prophet, a person whose message sprung up, or bubbled up from the Lord. He was the person of the Lord. The prophetic office is a call. The person must be sure of his call. He must be sure of the presence of God in his life. The presence of God will give a person confidence to pray for people for the Lord to respond (1 Sam 7:5, 9). God communicates with such people. Samuel was often praying to God and the Lord was responding. The communication between him and the Lord toward the institution of kingship was strong (1 Sam 8:6–9, 21–22). Therefore, a person cannot prophesy once or twice and claim to be a prophet. There is a very strong relationship between the prophet and the Lord.

As it was in the Old Testament when the Lord constantly revealed his will to the people through the prophet, so also he does in the New Testament through the apostle. Paul, for example, was being led by the Lord in his missionary journeys. The book of Acts shows how the Lord was directing him through dreams/visions (16:6–10; 23:11; 27:21–24), perceptions (27:10), and people who came his way (23:12–17). These things were constant but they were taking place in the ordinary way, meaning that God was leading him through regular day to day circumstances. For example, when there was a plot to kill him, the Lord used Paul sister's son, who happened to be there to unfold their plot (Acts 23:12–16). Meanwhile, the Lord had told Paul that he would testify about him in Rome. This is to say the Lord will cause all things to work in favor of his plan, and for the people he has called.

All that has been said gives evidence to the fact that God raises individuals who are available to serve his people. The Lord will do more for his people if he can find Christians who are available to be set apart for him. The challenge that the Lord has is the non-availability of people. He wants people who will sing his voice, and will not use the gift for money or fame. He does not do these in chambers but he enables people witness his hand on others. The Lord prepared Samuel as a prophet to serve the people of Israel, so also he prepared Paul to serve the Gentiles. God prepares people to serve his purpose in generations and not for personal gain.

DRAWS ATTENTION TO CHRIST

An important work of the Holy Spirit is to draw attention to Christ; he glorifies Christ (John 16:14). The true prophet or apostle has no ministry of his own; he says what the Lord wants him to say, and does what the Lord wants him to do. His ministry is like John the Baptist who says, "The one who has the bride is the bridegroom. The friend of the bridegroom, who stands and hears him, rejoices greatly at the bridegroom's voice. Therefore this joy of mine is now complete. *He must increase, but I must decrease*" (John 3:29–30 ESV, italics mine). The prophet or apostle is like the friend of the bridegroom whose duty is to serve the bridegroom. He is not to call attention to himself. Christ must increase, while he decreases.

The servant of God must not allow what others say about him supersede the person of Christ. The more people try to make him great, the more he must humble himself and give the glory to Christ.

People will always want to hail the persons God uses. As has been mentioned, in the book of Acts, the people of Lystra had wanted to offer sacrifice to Paul and Barnabas, because of the miracle they performed, but they stopped them (Acts 14:8–13). They pointed to them that they were also human beings, bringing the goodness of the living God to them. Peter declared that the household of Cornelius had received the Holy Spirit just as they received (Acts 10:48). By implication, he was saying both Jews and Gentiles were the same. The servants of the Lord need to know that all Christians are the same, and each has been granted spiritual gifts to serve, and each one is important.

A LIFE OF INTEGRITY

An apostle or a prophet must be a person of integrity. His life should be above reproach. When Samuel gave his farewell message, he could publicly declare that he had not taken any bribe or cheated the people:

> Samuel said to all Israel, "I have listened to everything you said to me and have set a king over you. Now you have a king as your leader. As for me, I am old and gray, and my sons are here with you. I have been your leader from my youth until this day. Here I stand. Testify against me in the presence of the Lord and his anointed. Whose ox have I taken? Whose donkey have I taken? Whom have I cheated? Whom have I oppressed? From whose hand have I accepted a bribe to make me shut my eyes? If I have done any of these, I will make it right." "You have not cheated or oppressed us," they replied. "You have not taken anything from anyone's hand." (1 Sam 12:1–4 NIV)

The prophet was saying that no person was cheated in his ministry. He did not use the people to accumulate wealth for himself. He did not use the people to acquire wealth for his friends. He did not use public funds to provide for his family members. He did not oppress the needy, neither did he act improperly. This is evidence that a prophet is to live above reproach.

When "an apostle" or "a prophet" begins to chase the young girls in the church, misuse church money, grab properties, and abuse people, you should know that he is not a messenger of God or has gotten out of fellowship. He is a deceiver, an imposter, or a person who is using the church for money.

Moses tells of how to know a true prophet:

> But a prophet who presumes to speak in my name anything I have not commanded him to say, or a prophet who speaks in the name of other gods, must be put to death." You may say to yourselves, "How can we know when a message has not been spoken by the Lord?" If what a prophet proclaims in the name of the Lord does not take place or come true, that is a message the Lord has not spoken. That prophet has spoken presumptuously. Do not be afraid of him. (Deut 18:20–22 NIV)

If the prophet predicts and it is fulfilled, then he is a true prophet. If he proclaims something in the name of the Lord, and it does not come true, he is not from the Lord, or the message does not come from the Lord. You must not fear him, for he was only presumptuous, applying "trial-and-error" method. Once he says many things, one of them may be fulfilled. There are many so-called prophets and apostles who use this method. Through this, they may have one of their predictions come true. Yet, such people only prey on the vulnerable people, such as the sick, poor, needy, and children in society.

Contrarily, Moses also tells us that fulfillment of prediction only does not show us that a person is a true prophet. Besides the text read, let us listen to him in chapter 13 of Deuteronomy:

> If a prophet, or one who foretells by dreams, appears among you and announces to you a miraculous sign or wonder, and if the sign or wonder of which he has spoken takes place, and he says, "Let us follow other gods" (gods you have not known) "and let us worship them," you must not listen to the words of that prophet or dreamer. The Lord your God is testing you to find out whether you love him with all your heart and with all your soul. It is the Lord your God you must follow, and him you must revere. Keep his commands and obey him; serve him and hold fast to him. That prophet or dreamer must be put to death, because he preached rebellion against the Lord your God, who brought you out of Egypt and redeemed you from the land of slavery; he has tried to turn you from the way the Lord your God commanded you to follow. You must purge the evil from among you. (Deut 13:1–5 NIV)

Moses says here, and in 18:20 above, that the Lord had clearly declared that you shall have no other God besides him. Therefore, if a prophet or an apostle claims to do some miracles but does something which leads to idolatry, he is not of God. He is a deceiver. We must understand the standard of God; his clear commandments must be the test of a true prophet. Once people deviate from them, no matter what they claim to do, they might be imposters. Do not entertain them. The standard rule of God has been laid for us to hold fast to as a safeguard against the tide. Consulting prophets must have been a practice during the time of Moses among the nations. Moses knew it would happen to his people. But under no circumstance, he warned, should something clearly contrary to the revealed word of God be accepted on the proclamation of a prophet. Kwabena J. Darkwa Amanor, a Ghanaian theologian, considers most of the contemporary prophecies of this nature as divination.[1]

Our Lord Jesus clearly gives us another test of a true prophet. You shall know them by their fruit:

> Watch out for false prophets. They come to you in sheep's clothing, but inwardly they are ferocious wolves. By their fruit you will recognize them. Do people pick grapes from thorn bushes, or figs from thistles? Likewise every good tree bears good fruit, but a bad tree bears bad fruit. A good tree cannot bear bad fruit, and a bad tree cannot bear good fruit. Every tree that does not bear good fruit is cut down and thrown into the fire. Thus, by their fruit you will recognize them. Not everyone who says to me, "Lord, Lord," will enter the kingdom of heaven, but only he who does the will of my Father who is in heaven. Many will say to me on that day, "Lord, Lord, did we not prophesy in your name, and in your name drive out demons and perform many miracles?" Then I will tell them plainly, "I never knew you. Away from me, you evildoers!" (Matt 7:15–23 NIV)

Jesus' test of false manifestation is simple. A bad tree cannot bear good fruit. The inward nature of such people has not changed; they are not born again. They merely wear the outward appearance of a good prophet. They call Jesus "Lord" and even perform some miracles and religious deeds, but they have not been saved! How do we detect these false prophets? Jesus shows, "You will know them by their fruits" (16). The fruit of the Spirit is evident in the true prophet or apostle. He manifests the fruit of the Spirit, or the virtues of the Beatitudes as Jesus shows

---

1. Amanor, *Prophecy of Divination*, 14–16.

in Matt 5. His lips are full of the testimonies of Jesus and of his praise. His body has been given to God as a living sacrifice. His aim is to win lost souls for Jesus and disciple them. Some people can pretend to be Christians and get involved in many religious activities and be somehow successful, but they are only acting. Their fruits bear evidence.

Chapter 30

Prophetic Flaws

It pleases the Lord to endow one person with many gifts for them to become a blessing to many. However, the person is still a human being with weaknesses. This chapter brings out the weaknesses of the prophets, and by implication apostles, which are set down as examples for other Christians. Samuel is cited in many areas.

TENDENCY TO HOLD ON TO ONE'S VIEW

There is the tendency to hold on to one's own view without allowing the Lord to have his own way. Samuel almost made this mistake when the people asked for a king. He thought the Lord should not give them a king. He was still holding on to his view when the Lord had already spoken (1 Sam 8:6–9, 18–22):

> But when they said, "Give us a king to lead us," this displeased Samuel; so he prayed to the Lord. And the Lord told him: "Listen to all that the people are saying to you; it is not you they have rejected, but they have rejected me as their king. As they have done from the day I brought them up out of Egypt until this day, forsaking me and serving other gods, so they are doing to you. Now listen to them; but warn them solemnly and let them know what the king who will reign over them will do." When that day comes, you will cry out for relief from the king you have chosen, and the Lord will not answer you in that day." But the people refused to listen to Samuel. "No!" they said, "We want a king

over us. Then we will be like all the other nations, with a king to lead us and to go out before us and fight our battles" When Samuel heard all that the people said, he reported it before the Lord. The Lord answered, "Listen to them and give them a king." (1 Sam 8:18–22 NIV)

Here, it appeared that Samuel was trying to convince the people to stop asking for a king, but the Lord had already agreed. It appeared that Samuel was speaking on behalf of God, but 1 Sam 12:1–3 betrays his intention; he was thinking of his sons:

> Samuel said to all Israel, "I have listened to everything you said to me and have set a king over you. Now you have a king as your leader. As for me, I am old and gray, *and my sons are here with you*. I have been your leader from my youth until this day. Here I stand. Testify against me in the presence of the Lord and his anointed. Whose ox have I taken? Whose donkey have I taken? Whom have I cheated? Whom have I oppressed? From whose hand have I accepted a bribe to make me shut my eyes? If I have done any of these, I will make it right." (1 Sam 12:1–3 NIV, italics mine)

Samuel was saying he had listened to them and given them a king and that he never cheated them in any way, but why did he have to bring up his sons? His sons were corrupt (1 Sam 8:1–2). They were not living the way of the Lord as Samuel was. Yet mentioning them here means Samuel had wanted his sons to have been chosen as leaders. He was still not happy about the choice of the people whereas his own children too were not right before God. The sin of Eli was that he honored his sons more than God (1 Sam 2:28). While we may not be able to control our adult children, we can dishonor them by not giving in to their demands. Each person will stand before God's judgment as an individual. If Eli had taken them from office after reprimanding them and seeing no change, he would not have been guilty. Apostles, prophets, bishops and founders of churches and ministries need not place their children who dishonor the Lord in positions. Positions and offices should be assigned to all whether children or not who honor the Lord.

Once a prophet holds on to his view or holds something against another person, it is very possible that he will prophesy according to his flesh. Negative thoughts about a person, jealousy, or anger can all lead prophets to prophesy against a person. Once you know an insight of any issue, a behavior or a characteristic trait of a person, do not use it to prophesy. What you need to do is to speak to it. In other words, share your mind on the issue with the right person. Prophesying into it is trying to use prophecy to control the situation. This is manipulation; this will be picked up in the next point.

The reliable prophet is the one who empties himself of all his personal views, accepts whatever the Lord tells him, and carries on with his ministry.

USING PROPHECY TO MANIPULATE

Linked with the tendency to hold on to one's view is using prophecy or position to manipulate. Samuel had earlier told Saul to wait for him at Gilgal to offer sacrifice. This might have taken place already as he and Israel gathered at Gilgal and Saul was reaffirmed as the king of Israel (1 Sam 10:8; 11:14–15). Then two years later, when the people were going to war, the unfortunate thing happened. Instead of Saul waiting for Samuel to come to offer the sacrifice, he did it himself as pressure was mounted on him. Read the account of 1 Sam 13:6–15:

> When the men of Israel saw that they were in trouble (for the people were hard pressed), the people hid themselves in caves and in holes and in rocks and in tombs and in cisterns, and some Hebrews crossed the fords of the Jordan to the land of Gad and Gilead. Saul was still at Gilgal, and all the people followed him trembling. He waited seven days, the time appointed by Samuel. But Samuel did not come to Gilgal, and the people were scattering from him. So Saul said, "Bring the burnt offering here to me, and the peace offerings." And he offered the burnt offering. As soon as he had finished offering the burnt offering, behold, Samuel came. And Saul went out to meet him and greet him. Samuel said, "What have you done?" And Saul said, "When I saw that the people were scattering from me, and that you did not come within the days appointed, and that the Philistines had mustered at Michmash, I said, 'Now the Philistines will come down against me at Gilgal, and I have not sought the favor of the Lord.' So I forced myself, and offered the burnt offering." And Samuel said to Saul, "You have done foolishly. You have not kept the command of the Lord your God, with which he commanded you. For then the Lord would have established your kingdom over Israel forever. But now your kingdom shall not continue. The Lord has sought out a man after his own heart, and the Lord

has commanded him to be prince over his people, because you have not kept what the Lord commanded you." And Samuel arose and went up from Gilgal. The rest of the people went up after Saul to meet the army; they went up from Gilgal to Gibeah of Benjamin. (ESV)

Samuel told Saul to wait for seven days. Saul waited until the seven days Samuel promised had passed. Meanwhile, in the Old Testament, the Lord had instructed the priest that whenever the people were going to war, the priest should go ahead to encourage the people:

> When you are about to go into battle, the priest shall come forward and address the army. He shall say: "Hear, O Israel, today you are going into battle against your enemies. Do not be fainthearted or afraid; do not be terrified or give way to panic before them. For the Lord your God is the one who goes with you to fight for you against your enemies to give you victory." (Deut 20:2–4 NIV)

Such instructions were to strengthen the people and reinforce the command of the Lord not to fear the people for his presence was with his own. This was meant to be the first instruction so that the soldiers would not be afraid. Take notice that the passage begins with, "When you are about to go into battle." Here, the priest waited until the people started leaving the battle ground before coming. As if Samuel had trapped Saul, he just came in at the time when Saul offered the sacrifice. Then, when he saw what Saul had done, he condemned his action and pronounced doom on him. He, then, continued to say what the Lord was going to do in such a way that was to create enmity between Saul and the next king. Samuel did not address the people, as the Scriptures required of the priest. He was so annoyed that he failed to do that. Saul was wrong, yet the prophet also erred for waiting for the people to scatter before coming. More so, his words were too strong, creating enmity between Saul and the next king. Examine this:

> "You acted foolishly," Samuel said. "You have not kept the command the Lord your God gave you; if you had, he would have established your kingdom over Israel for all time. But now your kingdom will not endure; the Lord has sought out a man after his own heart and appointed him leader of his people, because you have not kept the Lord's command." (1 Sam 13:13–14 NIV)

From this, it can be surmised that Samuel contributed to the failure of Saul. Already he was not happy about the issue of the kingship. In addition, he had wanted his sons to be considered. Saul was treading on a very slippery ground, which needed extreme care and complete reliance on God, something which Saul lacked.

After this incident, all the weaknesses of Saul began to manifest. In 1 Sam 14, which follows this, Saul gave instructions to the soldiers who were in the battle front not to eat. This almost led to the execution of his own son Jonathan. In chapter 15, he disobeyed the instruction of the Lord through Samuel to execute the Amalekites, yet he wanted to be honored. In chapter 16, he was possessed by an evil spirit. In chapter 17, he could not lead Israel in battle as he used to do. In chapter 18, he started chasing David to kill him. He had become a completely confused person. Saul came to the scene without any mentoring; he needed a mentor who could have trained him. But he did not have one. Samuel was not the type who was prepared to assist Saul. Pray that your leader's spirit will not go against you. When the leader's spirit goes against you, it becomes difficult for you to succeed. However, the good news is that you can still succeed if you rely on God and stay in him. This reliance on God was what Saul lacked. He was not a man of prayer or a man who read or studied the word of God. This was his greatest weakness, and it was his failure to depend on God that led to his downfall.

Apostles, prophets, mentors, or leaders should do all they can to help their mentees be successful. Leaders should not undermine the people who take over from them. I am afraid Samuel was not good at this. Initially he appeared to have rejoiced in the failure of his successor. However, later on, it would appear that he regretted his attitude toward Saul, and mourned for him. He also realized that if he continued treating Saul the way he used to do, Saul could kill him. He was afraid for his own life (1 Sam 16:1–2).

When a person says, "Thus says the Lord," it is supposed to be mandatory or when there is an issue at stake and a prophet says, "Thus says the Lord," the people are supposed to comply with it. If a prophet or an apostle always uses prophecy or "the Spirit directs" along this line, he is manipulating the system. There is a convention within the administration of the Church of Pentecost, which does not allow the chairman of the church or anyone chairing a meeting of the church to prophesy, as he steers the affairs of meetings. The reason is that once he says, "Thus says the Lord," it should never be debated. But the reason for the executive council and other executive committee members is for them to discuss issues and fine-tune them for the consideration of the governing bodies. Thus, the one steering the affairs of the meeting should not use the name of the Lord to stop the rest of the members from sharing their minds on issues which are raised.

The best way of presenting issues, which the Lord has communicated to such bodies is to say, "I feel the Lord has placed this on my heart for consideration," or present the issue as an idea that has dropped on your heart. In an institution like a church, there is not only one person who knows or who holds the mind of God, others also have the mind of God. They should be allowed to speak into issues. When Elijah thought that he was left alone, the Lord revealed to him that He had left seven thousand people for himself. The Lord will always allow others to see as you see. Do not use prophecy to manipulate a system.

POTENTIAL TO INCITE TROUBLE

Linked with the tendency to manipulate is the strong possibility of inciting trouble for families, societies, churches and nations. The division between the two nations of Israel developed from the way Samuel handled Saul. The people demanded for a king, and the Lord gave them Saul. Since Samuel was not happy, he kept on saying discouraging words toward the kingship (e.g., 1 Sam 8:18; 9:20; 12:1–3, 16–19, 25). Then, later he (Samuel) failed to discharge his duties fully as he should, until there was a great pressure on Saul, which he could not stand, and he fell. Samuel's reaction when Saul fell could be taken as the outcome of Samuel's inner anger:

> "*You have done foolishly*. You have not kept the command of the Lord your God, with which he commanded you. For then the Lord would have established your kingdom over Israel forever. But now your kingdom shall not continue. *The Lord has sought out a man after his own heart*, and the Lord has commanded him to be prince over his people, because you have not kept what the Lord commanded you." And Samuel arose and went up from Gilgal. The rest of the people went up after Saul to meet the army; they went up from Gilgal to Gibeah of Benjamin. (1 Sam 13:13–15 ESV, italics mine)

Addressing the king as acting "foolishly" before his people was quite strong; "your kingdom shall not continue" was also strong. Then, at another time, he said, "the Lord has torn the kingdom of Israel from you this day and has given it to a neighbor of yours, *who is better than you*"; this too was strong (1 Sam 15:28 ESV, italics mine). Samuel did not need to say more than he was required to say. If his spirit was opened, he could have helped Saul to succeed since he did not know the word of God and did not consult the Lord in prayer himself. Although the people put pressure on Saul, and Samuel also did not support him, if Saul had helped himself by reading the word of God and praying, he could have been successful. Saul was responsible for his own downfall. Despite all that happened, the Lord allowed him to reign for forty years. The Lord had given him to the people.

The people wanted a king and the Lord gave them one. As Samuel continued to say all these words to their king, he was going to create trouble. It was these sorts of sayings from Samuel that ignited the trouble between Saul and David. Already Saul was looking for the one person to whom Samuel claimed was better than he. When, therefore, Samuel went to anoint David and later the women sang for David after he had killed Goliath, the trouble had ignited. The nation was divided between Saul and David. Majority of the people supported Saul, otherwise, he could not have ruled for forty years. Even when Saul died, it took David seven years before he was instituted as the king of the whole Israel. Despite David's successes, Samuel had earlier on created problems for him. Strong pronouncements from prophets, as typical of Samuel, need to be seasoned with "salt," otherwise, they leave indelible troubles for societies.

The presence of Samuel was causing great fear to the people. Examine when the people of Bethlehem said, "When he arrived at Bethlehem, the elders of the town trembled when they met him. They asked, 'Do you come in peace?' Samuel replied, 'Yes, in peace; I have come to sacrifice to the Lord'" (1 Sam 16:4–5 NIV). They knew he had been causing trouble. The people were afraid of his presence in their town. Moreover, remember, he was a Nazirite, a person with dreadlocks (the hairstyle made popular by Rastafarians).

There were other prophets in the Bible whose messages caused problems, because they were not able to manage them well. One of such prophets was Elisha. When he met Hazael, who had been sent by his master, King Ben-hadad, he told him everything he had seen about him and his future dealing with Israel (2 Kgs 8:7–14). Hazael did not wait for these things to materialize, he immediately went and killed his master and started implementing the revelation.

God's messages presented in harsh ways, however, cost some prophets their lives. This includes Zachariah, the son of the high priest Jehoiada (2 Chr 22:20–22).

The good thing to note is that God's messages can be presented in a way that can lead to repentance and peace. Nathan was one of the prophets who could handle the messages of God in a wise way. He was able to bring David to repentance (2 Sam 12:1–14). David's sin was known, but the prophet was able to bring it out in such a way that broke David's heart, before the prophet pronounced the judgment of God. Isaiah was another prophet who had strong messages but was able to work with four kings of Judah—Uzziah, Jotham, Ahaz, and Hezekiah (2 Chr 26–33). He presented God's message to the wicked King Ahaz so well that although he did not accept it, there was peace between them (Isa 7). King Hezekiah, for example, was able to receive his messages, which brought deliverance to the nation and himself (Isa 37–39).

Those with prophetic messages must pray and present their messages in such ways that will not bring divisions among family members, churches and nations. The apostle should not misuse the authority given to him by the Lord. Paul shows that the authority given to us, leaders, is for building up the church, not to tear people down. He writes, "This is why I write these things when I am absent, that when I come I may not have to be harsh in my use of authority—the authority the Lord gave me for building you up, not for tearing you down" (2 Cor 13:10 NIV).

PROPHESYING FROM OTHER VOICES

There is constantly the tendency to prophesy from other voices, especially the flesh. As mentioned already, Samuel nearly made this mistake. When he was to anoint one of the sons of Jesse, he looked at Eliab's appearance, and thought he was the one (1 Sam 16:6–7). But the Lord said no, he wasn't. The human flesh was directing Samuel here. The prophet may speak from the flesh if he does not always remain with the Lord. Talking with people on particular issues may influence the human mind to speak from that angle in prophesying.

A more serious one is speaking from evil spirits. Saul was filled with the Holy Spirit and prophesied:

> As Saul turned to leave Samuel, God changed Saul's heart, and all these signs were fulfilled that day. When they arrived at Gibeah, a procession of prophets met him; the Spirit of God came upon him in power, and he joined in their prophesying. When all those who had formerly known him saw him prophesying with the prophets, they asked each other, "What is this that has happened to the son of Kish? Is Saul also among the prophets?" (1 Sam 10:9–11 NIV; also 1 Sam 10:6–7)

Later on, when he nursed envy and jealousy against David, an evil spirit filled him, and he prophesied but he wanted to kill David.

> And from that time on Saul kept a jealous eye on David. The next day an evil spirit from God came forcefully upon Saul. He was prophesying in his house, while David was playing the harp, as he usually did. Saul had a spear in his hand and he hurled it, saying to himself, "I'll pin David to the wall." But David eluded him twice. (1 Sam 18:9–11 NIV)

The sequence is that Saul kept a jealous eye on David before the evil spirit took control of him to kill David. The thought of killing him was already in his mind. The evil spirit was enforcing what he had conceived already. Often this is what evil spirits do, enforcing people to carry out their own evil inclinations. When the Spirit of God came upon Saul he prophesied, when an evil spirit also came upon him, he prophesied. The most complicated aspect is that later on, the Spirit of God fell upon him and he prophesied again (from the Spirit of God):

> So Saul went to Naioth at Ramah. But the Spirit of God came even upon him, and he walked along prophesying until he came to Naioth. He stripped off his robes and also prophesied in Samuel's presence. He lay that way all that day and night. This is why people say, "Is Saul also among the prophets?" (1 Sam 19:23–24 NIV)

How could a person know whether Saul was prophesying from God or the devil? This is one of the reasons why there is the need to judge prophecy, whether it comes from an ordained prophet or apostle. All manifestations need to be examined by the word of God and people of God (1 Cor 14:29–33; 1 Thess 5:19–22).

Earlier, we referred to the story from 1 Kgs 13:13–34 about a young prophet and an older one, who claimed an angel spoke to him, but he was lying (1 Kgs 13:18, 20–21). His lie led the younger prophet to death, yet the word of God came to him afterwards, and he prophesied again. We must weigh everything that people claim to have received from the Lord.

HOLDING ON TO THE WRONG MESSAGE

There is the tendency to hold on to one's mistake when he goes wrong. Samuel nearly got it wrong by attempting to anoint Eliab, but he corrected it. Nathan got it wrong when David consulted him about building a temple for the Lord. He asked David to do what was in his heart, but that was not God's will. Later, Nathan went back to correct it (2 Sam 7:1–3, 4–17).

Prophets are human beings and they can get it wrong. Paul has said, "For now we see in a mirror dimly, but then face to face. Now I know in part; then I shall fully, even as I have been fully known" (1 Cor 13:12). The prophet may interpret his own impressions as the word of God. This may cause him to prophesy from his interpretation or understanding. A prophet or an apostle must be able to say I got this one wrong, rather than to hold on to something that is wrong. Holding on to a wrong message may mislead many people, especially younger Christians.

TENDENCY TO PLEASE PEOPLE

There is also the tendency to please people. This may come about if pressure is mounted on the prophet to prophesy when he has not got a message. There are many occasions when people expect prophets to prophesy. These include December 31 watch night services, election periods, economic hardships, droughts, famines, plagues, national calamities, when there are misfortunes, when fasting are observed, and when a "famous" person is sick. During such periods, pressure is mounted on prophets to prophesy or an apostle to bring a revelation. People often know what they want to hear, and there is the strong tendency to "sing" to what the people want to hear. In the Old Testament, some prophets were giving vain comfort instead of calling people to repentance. Jeremiah shows his concern in Lamentation, and so did Ezekiel:

> The visions of your prophets were false and worthless; they did not expose your sin to ward off your captivity. The oracles they gave you were false and misleading. (Lam 2:14 NIV)

> I will spend my wrath against the wall and against those who covered it with whitewash. I will say to you, "The wall is gone and so are those who whitewashed it, those prophets of Israel who prophesied to Jerusalem and saw visions of peace for her when there was no peace, declares the Sovereign Lord." (Ezek 13:15–16 NIV)

These prophets were prophesying what the people wanted to hear. This trend continues, where people often pronounce God's blessing instead causing people to turn away from their sins. In every generation, people want to hear of blessings instead of rebuking or repentance. The messengers of God must hear from him, and speak what he says.

TENDENCY TO GOSSIP ON REVELATIONS

The Lord may reveal something to you concerning a person. You must keep it and never share it with others in a form of gossip. Samuel was able to keep the revelation until Eli asked of it. His responsibility was not to go about telling people that the Lord was going to destroy the family of Eli. That would have been prophetic gossip.

Interpretations of revelations are difficult. Sometimes the meaning you give to revelations may not be the same as what the Lord intends to communicate, thus speaking to others on such things may amount to slandering or gossiping. You may only share with another, if you intend to have a rather mature contribution to the revelation.

Unfortunately, many people pass on such obscure revelations to others and create unnecessary tension in families, churches and societies.

TENDENCY TO BE SUPER SPIRITUAL

There is the tendency to feel very special and awesome. One of the things Samuel did that was good was that when the Lord spoke to him, he continued to do the work that he used to do. Once a prediction comes true, some people may begin to make the prophetic person what he is not, and if he is not careful, he will assume that position. Often, it is the people who cause the humble people of God to sway.

The prophet must remain a normal person with passions and desires. He should not make himself different from others to pretend to be above them spiritually. The gift of the prophet is of the same grace that the Lord gives to people as apostles, evangelists, pastors and teachers. The Lord is the source of all.

Once I was traveling on a train in the UK and saw somebody who appeared to be a pastor, reading his Bible. I greeted him but he failed to respond. The way he looked at me showed that he was in a very high realm. Perhaps, he felt very spiritual at the time so he thought he could not respond to someone's greeting. Spirituality includes one's relationship with others; one must show love to others as Christ would do.

Chapter 31

How to Test Prophetic Utterance

THE CHALLENGE OF TESTING PROPHECY

All we have discussed so far should help us identify a true prophet, apostle, or a messenger of God. However, one of the greatest challenges the church continues to face from the New Testament times till today is the importance of testing prophecy, and other manifestation of the Holy Spirit. Many people assume that once the Lord is speaking, there is no need for testing. Attempts to question the validity of a prophetic utterance may paint a person as a skeptic. Nonetheless, the Lord Jesus Christ himself spoke about the need to test prophets. Similarly, apostles including John, Peter, Paul, and Jude all spoke about false prophets and the need to judge them. Although judging prophecy is implicit in the discussions made, this chapter will still throw some light on it.

MONTANISM AS AN EXAMPLE OF DIFFICULTY OF TESTING PROPHECY

One of the first challenges the early church had with the testing of prophecy was the emergence of a movement which was later called Montanism, named after its leader Montanus. Montanus was a new convert who started to prophesy around AD 135.[1] Some of the reports show that he was a priest of Apollos (or Cybele) before he became Christian. He claimed to prophesy under the power of the Holy Spirit. He was joined by two

---

1. Scholars are not certain about the date. It is dated between AD 135 to 177.

women, Prisca (Priscilla) and Maximilla, who also claimed to prophesy under the inspiration of the Holy Spirit. Later, their followers claimed to trace their prophetic gifts to prophets Quadratus and Ammia who were members of the church of Philadelphia. These two prophets were believed to have been part of a prophetic line dated back to Agabus and the four daughters of Philip in Acts 21:8–10.[2] The mode of their prophecy was first a concern. Some accounts indicate that on the pretext of possession, Montanus would be in a sort of frenzy and ecstasy, and then begin to babble and utter some strange things, and prophesy in a manner which was contrary to the tradition handed over to them from the beginning. Under such inspiration, the prophets claimed they could not resist the spirit. The teachings were initially accepted but some new things which emerged from their teachings became a concern to the leadership.

Their claim to be inspired by the Holy Spirit implied that some things could be added to the teaching of the apostles and, thus, the prophecies had to be accepted without testing. They prophesied that the New Jerusalem would soon descend to the earth between two towns in Phrygia, Pepuza and Tymion. The leaders and their adherents went to settle there. They emphasized religious moral rigorism from their followers: females were forbidden to wear ornaments; virgins were asked to wear veils; marriage was discouraged, and second marriage after the death of a spouse or divorced was prohibited. They promoted long periods of fasting, and required followers not to flee from martyrdom. Their strict emphasis on morality attracted some key leaders, but others were really concerned about the new teachings. As the movement was not ready to obey the directives of the leadership, Montanism was considered a heresy and was therefore suppressed. However, it had some followers until the eighth century, when it is said that Emperor Leo III ordered their conversion and re-baptism. Some accounts show that they refused, locked themselves in the place of worship, set the building on fire, and destroyed themselves.[3]

---

2. "Among those that were celebrated at that time was Quadratus, who, report says, was renowned along with the daughters of Philip for his prophetical gifts. And there were many others besides these who were known in those days, and who occupied the first place among the successors of the apostles." Eusebius of Caesarea, *Church History*.

3. Shelton, *History of the Christian Church*, 267–72; Frend, *Early Church*, 69–71

TESTING, SPONTANEITY, AND THEIR CHALLENGES

The following is to help you to test whether a given prophecy is from God or not. In other words, a good prophet may occasionally speak from the flesh if he is not constantly in fellowship with the Lord. This is one of the reasons why the Bible entrusts us to test all prophecies. Every mature Christian should be able to weigh a prophetic utterance to find out whether it is from the Lord or from other sources. The knowledge of the Scripture helps in this exercise. However, often people want to have a simpler way of knowing how to test a prophecy. The following may be helpful:

The Bible directly instructs Christians not to despise prophecy, however, we are to test it:

> Rejoice always, pray without ceasing, give thanks in all circumstances; for this is the will of God in Christ Jesus for you. Do not quench the Spirit. Do not despise prophecies, but test everything; hold fast what is good. Abstain from every form of evil. (1 Thess 5:16–22 ESV)

The text implies that failure to test prophecy is overlooking the instruction of God. Thus, testing prophecy should not become difficult for people who think that testing is like discarding it. With the teaching of Moses, the Lord Jesus and the apostles, it is absolutely important that everyone tests an utterance of prophecy to know its source, so as not to be deceived by the evil one. In many circumstances, prophecy thrives on spontaneity. Many people think that the one with the gift of prophecy should be allowed to speak as one receives the message from the Lord. In fact, some people even believe that once the message is not spoken immediately it is no longer prophetic. However, it has already been shown that the Old Testament prophets did not have the luxury of sharing their messages in church buildings. In many cases, the Lord gave the messages to them through prayers and they had to carry the messages to where the Lord would direct them. Some of them wrote or dictated to others to write (Jer 17:19–21; 29:1–3; 36:1–2; 45:1–2; Isa 7:3–4). While spontaneity is an important aspect of prophecy, when it comes to directive prophecy, that is, a prophetic message which gives instructions to church or church leaders, it is appropriate that these are written down for consideration by the collective leadership before it is passed on to the church.

Hill, a prophet himself, sees this as the first causality of the institutionalization of prophecy.[4] Fairly, it has been observed that anytime spontaneity is allowed in the prophetic, there is bound to be institutional growth. However, sooner than later, there will be chaos, which becomes a great concern to leadership. This concern eventually leads to control of the prophetic, which in due course brings about institutionalization. Institutionalization can be well handled by charismatic leaders who, upon seeing the dangers take the lead to lay down principles for judging prophecy. Conversely, on the demise of such leaders if their successors are not able to catch the spirit in which they set down the principles, the charisma is bound to die. Nevertheless, it is better to lay down principles to guide the prophetic than to leave impostors to cause disorder leading to the mass destruction of people. Father Sullivan's interpretation of Matt 7:22–23 is relevant for us: "Their description as 'ravenous wolves who can come in sheep's clothing' suggests that the bad fruit which they bear can be understood as the harm which they do to the Christian communities in which they exercise their pretended gift of prophecy."[5]

There have been great disasters in areas where the prophetic ministry was not managed well. In time past, some people claiming to hear from God have emerged, deceiving many into selling out their material possessions in anticipation of the second coming of Christ and the imminent destruction of the world. A United States citizen, faith preacher, and healer James Warren Jones (Jim Jones) led his followers in 1978 to commit mass suicide in Guyana. Similarly, in the year 2000, an estimated number of 338 members of the Movement for Restoration of the Ten Commandments of God in Uganda all died in a devastating fire which was considered a group suicide initiated by their leader.[6] Currently, there are many of such prophetic gimmicks and manipulations going on in many countries on the guises of prophecies. People are commanded to eat grass, instructed to drink poison, some are stepped on, and women are requested to remove their underwear. It is better to manage prophecies than allow people to destroy themselves. The house of God is a place of order where every gift must be used for the building up of God's people (1 Cor 14:1–5, 33, 39–40).

---

4. Hill, *Prophecy Past and Present*, 258.
5. Sullivan, *Charism and Charismatic Renewal*, 106
6. Venter, "Doomsday Movements in Africa," 156–73.

BASIC ISSUES TO CONSIDER

Writing down prophecies and sharing with church leaders should all be part of testing prophecies. These exercises are all spiritual activities. Something as briefly as stated here may help to test the genuineness of a given prophecy.[7]

- Does the prophetic utterance conform to the standard principles of Scripture? If the prophecy is not based upon the word of God, but goes against it, you must know outright that it does not come from the Lord. The Lord will not contradict himself that way.

- Does the lifestyle of the person who uttered it conform to Scripture (Matt 7:15–16)? Jesus emphasizes that by their fruits you shall know them. One of the things that many false prophets cannot copy is living the true life of the Christian. They can talk, convince, preach and even claim to perform miracles. But they cannot live the true Christian life. You will know them by their fruits. This is one of the best ways to find out a true prophet.

- Does it edify, exhort, encourage or create confusion (1 Cor 14:3)? Prophecy is supposed to encourage people, thus, when prophecy divides and causes confusion, care needs to be taken. Prophecy is supposed to edify.

- Do the individual Christians around have inner witness regarding the authenticity of the prophetic utterance (1 Cor 14:33)? The Spirit of God in the people will give them peace as a true prophetic utterance is taking place. When there is no inner peace concerning a prophecy, care needs to be taken.

- Does the body have cooperative peace regarding the content of the prophecy (1 Cor 14:33; cf. 1 Cor 14:24–26)? The body of Christ is supposed to be building up through the prophetic message. If the message is not building the body but creates confusion and tension, the Lord might not be in it.

- Does sanctified common sense accept it as of the Lord or reject it (cf. 1 Cor 14:36–40)? The Lord has given us common sense to use. If what the prophecy says completely goes against sanctified common

---

7. This is developed from the Church of Pentecost's handbook of testing prophetic utterance. The Church of Pentecost General Headquarters, *Ministers' Hand Book*, 89–90.

sense of the believer, care needs to be taken. For example, if a prophecy directs you as an individual to drink petrol, you must ask yourself of the benefits of drinking petrol. Again, in what way does the church or the people around benefit from you drinking petrol? Common sense is one of the best gifts that the Lord has given to us, especially as Christians. We must make good use of it.

- Once an utterance or a manifestation completely goes against some of these, you must be careful to accept it. Remember you are responsible for hearing the voice of God yourself. You cannot blame someone for deceiving you. The Holy Spirit is in you; you must not be deceived by others. This is where John's teaching is extremely important:

> I am writing these things to you about those who are trying to lead you astray. As for you, the anointing you received from him remains in you, and you do not need anyone to teach you. But as his anointing teaches you about all things and as that anointing is real, not counterfeit—just as it has taught you, remain in him. (1 John 2:26–27 NIV)

The Apostle John has said it all. The Holy Spirit lives in you to show you the truth. Do not despise the true word of God and accept what is not true. May the Lord be with you!

Conclusion

This study has shown that since creation God has been communicating with human beings. In the Old Testament, his spokesperson was the prophet; although God also used some apostolic figures, such as Joseph, Moses, Deborah, and Nehemiah, the prophet was the messenger of God during the period. The Lord raised prophets and then called them. The call had to come in such a dramatic way that left an indelible mark on the person, who could no longer live for himself. A number of gifts constituted a prophet. These include the gift of prophecy, the word of knowledge (including visions and dreams), the word of wisdom, the discerning of spirits, the gift of teaching, the gift of exhortation, and the gift of music. The prophet was a gift to God's people.

The functions of the prophet included reminding Israel of the terms of God's covenants, explaining the principles underlying the law of God and speaking to contemporary issues. He had access to the council of God, carried the authority of God, foretold the future, and interpreted signs.

The operation of prophecy was slightly changed in the New Testament. The Old Testament indicated that in the new covenant, the Holy Spirit would fall upon all flesh. This was fulfilled in the New Testament, where there was the potential for everybody to prophesy. Yet, it was shown that some could possess the gift of prophecy and others could be called to the office of the prophet. The gift of speaking in diverse tongues and the gift of interpretation,[1] which were not in the Old Testament were shown as additional gifts that could be exercised by the New Testament prophet.

---

1. With the possible exemption of Daniel, who interpreted the handwriting on the wall (Dan 5).

CONCLUSION

The coming of our Lord Jesus Christ changed the system where the prophet was the messenger of God. Our Lord Jesus was not just a prophet, He was presented as God's word himself. In Jesus, the ministration of God's word was metamorphosed from just being a spoken word from God to an embodiment of the human personality. The very human nature of Jesus was the word. He did not need to say, thus says the Lord. When he opened his mouth, it was the word of God, when he acted without speaking it was God's word. Thus, the Lord Jesus operated as the apostle par excellence. In him combined the offices of the leader (king), the prophet, and the high priesthood. Consequently, after his death and resurrection, his chosen, trained, empowered, and commissioned apostles, continued to do his work.

It was pointed out that his death and resurrection began an era, which was termed as the apostolic age. In this era, the apostles become the mouthpiece of God, the messengers of God. The first group of apostles were the Twelve selected by the Lord Jesus during his ministry on earth, and the additional one appointed by eleven apostles after the death of Judas. The next group of apostles were the two—James and Paul—who were called after the resurrection of Christ. Their apostolic callings were shown as something that the Lord Jesus used to demystify the apostolic office as limited to the Twelve. It was contended that besides these two well-recognized apostles, there were other persons whose ministries validated them as apostles. These included Jude, Barnabas, Apollos, Silas, Timothy, and Titus. Like the prophet, the apostle must have "a call," "leadership and administration or governance ability," and "signs, wonders and miracles." "Signs, wonders and miracles" often followed the one who possessed the gift of faith, the gifts of healing and the gift of miracles. These graces were shown as the basic gifts of the apostolic office.

The foundational differences between the apostle and the prophet are that the functions of the prophets in the Old Testament fundamentally helped the leaders or the kings to govern the people of God, explaining the contents of God's ways to them, and warning Israel of the repercussion of failure to obey God's covenant. The prophets were not the leaders of God's people. In contrast, the apostles carried the word of God along to the people and also led them. The apostolic office was shown to be a combination of the ministry of the prophets and that of the Lord Jesus Christ.

This also implies that our Lord Jesus' era was different from the apostolic era. The coming of our Lord Jesus demonstrated to us that God could still speak through a person without saying, "Thus says the Lord."

And that the human body is not necessarily evil. However, Jesus was first, the word of God, before he was clothed with the human body. Whereas, with the apostles, the flesh comes first before the word. What this means is that the ministry of the apostles would come about through the revelation of the Lord Jesus (the word) in the human body, and mixed with the personality of the person, before presentation. The implication of this is that if the individual apostle has not completely surrendered to the Lord there could be pollution of the word. Nevertheless, in Jesus there could never be pollution. Thus, an apostle must live a consecrated life.

The original apostles worked with leaders including elders or bishops and deacons. These officers were in charge of the local churches with the apostles having general oversight of the work. The apostles could visit or send others to visit and spend some time with the believers, strengthening and encouraging them. They could also write letters to direct or strengthen the believers. They governed the church, and were the stewards of God's treasure.

One of the purposes of the study was to find out why there was a drop from the apostles to bishops in the "governance" of the church. An analysis of the lives of some church fathers and available literature came out with some possible reasons that caused the drop from apostles to bishops as leaders of the church. The church fathers, who had been ordained as bishops, did not ordain other people as apostles, neither did they recognize themselves as apostles. The church fathers considered themselves as the successors of the apostles. They built upon the ministry of the apostles. What this means is that the Lord has not come out with a new order besides that which was climaxed in the apostles—that is, the Holy Spirit combining with the human personality to communicate the voice of God to people. In other words, apostles continue to lead the people of God.

Accordingly, it came out that some church fathers operated as apostles, yet they were not designated as apostles. It was also made known that apostles had always been in the church, although they had not been labeled so. It was pointed out that still, in many denominations, bishops or arch-bishops, and superintendent ministers function and operate as apostles. However, there appears to be a collective fear within many denominations to confer the name apostle on such people. Taking a cue from James, who brought to the attention of his audience that Elijah was a prophet like us, it was argued that the original apostles need to be considered as human beings just as we are. They were granted the grace to do the work of the Lord because they availed themselves to the Lord. The God who used them is the same who works today and needs people who are available to do the work of the ministry. The contemporary church was entreated not to mystify the term apostle or deify the "Twelve," but rather pray to the Lord of the harvest to raise more apostles and prophets in the church of today. The world is speeding so much that we need apostles and prophets of high caliber in our generation to spearhead the kingdom business. The question, therefore, is not, "Are there apostles today?" but that the Lord will raise more apostles for our generation.

It was pointed out that the Lord would continue to communicate with his people. God's people, especially apostles and prophets, would continue to receive revelations from the Lord. Therefore, a chunk of a session was allocated to discussing how to receive a revelation. It was shown that the starting point of a revelation is the prompting, which is like a flashing light or an enlightenment. It develops into an idea or a thought which then becomes a burden. The burden is formed by adding understanding to the prompting and the idea. The burden needs to be expressed through words. Two types of words were identified: divine words and human words. The divine words are words that are received through the human spirit, which is married with the Holy Spirit. These words are short, simple, and sharp. The divine words alone may be too strong for human consumption, hence, the need for human words in delivering the message. The human words come through a person's experience in life, maturity in the Lord, knowledge of Scripture, and how they are able to apply the Scripture to life situations. The burden would only be offloaded after the task had been discharged successfully. Once the burden had been released, it meant that the servant of God had discharged his duty faithfully.

It was emphasized that God always speaks, but sometimes people do not hear because of some hindrances. Often, people want to hear the voice immediately without paying the price of waiting or living right before God. The pressure of the people could cause some prophets to prophesy without hearing from God. Sin in people's lives could distort the voice of God. A determined mind might also hinder people from hearing God's voice.

It was established that apostles and prophets are human beings who experience human limitations. On the positive side, a good prophet carries along the presence of God. The Lord himself endorses the person, and so do others recognize him as the servant of God. Besides, the servant of God must live a life of integrity.

Some of the flaws which could bring the downfall of prophets and apostles were brought out. There is the tendency to hold on to one's view despite the fact the Lord might be directing him differently. The Prophet Samuel was cited as an example of a good prophet who nearly held on to his view, when the Lord instructed him on the request made by the Israelites. There is also the tendency of using prophecy to manipulate decisions. The prophet or apostle could also incite troubles for families, societies, churches, and nations. More serious is the possibility that the prophet or apostle could prophesy from other voices, especially the flesh. Unless the prophet or the apostle is broken in spirit, there is the tendency to hold on to one's mistake when he goes wrong. There is also the tendency to please people. This comes about if pressure is mounted on the prophet to prophesy when he has not received a message from the Lord.

It was emphasized that for the fact that apostles and prophets were human beings who could also fall into the trap of the evil one, there was always the need to test all manifestations. Citing from the early church experience, where some manifestations were tested and rejected, it was pointed out that the need to test prophecies must not be taken lightly. Failure to test prophecy is overlooking the instruction of Scripture, which is of itself disobedience. In many circumstances, prophecy thrives on spontaneity and, thus, many people think that those with prophetic messages should be allowed to speak, without any delay, since they receive their messages from the Lord. Some people even believed that nothing besides spontaneity was prophecy. However, it was pointed out that while spontaneity is an important aspect of prophecy, when it comes to directive prophecy, that is, a prophetic message which gives instructions to church or churches leaders, it is always appropriate that they are written down or shared first with the leader for the collective leadership consideration before passing on such messages to the church.

It was reiterated that the knowledge of Scripture should help every mature Christian to weigh a prophetic utterance to find out whether it was from the Lord or other sources. Nevertheless, a simpler way of knowing how to test prophecy includes asking the following questions. Does the prophetic utterance conform to the standard principles of Scripture? Does the lifestyle of the person who uttered it conform to Scripture? Does it edify, exhort, encourage, instill fear, or create confusion? Do the individual Christians around have inner witness regarding the authenticity of the prophetic utterance? Does the body have cooperative peace regarding the content of the prophecy? Does sanctified common sense accept it as of the Lord or reject it? People need to be seriously careful about manifestations that fail to meet these standards. Apostles and prophets are the messengers of God.

Bibliography

1 Clement. Sacred Text, 1926. https://www.sacred-texts.com/bib/lbob/lbob15.htm.

Adams, Noah. "What Hymn Did Jesus Sing at the Last Supper?" https://www.cbcelgin.net/single-post/2018/03/28/What-Hymn-Did-Jesus-Sing-at-the-Last-Supper.

Agnew, Francis H. "On the Origin of the Term *Apostolos*." *Catholic Biblical Quarterly* 38 (1976) 49–53.

———."The Origin of the NT Apostle-Concept: A Review of Research." *Journal of Biblical Literature* 105 (1986) 75–96.

Ahn, Yongnan Jeon. *Interpretation of Tongues and Prophecy in 1 Corinthians 12–14: With a Pentecostal Hermeneutics*. Blandford Forum, UK: Deo, 2013.

Amanor, Kwabena J. Darkwa. *Prophecy of Divination*. Achimota, Ghana: Crossroads, 2016.

The Apostolic Church. *The Apostolic Church: Its Principles and Practices*. Penygroes: Apostolic, 1937.

The Apostolic Constitution. New York: Appleton, 1848. https://www.britannica.com/topic/Apostolic-Constitutions.

The Assemblies of God. "The Twenty Third General Council: Minutes and Constitution with Bye Laws Revised." Seattle, Washington, September 9–14, 1949.

Aune, David E. *Prophecy in Early Christianity and the Ancient Mediterranean World*. Grand Rapids: Eerdmans, 1983.

Barclays, William. *The Book of Hebrews*. New Daily Study Bible series. London: Westminster John Knox, 2002.

Barnett, P. W. "Apostle." In *Dictionary of Paul and His Letters*, edited by Gerald F. Hawthorne, 45–51. Nottingham, UK: InterVarsity, 2018.

Barrett, C. K. "Shaliah and Apostle." In *Donum gentilicium: New Testament Studies in Honour of David Daube*, edited by Ernst Bammel et al., 88–102. Oxford: Clarendon, 1978.

Bickle, Mike. *Growing in the Prophetic*. With Michael Sullivant. Eastbourne, UK: Kingsway, 1995.

Bilezikian, Gilbert. *Beyond Sex Roles: What the Bible Says about a Woman's Place in Church and Family*. Ada, MI: Baker, 1989.

Blum, Edwin A. "Jude." In *The Expositors Bible Commentary*, edited by Frank E. Gaebelein et al., 381–96. Grand Rapids: Zondervan, 1981.

Body, D. D. "Irvin, Edward." In *The New International Dictionary of Pentecostal and Charismatic Movements*, edited by Stanley M. Burgess, 803–4. Grand Rapids: Zondervan, 2007.

Brown, Raymond E. *An Introduction to the New Testament*. New York: Doubleday, 1997.

Cannistraci, David. *The Gifts of Apostle: A Biblical Look at the Apostleship and How God Is Using It to Bless His Church Today*. Ventura,CA: Regal, 1996.

Cartledge, David. *The Apostolic Revolution: The Restoration of Apostles and Prophets in the Assemblies of God in Australia*. Chester Hill, Australia: Paraclete Institute, 2000.

Chironna, Mark. *The Prophetic Perspective: Seeing and Seizing Our God-Intended Future*. Shippensburg, PA: Destiny Image, 2013.

The Church of Pentecost. "Annual Report on Volta Region for the 24th Session of the Church Council." Kumasi. 12–14 April, 1986.

The Church of Pentecost General Headquarters. *Minister Hand Book*. Accra: Pentecost, 2018.

Clarke, Adams. "Ephesians 2:20." In *Adam Clarke's Commentary*. Electronic database. Biblesoft, 2006.

Deere, Jack. *Surprised by the Voice of God: How God Speaks to Us Today*. Eastbourne, UK: Kingsway, 1996.

The Didache. Translated and edited by J. B. Lightfoot. Zeeland, MI: Legacy Icons, 2016. https://legacyicons.com/content/didache.pdf.

Editors of Encyclopaedia Britannica. "Shepherd of Hermas". *Encyclopedia Britannica*, October 15, 2021. https://www.britannica.com/topic/Shepherd-of-Hermas.

Eusebius of Caesarea. *Church History*. Documenta Catholica Omnia, AD 340. http://www.documentacatholicaomnia.eu/03d/0265-0339,_Eusebius_Caesariensis,_Church_History,_EN.pdf.

Evans, Roderick Levi. *The Apostolic Ministry: Exploring the Apostolic Office and Gift*. Camden, NC: Abundant Truth, 2005.

Fee, Gordon D. *The First Epistle to the Corinthians*. Grand Rapids: Eerdmans, 1987.

Fife, Eric S. *The Holy Spirit: Common Sense and the Bible*. Grand Rapids: Zondervan, 1978.

Frend, W. H. C. *The Early Church: From the Beginnings to 461*. London: SCM, 1982.

Geitvett, R. Douglas, and Holly Pivec. *God's Super-Apostles: Encountering the Worldwide Prophets and Movements*. Wooster, OH: Weaver, 2014.

General Council of the Assemblies of God. "End Time Revival—Spirit-Led and Spirit-Controlled: A Response Paper to Resolution 16." Statement adopted by the General Presbytery of the Assemblies of God, August 11, 2000. https://static1.squarespace.com/static/57982559be6594e06f6f1dbd/t/57e06f8ee6f2e1f209ba906a/1474326416763/pp_endtime_revival.pdf.

Gibson Annor Antwi. *Myth or Mystery: The "Bio-Autobiography" of Apostle Professor Opoku Onyinah*. London: Inved, 2016.

Goll, James W. *The Coming of Prophetic Revolution: A Call for Passionate Consecrated Warriors*. Grand Rapids: Chosen, 2001.

Grudem, Wayne A., ed. *Are Miraculous Gifts for Today? An Investigation into the Ministry of the Spirit of God Today*. Dallas: Biblical Studies, 2005.

———. *The Gift of Prophecy in the New Testament and Today*. Eastbourne, UK: Kingsway, 1998.

Guignebert, Charles. *The Jewish World in the Times of Jesus*. New York: University Books, 1959.

Gyimah, James S. "The Ministry of Apostles and Prophets." In *Tell the Next Generations: Lecture Notes on the Annual Themes of the Church of Pentecost*, vol 3, edited by Opoku Onyinah. Accra: CoP Literature Committee, 2013.

Hamon, Bill. *Apostles and Prophets and the Coming Moves of God: God's End-Time Plans for His Church and the Planet Earth*. Santa Rosa Beach: Christian International, 1997.

———. *The Eternal Church*. Santa Rosa Beach, FL: Christian International, 1981.

Hathaway, Malcom R. "The Role of William Oliver Hutchinson and His Apostolic Faith in the Formation of British Pentecostal Churches." *Journal of the European Pentecostal Theological Association* 14 (1996) 40–54.

Hendriksen, William. *Luke*. New Testament Commentary. Edinburgh: Banner of Truth, 1979.

———. *Romans*. Vol. 1, *Chapters 1–8*. Edinburgh: Banner of Truth, 1980.

Hill, Clifford. "The Debate over the Muratorian Fragment and the Development of the Canon." *Westminster Theological Journal* 57 (Fall 1995) 437–52.

———. *Prophecy Past and Present: An Exploration of the Prophetic Ministry in the Bible and the Church Today*. Ann Arbor: Servant, 1991.

Hill, David. *New Testament Prophesy*. Atlanta: John Knox, 1979.

Hocken, Peter. "Charismatic Movement." In *International Dictionary of Pentecostal and Charismatic Movements*, edited by Stanley M. Burgess, 477–520. Grand Rapids: Zondervan, 2007.

———. *Streams of Renewal: Origins and Early Development of the Charismatic Movement in Great Britain*. Exeter: Paternoster, 1986.

Hoppin, Ruth. *Priscilla's Letter: Finding the Author of the Epistle to the Hebrews*. Fort Bragg, CA: Lost Coast, 2000.

Ignatius. *To the Philadelphians*. Salem Web Network, 2019. https://www.biblestudytools.com/history/early-church-fathers/ante-nicene/vol-1-apostolic-with-justin-martyr-irenaeus/ignatius/epistle-of-ignatius-philadelphians.html.

Irenaeus of Antioch. *Against Heresies*. https://www.newadvent.org/fathers/0103.htm.

———. *To Polycarp*. Eerdmans, 1967. https://www.catholicculture.org/culture/library/view.cfm?recnum=3836.

Jacobs, Cindy. *The Voice of God: How God Speaks Personal and Corporately to His Children Today*. Minneapolis: Chosen, 2014.

Johnson, Alan R. *Apostolic Functions in the 21st Century Missions*. Pasadena: William Carey, 2009.

Jones, Evan David. "Williams, Daniel Powell ('Pastor Dan'; 1882–1947), Founder and First President of the Apostolic Church." *Dictionary of Welsh Biography*, 2001. https://biography.wales/article/s2-WILL-POW-1882.

Joyner, Rick. *The Apostolic Ministry*. Fort Mill, SC: MorningStar, 2004.

Kinnear, Angus I. *Against the Tide: The Story of Watchman Nee*. Eastbourne, UK: Victory, 1974.

Koduah, Alfred. "The Role of Directive Prophecy in the Selection of Ecclesiastical leadership: The Church of Pentecost Experience." In *Impacting Generations: Hearing and Obeying the Lord*. Accra: Literature Committee of the Church of Pentecost, 2016.

Kraybill, Donald B. *The Upside-Down Kingdom*. Rev. ed. Waterloo, ON: Herald, 1990.

Lathrop, John N. *Apostles, Prophets, Evangelists, Pastors, and Teachers: Then and Now*. Maitland, FL: Xulon, 2008.

Lim, David. *Spiritual Gifts: A Fresh Look*. Springfield, MO: Gospel, 1991.
Lockyer, Herbert. *All the Apostles of the Bible*. Grand Rapids, Zondervan, 1972.
Luce, Ron. *Faith at the Speed of Light: Experiencing Exponential Growth while Surfing the Wave of Change*. Tustin, CA: Trilogy Christian, 2019.
Luxmoore, Jonathan. "As Dutch Parishes Close, Some Catholics Just Quit Going to Church." *American: The Jesuit Review*, January 21, 2020. https://www.americamagazine.org/politics-society/2020/01/21/dutch-parishes-close-some-catholics-just-quit-going-church.
Martin, Walter. *The Kingdom of the Cults: The Definitive Work on the Subject*. Edited by Ravi Zacharias. Minneapolis: Bethany House, 2003.
McBirnie, William Steuart. *The Search for the Twelve Apostles*. Wheaton, IL: Tyndale, 1979.
McDonnell, Killian, and George T. Montague. *Christian Initiation and Baptism: Evidence from the First Eight Centuries*. 2nd ed. Collegeville: Liturgical, 1994.
McDowell, Sean. *The Fate of the Apostles: Examining the Martyrdom Accounts of the Closest Followers of Jesus*. Farnham, UK: Ashgate, 2015.
Nee, Watchman. *The Ministry of God's Word*. New York: Christian Fellowship, 1971.
———. *The Spiritual Man*. New York: Christian Fellowship, 1977.
Onyinah, Opoku. "Divine Healing." In *Tenets of the Church of Pentecost*, edited by Opoku Onyinah et al., 295–339. Accra: Church of Pentecost, 2020.
———. *God with Us*. Accra: Pentecost, 2007.
———. *No One Will See God and Live*. Accra: Pentecost, 2010.
———. *Spiritual Warfare: A Centre for Pentecostal Theology Short Introduction*. Cleveland: CPT, 2012.
Patzia, Arthur G. *Ephesians, Colossians, Philemon*. New International Bible Commentary. Peabody: Hendrickson, 1990.
Petts, David. *Body Builders: Gifts to Make God's People Grow*. Mattersey, UK: Mattersey Hall, 2002.
Polycarp. *To the Philippians*. Palmer Translation, 2015. https://bibletranslation.ws/down/Polycarp_Epistle_To_The_Philippians.pdf.
Price, Paula A. *The ABC's of Apostleship: An Introductory Overview; Apostleship from God to You*. Book 1. Tulsa: Flaming Vision, 2009.
———. *The Prophetic Handbook: A Guide to Prophecy and Its Operation*. New Kensington, PA: Whitaker, 2008.
Riss, Richard M. "Latter Rain Movement." In *International Dictionary of Pentecostal and Charismatic Movements*, edited by Stanley M. Burgess, 832–33. Grand Rapids: Zondervan, 2007.
———. "Latter Rain Movement of 1948." *Pneuma* 4 (1982) 32–45.
———. *A Survey of 20th Century Revival Movements in North America*. Peabody: Hendrickson, 1988.
Robeck, Cecil Mel. "Christian Unity and Pentecostal Mission: A Contradiction?" In *Pentecostal Mission and Global Christianity*, edited by Wonsuk Ma et al., 182–206. Oxford: Regnum, 2014.
———. "Discerning the Spirit in the Life of the Church." In *The Church in the Movement of the Spirit*, edited by William R. Barr and Rena M. Yocum. 32–33. Grand Rapids: Eerdmans, 1994.
———. "Evangelism and Ecumenism: One Hundred Years after Edinburgh, Part I." *Lutheran Forum* 44 (Summer 2010) 33–39.

———. "Fuller's Ecumenical Vision." *Theology, News & Notes* 57 (Fall 2010) 19–22, 28. http://documents.fuller.edu/news/pubs/tnn/2010_Fall/6_ecumenical_vision.asp.

———. "Pentecostal Ecumenism: Overcoming the Challenges—Reaping the Benefits." Part 1. *Journal of the European Pentecostal Theological Association* 34 (2014) 113–32.

———. "Pentecostal Ecumenism: Overcoming the Challenges—Reaping the Benefits." Part 2. *Journal of the European Pentecostal Theological Association* 35 (2015) 5–17.

———. "Roman Catholic—Pentecostal Dialogue: Challenges and Lessons for Living Together." In *Pentecostal Power: Expressions, Faith and Politics of Latin American Pentecostalism*, edited by Calvin Smith, 249–76. Leiden: Brill, 2010.

Ruthven, John. *On the Cessation of the Charismata: The Protestant Polemic on Postbiblical Miracles*. Sheffield: Sheffield Academic, 1997.

Schillebeeckx, Edward. *The Church with a Human Face: A New and Expanded Theology of Ministry*. London: SCM, 1985.

Schmithals, Walter. *The Office of Apostle in the Early Church*. Translated by John E. Steely. Nashville: Abingdon, 1969.

Shelton, Henry. *History of the Christian Church*. Vol. 1, *The Early Church History*. 1894. Peabody: Hendrickson, 1988.

Starr, Lee Anna. *The Bible Status of Woman*. Zarephath, NJ: Pillar of Fire, 1955.

Strachan, Gordon. *The Pentecostal Theology of Ewald Irving*. 1973. Peabody: Hendrickson, 1988.

Sullivan, Francis A. *Charism and Charismatic Renewal: A Biblical and Theological Study*. Eugene, OR: Wipf and Stock, 1982.

———. *From Apostles to Bishop: The Development of the Episcopacy in the Early Church*. New York: Newman, 2001.

Synan, Vinson. *An Eye Witness Remembers the Century of the Holy Spirit*. Grand Rapids: Chosen, 2010.

Taylor, Nicholas H. "Apostolic Identity and the Conflicts in Corinth and Galatia." In *Paul and His Opponents*, edited by Stanley E. Porter, 99–127. Leiden: Brill, 2005.

———. "Conflict as Context for Defining Identity: A Study of Apostleship in the Galatian and Corinthian Letters." *HTS Teologiese Studies / Theological Studies* 59 (2003) 915–45.

Thomas, John Christopher. *A Pentecostal Reads the Book of Mormon: A Literary and Theological Introduction*. Cleveland, TN: CPT, 2016.

Thomas, Marcus. *The God of Our Fathers: Belting the Globe with the Gospel*. Belfast: Ambassador International, 2016.

Turner, Max. *The Holy Spirit and Spiritual Gifts*. Rev. ed. Carlisle: Hendrickson, 2009.

Venter, Peter M. "Doomsday Movements in Africa: Restoration of the Ten Commandments of God." *HTS Teologiese Studies / Theological Studies* 62 (2009) 156–73.

Vine, W. E. "Prophecy, Prophesy, Prophesying, Prophets." In *Vine's Expository Dictionary of Biblical Words*, edited by W. E. Vines et al., 221–22. Nashville: Nelson, 1985.

Wagner, C. Peter. *Apostle and Prophets: The Foundation of the Church*. Ventura: Regal, 2000.

———. *Apostles Today: Biblical Government for Power*. Bloomington, MN: Chosen, 2006.

———. *Church Quake: How the New Apostolic Reformation Is Shaking Up the Church As We Know It.* Ventura: Regal, 1999.
———. *The New Apostolic Churches.* Ventura: Regal, 1998.
Word in Life Study Bible. Electronic ed. Logos Library System. Nashville: Nelson, 1997.
Worsfold, James E. *The Origins of the Apostolic Church in Great Britain: With a Breviate of Its Early Missionary Endeavours.* Thorndon, New Zealand: Julian Literature, 199.

Subject Index

Aaron
    assisting Moses, 23, 24, 119, 135
    as the high priest, 137
    with Miriam challenged Moses, 25
Abel, 14, 15
Abimelech, 17, 22
Abraham
    called to keep the way of the Lord, 44
    God addressed as a prophet, 17, 21, 22–23
    God made a covenant with, 95–96
    God spoke to, 16–17
    listening to Sarah and taking Hagar, 287
    Lord sent angels to, 64
Activate Churches (organization), 5
ACTS churches, 4
Adam and Eve, 14, 43
administration of the church, 164–166, 190–193, 208
African countries, revival going on in many, 264
Agabus, as a prophet, 128, 225, 325
Against Heresies, by Irenaeus, 249
King Agrippa, Paul and, 141–142
Ahab, 298
King Ahaz of Judah, 102, 103–104, 319
Ahijah (prophet), 28, 101
AI (artificial intelligence), ethics of, 263, 264
all are one, in Christ Jesus, 206
almah, translated as young woman or a virgin, 104

Amalekites, 316
Amaniampong, James Osei, 305
Amanor, Kwabena J. Darkwa, 310
American Orthodox church, regarding Aquila as an apostle, 160
Ammia, 325
Amos, 28, 99, 105
Ananias, 62–63, 141, 149–150, 233
Ananias and Sapphira, sins of, 62
ancient literature, apostleship deductions from, 252–258
Andrew, listed as an apostle, 138
Andronicus, 161
angelic visitation, 64, 171
Anicetus, bishop of Rome, 247
Aninkorah, Emmanuel David, 1
anointing, purpose of, 222
answer, wanting an immediate, 297
Apelles, "tested and approved in Christ," 231
Apollos
    as author of the book of Hebrews, 78
    continued apostolic work, 230
    demonstrated the gift of teaching, 77
    mentored by Priscilla and Aquila, 159
    ministry of, 157–158, 331
apostle(s). *See also* disciples
    ability to teach, 186
    after the death of the original, 235–242
    appointed bishops or elders and deacons, 2, 242, 244

(apostle(s) continued)
of blessed memory, 241
call and training of other besides the original twelve, 151–160
carrying the word of God and also leading, 226
in church history, 257–258
clear sense of God's call, 142
Clement on, 244
compared to evangelists, 184–185
concern about the needy and the vulnerable, 210
constitution of, 162–173
continuing to lead the people of God, 332
criteria for a new, 139–140
dealing with sin, 195, 196
denominations fearing the term, 260
discovering additional, 11
disputing on who was the greatest among them, 148
faded away as a term, 242
faded out leaving the prophets, 239, 252
as the focus of the New Testament minister of God, 10
as foundation layers, 181
functions of, 11, 172, 190, 202, 208, 215
gift of as evident, 303
God using "to interpret the times," 195
grace to impart spiritual gifts, 203
Holy Spirit continuing to reveal things to, 207
human limitations of, 332–333
identifying, 11, 134–143, 162, 174–177
integrity of, 308
involved in the charismata, 262
James as, 152
Jesus appointed twelve, 2, 19–20
Jesus as, 137–138
Jesus continuing his work through, 176
leading people to receive baptism in the Holy Spirit, 204
limitations of, 257, 301
living above reproach, 267, 308–309, 332
making of, 144–161
managed charismata in the New Testament, 261
martyrdom of all, 199
Matthias added to, 229
meaning "to send," "to send off" or "away," or "to send forth," 136–137
as the messenger of God in the New Testament, 11, 31, 130, 132, 221
ministry of, 142–143, 163
miracles of, 172
as the mouthpiece of God, 20–21, 331
mystified the number twelve, 140
need for, 259–267
needing preparation, 146–147
never took it easy, 199
in the New Testament called by the Lord, 222
not healing by their power, 172
not misusing authority, 319
not ruling the church alone, 218
not taking glory for themselves, 171
office and ministry of used interchangeably, 9
in the Old Testament, 134–137
Old Testament approach, 21
ordination of, 222, 242
others functioning as besides the Twelve and Matthias, 140
oversight of the churches, 230
oversight of the work, 332
period of, 20–21
placing the right person in the right church, 192–193
Polycarp as, 248–249
portrayed in the *Didache* as itinerant teachers, 238
promoting unity in the body of Christ, 211
prophets or teachers later recognized as, 183
raising for our generation, 333

SUBJECT INDEX

receiving revelations, 205, 271
recognizing, 11
representing Christ, 144
respected as men but should not be deified, 261
responsibility for calling, 266–267
revelation within his very personality, 206
singing of, 91
spiritual authority of, 202–207
spiritual gifts, 163–164
as stewards managing the household of God, 165
teamwork of, 215–220
thinking of the entire body of Christ, 213
training leaders, 196–198
training of the twelve, 144–149
transmitted governing of the church to the bishops, 251
on to the true word of God, 191
types of, 173, 173n8
understanding the ministry of Christ, 145
visiting, could stay for a day, 236–237
as a witness of the resurrection, 175
worked with leaders, 332
writing letters to churches, 189, 230
writing to believers, 191–192
apostles and prophets
church built on the foundation of, 2
confronting contemporary challenges, 266
existing from the Old Testament period to date, 10
limitations of, 11
many attacking the concept of, 7–8
needing high caliber in our generation, 333
needing to receive new revelation, 265
recognizing by their fruits and works, 266
tracing and finding out the role of in the Bible, 9
apostleship, 162, 252–258
apostolic age, beginning of, 331

apostolic call, of Paul, 140
Apostolic Church, 4, 6
Apostolic Church of New Zealand. *See* ACTS churches
Apostolic Constitution, 160, 255
apostolic era, 20, 21
Apostolic Faith Church, 4
apostolic figures, in the Old Testament, 221, 330
apostolic ministry
  of Apollos, 157
  bringing a harvest, 184
  confirmed with signs and wonders, 266
  founding or establishing local churches, 182
  needing people truly endowed with, 266
  oversight of the churches, 188
  of Paul as an example, 230
  stirring satanic strongholds, 199
  visible things happening through, 166
apostolic office
  basic gifts of, 172, 331
  Clement functioned in, 245
  not functional in the *Shepherd of Hermas*, 241
apostolic succession, in the Catholic Church, 254–256
apostolic work, in the ministry of Paul, 229–230
apostolicity, 246, 256–257, 259–262
Apphia, addressed as "our sister," 231
Aquila and Priscilla, 198, 231
Archippus, as "fellow soldier," 231
Aristarchus, 198, 231
Aristobulus, household of, 231
artificial intelligence (AI), 263, 264
Asaph, leading music in worship, 89–90
Assemblies of God, 3–4, 6, 7, 213, 229
assignment, sending someone on, 137
associates, of Paul, 160–161, 233–234
atonement, 36
attention, drawing to Jesus Christ, 307–308
audible voice, hearing, 64

authority
    to administer discipline, 81
    bishopric episcopal, 246
    collegial and prophetic, 255–256
    of elders, 187
    of the Father, 148
    given by the Lord, 319
    of interpreting the law, 45
    of John the Baptist to baptize Jesus, 61
    of a king, 129
    of Moses, 23–24, 25
    not misusing, 319
    of presbyters, 244
    prophets carrying, 109
    spiritual, 202–207
availability, to the Lord, 41–42
Azariah, friend of Daniel, 136
Azusa Street, manifestation of spiritual gifts, 3

bad tree, not bearing good fruit, 310
Barak, 25, 89
Barnabas
    already working with Saul, 183
    as an apostle, 154, 331
    appointing and training leaders, 197
    appointing elders, 187
    as the author of Hebrews, 155
    continued apostolic work, 230
    doing miraculous signs and wonders, 166
    of great help to Paul, 150, 151
    Holy Spirit directed his appointment, 233
    Joseph as the real name of, 153
    as one of the finest brothers in the New Testament, 153–155
    as one of the first to sell his land, 210
    planting and growing church as, 182
    as a prophet in the New Testament, 128
    saw the need for teamwork, 216
    stopping the people from worshipping them, 171
    trained John Mark, 154, 198
    went with Mark, 219
    working with Paul, 150–151, 216, 245–246
Bartholomew, listed as an apostle, 138
basic gifts, for prophets and apostles, 224–225
being in the Spirit, 279
believers
    first called Christians in Antioch, 154
    focusing on the Lord and his kingdom, 274
    gift of prophecy exhorting, 52
    needing to pray and read, 275
    potential to prophesy, 125–130
    suffering for Jesus' sake, 146
    testing all things including prophecy, 72
Belshazzar, Daniel working with, 136
King Ben-hadad, killed by Hazael, 318–319
Bezalel, 87–88
Bible
    on apostles, 2, 222
    apostles and prophets role in, 9
    books of writing prophets in, 28
    canticles in, 84n5
    as the inspired word of God, 285
    not contradicting itself, 71
    not teaching that "apostles today must govern the church," 8
    people the Lord used in, 260–261
    signs in, 106
    on testing all prophecies, 326
    types of ministers in, 9–10
    word of God in, 207
    words preferred in, 285
Bible Society, 176
biblical words, divine words as often, 279
birth of a son, as a sign, 104
bishop, office of, 241
bishopric (episcopal) authority, development of, 246
bishops
    appointment of, 239

SUBJECT INDEX

assisting the work of the apostles in the New Testament, 10
became more prominent than "elders," 242
functioning as apostles in many denominations, 260
infallibility of, 254
as leaders of the local churches, 253
leading the church with elders, 239
as the managers of the church, 227
as representatives of apostles with deacons, 244
as successors of the apostles, 11, 157, 250–251, 252, 253
taking the place of Christ himself through ordination, 254–255
variety of titles of, 255
blessings, people wanting to hear about, 322
body of Christ, 211–214, 217, 328
Branham, William, 5
Brown, Michael, 8–9
burden, 276–282, 283, 333
burning coal, as a token of forgiveness, 36
busybodies, 211

Cain, 14, 15
call
  accepting with fear and trembling, 40
  of an apostle, 164, 331
  of the apostles by Jesus, 8, 138–140, 331
  of Barnabas, 154
  coming with a revelation, 223–224
  of Ezekiel, 38
  heard by Isaiah, 36–37
  of Moses, 24, 134–135
  of Paul, 140–143, 229, 230
  of prophets, 35–40, 330
  training following, 145
Calvin, John, 257, 262
canon of Scripture, Jude's book accepted in, 153
canonical prophets, not seen as healing the sick, 109
canticles, as songs in the Bible, 84n5

Carey, William, 262
cases, handled by apostles, 192, 230
Catholic Church, apostolic succession in, 254–256
centrality of Christ, Irenaeus affirmed, 249–250
cessationism, 2, 8
chairmanship, aspect of from James, 253
challenges, preview of some modern, 262–265
chaos, of great concern to leadership, 327
charismata, 253, 261
charismatic leaders, judging prophecy, 327
Charismatic renewal, within mainline churches, 6
Charismatic Renewal Movement, 256
charisms, ordination of a bishop coming with, 255
chief cornerstone, Jesus Christ as, 165, 181
Child Evangelism Fellowship, 176
children, going wayward, 32
chip implants, in the brain, 263
choice, training by, 145
chosen ones, the Lord providing for, 213
Christ. *See* Jesus Christ
Christ Apostolic Church of Ghana, 4
Christ Apostolic Church of Nigeria, 4
Christian giver, Barnabas as a good example of, 210
Christian initiation, of baptism and confirmation, 256
Christian life, needing to be a life of prayer, 203
Christian Ministries International, 172
Christianity, slowing growth of, 264, 265
Christians
  backsliding, 294
  being obedient to receive revelation, 274
  dangers of unbroken, 275

(Christians continued)
   diminishing number of young world-wide, 265
   doing the wrong thing as suffering for Christ, 201
   encouraging to be models of ethical behavior, 267
   making others disciples of Christ, 37
church
   ability to supervise, 188–189
   in Antioch, 245
   comprising both Jews and Gentiles, 206
   contemporary not mystifying the term apostle, 333
   dealing with challenges in, 193–196
   government of, 190–201
   of Rome associated with Peter and Paul, 250
church fathers, 243–251
   not considering themselves as apostles, 252
   not ordaining apostles, 259, 332
   some operated as apostles, 332
   as the successors of the apostles, 259
church history, apostles in, 257–258
Church of God, opposed the Latter Rain movement, 6
church of God, praying for more apostles and prophets in our generation, 261
Church of Pentecost, 1, 4, 43, 316–317
Church of Scotland, 3
church officers, 187–188, 187n7
church unity, promoting, 213
churches
   apostles visiting and sending personal representatives, 230
   appointing bishops and deacons, 239
   beginning new, 182–185
   growing, 185–188
   independent, 6, 266–267
   laying a good foundation in, 224
circumcision, 193
classical Pentecostals, 6, 55, 60

cleansing, by washing through the word, 281
Clemens Alexandrinus, calling Clement an apostle, 245
Clement of Alexandria, 240n5
Clement of Rome, 153, 231, 243–245
commandments, of God as the test of a prophet, 310
common sense, accepting prophecy, 328–329
communication
   of prophets with the Lord, 115
   between Samuel and the Lord, 306–307
company of prophets. *See* school of the prophets
confession, in Daniel's prayer, 110–111
convention center, Church of Pentecost putting up, 168
Corinthian church, 126, 156, 204
corrupters, multiplied in the last days, 237
council of God, access to, 102–108
Council of Jerusalem, James as chair of, 152
council of the Lord, standing in, 27
counseling, lifting up a believer, 52
covenant
   beginning of the new, 123
   broken by rebellious people, 38
   of the Lord with Abram, 284
   prophet becoming the interpreter of, 10
   reminding Israel of the terms of God's, 95–98
coworkers, of Paul, 230–232, 233
craftsmanship, gift of, 87–88

Daniel
   as an apostolic figure in the Old Testament, 136
   on how knowledge would increase, 106
   interpreting the dream of Nebuchadnezzar, 67
   Lord sent angels to, 64
   often seen praying, 110

re-dreaming the dream of Nebuchadnezzar, 225
as a writing prophet, 28
Darius, Daniel working with, 136
daughters, of Philip, 128
David, 80–81, 84, 88, 89, 90, 319
Day of Atonement, 36
deacons (*diakonos*)
appointment of, 208, 233, 239
attention to prayer and the ministry of the word, 202
with the gift of service or help, 185–186
"dead traditions," seeking something more than, 2
death, ministering to people, 280
Deborah, 25, 28, 89, 135, 221
dedication, of parents, 32–33
deep revelation, 284
Demas, as "fellow worker" by Paul, 231
Demonstration of Apostolic Preaching, by Irenaeus, 249
denominations, 211, 257, 259–260
depression, Jeremiah showing signs of deep, 114
devil. *See also* evil one; Satan
accusing believers who live in sin, 274
attacking true apostles of Christ, 199, 200
manifestations stemming from, 69
sinning from the beginning, 295
speaking to everybody, 74
stirring up a church, 193
Didache, 235, 236, 237, 238, 242
differences, between apostles and prophets, 221–226
directive prophecy, 4, 4n14, 326, 334
discerning of spirits, gift of, 69–74
discernment, 74, 129
disciples. *See also* apostle(s)
afraid of Paul, 150
filled with the Holy Spirit, 123
as learners, 144
making others the, 37
ready to receive the new, 265–266
on the road to Emmaus, 176

diseases, healing diverse forms of, 169
disobedience, putting aside every act of, 274
dissimilarities, of prophets and apostles, 224–225
district, defined, 187n7
diverse kinds of tongues, gift of speaking in, 56–57
divided tongues, of fire, 123
divine authorizations, 266
divine encounters, 142
divine words
to Abraham to leave his country, 284
coming from the Holy Spirit directly, 282
difference from human thoughts, 281–282
expressing the burden, 277–278
formation of, 279–281
polluting with human words, 283
received through the human spirit, 333
taking some days or weeks in deep revelation, 284
doctrines, laying sound foundation in, 181–182
donations, to the believers in Jerusalem, 187
dreams
God speaking to Abraham and Jacob in, 16–17
as images during sleep, 62
prophet(s) having, 206, 225
related to the office of a prophet, 64
from the soulish realm, 280
understanding the meaning of, 66–67
Du Plessis, David Johannes, 6n22

early church, not having the complete Scripture, 2
Ecclesiastes, advising that two are better than one, 220
ecumenical council, bishops assembled in, 254
ecumenical issues, Mel Robeck working on, 213

edification, 52, 56
elders
  apostle(s) working with, 230, 332
  appointed by the apostles, 216–217, 232
  appointing the apostles, prophets and teachers, 217
  assisting in the governing of the churches, 187, 188
  assisting the work of the apostles, 10
  bishops became more prominent than, 242
  bishops leading the church with, 239
  chosen by Moses, 119–120
  exercising authority over the people, 187
  laid hands on Timothy, 217
  as leaders of the local churches, 253
  as *presbuteroi* in the *Shepherd of Hermas*, 241
Eli
  honoring his sons more than God, 295, 313
  the Lord speaking to, 291
  Samuel serving, 33, 34
  sons of disobeying the Lord, 34, 43, 293
  speaking to his sons about their sins, 42
  taught Samuel how to respond to the Lord, 44
Elijah
  asked to ordain others, 223
  claimed he was standing in God's council, 27
  as a man just like us, 95
  as a non-writing prophet, 28
  not physically ordained or anointed, 222
  raising the dead, 109
  taken up to heaven, 122
  on worshiping the Lord rather than Baal, 80
Elijah and Elisha, schools of the prophets during the time of, 29
Elim Bible College, 1–2
Elisha
  anointed a prophet, 222
  guidance to King Joram of Israel, 103
  interacted with some of the sons of the prophets, 30, 120–121
  miracle of multiplication to settle debts, 121
  as a non-writing prophet, 28
  not managing his message well, 318
  prayer to cause blindness to the Syrians, 109
  raising the dead, 109
  requested a musician to play for him, 30, 91
  saw the evil that Hazael would do to Israel, 62
  trained others, 224
Elizabeth, 61
Elkanah, Eli blessing, 44
Elymas, Paul caused blindness to, 305
embodiment of gifts, of an apostle, 162–164
empty prophets, 241
enlightenment or light, in a person's spirit, 271
Epaphras, as "fellow prisoner," 231
Epaphroditus, as Paul's fellow worker, 160–161
Epenetus, acknowledged by Paul, 231
Ephraim. *See* Israel
epileptic boy, apostles attempted to heal, 147
episcopacy (government of a church by bishops), 254
episkopos (bishops), 239. *See also* bishops
Equippers Churches, 5
Erastus, discipled by Paul, 198
eternal life, Jesus having the words of, 147
euangelizo, meaning to announce the good news, 51
Euodia, as a "loyal yokefellow" of Paul, 231
Euodia and Syntyche, Paul pleading with, 192
Eusebius, on Clement, 245

SUBJECT INDEX

evangelicals, on a restoration of spiritual gifts, 229
evangelistic gift, 185
evangelistic-apostles, like Peter, 173
evangelists, 76, 184–185
Eve. *See* Adam and Eve
events, of spiritual significance as sings, 106–107
evil behavior, not following, 45
evil one, 334. *See also* devil
evil spirit(s), 69, 71, 73, 319–320
exhortation, gift of, 78–83, 184
exponential change, opportunities for, 262
Ezekiel
  on the "hand of the Lord upon me," 271, 272
  as prophet to the exiles in Babylon, 38
  received the word of God, 273
  on repentance, 98
  on the Spirit falling upon all, 124
  on suffering because of fathers' sins, 99–100
  taken captive along with King Jehoiachin, 38
  visions of God, 62
  on visions of prophets, 321–322
  as a writing prophet, 28

face to face, the Lord speaking to Moses, 18
failure
  to discipline, 296
  to test prophecy, 326, 334
faith, 167–168, 169, 170, 196
Faith at the Speed of Light (Luce), 262
fake prophet or dreamer, putting to death, 309
the fall, God speaking to people after, 14–15
false apostles and teachers, 199–200
false doctrines, apostles dealing with, 196
false manifestation, Jesus' test of, 310
false prophets
  aound when the *Didache* was written, 237

bred by the school of the prophets, 30
cannot copy the true life of the Christian, 328
detecting, 310
multiplied in the last days, 237
false teachers, Jude warning about, 192
the Father. *See also* God
  declaring Jesus as his beloved Son, 282
favoritism, not showing, 209–210
fear, to confer the name apostle, 332
Fee, Gordon, 7, 9
Fife, Eric S., 261
filling of the Spirit, Paul associated music with, 83
first fruits, given to prophets or to the poor, 239
flaws, bringing downfall, 334
the flesh, 20, 319, 334
flesh and blood, as a source of manifestations, 69–70
"fleshy" things, true ministers seeing as vain, 33–34
floating iron, miracle of performed by Elisha, 30, 121
foretelling (predictive), from the prophet, 27
forgiveness, 36, 82, 296
formation
  of the burden, 277
  of the divine words, 279–281
  of human words in people, 285–289
"forth telling," from the prophet, 27
foundation layers, 181–189, 224
foundational work of the church, 165–166
founding fathers of Protestant denominations, 257
friend of the bridegroom, prophet or apostle as, 307
fruit
  knowing a true prophet by, 310
  of the Spirit, 274
Full Gospel Business Men's Fellowship, 5–6

Full Gospel Business Men's Fellowship International, 177
fund-raisers, gift of exhortation good for, 82–83
future, foretelling by prophets, 103–106

Gabriel (angel), message from, 218
Gad, 26, 28, 30, 120
Gaius of Derbe, accompanied Paul, 198
Gamaliel, 65–66
Geivett, R. Douglas, 8
Geivett and Pivec, on NAR teachings about apostles, 8
general wisdom, 66
generosity, 211
genes, scientists mapping, 263
Gentile Christians, not knowing much about Old Testament prophets, 182
Gentile churches, uniting with the church in Jerusalem, 212
Gentiles
  accepting Christ Jesus as their Lord, 193
  being the light to, 106
  gift of the Holy Spirit poured out on, 54
  as heirs together with Israel through the gospel, 206
  saved by grace, 194
Gideon, Lord sent angels to, 64
Gideon's International, 176
gift(s)
  coming upon a person, 162–163
  of confirmation, evangelist having, 184–185
  constituting a prophet, 330
  constituting the prophetic office, 10
  of healing, 169–173
  helpful to prophets, 129
  identifying an apostle, 163
  important for the church of the 21st Century, 7
  as irrevocable, 275
  no sharp line of demarcation between, 226
  of a pastor, 186
  sent to the elders, 188
  of the Spirit including prophecy, 127
"the gift of a prophet," 10
The Gift of Apostles (Cannistraci), 6
gift of craftsmanship, 87–88
gift of discerning of spirits, 69–74
gift of diverse kinds of tongues, 56–57
gift of exhortation, 78–83, 184
gift of faith, 167–168, 170
gift of interpretation, 57–59, 330
gift of leadership, 164, 186, 225
gift of miracles, 169
gift of music, 83–91, 185
gift of prophecy, 51–52
  Miriam endowed with, 25
  possessing, 11, 330
  a prophet must have, 128
gift of service or help, 185–186
gift of serving, 186
gift of showing mercy, 186
gift of songs, Deborah and Miriam having, 26
gift of speaking in diverse tongues, 53–57, 330
gift of teaching, 75–78, 164, 186
gift of the word of knowledge, 60–65, 72
gift of the word of wisdom, 65–69, 128–129
gift of wisdom, 68
gimmicks and manipulations, as guises of prophecies, 327
glory of the Lord, seen by Ezekiel, 38
Gnostic teaching, Irenaeus on, 249
God. *See also* Lord
  allowing Jeremiah experience, 114–115
  allowing Noah to use his own wisdom, 16
  answering Jeremiah's prayer, 112
  blessing all who call upon him, 34
  called Abraham to leave his country, 284
  calling to Samuel three times, 42
  causing all things to work together for good, 219

SUBJECT INDEX

communicating with human beings, 13
continuing to speak after the fall, 14–15
created human beings in his image, 286
dialogue with Cain, 15
endorsement of a person, 304–305
kingdom of, 106, 208–214
knowing the end from the beginning, 105
law of. *see* law of God
making Jesus perfect through suffering, 286
mercy of, 80
messengers of. *see* messengers of God
potential to hear from, 128
in the presence of the council of, 27
raising individuals to serve his people, 307
raising people of apostolic ability, 262
repeating the call until our ears are opened, 42
revealing himself, 26, 42–43
revealing the dream of Nebuchadnezzar to Daniel, 62
sending Moses to deliver his people Israel, 135
speaking always, 21, 259, 333
speaking through people, 286
speaking to both apostles and prophets, 224
speaking to Noah, 15–16
speaking to whoever he wished, 27
special presence of, 271
working in the form of the Trinity, 219
God's Super-Apostles: Encountering the Worldwide Prophets and Movements (Geivett and Pivec), 8
God's will, knowing that suffering could be, 146
God's word. *See* word of God
good prophet, carrying along the presence of God, 333–334
good tree, bearing good fruit, 310

Gospel of John, written by the Apostle John, 249
Gospel of Luke, written by Luke, 249
Gospel of Mark, said to be written by John Mark, 198
gospels, Irenaeus first to list the four, 249
gossip, prophets never sharing, 322
"governance" of the church, 332
governing office, of apostles as temporary, 8
government, of the church, 190–201
grace
  apostle(s) imparting, 203
  calling by, 145
  Gentiles saved by, 194
  God granted to Paul, 305
  of God not taking for granted, 293
  of "open vision," 306
  Paul on the administration of God's, 191
graces, associated with apostleship, 175
Great Britain, Islam as the dominant religion, 264
Grecian Jews, 150, 208
Grudem, Wayne, 76
guinea fowl, stolen, 200–201
Gyimah, James, 166

Hagar, Abraham taking, 287
Haggai, on economic hardship, 107
Hama, Jude, as an apostle of ecumenism, 214
Hamon, Bill, 172
Hamon, Riss and Bill, 5
Hananiah, 136, 280
Hannah, 32, 44
hard teaching, Jesus giving, 147
harp, seeking out a skillful player on, 84
harvest, apostolic ministry bringing, 184
Hazael, killed his master, King Benhadad, 62, 318–319
"he who has ears," meaning of, 44–45
healing, 109, 111, 147, 169–173

hearing from the Lord, hindrances to, 291–299
Hebrews (book of)
  author of, 78, 155, 158, 159
  challenging pastors, 34
Heman, organizing and leading music in worship, 89–90
heresies, 247, 252–253
Hermas, message of, 240
Hermes, Paul called, 171
Herod, attempting to kill all firstborns of the Jews, 282
Herodian, relative of Paul, 231
Hezekiah, healing of, 109
King Hezekiah, receiving Isaiah's messages, 319
high priest
  Eli as, 42
  Jesus Christ as, 174, 331
  office of, 137
Hill, Clifford, 106, 327
Hill, David, 109–110
hindrances, to hearing from the Lord, 291–299
holding on to one's view, tendency to, 334
Holy Catholic Apostolic Church, 3
Holy Spirit
  baptism of, 54, 204, 256
  bringing to memory human words, 283
  bringing words to us, 278
  caused John to leap in joy in the womb, 61
  descended during prayers, 202
  divine words supplied by, 277
  drawing attention to Christ, 307
  falling on all flesh, 119–124, 330
  fell on Cornelius and his household, 54–55
  filling of sanctified John, 61
  given through the laying on of hands, 53–54
  giving life, 283
  guiding, teaching and informing the apostles, 20
  guiding the believer, 124
  indwelling of, 286
  inspiring a Christian to receive a new song, 85
  interpretation of, 207
  living in you, 329
  outpouring of, 3, 261
  performing miracles, 169
  predicting the birth of the Messiah, 104
  purposes of, 306
  quenching, 280
  separating Barnabas and Paul, 183
  song received through inspiration of, 19
  speaking to Ignatius, 246
  speaking under the inspiration of, 51
hope, "lamp of God" referring to, 42n7
Hophni, son of Eli, 295
Hoppin, Ruth, 159–160
horizontal apostles, 173n8
Hosea, young when called, 39
house of God, as a place of order, 327
Huldah, as a non-writing prophet, 28
human beings. See also people
  errors of, 127
  God communicating with, 13, 14
  limitations of, 219
  not accepting the praise of, 147–148
human flesh, directing Samuel, 319
human nature of Jesus, as the word, 331
"human organizations," Latter Rain movement opposed to, 5
human thoughts, difference of divine words from, 281–282
human words
  added to the divine message, 284, 285
  applying the Scripture to life situations, 333
  formation of in people, 285–289
  making divine words understandable, 282
  need for before release, 283
Hutchinson, William Oliver, 4
hymns, 83, 84

SUBJECT INDEX

hyphenated apostles, 173n8
hypocrites, listening to God's word from, 45

Iddo, 26, 28
ideas, as a stage in receiving revelation, 272–275
identification, of an apostle, 134–143, 162, 174–177
idolatry, 79, 97, 107
Ignatius of Antioch, 245–246
ignorance, 29, 291–292
Immanuel, meaning "God with us," 105
"immediate answer," as too demanding, 297
independent churches, 6, 266–267
individuals, led by the Spirit, 217
inexperience, not an obstacle for the Lord, 39
infallibility, 254, 256
inner witness, Christians having, 328
inspiration, 51–59, 87
institutionalization, controlling the prophetic, 327
integrity, 308–311, 334
intelligence, boosting, 263–264
intercession, Daniel's prayer of, 110–111
interdependence, of apostles and elders, 217
International Fellowship of Evangelical Students, 176
Internet of Things, 262
interpretation
  gift of, 57–59, 330
  of signs, 106–108
Irenaeus, 240n5, 246, 247, 249–251
Irving, Edward, 3
Isaac, God spoke to, 16–17
Isaiah
  assuring Ahaz of God's love to David, 102–103
  brought the word of God to Hezekiah, 109
  called and sent, 135
  called to discipleship, 37
  on a contemporary issue, 104
  heard: "A voice said, 'Shout!'" 272, 273
  inspiration of the Holy Spirit, 104
  messages working with four kings of Judah, 319
  prayed with and for the people, 111
  prophesied on a light to the Gentiles, 206
  prophesied to the people of Judah, 35–37
  received unconditional forgiveness, 36
  on repentance, 98
  requesting for what to say, 272
  as a writing prophet, 28
  young when called, 39
Isaiah type of prophets, assisting the kings, 136
Isaiah's wife, as a non-writing prophet, 28
Islam, 264, 265
Israel, 96, 97, 106, 122
issues, presenting, 317

Jabin, attacking Israel, 101
Jacob, God spoke to, 16–17
Jahaziel, the son of Zechariah, 28
James (natural brother of Jesus)
  calling of, 151–152
  championed the Jewish mission, 174
  dealt with social challenges in the church, 195–196
  on Elijah, 95, 260, 332
  on Gentiles bearing the name of God, 194
  identified as an apostle, 229
  as leader of the church in Jerusalem, 152, 253
  not directly ordained, 222–223
  Paul and, 331
  on the purpose of suffering, 66
  as a servant of Jesus, 176
  transformed into a great apostle of the Lord, 152
  warning church leaders not to show partiality, 209
  on wisdom, 66

James, Peter, and John, teamwork of, 215–216
James, the brother of John, executed, 199
James and Jude, two brothers of Jesus, 140
James the son of Alphaeus, listed as an apostle, 138
James the son of Zebedee, listed as an apostle, 138
Jeduthun, organizing and leading music, 89–90
King Jehoash of Israel, calling Elisha "my father," 103
Jehovah, speaking to Samuel, 44
Jehu son of Hanani, 27, 28
Jeremiah
 appointed as a prophet before he was born, 31
 called as a prophet for the nations, 40
 cursed the day he was born, 113–114
 depressed by God not answering, 112–113
 disobeyed God, 114
 on a drought as the act of God, 107
 hesitated to accept his call, 39–40
 ministered life to people by foretelling doom, 280
 ministry of, 111
 praying for the people, 114
 spoke about the destruction of Jerusalem, 105
 ten days before he heard from the Lord, 297
 told to go to everyone, 135
 visions of prophets as false and worthless, 321–322
 wanting to take God's place, 114
 as a writing prophet, 28
Jerome, on Clement, 245
Jesus Christ
 accusing the religious leaders of failure to interpret the times, 107–108
 as an apostle, 137–138
 appearances of after his resurrection, 151–152
 asked his disciples who they thought he was, 35
 under the authority of the Father, 148
 baptism in the name of, 55
 baptized in water and received the Holy Spirit, 282
 baptized John with the Holy Spirit, 61
 brothers of, included in the list of apostles, 153
 building his church on "this rock," 165
 called Paul, 142
 called the original twelve apostles, 138–140, 174, 229
 called two other apostles, 174
 centrality of, 249–250
 combined the offices of the leader (king), the prophet and the high priesthood, 174, 331
 commissioned Mel Robeck, 213
 controlling the world while in Mary's womb, 61
 disobeyed man-made rules of the Pharisees, 46
 drawing attention to, 307–308
 on false prophets, 238
 fasted forty days and forty nights, 286
 fed five thousand people, 147
 as God's word, 20, 21
 helping those being tempted, 287
 Irenaeus on, 250
 isolating himself in prayer, 203
 on John the Baptist, 260
 knowing the person of, 145–146, 176
 led by the Spirit into the desert to be tempted, 69
 as the manifestation of the word of God, 19
 on the payment of tax to Caesar, 68–69
 period of, 18–20

SUBJECT INDEX

Psalm 22 intertwining with the death of, 90
rebuked Peter and accused him of being Satan, 146
rose from the grave and spoke to Peter, 139
sang with his disciples, 91
on the scribes and Pharisees, 45
as the second part of Isaiah's prophecy, 104
seeing as a different person, 283
as the Son of Man, 282
Spirit of life in, 275
on testing prophets, 324
on unity and teamwork, 219
washed the feet of his apostles, 149
on the woman caught in adultery, 68
Jewish Christians, felt Gentile Christians should observe the Mosaic laws, 193
Jews, stirred persecution in Antioch, 199
Joanna, the wife of Cuza, 158n8
Joel, 65, 122, 206
John (apostle)
on the angel in the book of Revelation, 260
disciplining a man called Diotrephes, 189
on false prophets, 324
fasting and praying, 203
ministry depicting a prophet and a teacher, 172
Polycarp a disciple of, 246
praying for people of Samaria to receive the Holy Spirit baptism, 54
prophetic ministry of, 225
receiving revelation for the people of God, 226
showing Jesus Christ as the Son of God, 285
in the Spirit when the Lord Jesus Christ revealed himself, 279
on those trying to lead you astray, 329

John brother of James, listed as an apostle, 138
John the Baptist, 55, 61, 260, 307
Jonah, 28
Jones, James Warren (Jim), 327
Joroboam, 97
Joseph, as the real name of Barnabas, 153
Joseph (human father of Jesus), 282
Joseph (son of Jacob), 67, 136
Joshua, 79–80, 120, 135, 221
Judah, 97
Judas, as the Greek form of Judah, 139
Judas and Silas, sent to deliver the message from the Jerusalem Council, 216
Judas Iscariot, 138, 139
Judas son of James, or Judas Thaddaeus, 139
Judas the Galilean, killed and his followers scattered, 65
Jude (natural brother of Jesus)
as an apostle, 152–153, 331
apostolic prowess of, 229
call to apostleship, 140n2
on edifying yourself, 56
on false prophets, 324
on false teaching, 191–192
letter of, 189
Junias (a woman), Paul called outstanding, 161
justice, prophets demanded for the poor, 100

King, The Lord of hosts, seen by Isaiah, 36
king of Israel, Messiah as, 106
kingdom of God, 106, 208–214
kingdom oriented organizations, examples of, 176–177
kings, 101, 129, 222
Kinsey, Alfred, 32
knowledge, 16, 60, 61, 262–265, 334
Knox, John, 262
Kraybill, Donald, 99
kubernesis, directing the affairs of the church, 191

lamp of God, in the tabernacle, 42n7
Langham Partnership International, 177
languages, speaking, 53, 56
Lappidoth, Deborah the wife of, 25
Lathrop, John P., 223
Latter Rain movement, 5, 6
law of God, 18, 45, 99–101, 295
lawlessness, sin as, 295
laying on of hands, 5, 53–54, 204, 205, 217, 233
leaders
  ability to train, 196–198
  following the footsteps of, 35
  not undermining people taking over from them, 316
  prophets as, 109–110
  qualifications of, 232
  selection of, 232–233, 253
leadership
  dropped from apostles to bishops, 11, 227
  gift of, 164, 186
  invested into Peter by Jesus, 165
  offering guidance to, 102
  role showing apostolicity, 253
  as servanthood and service, 148–149
"leadership ability," of an apostle, 190
Lebbaeus, listed as an apostle, 138
letter of the law of God, following, 99
letters
  of Ignatius to the churches and to Polycarp, 246
  individuals writing for Paul, 220
  writing of by apostles, 189, 230
Levites, 90, 276
life, Holy Spirit giving, 283
lifestyles, of prophets, 110, 328
light, translating into an idea or a thought, 272
limitations, of apostles and prophets, 257, 301
Lindsay, Gordon, 5
living for the Lord, 41, 42
Lord. *See also* God
  allowing to speak to you, 127
  calling each individual differently, 142
  calling prophets, 31, 119
  chose prophets as special vessels, 95
  communicating with his people, 333
  confirming to Eli that he was raising a prophet, 47
  constant revelation from, 306–307
  forgiving once people repent of their sins, 296
  on the importance of teamwork, 218
  instructed Moses to write the laws in songs, 89
  instructed the priest to encourage the people in war, 315
  Jeremiah and, 39, 40
  not allowing words uttered by Samuel to fall to the ground, 304–305
  preparing Samuel as a prophet, 33
  relying wholly on, 146–147
  requiring obedience more than sacrifice, 296
  revealing his will through apostles, 307
  showing love when people repent, 112
  spoke to Samuel in his own timing, 297
  spoke to the Hebrews as a nation (Israel), 64
  told Jeremiah to stop praying for the welfare of the people, 114
  wanting Samuel to to have the training of Eli, 44
  will of dawning upon an apostle, 225
lordship, apostleship not an office of, 149
loved ones, disciplining as part of mentoring, 296
Luce, Ron, 262
Lucius of Cyrene, 128
Luke, 154, 197–198, 231, 285
Luther, Martin, 158, 257, 262
Lyft rides, 263, 263n10

SUBJECT INDEX

Madonna Louise Ciccone, 32
Maher-Shalal-Hash-Baz ("Quick to the Plunder, Swift to the Spoil"), 104
mainline churches, renewal within, 6n22
man of God, not needing to blow his own horns, 304
man of God's word, prophet as, 95–101
Manaen, as a prophet, 128
Mani of Persia, claimed to be the last apostle, 2
Manichaeism, 2
manifestations
  distinguishing whether from God or not, 69
  of the gift of knowledge, 62–65
  of the gift of teaching, 76–77
  knowing the source of, 71
  testing, 72, 320, 334
manipulation, using prophecy for, 314–317
Marcion, Polycarp's encounter with, 247
Mark, 154, 198, 285
Mark, John, 198, 219, 231
market place apostles, 173n8
Mary (convert), 231
Mary (mother of Jesus), 61
Mary (mother of Mark), 198
Mary Magdalene, 158n8, 176
massaw, translating as burden, 276–277
masses, causing leaders to respond to them, 292–293
Matthew, 104–105, 138, 285
Matthias, 138–140, 175
Maximilla, 325
McBirnie, William Steuart, 139, 182, 199
McDonald, Sean, 199
McDonnell, Killian, 255
McKeown, James, 305
medical healing, 169
medical prevention, adding years onto life, 263

members, of the body of Christ, 217
mentees, 35, 316
mentors, need for, 43–46
mercy, 80, 114, 186
Mercy Ships, 176
message(s)
  as the "burden," 276
  delivery of, 289–290
  of doom concerning Eli's family, 47
  getting people to act on, 289
  holding on to the wrong, 321
  of prophets, 110
  received by prophets, 27
  types of, 283
messengers, 122, 149
messengers of God, 14–21, 262
  apostles as, 20, 331
  needed to lead the church of God, 260
  prophets and apostles called as, 221–222
Messiah, 104, 105–106, 285
Micah, 28, 28–29n5
Micaiah, 280–281, 298
Michael (archangel), 218
mind of God, 317
ministering, the word at the highest level, 289
ministers, itinerant, 242
ministry
  of the apostles, 21, 173n8, 332
  of Barnabas in Antioch, 154
  of Isaiah as discouraging, 37
  of Jeremiah as difficult, 40
  as a matter of being faithful to the Lord, 37
  people trained, appointed and released for, 197
  seeing the challenge of, 39–40
ministry gifts, as persons themselves, 163
miracles, 109, 166, 169, 170
Miriam (sister of Moses and Aaron), 24–25, 24n3, 28, 88
Mishael, friend of Daniel, 136
mission churches, of ACTS, 5
missionaries, doing the work of the apostles, 4

missionary journeys, of Paul, 292
Mohammed, 2
Montague, George T., 255
Montanism, 324–325
Montanus, 324–325
morality, emphasis on in Montanism, 325
Mormon (book of), 3
Mormons, 3
Mosaic law, 192, 194
Moses
    as an apostolic figure, 221
    asked to ordain others, 223
    authority from God to command Pharaoh, 23–24
    call of and mission assigned to him, 134–135, 142
    comparing Jesus to, 137
    considered "above" the prophet, 18, 21, 23
    constantly hearing from God, 119
    experience of, 272–273
    on fulfillment of prediction only, 309
    God training in the wilderness, 145
    got to a time when the Lord said he had received enough, 293–294
    hesitated to accept the call of the Lord, 24
    on how to know a true prophet, 309
    instructed to write the law in songs, 89
    leadership ability of, 225
    limited by the priestly functions of Aaron, 135
    not healed of stammering, 220
    not physically ordained or anointed, 222
    overburdened with the work of leading the people, 119–120, 277
    saw a visible light, 272
    "speaking to God face to face," 17–18
    told the Israelites their life as a nation depended upon obedience, 79
    wishing all of God's people would be prophets, 119–120

Moses and Miriam, writing new songs to the praise of God, 88–89
Moses type of leaders, needed to work with the high priests, 174
Moses type of prophets, 136
mourning devotion, song written during, 85–87
mouthpiece of God, 22, 129, 255
Movement for Restoration of the Ten Commandments of God, group suicide of, 327
multiplication, miracle of, 30, 121
Muratorian Canon, rejected *Shepherd of Hermas*, 240n5
music, gift of, 83–91, 185
"my partner and coworker," Titus as to Paul, 156–157
mysteries, speaking to God, 55

nabi (ecstatic spokesman), 23, 23n1, 24, 26
NAR. *See* New Apostolic Reformation (NAR)
Nathan
    handling the messages of God in a wise way, 319
    helpful to King David in his life and kingship, 30, 120
    incorrect on David building a temple, 321
    as a non-writing prophet, 28
    rebuked David in a wise way, 80–81
nation of Israel, divided between Saul and David, 318
natural healing, 169
natural wisdom, 65–66
Nazirite, Samuel as, 32, 318
nebiyah, as the feminine form of the Hebrew *nabi*, 25
Nebuchadnezzar, 67, 136
Nee, Watchman, 9–10, 262
needy persons. *See* the poor
negative thoughts, of prophets, 313–314
Nehemiah, 136
Nelson, Thomas, 294
networking, the church in Jerusalem, 211–212

SUBJECT INDEX

New Apostolic Reformation (NAR), 6–7, 8, 172, 172n6
New Jerusalem, 325
new song, receiving, 85
New Testament
  on apostles working together with the elders, 230
  church, 91, 192
  on gifts people possess, 127
  identifying the apostle (messenger), 137
  pointers on what constitutes an apostle, 175
  prophets in, 10–11
  system still operating, 260
"new" things, as revelations, 207
Noadiah, non-writing prophet, 28
Noah, 15
Noble-Atsu, Daniel Kwame, 1–2
non-availability of people, challenging to the Lord, 307
non-writing prophets, in the Old Testament, 28
northern kingdom (Israel), rejected the law, 97
Ntumy, M. K., 272
nurse, gladly assisting the aged, 186

obeying, "in the Lord," 46
office of the prophet, 64, 330
offices, assigning to all who honor the Lord, 313
Oholiab, helping Bezalel, 88
oikonomia, as stewardship over the church, 191
oil, as a symbol, 222
Old Testament
  apostles in, 134–137
  apostolic figures in, 10
  prophecies fulfilled in the New Testament, 119
  spokespersons of God as prophets, 330
older man, treating as your father, 209
older prophet, led a younger prophet to death, 70–71, 320–321
older women, treating as mothers, 209

one body and one Spirit, Paul recognizing, 211
Onesiphorus, served Paul and was not ashamed, 185
"open vision," endowing with the grace of, 306
operation, of prophecy in the New Testament, 330
Operation Mobilization, 176
ordination
  of apostles, 144
  of bishops and deacons, 242
  for both Timothy and Titus, 234
  of officers as an ongoing activity, 232
  as a symbol, 222
Origen, accepted the *Shepherd of Hermas*, 240n5
Osborn, T. L., 5
other voices, prophet or apostle prophesying from, 334
outpouring of God's Spirit, Joel on, 122
overseer as bishop (*episkopos*), qualifications for, 232
overseers (bishops) and elders, 233
Oye, Florence, 218

Paintsil, Joseph Egyir, 278
paralytic (Aeneas), Peter's ministry of, 170
parents, 32–33, 43
parthenos, translated as a virgin, 104
pastor (shepherd), referencing our Lord Jesus, 260
pastoral-apostles, like James, 173
pastors
  apostle positioning, 193
  with the gift of service or help, 185–186
  as heavier than the term "apostle," 260
  needing the gift of leadership, 186
  responsibility placed on, 34
  rights of, 41
  shepherding a church, 185
  transfer of all who had the gift of prophecy, 205

(pastors continued)
    who do not know the Lord, 33
pastor-teacher, shepherding the church, 186
Patriarchs, God spoke to, 16–17
Paul
    on accepting a repentent sinner, 82
    on the administration of God's grace, 191
    on Apollos, 77–78
    apostleship of, 303
    appointing and training leaders, 187, 197
    appointing associates, 233–234
    asked Romans to offer their bodies to God, 80
    on authority given to leaders, 319
    authorized leaders to minister disciplinary measures, 81
    aware of spiritual gifts, 203–204
    Barnabas and, 184, 188, 220, 308
    on believers prophesying, 125–126
    blinded Elymas, 305
    broke fellowship with Barnabas, 219
    building the church, 126
    call of, 140–143, 229, 230
    championed the Gentile mission, 174
    on children obeying parents in the Lord, 46
    on Christians not being beggars, 211
    on circumcision, 194
    Clement of Rome close to, 243n2
    concern about the poor, 209
    concern for all the churches, 192
    coworkers of, 230–232
    deliverance of the demon-possessed slave girl, 73
    discouraging division among the people of God, 219
    established the church in Corinth, 188
    as an example of working hard, 210–211
    on false prophets, 324
    as the final apostle, 8
    guidelines on the operations of prophecy, 238
    healing during his ministry, 171, 172
    on his apostleship and the rights of apostles, 153
    on husbands loving wives, 281
    on imparting spiritual gifts, 261–262
    individuals wrote his letters for him, 220
    on interpretation of tongues, 59
    introduced by Barnabas at Jerusalem, 183
    on issues in Corinth, 195
    on keeping the unity of the Spirit, 211
    laid his hand on Timothy, 233
    on living for the Lord, 41
    longing to impart spiritual gifts to the Romans, 204
    on the Lord destroying the wisdom of the world, 66
    mentioning "varieties of tongues," 56
    mentored by other disciples, 149
    mentoring Timothy, 44
    miraculous signs and wonders, 166
    missionary journeys of, 307
    needing a person of equal status to minister with, 156
    networked churches, 212
    not discharging burden with human words, 278
    on not limiting yourself with ignorance, 292
    not soliciting money to take care of himself, 200
    ordained Timothy, 223
    ordination of, 222–223, 223n2
    planted and Apollos watered, 157
    planting and growing church as, 182
    praying and singing hymns when delivered from prison, 91
    praying on his weaknesses, 287
    on the purpose of prophecy, 52

SUBJECT INDEX 363

rebuked a man having sexual relations with his stepmother, 81
rebuked Peter, 81–82, 257
on receiving the baptism of the Holy Spirit, 205
recruited many people in his team, 198
recruited Silas, 155–156, 197
referring to apostles and prophets in the New Testament, 182
remembering all those who worked with him, 231–232
responsibility to manage God's church, 166
on revelation strengthening the church, 289
saw the resurrected Jesus, 175
selection of leaders, 232–233
sent to the Gentiles, 141
Silas and, 156
on the source of manifestations, 72
on speaking in tongues, 261
speaking well of Mark, 219
spent days with the disciples in Damascus, 150
stayed with the disciples to learn from them, 150
stirring Timothy not to neglect his gift, 217
stoned and dragged out of Lystra, 199
stopping the people from worshipping him, 171
on taking away the messenger of Satan, 203
on teaching as a gift from the Lord, 75–76
teamwork of, 155, 216
on testing everything, 72
told Timothy to fan into flame the gift of God, 204
trained in the ministry as he moved around, 184
trained many people, 224
training of, 149–151
using the terms elders and overseer or bishop, 233

vision of a man asking him to come to Macedonia, 224
visiting the churches and strengthening them, 189
on the weapons we fight, 274
works of as more numerous than Peter, 292
paying attention, to the Lord and allowing him to speak, 47
Pentateuch (five books of Moses), torah as, 99
Pentecost, day of, 53, 123
Pentecostal Christians, on outpouring of the Spirit, 123
Pentecostal church, needing spiritual gifts, 205
Pentecostal Holiness Church, 6
Pentecostal members, receiving songs instead of writing, 19n1
Pentecostals, 4, 53, 229
people. *See also* human beings
in the Bible as normal people like us, 260–261
of charisma attracting following, 172
handling with care and respect, 209
recognition by many, 305–306
standing before God's judgment, 313
as the subject matter of gifts, 163
wanting to combine the worship of YAHWEH with the worship of Baal, 80
wanting to hail the persons God uses, 308
wanting to offer sacrifice to Paul and Barnabas, 308
Persis, worked very hard in the Lord, 231
Peter
as an apostle, 138
assumed leadership, 139
on both Jews and Gentiles as the same, 308
Clement of Rome close to, 243n2
concern for all Christians, 212–213
confirmed Jesus was the Holy One of God, 146, 148

(Peter continued)
  on the day of Pentecost, 122–123
  directed through revelation to visit Cornelius, 54, 204–205, 224
  on false prophets, 324
  fell into a trance and saw heaven opened, 63
  on fulfillment of Joel's prophecy, 65
  given keys, 165, 223–224
  good relations and teamwork of, 216
  intimidated by the leadership of James, 152
  John and, 170, 204, 215, 220
  ministry of, 172, 189
  name always listed first, 139
  on the outpouring of the Spirit, 123
  praying for people of Samaria to receive the Holy Spirit baptism, 54
  realized that God had granted Paul special grace, 305
  rebuked by Paul, 81–82, 257
  representing the twelve apostles, 165
  seen fasting and praying, 202
  showed that God accepted the Gentiles, 194
  on Silas assisting him to write, 156
  Simon and, 72–73, 261
  on suffering, 146
petition, in Daniel's prayer, 110–111
petrol, prophecy directing the drinking of, 329
Petts, David, 7, 9
Pharaoh, 23, 67
Pharisees, 45–46, 68–69, 169, 193
Philemon, as "dear friend" and "fellow worker," 231
Philip, 138, 188, 224
Phinehas, son of Eli, 295
Phoebe, as a deaconess, 231, 233
Pivec, Holly, 8
Plato, on ignorance, 291
plea, for more apostles and prophets, 265–266
pleasing people, tendency to, 321, 334
pleasures, rejecting worldly, 41

plot to kill Paul, 307
political leaders, offering spiritual guidance to, 102–103
Polycarp (bishop of Smyrna), 246–249
the poor
  ability to care for, 208–211
  false prophets preying on, 309
  prophet not oppressing, 308
  trampling on the heads of, 100, 105
positions, assigning to all who honor the Lord, 313
potential to prophesy, of every believer, 125–130
power, in corporate recognition and prayer, 261
praise, apostles not accepting from human beings, 147–148
prayer
  on the building of God's kingdom on earth, 286
  cannot change the mind of God, 115
  fasting and, 147
  Jeremiah sinning in his, 114
  by Jesus before choosing the apostles, 138
  as one of the ministries of Jesus here on earth, 202
  prophets as men of, 110–115
  types of, 110
praying, 56, 279, 292
preachers, gift of exhortation good for, 82–83
preaching, not the same as prophecy, 51
presbuteros (elders), 188, 239. *See also* elders
presbyteries, role in the government of the church, 217
presbyters, as the term used by Clement, 244–245
presence of God, 109–115, 303, 306
presiding, over church issues, 190
pressure of the people, on prophets to prophesy, 292–293, 321, 333
pride, Paul discouraging, 126
priesthood, as a sacrificial service by practice, 33

principles, laying down, 327
Prisca (Priscilla), claimed to prophesy, 325
Priscilla, ministry of as apostolic in nature, 158–160
Priscilla and Aquila, 77, 157, 159, 160
Prison Fellowship, 177
proisteni, as "the one who leads," 190
promptings, 271–272, 333
prophecy
   compared to teaching, 76
   on the day of Pentecost, 123
   defined, 51, 76
   edifying the church, 52
   false, 328
   gift of, 11, 25, 51–52, 128, 330
   as greater than speaking in tongues, 125
   indicating the Lord speaking to you, 126
   as infallible initially within the Apostolic Church, 4
   purpose of, 52
   putting too much pressure on, 297
   on the Spirit falling on all people, 121–124
   spontaneous message of, 283
   supposed to encourage people, 328
   testing, 70, 320, 324, 326, 328, 334–335
   using to manipulate, 314–317, 334
prophesying
   as evidences of God's Spirit falling on a person, 120
   as going above speaking in tongues, 126
   music associated with, 30, 90
   from other voices, 319–321
   in turn for everyone to be instructed and encouraged, 125–126
prophet(s)
   allowing others to judge their messages, 238
   apostles and, 11, 222–223
   bringing the mind of God, 101
   calling of, 11, 222
   on chastity, 80
   as chief priests, 238–239
   as common people living in society, 95, 333
   constitution of, 10
   on contemporary issues, 101
   finding out the life story of, 31
   as the focus of the Old Testament minister of God, 10
   foretelling the future, 103–106
   functions of, 10, 330, 331
   getting it wrong, 321
   gift of as evident for people around, 303
   as a gift to God's people, 330
   God speaking through, 18
   as God's messenger in the Old Testament, 22–30
   having a vision or dream on an issue, 206
   Hermas spoke extensively about, 241
   identifying, 11, 303–311
   identifying the type of spirit, 74
   instruction concerning in the *Didache*, 237
   integrity of, 308
   interpreting impressions as the word of God, 321
   interpreting the times, 108
   introduction to, 16–18
   known by God, 23
   limitations of, 301
   as the main minister of God's word, 129
   making of, 31–47
   on the meaning of God's law, 101
   as messenger of God, 31, 221
   need for, 259–267
   needing the gift of prophecy, 52
   in the New Testament, 117, 182
   not accumulating wealth, 308
   not all who prophesied were, 28
   not living above reproach, 308–309
   not physically ordained in the Bible, 222
   as not the leaders of God's people, 331
   offering thanksgiving, 239

(prophet(s) continued)
  in the Old Testament, 135, 206, 226, 321
  people consulted for guidance, 101
  prominent in the books of Samuel, 120
  prophesying what the people wanted to hear, 322
  receiving revelations from the Lord, 271
  remaining a normal person with passions and desires, 322–323
  reminded Israel of the contents of the law, 98
  reminding about the terms of the covenant, 97
  seeing visions, dreams, and hearing the Lord, 225
  speaking initially to their own situations, 106
  speaking to spiritual and political leaders, 102
  speaking with the intent of allowing others to speak, 238
  standing in the council of the Lord, 27
  teachers and, 183, 217
  terms used to describe, 26–27
  types of in the Old Testament, 28
  understanding the times, 266
  used by the flesh or a devil, 70
  visions of, 62
  working with the apostle in the New Testament, 130
propheteia, meaning "to speak the mind of God" or "foretelling," 51
prophetess, Deborah as, 25–26
"the prophethood of all believers," 124
prophetic call, 40
prophetic flaws, 312–323
prophetic insight, demonstrated by Polycarp, 248
prophetic message, 52, 237, 319
prophetic ministry, posing challenges, 237
prophetic office, 30, 35, 306
prophetic traditions, 95
prophetic utterance, 241, 324–329

prophetic-apostles, like John, 173
"prophets group," in the New Testament, 128
protection, Jeremiah's prayer of, 111
Protestant Christians, issues posing challenges to, 254
Protestant churches, on spiritual gifts ceasing, 229
Protestants, 256–257
Proverbs, on training up a child, 33
Psalm 22, as very prophetic, 90
psalms, making music out of, 84
punishment, of Eli's sons affect Eli's family, 296

Quadratus, 325, 325n2
"Queen of Pop," 32

rabbinic writings, 99
rains, people defied to attend meetings, 1
rebuking others, when they sin, 80
reception, of divine words, 278
regional superintendent, appointment of, 1
relationship with the Lord, apostles strengthening, 202–203
reliance on God, 146, 316
religious practices of the people, accepted by God, 100–101
repentance, 98, 112
representatives, of apostles sent to visit churches, 189
responses, of God to prayer, 115
responsibility, as burden, 277
results, already determined, 297–298
resurrected Jesus, 175
revelation(s)
  based on the Scripture, 288
  breaking the flow of, 274–275
  churches not making room for, 289
  gifts of, 60–74, 225
  of God, 46
  gossiping on, 322
  interpretations of as difficult, 322
  Jesus not needing to receive, 19
  leading to Christ, 288
  from the Lord, 306–307, 333

SUBJECT INDEX

not making you a prophet, 47
passing on obscure, 322
Paul writing to Ephesus about, 206
prophets and apostles having from God, 223–224
receiving, 11, 205–207, 269, 271–290, 333
types of, 283–285
understanding and explaining, 65
within the body of the messenger, 225
revelatory message, preaching once, 290
righteous life, 240
rights, of pastors, 41
Robeck, Cecil Mel, Jr., 213
Roberts, Oral, 5
Roman church, apostolic tradition of, 250
Rufinus, on Clement, 245
Rufus, "chosen in the Lord," 231

Sabbath day, keeping holy, 112
salvation, Jesus as the author of, 287
Samaria. *See* Israel
Samaritan's Purse, 177
Samuel
   anointed Saul as a king and later David, 222
   as an apostolic figure, 221
   asked Saul to wait, 297
   asked to ordain others, 223
   attempting to anoint Eliab, 321
   chose to live for the Lord, 42
   consultation of Saul, 101
   contributed to the failure of Saul, 315, 316
   created problems for David, 318
   dedicated to God at three years old, 32
   difficulty accepting the "yes" answer on kingship, 297–298, 312, 317
   directed to call Saul as a king, 306
   established a school of prophets, 29–30
   God revealing himself to, 42–43
   got closer to Eli than to his sons, 34
   heard the voice of the LORD as the voice of Eli, 43, 46, 64, 142, 272, 291–292
   kept on doing what he used to do, 47
   leading according to instructions from the Lord, 135
   life story as a case study, 10, 31
   listened to Eli, the high priest, 42
   mentoring a group of prophets, 292
   ministry of felt by the entire nation, 305
   mourned for Saul, 316
   nearly anointed the wrong son of Jesse, 298, 319
   not addressing the people, as the Scriptures required, 315
   not physically ordained or anointed, 222
   not prepared to assist Saul, 316
   on not taking any bribe or cheated the people, 308
   not telling people that the Lord was going to destroy the family of Eli, 322
   on obedience as better than sacrifice, 296
   praying for the people and teaching them, 111
   praying to God, 306
   presence of causing great fear to the people, 318
   as a prophet, 26, 41–47, 303, 304
   reaction when Saul fell, 317–318
   receiving from the Lord, 46
   requested the Lord send rain, 305
   response to the Lord, 46–47
   saying more than he was required to say, 318
   as a seer and a prophet, 26, 306
   serving Eli even at night, 34
   sons of as corrupt, 313
   told Saul to wait for seven days, 315
   trained others, 224
   trapped Saul when Saul offered the sacrifice, 315
   as a writing prophet, 28

sanctified common sense, accepting prophecy, 328–329
Sapphira, 62
Satan, 146, 200. *See also* devil
satanic oppositions, 199–201
Saul (king)
    consultation of by Samuel, 101
    disobeying because of pressure from the people, 292
    looking for the one person Samuel claimed was better, 318
    needed a mentor, 316
    offering the sacrifice due to pressure, 314
    prophesied but wanted to kill David, 320
    prophesied filled with the Spirit of God, 71
    responsible for his own downfall, 318
    Samuel contributing to the failure of, 316
    waited until the seven days Samuel promised had passed, 315
Saul (Paul), as a prophet in the New Testament, 128
savior of the world, John presenting Jesus as, 285
scepter of righteousness, 130
Schillebeeckx, Edward, 255–256
school of the prophets, 29–30, 120, 121, 122
scribes and Pharisees, example of, 45
Scripture
    canonization of, 259
    giving no indication of apostles after the original, 8
    helping every mature Christian to weigh a prophetic utterance, 334
    knowledge of important in the prophetic ministry, 279
    receiving insight into, 60
Scripture Union, 176
Secundus, accompanied Paul, 198
seed of God, 295
seer, 26, 306
self-deception, practicing, 294
self-driving cars, 263

self-serving or perverted ways, 294
"the sent one," Moses as, 135
servant, not greater than his master, 149
servant of all, leader becoming, 148
"a servant of Jesus Christ," Jude seeing himself as, 153
servants of the living God, prophets as, 110
service or help, gift of, 185–186
serving, gift of, 186
serving heart, of Samuel, 33–35
seventy elders, chosen by Moses, 119–120
Shemaiah, as a non-writing prophet, 28
Shepherd of Hermas, 239–241
showing mercy, gift of, 186
sick people, Peter's shadow falling on them, 170
signs, 104, 106–108, 166
signs, wonders and miracles, marking an apostle, 166–173
Silas
    addressed as a prophet and then as an apostle, 197
    as an apostle, 155, 331
    continued apostolic work, 230
    Paul going with, 219
    played an active role, 156
    praying and singing hymns, 91
    prophetic gift of, 155
Simeon, as a prophet in the New Testament, 128
similarities, between apostles and prophets, 221–224
Simon, 54, 72
Simon the Canaanite, listed as an apostle, 138
sin
    blurring the light, 273
    distorting the voice of God, 333
    of Eli's sons, 293
    keeping people from hearing the voice of God, 293–297
    by pastors without repentance, 33–34
    prophets condemned, 100

SUBJECT INDEX 369

revealing through the gift of knowledge, 62
sinful lives, of members of church in Corinth, 195
sinful thought, mastering a person, 274
singing, 56–57, 91. *See also* songs
Sisera, 25, 101
situations, special insight into difficult, 65
Smith, Joseph, 3
social justice, within the Christian community, 209
Solomon, wisdom of, 67–68
Son of God, 295
Son of Man, Jesus as, 282, 285
songs, 26, 83, 84, 85–87, 91. *See also* singing
sons of the prophets. *See* school of the prophets
Sopater of Berea, accompanied Paul, 198
Sosthenes, called "brother" by Paul, 231
soul, of one who sins, 100
soulish life, of Hananiah, 280
soulish realm, prophecy and dreams from, 280
sources, of manifestations, 69
South Korea, demise of the revival in, 264–265
southern kingdom, as Judah or the House of David, 97
sovereign will of God, miracles and, 169
speaking, under inspiration, gifts of, 51–59
speaking in diverse tongues, gift of, 53–57, 330
speaking in tongues, 53, 55–56, 59, 123
Spirit of God
  came upon David, 85
  compelling Paul to go to Jerusalem, 225
  demonstration of the power of by Paul, 166
  needing to walk in to exercise spiritual gifts, 204
  as not needing consultation, 241
  poured on all flesh, 121
  prophet carrying, 109
  respecting in all of us, 127
  as the source of manifestations, 70
  upon the corporate nation of Israel, 119
spirit of the law, understanding, 101
spirits, gift of discerning of, 69–74
spirits of prophets, 127
spiritual authority, of apostles, 202–207
spiritual gifts, 203–205, 255
spiritual guidance, to political leaders, 102–103
spiritual things, condemning, 295
spiritual words, expressing spiritual truths in, 278–279
spirituality, including showing love to others, 323
spokesperson, of God instructing others, 23
spontaneity, 326, 327, 334
stages, in receiving a revelation, 271
standards, for testing manifestations, 334–335
stanzas, in hymns, 84
Stephen, Paul approving of the death of, 141
stolen goods, woe to him who piles up, 100
studying, as necessary, 292
suffering
  for being a Christian, 201
  believers not understanding the purpose of, 66
  Ezekiel on, 99–100
  God making Jesus perfect through, 286
  as God's will, 146
Sullivan, Father, 327
Sullivan, Francis A., 157
Sunday school children, asking volunteers to teach, 78
super spiritual, tendency to be, 322–323

surrender, measure of one's, 223
Susanna, accompanied Jesus, 158n8
Synan, Vinson, 5, 7
syncretism, 205n3
Syntyche, as a "loyal yokefellow" of Paul, 231

talents, compared with gifts, 77n3
Talmud, 99
tambourine, in Miriam's hand, 88
Taylor, Hudson, 262
teacher-apostles, like Apollos, 173
teachers, instructions on in the *Didache*, 235, 236
teaching, gift of, 75–78, 164, 186
"The Teaching of the Lord to the Gentiles by the Twelve Apostles." *See Didache*
teams
 apostles working in, 215–220, 231–232, 266
 Ignatius desiring to work with, 246
technology, use of modern by people online, 262
temple priests, consecrated at the age of thirty, 38
temptations and trials, Christians going through, 287
tent makers, Paul, Priscilla, and Aquila as, 159
Tertullian, rejected *Shepherd of Hermas*, 240n5
theology, doing local, 205
Theudas, 65
Thomas, 138, 175
thoughts, becoming polluted, 274
"Thus says the Lord," using to manipulate, 316
Timothy, 155–156
 accompanied Paul, 198
 as an apostle, 155, 197, 331
 body of elders laid hands on him, 233
 continued apostolic work, 230
 elders laid their hands on, 217
 mentored by Paul, 44
 Paul laid his hands on, 204
 recruited into the apostolic team, 197
 sent to visit and minister to the churches in Macedonia, 155
 spoken well of by his local church, 197
Titus
 as an apostle, 331
 continued apostolic work, 230
 left in Crete to appoint elders, 217
 requested by Paul to appoint elders, 232
 role in Paul's ministry, 156–157
 working with the Corinthian church, 186
tongues. *See* speaking in tongues
torah, 96, 99
training
 following a calling, 145
 of musicians, 91
 as ongoing in the church, 197
 of Paul, 149–151
 of the twelve apostles, 144–149
trances, 63, 64
"trial-and-error" method, prophet not applying, 309
trials, 286, 288
Trinity, form of, 219
Trophimus, accompanied Paul, 198, 231
trouble, potential to incite, 317–319
true prophet, 241, 303–311
Tryphena, "working hard in the Lord," 231
Tryphosa, "working hard in the Lord," 231
"turning aside to see," as the Moses experience, 272
twelve apostles
 call of, 8, 138–140, 331
 mystification of the number of, 5n17
Tychicus, accompanied Paul, 198, 231

unbroken Christians, dangers of, 275
unity, in the body of Christ, 214
Urbanus, "fellow worker in Christ," 231

SUBJECT INDEX

Uriah, spoke once and never prophesied again, 28
Uriah the Hittite (husband of Bathsheba), 80–81
"usership," as a subscription of automobiles, 263
King Uzziah, 36

Valens, mishandled funds, 247
varieties of tongues, gift of speaking in, 56
Vatican II, of the Catholic Church, 254
vengeance, Jeremiah maintained his prayer of, 113
vertical apostles, 173n8
view, holding on to one's own, 312–314
virgin, Christ born of, 104
visions, 43, 62, 64, 275
voice of God, 18, 292, 329
voices, prophesying from other, 319–321
the vulnerable. *See* the poor

Wa central church, woman claiming to be a prophetess at, 74
Wagner, C. Peter, 6, 7, 173n8
"watchman," Ezekiel's unique ministry to Israel as, 38
weaker brethren, encouraging, 82
weaknesses, 287, 312
Wesley, John, 257, 262
"whole word of God," apostles considering, 194
widows, placed on a list for assistance, 209
will of God, 115, 138, 147, 289
willful sin, warning against, 294–295
Williams, Daniel Powel, 4
Williams, William Jones, 4
wisdom, 16, 66, 68, 253
"wisdom and knowledge," management with, 165
the wise, knowing they are limited, 291
women, apostleship of, 158–160
wonder, defined, 166

word
  gifts of the, 75–91
  ministration of, 164
word of God
  becoming part of an apostle, 207
  bringing into contemporary issues, 206
  bringing to the people, 109
  coming first before the flesh in Jesus, 20
  God commanded Ezekiel to eat, 38–39
  Jesus as, 331–332
  listening to whatever is truly taught from, 45
  personifying in us, 285–286
  polluting, 288
  prophecy not based upon, 328
  success and failure becoming, 287
  washing with, 281
word of knowledge
  gift of, 60–65
  gift of discerning of spirits similar to, 72
  Jesus as, 19
  needed to have visions and intuitions from God, 129
  through a vision, 128
word of wisdom
  gift of, 65–69, 128–129
  Jesus as, 19
words, preference for in the Bible, 285
"words without" (human words), adding to divine words, 281, 281n2
workers, Paul rescheduling, 192–193
World Vision International, 177
worldly or earthly wisdom, 66
worldly pleasures, rejecting, 41
worship
  in Daniel's prayer, 110–111
  edifying the church, 52
  importance of music in, 83
  in Jeremiah's prayer, 111
writing of letters, by apostles, 189, 230
writing prophets, 28, 109
wrong message, holding on to, 321
Wycliffe, John, 257, 262
Wycliffe Bible Translations, 176

Yeboah, M. K., 73–74
younger men, as brothers, 209
younger women, as sisters, 209
youth, fewer identified as Christians in Korea, 265
Youth for Christ, 177
Youth with a Mission, 177
Zachariah (son of the high priest Jehoiada), 319
Zadokite priesthood, priestly family of, 38
Zechariah, 39
Zedekiah, 280–281, 298
Zeus, Barnabas identified as, 171

Scripture Index

OLD TESTAMENT

Genesis

	24
1:26—3	14
1:28 ESV	14
3:8 NKJV	14
4:2–9	15
4:3–16 NIV	15
6:13–14 ESV	15
8:6–12 ESV	16
12	16, 95
12:1–3	95
12:1–3 ESV	96
12:1–3 NIV	284
12:3	16
13:14	16
15	95
15:1	16
15:1–21	95
15:12–14	16–17
15:12–14 ESV	17
15:12–21 NIV	284
15:18–21 ESV	96
17:9–14	193
18:1–2	64
18:19 NIV	44
20:7 ESV	17
20:7 NIV	22
28:12–17	17
28:12–17 ESV	17
37	136
39	136
40	136
41	136
41:25–34 NKJV	67

Exodus

2:11–15	145
3:1–2	272
3:1–3 NIV	272
3:7–15 NIV	135
3:18	187
4:10–17	220
4:14–16 NIV	24
4:15 NIV	24
4:24–26	193
7:1	24
7:1–3 NIV	23
7:10	135
7:12	135
7:13	135
7:14	135
7:15	135
7:16	135
12:24	193
12:45–49	193
15:1–2 NIV	88
15:1–18, 21	83
15:20–21 ESV	25
15:20–21 NIV	88
15:21	84n5
19:4	96
19:4–6 ESV	96
20:6	99
20:18–20	64
24:1–9	96

(Exodus continued)

25:5 ESV	276
27:21	42n7, 193
31:1–6 NIV	88

Leviticus

12:3	193
16:12–13	36
16:31	193
22:18	193
23:21	193
23:29	193
23:31	193
24:1–4	42n7

Numbers

4:15 ESV	276
4:19 ESV	276
4:24–25 ESV	276
9:14	193
11:16, 24	187
11:28	120
11:29–30 NIV	120
12:2 NIV	25
12:6–7 ESV	25
12:6–8 NKJV	18
15:15	193
15:15–16	193

Deuteronomy

1:12–13 ESV	277
3:23–28 ESV	294
4:15, 36	64
5:23–24	64
10:16	194
13	309
13:1–5 NIV	309
18:20	310
18:20–22 NIV	309
20:2–4 NIV	315
27:1	187
30:6–7	194
31:19 NIV	89
31:30 NIV	89
32:44–47 ESV	89
32:46–47 ESV	79
34:10 ESV	23

Joshua

1:2–9	96
21:43	96
24:14–18 ESV	79

Judges

4:4	25
4:4–10	26, 101
4:4–10 ESV	25
4:17–22	26, 101
5:1–3 NIV	89
5:1–31	26
6:11–12	64
13:5	32

1 Samuel

1:11	32
1:11 ESV	32
2:1–10	84n5
2:11	34
2:12	33, 34
2:12 NKJV	43
2:12–17	33
2:18 NLT	42
2:20–21 NLT	44
2:21	304
2:22–26	295
2:23–25 NLT	42
2:24–28	32
2:27	28
2:27–36	293
2:28	313
3:1	34
3:3	42n7
3:7	43
3:8–10	272
3:9 ESV	44
3:10 NIV	46
3:10–14 NIV	64
3:10–15	47
3:13–14 ESV	293
3:15	47
3:15 NIV	46
3:19–21	303
3:19–21 NIV	304
3:19a	304
3:19b NIV	304
3:20	26, 305
3:21	306

4:1	305	16:14 NIV	71
7:5	306	17	316
7:5–6	111	17:34–37 NIV	167
7:8–9	110	17:45–47 NIV	168
7:9	306	17:51	168
8	101	18	316
8:1–2	313	18:9–11 NIV	320
8:4–7	298	18:10–11 NIV	71
8:6–9	306, 312	19:20	29
8:18	317	19:20–23	122
8:18–22	298, 312	19:22–24 NIV	71
8:18–22 NIV	313	19:23–24 NIV	320
8:21–22	306	22:5	26, 30, 120
9:9	26, 306		
9:11	26, 306	**2 Samuel**	
9:15–17	306	7:1–2	28
9:15–27	306	7:1–3	321
9:18–19	26	7:2ff	30, 120
9:20	317	7:4–17	321
10:1–8	306	12:1–14	319
10:5	292	12:1–17	120
10:5 NIV	29	12:1ff	30
10:6–7	320	12:7–12 NIV	81
10:8	314	21:17	42n7
10:9–11 NIV	320	24:11	26, 28, 30, 120
10:10	120		
10:10–11 NIV	71	**1 Kings**	
11:14–15	314	1:32	38
12:1–3	313, 317	3:23–27 NKJV	67
12:1–3 NIV	313	4:20–21	96
12:1–4 NIV	308	11:36	42n7
12:16–18 NIV	305	12:16–24	97
12:16–19	317	12:25–33	97
12:23–24 NIV	111	13	70
12:25	317	13:1 ESV	97n1
13:6–10	292	13:1–32	97n1
13:6–15 ESV	314–15	13:13–34	320
13:7–8	297	13:18	70
13:13–14 NIV	315	13:18, 20–21	320
13:13–15 ESV	317	13:18–22 LNT	70
14	316	13:20–21	320
15	316	14:1–18	101
15:22–23 NKJV	296	16:7	27, 28
15:28 ESV	318	17:1 ESV	27
16:1–2	316	17–18	28
16:4–5 NIV	318	18:20–21 ESV	80
16:6–7	298, 319	18:38–40 ESV	80
16:13–23 NKJV	85	18:39	169
		19:5–7	64

(1 Kings continued)

19:16–21	222
20:35	29
22:1–26	298
22:24–28 NIV	280, 298

2 Kings

1:3, 15	64
1:15–25	28
1:17	103
2:3	29, 122
2:3–5 NIV	29
2:5	29, 122
3:1	103
3:15	30, 91
4:1, 38	29
4:1 NIV	121
4:1–7	30, 121
4:38	29
6:1	29
6:1–7	30, 121
6:12 NIV	103
8:7–14	318
8:10–12	62
8:19	42n7
9:1	29
9:24	103
13:14 NIV	103
18:8–23	109
19:1–2	111
19:1–7	110
19:5–7	111

1 Chronicles

	29
21:1–7	88
21:9	26
23:5	88
23:5 NIV	90
25:1 NIV	30
25:1–7	89
25:1–8 NIV	90
25:7–8 NIV	30

2 Chronicles

9:29	26, 28
10:15	28
12:15	26, 28
13:22	26
18:1–34	298
19:2	27, 28
20:14–15 NIV	28
22:20–22	319
26–33	319
32:20	111
32:20–23	110

Ezra

10:8	187

Nehemiah

1:4–11	136
4–6	136
6:14	28
7–13	136
9:20	119

Psalms

	83
1:1–3 NIV	288
2	129
2:1–7 NKJV	129
22 NIV	90
45	129
45:1–7 NKJV	129
50:12	96
89:19	64
113–114	91
115–118	91
136	91

Proverbs

22:6 ESV	33

Ecclesiastes

4:9–12	220

Isaiah

1:11–17 NIV	101
5:25	106
6	111
6:1–4, 8 NKJV	36
6:1–7	64
6:5	36
6:7	36
6:8	37, 64
6:8 NIV	135
6:8 NKJV	36
6:8–9	222

6:9	37	14:11–12 ESV	114
6:9–10	37	14:19	106
6:11 NKJV	37	14:19–21 ESV	114
6:13 NKJV	37	16, 20, 21	105
7	319	17:12–18 NIV	111
7:3–4	110, 326	17:14	111
7:3–14	102	17:16–17	111
7:10–17 NIV	104	17:17–19	111
8	104	17:19–21	110, 326
8:3	28	17:19–27	112
8:3–4	104	18:19–23	113
8:5–8	96	18:19–23 GNT	113
13:1 NKJV	276	20	105
14:28 NKJV	276	20:7–9	113
22:1 NKJV	276	20:7–18 ESV	113
26:9–21	84n5	20:14–18	113
30:15–16 NIV	98	21	105
32:15	121	23:18 ESV	27
33:2–3	110	25:8–14	105
35:4–6	106	26:20	28
37–39	319	28:10–11 NIV	280
38:1–22	109	29:1–3	110, 326
40:6	273	29:17–19	105
40:6 NLT	272	29:27	23n1
42:6	206	30:3	105
42:6–9	106	30:11	105
42:18–20	37	30:24	105
42:24–25 NIV	98	31:13, 28	105
43:19	5	31:33	194
44:3–5	122	32:6–15	105
44:3–5 NIV	121	32:37–44	105
61:1	106	32:39–40	194
62:1	110	36:1–2	110, 326
63:10–14	119	42:1–7	297
		45:1–2	110, 326

Jeremiah

1:3	77n3		

Lamentations

1:4–5	222	2:9	64
1:4–5 ESV	31	2:14 NIV	321

Ezekiel

1:4–10 ESV	39		
1:7 NIV	135		
1:10	40	1:1, 28 NKJV	38
1:10 ESV	40	1:1 NIV	62
1:11–12	62	1:1–2	38
1:13 ESV	40	1:1–3	64
1:17–19 ESV	40	1:2	38
3:1–3	107	1:3	38, 271
11:6–10 NIV	98	1:28 NKJV	38
14:7–9 ESV	114	2:1–5	135

(Ezekiel continued)

2:7	38
3:1–3	38
3:14–17	271
3:17–21	38
5:14–15	106
8:1–4	64
11:19 NIV	194
13:15–16 NIV	322
14:6 NIV	98
18:2–4 NIV	100
18:17–18 NIV	100
21:33	273
22:8	23n1
29:17	38
33:1–9	38
33:21–33 NIV	273
33:22	271
36:26–27 NIV	194
36:26–28 ESV	124
36:26–28 NIV	121
37:1–2 NIV	271
37:10	23n1
39:29 NIV	121
44:15	38

Daniel

1:17	64
2	49, 62, 67, 136
2:17–19	110
2:19–45	225
2:23	49
3–6	136
5	58, 330n1
5:25–29 NKJV	58
5:26	58
5:27	59
5:28	59
6:10–11	110
6:19–28	136
8:5–17 NLT	110
9	106, 110
9:4 NLT	110
9:16	106
9:17–18 NLT	111
9:20–23	64
12:4	106

Hosea

8:1–2 NIV	97

Joel

2:28–29	206
2:28–29 NIV	122
2:32 NIV	122

Amos

1:1	62
2:6–8 ESV	105
2:6–8 NIV	100
2:13–16 ESV	105
3:7 ESV	27
5:21–25 NIV	99

Micah

	29n5
3:6	64

Nahum

1:1 NKJV	276

Habakkuk

1:1 NKJV	276
2:6–7 NIV	100
3:2–19	84n5

Haggai

1:6–11	107
2:2–4	119

Zechariah

1:9–19	64
2:3	64
7:11–14 NIV	98
12:10–11 NIV	122

Malachi

1:1 NKJV	276

NEW TESTAMENT

Matthew

1:22–23 NIV	105
1:23	104
3:15	61
3:17	64, 69
4:1	286
4:1–3 NIV	69
4:1–11	74
4:18—7:29	145
5	311
5:17–18 NKJV	18
6:13 NIV	287
7:1–16	328
7:15–23 NIV	310
7:16	310
7:22–23	327
8:26	170
9:18, 22	170
9:23–26	170
9:36	260
10:1–14	146
10:2–4	138
10:42	19
11:11	260
11:15 NIV	19
12:13–22	169
13:9 ESV	44
13:9 NIV	19
13:43 ESV	44
13:52	265
13:52 NASB	265
13:52 NASU	207
13:58 KJV	170
15:1–6	46
15:21–28	170
15:31	170
16	145
16:2–4 NIV	108
16:13–16 NIV	146
16:13–21	35
16:16 NIV	165
16:16–19 NIV	165
16:17 NIV	70
16:17 NKJV	20, 70
16:17 NLT	70
16:17–22	146
16:23	283
16:23–26	146
17:5	64
17:19–21	147
17:21 KJV	147n3
20:20–23	148
20:23	148
20:23 NLT	148
20:24–25 NLT	148
22:15–22 NKJV	69
23:1–3 NIV	45
23:1–3 NLT	45
23:37–39	285
25:32	260
26:27	260
26:30	91
26:36–46	202
27:55	158
28:18–20	165

Mark

	198
1:23–24 NIV	69
1:35	202
3:13	202
3:13–14	222
3:14	144
3:14 KJV	144
3:16–19	138
3:21	151
3:31–35	151
5:24–34	158n7
6:1–6	170
6:5	170
7:1–8	46
10:45	285
12.32–42	138

Luke

	249
1:15	61
1:27	104
1:34	104
1:34–35 NIV	104
1:42 NIV	61
1:43 NIV	61

(Luke continued)

1:44 NIV	61
1:46–55	84n5
1:68–79	84n5
2:8	260
2:15	260
2:18	260
2:20	260
2:29–32	84n5
2:32	206
4:1–13	69
5:1—6:41	145
5:16	202
6:12–13 NIV	138
6:12–16	202
6:13 NIV	144
6:14–16	138
7:36–50	158n7
8:1–3	158
8:1–3 NIV	158n8
8:8	19
8:50	170
9:1–6	19
10:17–20	146
13:10–17	169
14:35	19
16:2–4	191
19:10	285
22:24 NLT	148
24:45	176

John

	172, 249
1:1–3 NIV	20
1:12–13 NIV	20
1:14 NIV	20
3:16	285
3:29–30 ESV	307
6:1–13	147
6:14–15	147
6:60 NIV	147
6:63 NIV	289
6:63–64 NIV	283
6:68–69 NIV	148
6:70–71 NIV	138
7:5	151
7:37–38 NIV	266
8:7–10 NKJV	68
10:2	260
10:11, 14	260
11:46–50	169
12:28–29	64
13:12–17 NIV	149
14:23–24	19
16:12–13	20, 124
16:12–14 NIV	207
16:14	307
17	219
17:20–23 NIV	219
19:10–18	159
20:10–18	176
20:16 NIV	176
21:24–29	175

Acts

	149, 182, 223
1–2	152
1:6–11, 14	140
1:13	139
1:13—2:13	202
1:14	140, 152, 159
1:15–26	139
1:21–22 NIV	139
1:22	164
1:23–24	140, 175
2:1–4	53
2:1–4 NKJV	53
2:2–4	123
2–3	172
2:10–12 NKJV	53
2:11 ESV	123
2:38–39 ESV	123
2:38–39 NKJV	54
3:1–9	215
3:1–10	170
3:7	285
3:16	170
4:1–4	199
4:32–37 NIV	210
4:36–37	153
5:1–10	62
5:12	170
5:15–16	170
5:18	199
5:33–39 NIV	65
5:40	199
6	208
6:1–7	230, 233

Reference	Page
6:3–4	164
6:4	202
8	55
8:6–8	171
8:9–25	188
8:14	154, 189
8:14 NKJV	215
8:14–17	204, 261
8:14–19 NKJV	53
8:14–25	230
8:18–23 NKJV	73
9	223n2
9:1–5	141
9:1–9	222
9:1–19	233
9:3–16	140
9:4	64
9:5–6 NIV	149
9:10–19 NIV	63
9:15–16 NIV	216
9:15–18 NIV	150
9:26–28	154
9:26–30	150, 183
9:26–30 NIV	150
9:32	189
9:32–35	170
9:32–42	230
9:36–43	170–71
10	202, 224
10:1–48	54
10:9–19 NIV	63
10:13–16	224
10:19–20	224
10:34	34
10:44–48 NKJV	54
10:48	308
11	189
11:16–33	211
11:19–26 NIV	246
11:22–24	154
11:22–26 NIV	216
11:22–26 NKJV	151, 183
11:24 NIV	154
11:25–26	154
11:27–28	225
11:29	208
11:29–30 NIV	187
11:30	187
12:1–4	199
12:6–19	171
12:12–13	198
12:17	216
13	202, 223n2, 233
13:1	127, 128
13:1–3	183, 216, 217
13:1–3 NIV	246
13:1–3 NKJV	183
13:1–4	182
13:2	154
13:3	154
13:6–12	171
13:8–12	305
13–20	230
13–21	189
13:38–39 ESV	296
13:43	199
13:50	199
14:1	184
14:3	166
14:3 NIV	166
14:4	154, 183
14:8–10	171
14:8–13	308
14:9–10	170
14:11–18 NIV	171
14:14	154, 183, 203, 217
14:20 NKJV	199
14:21 NIV	184
14:21–23	197
14:23	188, 232
14:23 NIV	188, 232
14:23 NKJV	217
15	152, 154, 188, 192, 194, 217
15 NIV	253
15:1–35	230
15:2	188, 217
15:4	188, 217
15:5	217
15:5 NIV	193
15:6 NKJV	217
15:7–12	253
15:8, 11	194
15:8–11	194
15:11	194
15:15–19 NIV	194
15:22	155, 216, 217

(Acts continued)

15:28–29 NIV	194
15:32	155, 182, 197, 216
15:36–40	154
15:39–41	219
15:40—18:5	155
16	224
16:1–3 NKJV	197
16:1—18:11	155
16:4	217
16:6–10	171, 307
16:8–10	198, 224
16:10	197
16:10 NKJV	198
16:15–30	171
16:16–18 NLT	73
16:25–27	91
16:25–30	156
17:5–9	156, 199
17:12 NKJV	184
17:19–21	5
18:1–4	198
18:12–17	199
18:17	231
18:18	159
18:18–29	231
18:24–26	157
18:24–26 NIV	77
18:26	157, 159
19:1–7 NKJV	55
19:5–7	205
19:11–12	171
19:12	171
19:18–19	198
19:21–22	155
19:22	198
19:23–41	199
20	198
20:4	155, 231
20:4–5 NKJV	198
20:7–12	171
20:17	233
20:22–24 NIV	225
20:28	188, 260n2
20:28 NIV	233
21:8–10	325
21:8–10 ESV	128
21:9	128
21:9–11	127
21:10	128
21:10–11	225
21:18–27 NIV	257
21:29	231
22:10–21 NIV	141
23:11	307
23:12–16	307
23:12–17	307
24–26 NIV	158
26:15–18 NIV	142
26:16	164
27:10	307
27:10 NKJV	225
27:11	191
27:21–24	307

Romans

1:1	140, 231
1:10–13	230
1:11	204n1
1:11 NIV	204
1:11–12 NIV	262
1:11–13	189
2:29	194
8:2	275
8:9–11	127
8:14	127
8:28	167, 219
11:29–30 ESV	275
12:1 ESV	80
12:4–6	51n1
12:6	51, 127
12:6–8 NIV	75
12:7	185
12:8	186, 190
12:8 ESV	78
14:19	52
15:20	159
15:25–27 NIV	209
15:25–29 NIV	212
16:1–3	231
16:1–16	231
16:3	159
16:3–5	159
16:7	161
16:17	219
16:20	182
16:21	155, 220

SCRIPTURE INDEX

16:23 NKJV	198

1 Corinthians

	72, 82, 195, 204
1:1	140, 231
1:4–8 NIV	203
1:7	203
1:12	195
1:12–13 NIV	157
1:19–21 NKJV	66
2:13 NIV	278
3	126
3:1–9	173
3:3–4	219
3:5–7 NIV	77
3:6	157
3:9–16	182
3:18–23 NIV	78
4:1–2 NKJV	165
5	82, 195
5:3–5 NLT	81
7:1	192
7:10–13 NIV	195
9:1	153
9:1–5	140
9:2 ESV	188
9:4–7 ESV	41
9:5	140, 153
9:5–6	154
9:5–6 NIV	153
9:15–17 ESV	41
10	119, 205
11:27–34	195
12:1	204n1
12:4–12, 28	127
12:8 KJV	60, 65
12:8–10 NIV	287
12:9	169
12:10	51, 53, 69
12:10 KJV	53
12:10 NKJV	57, 69
12:27–30	163
12:27–30 NIV	163
12:28	8, 56, 127, 163, 169, 185, 186, 191
12:28 NKJV	56
12:28–29 NIV	76
12:30	169, 204n1
12:30–31 NKJV	56
13:12	127, 321
14:1	126
14:1–5, 33, 39–40	327
14:2 NKJV	55
14:3	328
14:3 NKJV	52
14:4 NKJV	56
14:5	125, 126
14:5 NIV	125, 126
14:5–6	238
14:13–14 NIV	57
14:13–15 NKJV	56–57
14:15 NKJV	57
14:18–19 NLT	261
14:24–25	125
14:24–25 ESV	52
14:24–25 NIV	125
14:24–26	328
14:24–31	126
14:26	238
14:26 NIV	289
14:26 NKJV	83
14:26–33	127
14:26–33 NIV	127
14:27 NKJV	59
14:29	238
14:29–33	320
14:29–33 NIV	126
14:30–31	125, 238
14:33	327, 328
14:36–40	328
14:39–40	327
14:40	127, 238
15:3–8 NIV	151
15:7	253
15:7–8	140
15:9–10 NIV	206
16:1–6 NIV	212
16:8	159
16:10	189
16:12	157
16:12 NIV	78
16:19	159
16:21	220

2 Corinthians

	82, 204
1:19	155–56
2:5–11 ESV	82

(2 Corinthians continued)

2:6–11	247
2:12	156
2:13	186
5:7 NIV	167
7:5–7	156
7:5–16	186
8:1–3 NIV	212
8:23	156
10:4–6 NIV	274
10:8	52
11	196, 199
11:8–11	200
11:12–15 NIV	200
11:28–29 NIV	192
12:8	203
12:12	166
12:20	196
13:9	52
13:10 NIV	319
14:29–30 NKJV	72

Galatians

1:1	140
1:8 NIV	196
1:13–17 NIV	140
1:17–24	140
2:1–5	156
2:1–10	154, 216
2:9	154
2:9 NIV	152
2:9–14	140
2:10 NIV	209
2:11–13	152
2:11–14	257
2:11–14 NLT	82
3:2–3	204
3:5	203
3:5 NIV	204
3:26	206
5:16–17	204
6:15	194

Ephesians

	181
1:1	140
1:10	191
2:8–9	167
2:19–21 NIV	164, 181
2:20	2, 8, 127
2:20–22	182
3:1–3 NIV	191
3:2	164, 191
3:2–6 NIV	206
3:4–5 NIV	182
3:7–9 NIV	191
3:9 NIV	165
4:3–7 NIV	211
4:11	51, 127, 128, 256
4:11–12	5, 8, 162
4:11–12 NKJV	196–97
4:11–13 NIV	162
4:12	6
4:14–15	76
5:11–12	163
5:18–21 NKJV	83
5:19	83
5:21–24	253
5:25–27 NIV	281
6:1	46
6:1 NIV	46
6:21–22	231

Philippians

1:1	245
2:19–24	155
2:25 NIV	160
2:25–27	172
3:3	194
3:10 KJV	146
4:2	192
4:2–3	231
4:3	243

Colossians

1:6–7	189
1:25	191
2:11	194
3:16	83
3:16 NKJV	83
4:7 NIV	231
4:7–9	231
4:10 NKJV	198
4:11	219

1 Thessalonians

	72
1:1	155, 156, 197

2:6	155
2:7	197
3:1–6	155
5:16–22 ESV	326
5:19–21 NIV	72
5:19–22	70, 238, 320

2 Thessalonians
1:1	156
3:6–13 NIV	211

1 Timothy
1:1–3	155
3:1	188
3:1–7	232
3:1–8	188
3:1–16	232
3:4–5	190
3:7	233
3:8	233
3:12	190
3:15	232
4:11–16	155
4:14	233
4:14 NIV	217
5:1–2 NIV	209
5:2	188
5:3 NIV	209
5:9–10 NIV	209
5:17	188, 190, 232
5:22	232
5:23	172

2 Timothy
1:6	233
1:6–7	204
1:15–18 NIV	185
2:2–3 NIV	44
2:11	219
2:15 KJV	292
4:11	154, 198, 231
4:12	231
4:19	159, 231
4:20	198, 231
4:20–21	172

Titus
1:4–5	157
1:5	188, 217, 232
1:5 NIV	232
1:5–9	188, 232
1:6	232
1:7	157
3:12	231
3:12–13	189
3:12–14 NIV	192–93
3:13	157

Philemon
	231
1–2	231
23	198
23–24	231

Hebrews
	159, 286, 294
2:10–18 NIV	287
3:1	137
10:26–31 ESV	294
11:1	167
11:6 NIV	167
13:4–10	34
13:10 NIV	34
13:20	260
13:22–23	188

James
1:1	176, 188
1:1 NIV	152
1:2–5 NIV	66
1:7–8 NIV	196
1:21 NIV	196
2:1–4 NIV	210
2:14–20	196
3:13–15 NKJV	66
3:17 NIV	66
5:17–18 NIV	95, 260

1 Peter
1:1	188
1:1 NLT	212
2:25	260
4:10	51
4:14–17 NLT	201
5:1–2	260n2
5:12 NIV	156

2 Peter
2:1–22	196

(2 Peter continued)
3:15–16   305

1 John
1:4–10 ESV   295
1:9 ESV   296
2:26–27 NIV   329
3   196

3 John
  189
9   189

Jude
  196
1–3   188
1–5 NIV   192
3   189

20 NKJV   56

Revelation
172, 225, 260
1:9–11 NIV   226
1:10   203
1:10–11 NIV   279
2:7   44
2:11   44
2:17   44
2:29   44
3:6   44
11:15   44
13:9, 43   44
13:43   44
18:17   191
22:8–9   260

EARLY CHRISTIAN WRITINGS

Apostolic Constitution
  255
25   255
46   160

Clement of Alexandria
240n5

Clement of Rome
243, 253

1 Clement
introduction   245
1:13   244
3:12–15   243, 243–44n2
19:2–18   244
19:20   244
20:14   244
20:15   244
20:19   244
22:14   244

Didache "The Teaching of the Lord to the Gentiles by the Twelve Apostles"
235, 239, 241, 253
10:7   239

11:1–12   236
13:1–7   238
15:1–2   239
16:3   237

Eusebius of Caesarea
Church History
325n2

Ignatius of Antioch
245–46
To the Philadelphians
7:2ff   246
To Polycarp
7:2   246

Irenaeus
240n5
Demonstration of Apostolic Preaching
249
Against Heresies
3:1:1   251
3:4   246n5, 247, 249
3.1:2   250
3.11   249

3.11:1–2	250	Shepherd of Hermas	
3.4	247		239–41, 253
5.1	250	8:14–16	241

The Martyrdom of Polycarp

248n7

11:16 241
17:1–6 240
49:14–16 241
49:25–27 241

Origen

240n5

49:31 241
49:50–56 241

Polycarp, Bishop of Smyrna

246–49

101:16 241
102:12 241

To the Philippians

103:5 241
111:2 241

11:4 247
13:1 247

GRECO-ROMAN LITERATURE

Plato 291

www.ingramcontent.com/pod-product-compliance
Lightning Source LLC
Chambersburg PA
CBHW071230290426
44108CB00013B/1352